THE HALL OF MIRRORS

To Heidi

The Hall of Mirrors

War and Warfare in the Twentieth Century

Jim Storr

 Helion & Company

Helion & Company Limited
Unit 8 Amherst Business Centre
Budbrooke Road
Warwick
CV34 5WE
England
Tel. 01926 499 619
Fax 0121 711 4075
Email: info@helion.co.uk
Website: www.helion.co.uk
Twitter: @helionbooks
Visit our blog http://blog.helion.co.uk/

Published by Helion & Company 2018
Designed and typeset by Mach 3 Solutions Ltd (www.mach3solutions.co.uk)
Cover designed by Paul Hewitt, Battlefield Design (www.battlefield-design.co.uk)
Printed by Gutenberg Press Limited, Tarxien, Malta

Text © Jim Storr 2018
Maps drawn by George Anderson © Helion & Company Limited 2018

ISBN 978-1-912390-85-4

British Library Cataloguing-in-Publication Data.
A catalogue record for this book is available from the British Library.

For details of other military history titles published by Helion & Company Limited contact
the above address, or visit our website: http://www.helion.co.uk.

We always welcome receiving book proposals from prospective authors.

Contents

List of Figures

Introduction

What can we learn from war, and warfare, in the 20th century?

The 20th century was possibly the most violent in history. It is now a defined period in the past. A huge amount has been written about war, and warfare, during its course. So: what can we learn from war, and warfare, in the 20th century?

The question is possibly unanswerable. We could recite any number of facts. We could summon up a seemingly limitless number of lessons. In order to make the problem answerable, this book will focus on insight: 'accurate and deep understanding'. If we seek depth, we will occasionally have to go into detail. That may be in areas where others have not.

The outcome of war is largely unpredictable, so we shall not seek to predict the future. We shall seek insight into the largely human processes by which war is waged, and into the nature of collective violence. The main value of studying war and warfare is to enable one side to win. Armed forces do not get paid to come second, so insight into things which allow a protagonist to win will be an important area of discussion.

'The Hall of Mirrors' is a work of history, in the narrow sense of 'the study of past events'. More generally, it is a work of analysis. It is not history in the sense of 'a continuous, typically chronological, record of past events or trends'.

War is hugely important. It can shape continents, and can do so dramatically quickly. Four empires ceased to exist as a result of the 52 months of the Great (or First World) War. Eight new countries were born in Europe. As a result of the six years of the Second World War the border of the Soviet Union was effectively moved over 800km west, to the Oder (if not the Elbe). Japan and Germany renounced militarism. They ceased to be major players on the world stage for decades. Regrettably, war is hugely important. It is not futile, although it may appear so those taking part.

The Hall of Mirrors focuses on insight accessible to an English-speaking audience. One reason is to further limit the scope of the book. Another is the difficulty of gaining access to foreign-language sources. Yet another is to focus in part on British, British Empire and British Commonwealth armed forces. Britain was the only nation to fight through the whole of both World Wars. Even Germany did not. Britain did not fight in every war during the century, but it did suffer casualties due to enemy action in every year except 1969. So, although the book does not focus uniquely on Britain and British armed forces, a British perspective is useful when looking at the wars and warfare of the 20th century.

The first half of the 20th century was dominated by the two most destructive wars in history. Its second half was dominated by a war which could easily have been even more destructive, but did not happen: the Cold War. At the beginning of the 20th century, much of the world was colonised by European nations. By the 1980s almost all of the world had been decolonised. The world was not uniquely characterised by colonialism in the 20th century, but the geopolitical issues associated with it and (more importantly) decolonisation were significant.

War and warfare in the 20th century were characterised by mechanisation to an unprecedented extent. It was the first century of aerial warfare. It was the century of the Dreadnought battleship, the aircraft carrier and then the nuclear submarine. At the beginning of the century land warfare was largely dominated by mass-produced rifles and quick-firing field guns. Machineguns and tanks soon entered the picture. Yet, curiously, despite a massive global arsenal and with nuclear weapons hovering in the wings, the second half of the century was largely one of peace and improving prosperity for much of the world. Real incomes grew in the great majority of countries, albeit from pitiably low levels in many cases.

No single book appears to have tackled war this subject. There are great gaps in our understanding. There is, currently (in 2018) no consensus as to the contribution of the Allied Combined Bomber Offensive to the defeat of Germany in the Second World War. There is almost no discussion, and certainly no agreement, as to how the Western Allies defeated Germany in north west Europe in 1944-45. Yet both of those campaigns took place over 70 years ago.

There has been a vast amount of study and written work. Much of it is impressive. Arguably some of the more recent works on this subject have added very little to either our understanding or to consensus. We have, perhaps, reached the practical end of what the conventional study of history will usefully add. Several books, for example, treat the battle of El Alamein in some detail. The broad facts are all generally similar, but the accounts all differ significantly. Critically, the British Eighth Army failed to break through the German defensive positions on the first night. One book didn't mention that at all. Others glossed over it. So even what appear to be thoroughly well-researched and well-written accounts, produced decades after the events, can fail us.

Two things are clear from the recent historiography of the wars and warfare of the 20th century. The first is that massive amounts of archival research move the debate but slowly. The foot soldiers in the 'war on history' are the archival researchers. Many are doctoral students. They do the spadework, analyse their findings, and publish their results. To extend the metaphor, they have occasional tactical successes. Some of them are startling. But, writ large, few (if any) of those successes are at the operational or theatre level. That also applies to massively popular, immaculately researched, and commercially hugely successful blockbusters by famous writers. Hugely readable, they often say nothing new. They don't really attempt to.

The second point is that huge amounts of closely-argued academic argumentation have shifted the discussion scarcely at all. Perhaps the best example is the extensive discussion, in 'War in History' and elsewhere, as to whether or not there actually was a Schlieffen Plan. The proponents included Terence Holmes and Terence Zuber. 17 articles amounting to well over 150,000 words were published in 'War in History' between 1999 and 2015. The conclusion seems to be:

- there was no 'Schlieffen plan' in the form of a General Staff order or directive.
- Schlieffen conceived of a 'strong right hook' through Belgium with two powerful armies.
- the troops allocated to the 'plan' by Schlieffen did not match reality.
- what Moltke the Younger did in 1914, with the troops actually available, did not meet the expectations of Schlieffen's concept.
- after the war, the German army 'Establishment' wrote the official history so as to cast Schlieffen and the General Staff (but not Moltke the Younger) in a favourable light. The official history was, effectively, written so as to blame Moltke.

The first, second and fourth points are no surprise at all. The third and fifth constitute a minor corrective. Yet the effort, the vitriol, and the ink spilt has been staggering. Grown men published articles with titles such as 'Terence Holmes Reinvents the Schlieffen Plan – Again'[1]. One editorial called it 'great history'[2]. Seen from outside the confines of academic history it is, arguably, trivial. However, it does shed some light on a larger issue, which *is* addressed in this book. Of the various things that every British schoolboy used to be taught about the Great War, why on earth should he know that someone called Moltke the Younger had weakened the right wing of something called the Schlieffen Plan? More significantly, why have historians failed to ask *that* question? There seems to be something wrong with the Western study of war and warfare. It seems to be connected with the structure of academia.

In order to understand war, and warfare, we need to start with politics. Politics are the ways in which power is brokered in a society. Man realised long ago that he could use force, and then collective armed force, to acquire power within his society. As societies developed from tribes through nations to states, the use of collective armed violence to acquire and broker power became identified as 'war'. Where that was done for the purpose of the state it has been known as 'interstate war'. Where it was done for the purposes of factions *within* a state, it became known as 'civil war'. Where a faction embraced collective violence and rose up in order to seize power, that is now identified as an uprising, insurrection or insurgency. Hence the need for, and techniques of, counter-insurgency.

These terms, or definitions, are not sharply-defined (for example, when is a state a state?), categoric (what is the difference between an insurrection and a civil war?)

1   Zuber, Terence, 'Terence Holmes Reinvents the Schlieffen Plan – Again', *War in History*, 10:1 (January 2003), pp92-101.
2   Strachan, Hew and Showalter, Denis, Editorial, *War in History*, 11:1 (January 2001), pp1-2.

or exclusive (armed insurrections have been significant features of interstate wars. Consider, for example, the French Resistance of the Second World War). It is not appropriate to seek pedantic definitions in the complex and loosely-structured phenomenon known as war. 'Warfare' is simply the conduct of war.

War is a matter of politics. Politics considers how power is brokered in a society. It is a fallacy to suggest that war can be waged over religion or economics. The 37-year-long 'Troubles' in Northern Ireland between 1969 and 2006 had nothing to do with religion. Nobody gave two hoots for the nature of the Host in the Mass (or Communion); nor any other theological issue. The Troubles were about a power struggle between unionist, loyalist (and in practice mostly Protestant) factions and Republican (and generally Catholic) factions of the community. Religion figures in some wars, but theology is not the cause. The cause is the power to impose one faction's theology on another. Similarly for economics: the issue is not the particular commercial, economic nor fiscal matter in question. It is the power to impose one faction's wishes regarding that issue over others. War is about power, and politics is the way that power is brokered in a society.

It is common, but wrong, to think that religious or economic issues are the cause of a given war, rather than politics. That is to misunderstand the nature of politics. The fallacy arises because of a confusion between politics (the way that power is brokered in society) and normal political activity. In a largely peaceful society, politics is undertaken as 'normal political activity': the business of governments, councils, and elections.

Collective armed conflict has a taxonomy. One spectrum is that of wars, campaigns and battles. That gives rise to an equivalent spectrum of strategy, operational art and tactics. Strategy is the conduct of war through the planning, ordering and resourcing of campaigns in theatres of war. Tactics is the conduct of battles and engagements. Operational art is the link: it concerns the planning, sequencing, resourcing and conducting a series of battles within a theatre, in order to achieve the strategic objectives of the campaign. Alternatively, wars are waged as a series of campaigns; campaigns are waged as a series of (tactical) battles and engagements.

Those are the terms used here. Regrettably they are used far too loosely elsewhere. For some time a professor of war studies used to talk about 'the strategy of platoon houses' in Afghanistan. Platoon basing is a matter of tactics. Other writers use the term 'strategy' to mean 'the art of the general' or 'the craft of generals'. That gives free licence to charlatans. If you use that definition, you can write about almost anything you like. One writer on strategy dwelt at length on the tactics of the Battle of Britain: an obvious fallacy.

People often assume that the events of the past were inevitable. However, they also generally believe that the future is uncertain and unpredictable. Logically that cannot be so. At each moment in the past, the events which were about to occur were unpredictable. Thus what we now perceive as the past was, at the time, unpredictable. It did not seem to be inevitable. Human agency is one of the main reasons: we cannot predict human actions with any confidence. So in order to gain insight into the past we have to look at human behaviour in appropriate detail. It is also useful to look at alternative decisions that might have been made, if only to consider why they were not.

Trying to identify what we can learn from war and warfare in the 20th century could be seen as a fool's errand. No matter what one writes, a reader might say 'I already knew that'. Such things have little value. Identifying things to which the writer would respond 'I *didn't* know that' is more useful. Identifying things to which he or she might say 'I hadn't thought about that' would be better. So would things to which the response would be 'I hadn't thought about that *in that way*'. We shall try to identify as few of the first kind of issues as possible, in order to identify several of the rest.

'The Hall of Mirrors' looks at the course and conduct of wars. Their overall *course* is largely a result of the strategy. Their *conduct* is largely a matter of campaigns and tactics, informed in places by strategic decisions. Military organisations and technology also figure. The goal, however, is insight. Thus we shall not 'discuss the discourse', unless strictly necessary. We shall not look at 'great men' much, except in terms of human agency. Neither shall we dwell on 'great themes', social, high cultural, nor women's issues. They are largely irrelevant to our purpose. Every intellectual discipline has heuristics, biases and blind spots. That includes the study of war. We shall try to identify what they are in this case. 'The Hall of Mirrors' also contains little discussion of the nature and processes of command. That would merit another book all of its own.

Note on Sources

Captain Edmund Blackadder once referred to the object of one particular battle as being to move Field Marshal Haig's drinks cabinet "six inches closer to Berlin". Serious historians may object that Blackadder, the central role in BBC TV's 1989 series 'Blackadder Goes Forth', is fictional.

In researching for this book I have looked at a reasonable number of books. I have also conducted research in other areas. One is military operations research. I have contributed to some, read reports from some more, and conducted some of my own. The latter was, mostly, fairly straightforward numerical analysis.

I have attended at least 164 conferences, seminars or lectures relevant to this book. Well over 300 speakers presented their work, some of them several times. Very few of them were not, at the least, doctoral (i.e. PhD, or similar) candidates; or serving officers of at least the rank of colonel or equivalent. I have reviewed my notes from all of them.

I have visited over 300 battlefields. I studied the terrain, and the events of the battle, to the extent that time allowed. Some visits were brief. Some, such as to Cassino, lasted several days. I have visited some battlefields (such as those in Normandy) several times.

The peer-reviewed Journal 'War in History' first appeared in 1994. Its founding editors were Professors Hew (now Sir Hew) Strachan and Dennis Showalter. By 2016 it had run to 23 Volumes. They contain 911 articles or book reviews relevant to this book. All of the articles are peer-reviewed by internationally-known experts. The reviews are of similar quality. Very few of the authors are of less than doctoral standing. All 911 items were reviewed in preparing for this book.

I have had the honour and privilege of talking to, and on occasion interviewing, several veterans. They came from many ranks and many conflicts. The oldest was a veteran of the Manchester Regiment in the Great War. He had been awarded the Military Medal three times. Two of the youngest retired as (full) generals.

Captain Edmund Blackadder is an historical character to the extent that he features, in Rowan Atkinson's character, in the film and video history of the 20th century. He is, nevertheless, fictional. Nonetheless something prompted the writers of 'Blackadder' to create such a character, and set him in a series on the Western Front in the Great War. We shall probably never know what that was.

A Major John Blackader of the Cameronians (later the Scottish Rifles) fought at the battle of Maplaquet on 11 September 1709. So did a French Major General d'Artaignan. Blackader's commanding officer was mortally wounded, so he succeeded to command of the Cameronians that day.

Major General Charles Blackader, late of the Leicester Regiment, commanded the 38th (Welsh) Division on the Western Front from June 1916 to May 1918.

Acknowledgements

I am grateful to many people for their help, insight and guidance in writing this book.

I asked a number of academics for their views whilst conducting my research for this book. They include: Professor Sir Hew Strachan, Chichele Professor of the History of War at the University of Oxford; Professor Gary Sheffield, University of Wolverhampton; Professors Andrew Lambert and David Betz, King's College, London; and Doctors Peter Grey and Jonathan Boff of the University of Birmingham.

My editorial panel for the former online Journal of Military Operations have helped in many ways. They were: General Sir Rupert Smith; Lieutenant General Sir John Kiszely; Major General Julian Thompson (Royal Marines); Brigadier Justin Kelly (Australian Army); Professor Karen Carr (Cranfield University); Colonels Clint Ancker (US Army), Mike Crawshaw and John Wilson; Lieutenant Colonels Jan Frederik Geiner and Egil Dahlveit (both of the Norwegian Army); Doctor Eado Hecht (Bar-Ilan University); Major Gerry Long; William Owen and Dermot Rooney.

I have been fortunate to serve with a number of highly knowledgeable and professional officers over many years. Several have contributed significantly to my knowledge and understanding of the profession of arms. They include Major Generals Jonathan Bailey, Christopher Elliot and Mungo Melvin; Colonels Dirk Brodersen and Bruno Paulus (both of the German Army); Colonels David Benest, Richard Iron and Steve James.

In reviewing my notes I found that several of the ideas which I had thought were my own originated in things said by other people. From the ranks of military colleagues, for example, I should acknowledge suggestions or comments made by Brigadier Allan Mallinson and Major Gordon Corrigan.

Colleagues at the weekly University of Birmingham War Studies seminars have contributed in many ways. It would be unfair of me to mention any one of them except Professor John Bourne. His encyclopaedic knowledge of his subject and his perceptive, wry humour have been a great help over more than a decade.

German academic tradition uses the term 'Doktorvater' to mean 'doctoral supervisor'. In my case I owe a great deal to the late Professor Richard Holmes. His early death remains a great sadness to all who knew him.

Helion have, once again, done a wonderful job in publishing this book. I am particularly grateful to Duncan Rogers and Michael LoCicero.

I wish to thank them all.

1

The Dawn of the Century

Two major wars were underway at the beginning of the century: one in South Africa, the other in the Philippines. The British had been fighting in South Africa since 1899. Things had gone badly at first. In what became known as 'Black week', in December 1899, the British suffered three tactical defeats. It took several months for the British to reinforce, go over to the offensive, and turn the tide of the war. The British eventually deployed 488,000 men in South Africa. The Boers, or Afrikaners, never fielded more than 80,000 men.

There was considerable criticism of the British Army, not least in the British press. Some of it was justified. Some of it reflected shock that the British Army had been defeated by irregulars. Some of it reflected a failure to understand the changing conditions of modern warfare. The battle of the Modder River in South Africa had taken place in the same week as the battle of Omdurman in the Sudan, fought largely against tribesmen armed with little more than spears. The need to adapt the techniques of warfare against a thinking and educated 'western' enemy was exposed.

The British were initially short of cavalry. Two cavalry regiments were based in South Africa, and a brigade was moved from India before the outbreak of hostilities. However four of the five regiments were besieged in Ladysmith, and therefore were not available for the early stages of the war. More cavalry was rushed to South Africa by sea, but the horses were not given time to acclimatize. The units, and their horses, were then heavily overworked. It is questionable whether they ever really recovered during the war.

There were, however, several British successes. There had been two successful local sorties in the siege of Ladysmith. Both were well-handled night attacks. On other occasions, undetected night approaches preceded successful dawn assaults. A tactical envelopment was attempted at the battle of Belmont, and succeeded at the relief of Kimberley. Cavalry succeeded admirably at the battles of Klip Drift and Elandslagte. There were, nonetheless, several poor commanders. That is not unusual in a major war fought after extended periods of peace. Younger officers stepped up to fill the gap very well. Accounts stressed the need for individual initiative at low levels. They detected a structural link between firepower, dispersion and initiative. These were the actions of a professional army which had not fought a 'European' enemy for many years. It identified and learnt many lessons; some small, some large.

The war was fought 6,000 miles from home, with support from around the world (troops from Canada, Australia and New Zealand, and remount horses purchased in the United States). Only five years before, the French had needed British shipping to transport a force to Madagascar. In 1897 Germany had been unable to deploy a single battalion to Crete. In the Spanish-American War of 1898 the United States Army had logistic difficulties in Cuba, less than 100 miles from its own coast. Conversely the British Army had conducted 35 overseas campaigns since 1820. The Victorian Royal Navy had a uniquely global reach.

The reinforcements rushed to South Africa included several militia and yeomanry (cavalry) units. They showed some shortcomings, particularly in standards of training. That coloured the attitude of the Regular Army towards its reserves in the Great War.

It has been said that, at the time of the Boer War, the British Army had an ethos but no clear doctrine. That is, literally, true. However, Staff College teaching was based on the work of individuals such as Lieutenant General Sir Edward Hamley, Major General Sir Charles Callwell and Colonel George ('G F R') Henderson. Their books were published commercially, but they were the standard texts. They remained in use in various editions for several decades.

The British showed considerable restraint in South Africa. One particular concern was to not employ Indian troops, nor local indigenous fighting forces, aware of the impact that would have on relations with the Afrikaners. However, the British also relocated a considerable number of Afrikaners (mostly women and children) in internment, or what became known as 'concentration', camps. Neglect became widespread. That became known to the British public due to the activities of British civilian activists, and was eventually rectified.

The Afrikaner (or 'Boer') forces were irregulars, but they had a military history which went back to the Dutch East India Company of the 1650s. Several of their leaders were replaced in the middle stages of the war because they were found to be inadequate. Their successors were generally better educated but quite young. One of those replacements became the prime minister South Africa, General Jan Smuts.

On the other side of the world, the Philippine-American war had evolved out of the Spanish-American war of 1898. The Filipino population objected to what was seen as the American occupation of their country, and rebelled. The war had the character of a 'guerrilla', or small-scale, war. It might be more useful to consider it to be an insurgency, and therefore American operations as a counterinsurgency campaign.

There was a considerable amount of fighting and casualties on both sides. American social, political and economic development was probably more important than fighting in resolving the conflict. 500 American teachers relocated from the continental United States as part of the social development programme. They founded a number of the country's more important academic institutions, several of which survive to this day.

Atrocities were committed on both sides. One American general was court martialled for just that reason. Reprisals were carried out, but at the time reprisals were not contrary to the laws of war. Just as in South Africa, elements of the local population were relocated into what became known as concentration camps. Once again, neglect and deprivation occurred. Over 120,000 American soldiers were involved in the campaign, of whom perhaps 6000 were killed. About 50,000 Filipinos were killed through American military action. However, cholera broke out amongst the indigenous population and a further 200,000 Filipinos died.

One notable aspect of the war was the service of a number of veterans of the American Civil War. One was Lieutenant General Arthur MacArthur, who had been awarded the Medal of Honor at the battle of Missionary Ridge in 1862. He became the commander in chief of the US army in the Philippines. General Douglas MacArthur, of Second World War fame, was his son.

The US Army adapted and evolved. Only 14 years earlier it had waged the last major campaign of the Apache wars. It had learnt the need to adapt its tactics and its operational approach against an irregular indigenous enemy. That lesson was relearnt in the Philippines.

By the beginning of the 20th century, the Industrial Revolution was changing warfare dramatically. That was especially true at sea. The steam turbine had been invented in 1884. By 1900 it was being introduced to warships. The turbine was more compact than the steam reciprocating engines it replaced; it was reliable; it allowed greater speeds; but it led to huge increases in coal consumption. The need to stoke coal by hand could require up to 300 men per ship. Those features all had an important impact on ship design. By 1910 or so, battleships' gun turrets were probably the most complex man-made structures on earth.

Lightweight internal combustion engines and developments in aerodynamics allowed man to undertake powered flight for the first time in 1903. Flying was embraced by armed forces rapidly and with enthusiasm. The first take-off by an aircraft from a warship occurred in Weymouth Bay in England in 1912. Armed forces continued to develop and deploy lighter-than-air craft. Tethered observations balloons were used at Ladysmith, and powered airships were in military service by 1914.

There had also been a revolution in military technology on land. Modern rifles were the product of several parallel inventions: effective locking breeches, smokeless propellants, the conoidal bullet and the box magazine. Together they allowed infantry soldiers to produce effective fire out to ranges of several hundred metres, and to do so lying down behind cover. Machineguns had been deployed from the 1860s. At the beginning of the century they were big, typically mounted on artillery carriages, and relatively vulnerable. Smaller, tripod-mounted designs such as the Maxim (the British Vickers) were beginning to enter service.

There had been similar advances in land-based artillery. Fast-operating and efficient breeches, coupled to effective recuperating mechanisms, allowed field artillery to fire accurately and rapidly over distances of several thousand yards. Coastal artillery had adopted further improvements, such as prediction of fire and corrections for the effects of charge temperature, atmospheric pressure, wind, and barrel wear.

The telegraph and (radio) wireless telegraphy allowed considerable developments to signalling, both on and off the battlefield. The telegraph was widely used between continents, between countries, and on to the battlefield. Despatch riders, runners and semaphore were employed forward from there. Wireless telegraphy was in its infancy but developing rapidly, particularly at sea.

In some ways, intelligence was in its infancy. Its importance was broadly understood, but since most enemy information came from horsed cavalry, there was not much of it. Analysis and dissemination were not well developed. Some nations had moderately well-developed strategic intelligence services, typically using networks of military attachés and sometimes spies. The British government, for example, had been systematically intercepting correspondence since the middle of the 19th century.

Industrialisation had affected logistics in several ways. Transport between continents was by steamship. Transport between and within countries was generally by rail. Thus the railway network might dictate the conduct of land campaigns; but also vice versa. Armies depended on railways for operational movements and supplies. Transport at divisional level and below was generally by horsed wagon.

Canning and refrigeration greatly improved the supply of food to the troops and therefore their health. Advances in field hygiene, inoculation and other forms of preventative medicine were beginning to reduce the incidence and the consequence of disease: in the armed forces of developed nations, at least.

Those nations' navies were important and complex bureaucracies. Naval policy and spending was a significant public issue in several countries. So-called 'navy leagues' attracted both political and public attention.

Nowhere was that more true than in Britain. The naval budget was the single largest item of government spending. At the turn of the century Britain had a chain of coaling stations along its major shipping routes. About 44,000 Royal Navy seamen were stationed abroad, typically for three years at a time. In 1906 Admiral Sir John Fisher, the First Sea Lord (the professional head of the Royal Navy) introduced a revolutionary new type of warship. Named after the first ship of the class, HMS *Dreadnought*, it was designed around steam turbines, a main battery of big guns of one calibre (12 inches), a sophisticated fire control system, a high top speed, and a reasonable cruising range (albeit at relatively low speeds).

Dreadnought rendered practically all previous battleships obsolete. Fisher has been criticised for poor strategic decision-making in developing and deploying *Dreadnought*. That is naive. Britain's fleet was as large as those of any two other nations combined. If it was to maintain its operational lead it could not ignore technical development. Britain proceeded to build Dreadnoughts faster than any other nation. If it had not developed the Dreadnought, another nation (probably Germany) would have.

Below the battleships came the cruisers. They were primarily designed to patrol the world's sea-lanes. The Royal Navy had 121 cruisers in 1914. The next eight largest navies combined had a total of 177. The next class, destroyers, could only just remain at sea in bad weather. However, with a mixed armament of torpedoes and guns (of about four inch calibre), they could threaten battleships and cruisers whilst being able to destroy any ships smaller than themselves. Destroyer flotillas were a very useful component of fleets, although somewhat short-ranged. Submarines were in their infancy. Admirals were aware of their potential, but they were not yet particularly seaworthy nor seen as a major threat to warships.

Naval theory was well developed. The works of Sir Julian Corbett and Captain Alfred Mahan were studied around the world. That led to some uniformity of tactical and operational thinking. Tactics stressed the Nelsonian line of battle dominated by the battleship (and hence, increasingly, by Dreadnoughts), together with the necessary signalling and fleet manoeuvres.

Operationally, there was clear and mature understanding of issues such as control of the sea; the importance of maintaining a fleet in being (not least, to threaten the enemy's control of the sea); the use of the sea to move armies to other countries and continents; and war on trade (for which a reasonably well-developed body of international law existed).

Battleships were expensive. Although *Dreadnought* rendered most previous battleships redundant, the latter were not immediately scrapped. Several continued to serve well into the Great War.

If manned flight was in its infancy, aerial warfare had not yet been born. It did, nevertheless, attract considerable discussion and attention. Armed forces and their governments were well aware of the military potential of aircraft. Aircraft had to be bought out of military budgets and therefore competed for procurement funds with other warlike equipment. In 1914 naval and military air forces were small; but considerable thought, experimentation and development had taken place.

Warfare on land was beset by particularly difficult problems. The firepower of infantry, particularly when entrenched, had been remarked upon as long ago as the American Civil War. There was considerable debate as to infantry tactics. In Britain it focussed on the appropriate dispersion between soldiers in the firing line. Armies typically consisted of large numbers of rifle-armed infantry and smaller proportions of cavalry and artillery. The tactical problems caused by rifled bullets, and the sheer weight of fire which riflemen and machine gunners could deliver, were recognized but nowhere near solved.

The demise of cavalry, caused by improvements to infantry firepower, had been foreseen as far back as the Crimean War. Some cavalry commanders were notably socially and professionally reactionary, but others were amongst the keenest reformers. It had been noted, for example, that in the final months of the Franco-Prussian war 12 out of 16 Prussian charges had been effective. The issue was not *whether* cavalry needed to adapt and evolve, but *how*. The cavalry of the 1900s was quite different from that of the 1870s, and better for it. Machineguns were seen as important cavalry weapons. A reasonably well-informed debate as to the balance between the mounted charge and dismounted rifle fire was underway, but consensus had not been reached.

Theory and doctrine were generally well developed. In the German army, military doctrine had developed and evolved from the writings of Clausewitz and Moltke the Elder. It did not ignore modern challenges; it sought to adapt and evolve practice accordingly. Exercises and manoeuvres were keenly debriefed and lessons incorporated into doctrine. For example, reckless charges were discouraged; the importance of field defences was acknowledged; and it was recommended that troops should practice attacking them in peacetime. As Chief of the German Greater General Staff, Moltke the Younger managed to prevent the Kaiser from getting personally involved in the annual army manoeuvres, thus generally improving their conduct and the lessons identified.

Some armies very much wanted to believe in the power of the offensive. The 1904 French infantry regulations considered that forward movement would prove decisive and irresistible. They were wrong. Where rationalistic military thought and aspiration triumph over empirical reality, the results are often tragic.

The British Army learnt enormously from the Boer War. Skill at arms improved dramatically, due to assiduous practice with live ammunition. A British soldier fired 250 rounds per year in training (a German conscript fired only 100 in two years). Cavalry doctrine, training, and horse handling all received considerable attention. New field guns were introduced: the 18 Pdr of 1904 had the heaviest shell weight of any field gun in general service in 1914. It was a direct lesson from the Boer war.

A general staff was introduced. Formal doctrine (in the shape of Field Service Regulations) was published, and then revised. The army reserves were reorganised into the Territorial Army, and a host of other improvements were put in place. The selection of battalion commanders was radically improved through an exam-based selection process which tested tactical competence. Officer education was reviewed, including allowing university entrants to gain commissions directly without attending officer academies.

The defence of the British Empire was reorganised. The Dominions (Canada, Australia, New Zealand and South Africa) were included, to the extent of training officers for a truly imperial general staff. Individual officers were exchanged between Dominion and British armies for two years at a time. Individual, unit and formation training was enhanced. For example, compulsory military training was introduced in Australia in 1911. The New Zealand Army conducted unit-level exercises for the first time in 1912 and formation-level exercises in 1913. All these measures had a direct bearing on the course and outcome of the Great War.

Hundreds of fortresses were in use around the world in 1914. France fortified its eastern border with Germany after the Franco-Prussian war. Germany had fortified its western border with France in Alsace-Lorraine. There were fortifications throughout Switzerland. Italy had fortified its borders with both France and Austria. Belgium had heavily fortified its eastern borders with Germany. Russia had fortified many of the cities in Poland along its borders with Germany and Austria-Hungary. Many British ports (including several in Ireland, Australia and New Zealand) had coast defence fortifications. The United States had fortified its east (and to some extent its west) coast, originally against the British, at vast expense. And so on.

Some of the fortifications were of modern design, using large amounts of reinforced concrete and often incorporating turreted guns. However, there was a systematic problem with obsolescence, often due to the sheer cost of building fortifications; let alone upgrading them. British coastal fortifications did not employ turreted guns. They had lower, less obvious profiles and relied heavily on earth ramparts and traverses (albeit with large amounts of reinforced concrete around the gun positions, etc).

When war came, many fortifications would be found wanting. Typically they were sited on the crest of hills, and the defences were often concentrated in keep-like areas. They were therefore vulnerable to concentrated artillery fire. In some cases the concrete was of poor quality. Nevertheless, the best fortifications of the early 20th century could be very tough indeed.

Nationalism was becoming an issue, particularly in central and eastern Europe. Nations in the Balkans, the Czechs and the Poles were making the case for their own states. The same applied, for example, to the Armenians in Ottoman Turkey. In the summer of 1914 the most pressing political problem in Britain was a relatively limited form of devolution for Ireland, known as 'Home Rule'. (The relevant bill was passed into law, but its enactment was immediately deferred with the beginning of the Great War). There was also a growing sense of the identity of the industrial working class. Socialism was becoming popular in several western nations.

The media had become a major factor. In many countries newspapers were cheap and widely read. However euphemism, evasion, circumvention and wilful distortion in reporting military matters were widespread. Simple, clear, direct language was rarely used. Some writers consciously distorted issues. Others just didn't bother to check their facts. In several countries the population developed an unrealistic understanding of war, which may have contributed to the popular support for war and eager volunteering of 1914.

Much of the war and warfare of the early 20th century now seems Eurocentric, for good reason: it was. Much of the Americas were at peace, not least due to the isolationist Monroe doctrine in the United States. Most of Africa was colonised, and colonial nations rarely warred against each other. Similar considerations applied to much of Asia.

Europe had largely been peaceful in the 19th century. That was partly a consequence of the post-Napoleonic system. The five major powers (Prussia, now Germany; Austria, now Austria-Hungary; France; Russia; and Great Britain) maintained a system of international diplomacy which, by and large, prevented major wars in Europe. Smaller countries such as the Netherlands, Denmark and Switzerland protected themselves quite effectively through neutrality.

However, there were 'new kids on the block'. Italy, relatively recently united, suffered from irredentism: a desire that everything that was once Italian (or Roman) should be part of the new country. Serbia suffered from rabid nationalism, interpreted in some undefined (and conveniently indefinable) manner that a greater Serbia should arise again. Japan, in the throes of modernization, also developed a strident nationalism and militarism which would cause problems for much of the early 20th century.

Colonial areas were largely, but not entirely, peaceful. Most colonies had been effectively pacified and were being developed to some extent. There were some colonial revolts. Some, like the Herero Revolt in German South West Africa, were suppressed viciously with great loss of life. But broad swathes of the globe were largely at peace. The colonial powers had developed pacification techniques which were largely effective, if sometimes brutal. The British Empire in India relied on what has been described as a massive bluff. Most of its army consisted of locally-recruited indigenous forces. Indians, both soldiers and civilians, believed that they would be ruled well and fairly. By and large, they were. The British Indian Army served effectively and loyally throughout the period, so the largest empire the world has ever seen was largely at peace for decades.

Russia was expanding eastwards into Manchuria. It had a summer port in Vladivostok, and opened an all-weather harbour at Port Arthur under a lease with China. Japan had captured the area in 1894 but had been forced, by western pressure, to hand it back to China. Japan and Russia collided. War broke out in 1905.

The Russian army showed many of its old characteristics. The soldiers were brave, dogged and obedient. Units and formations were often slack. The army had *some* capable leaders. Intelligence was generally poor. These traits, identified in the Russo-Turkish Wars of 1877-8, would be seen right up to the Second World War.

The Japanese army was relatively well organized, well-trained and well-equipped. Japan also had a modern, well-equipped navy. Soon after the outbreak of war Russia sent a fleet from the Baltic around the south of Africa to relieve Port Arthur. The Japanese navy learnt that it was coming and gave battle at the Tsushima Strait. The outcome was a massively one-sided success for the Japanese. After heavy fighting on land, the war ended with clear operational and strategic success for Japan.

Unfortunately the Japanese had, or soon developed, a misguided sense of racial superiority (for example, over the Chinese) and a sense that the western nations were decadent. A perception of supremacy at sea, linked to issues such as the Samurai code of honour and hyper-nationalism, were interpreted by army and navy officers to imply almost divine invincibility. Those attitudes led inexorably towards tragedy in 1945.

There were many lessons to be learned from the Russo-Japanese war. At sea they reinforced belief in the power of the line of Dreadnought battleships. The effective-ness of the torpedo was, if anything, over-stressed. On land, it was observed that reasonably well-constructed trenches were almost impregnable; a lesson that had been identified in the American Civil War. The British deduction was to reinforce the need for more artillery. Nonetheless, trench positions *could* be taken, and were, if the attack was pressed heavily enough and the attacker was prepared to take significant casual-ties. Cavalry was poor on both sides. In the case of Russian Cossacks, that came as a surprise to western observers.

There was, however, a problem of perception. The nations involved were seen as being 'oriental'. In the Russian case that was due to eastern European Orthodoxy and a sense of 'otherness'. In the Japanese case it was due to Asiatic inscrutability. Therefore there was recognition that tactical and perhaps operational lessons *had* been identified. Conversely there was also a sense that those lessons might not apply to western nations.

The Ottoman Empire had been seen to be in decline for centuries. The Young Turk movement broke out in 1906 amongst Turkish army officers stationed in European Turkey, which at the time stretched as far west as the Adriatic Sea. Several Balkan countries believed that Turkey's European provinces were vulnerable. That perception was the main rationale for the First Balkan War of 1912-13.

The Serbian, Bulgarian, Greek and Montenegrin armies were quite numerous and reasonably well equipped, trained and led. The Turkish army was heavily outnumbered in its European provinces and was in the midst of modernization. The Turks attempted to appeal to a sense of Ottoman sense of unity which largely failed, not least in due to the number of non-Turkish and non-Moslem soldiers in the army.

Serbian, Greek and Montenegrin forces quickly overran Turkey's western European provinces. Bulgaria mobilised over 400,000 men in two months and directed the bulk of its army towards Istanbul. The Bulgarian army besieged the city of Adrianople (Edirne), about 160 miles beyond its border, which was protected by fairly modern German-designed fortifications. The Bulgarian army had no medium or heavy artillery. A five-month siege developed. The Bulgarians were then reinforced by a Serbian army with heavy artillery. Adrianople then fell after a two week bombardment followed by two well-conducted night attacks. Bulgarian attempts to attack Constantinople had been thrown back, as were Greek landings in the Gallipoli area. As a result of this First Balkan War, the Ottoman Empire lost most of its European provinces.

However, several Balkan states felt that Bulgaria had benefitted too much from the peace settlement. Bulgaria's new provinces were attacked by Serbian, Greek and Montenegrin forces in the Second Balkan War of 1913. Bulgaria might have repulsed that attack, but was then invaded from the north by Romanian armies. Romania wanted to annexe southern Dobruja, which had some ethnic Romanian population. Turkey also attacked, and reoccupied Edirne. Now heavily outnumbered, Bulgaria sued for peace. Serbia, Greece and Montenegro gained territory in the south and west. Romania gained southern Dobruja. Turkey kept Edirne. The war lasted for less than two months.

The events that led to the outbreak of war in 1914 were rooted in the past. The post-Napoleonic settlement in Europe had lasted for decades. Then in the 1860s and 70s Prussia fought and won short wars against Denmark, Austria-Hungary and France. The first treaty of Versailles brought the Franco-Prussian war (the third War of German Unification) to an end. King Wilhelm of Prussia was crowned Kaiser of the newly-created German Empire in the Hall of Mirrors in Versailles on 26th February 1871. The post-Napoleonic balance of power had shifted radically.

Wilhelm died in 1888. He was succeeded by his son and then, within three months, by his grandson, Kaiser Wilhelm the Second. Although a grandson of Queen Victoria, Wilhelm the Second had a very odd attitude towards Britain. It alternated between anger and envy. He started what became a 'Dreadnought race' in order to build a navy to challenge the British Royal Navy. Wilhelm was disliked by many of the kings and emperors of Europe, many of whom were his relations. By the early 20th century he had alienated an impressive array of countries.

Remarkably, all five of the great powers in Europe chose to go to war simultaneously in 1914. Most German leaders wanted war. They feared a resurgent Russia. They believed that it was necessary to fight a war before time ran out, and that there was currently a favourable window of opportunity. The older generation of Prussians had fought through three wars which had been short, victorious, and waged outside German territory. Many Germans assumed that military success in any forthcoming war was, effectively, guaranteed.

France did not necessarily want war, but if war broke out France wanted it sooner rather than later. Revenge for the events of 1870 were a factor, as was the desire to regain Alsace and Lorraine. The wider issue, however, was the pre-eminence of Germany in Europe.

Russia had rebuilt her armies after the Russo-Japanese war. Its economy was developing rapidly. Strategically she depended on the use of the Dardanelles for her exports; particularly grain. Russia saw herself as protector of the Slavs, especially those in the Balkans, and of the Orthodox religion. Russian politicians had designs on liberating Constantinople (Istanbul) from the Turks. The defeat of Bulgaria in the Second Balkan War was seen as a blow to Russian prestige, to the benefit of Austria-Hungary. Russia's goal of controlling the Dardanelles was considered to have been set back considerably. Thus in the summer of 1914 Russia saw it to be in its interests to support Serbia, almost regardless of the pretext.

The Austro-Hungarian empire included several ethnic minorities. It had been involved in the Balkans for centuries. It found Serbia to be quarrelsome and problematic. Austria-Hungary had several legitimate interests in the Balkans, and saw Serbian nationalism as a particular threat. The chief of the Austro-Hungarian general staff, Field Marshal Franz, Freiherr (later Graf) von Hötzendorf,[1] was an interesting personality. In 1913 he had urged the Austrian Emperor to declare war on Serbia 25 times. Wiser councils, especially that of Archduke Franz Ferdinand (the heir apparent) had prevailed. Franz Ferdinand intended to relieve von Hötzendorf of his appointment after the summer manoeuvres of 1914.

Britain was an imperial trading nation. Its long-term interest and declared position was to support peace in Europe. Peace was good for trade. Trade was good for Britain. However, peace was not to be maintained at any price. Britain had worked for centuries to avoid the emergence of any single dominant power in Europe. Britain had an informal agreement with France to declare war on a Germany if the latter violated Belgian neutrality. The German fleet was the only significant threat to Britain's preeminent trading position. From Belgian ports German naval units could easily interrupt the coastal and North Sea trade upon which much of Britain, and critically the port of London, depended. In 1914 London was the busiest port in the world. Unusually for both countries, Britain was allied to Japan.

---

1   Also known as 'Conrad' or 'Conrad von Hötzendorf'.

Most European countries were democratic to some extent, but there were only three republics in Europe. Kings and emperors still held important roles. Parliaments were generally not sovereign. Ministers (and prime ministers) were generally appointed by, and worked for, their king or emperor. In practice many ministers worked *around* their sovereigns. But in practically every case the only point at which government, foreign affairs and military issues came to a head was with the person of the king or emperor. Their individual personalities were therefore a significant issue; as were the ways in which ministers, generals and admirals worked to and for them.

With the assassination of Franz Ferdinand, Europe began to slide towards war in what became known as the July Crisis. Much of Europe was on holiday. At this point a remarkable woman, a granddaughter of Queen Victoria, stepped into the spotlight. Queen Marie of Romania invited several of the protagonists to join the royal family at the summer palace of Peleş near Sinaia. Von Hötzendorf was one of the guests. The intention was to hold a series of informal discussions about the July Crisis out of sight of the European media, and (crucially) away from easy access to the telegraph system.

Sinaia is not far from the border with Transylvania, at the time or part of the Austro-Hungarian Empire. At about the same time an invitation was received by the Austrian Frau Gina von Reiningshaus and her husband. It asked them to join acquaintances in Kronstadt (modern Braşov), just inside Transylvania. Frau von Reiningshaus was von Hötzendorf's mistress. A day or so after the Reiningshausens arrived a note was passed to Gina, seemingly from von Hötzendorf. It asked her to join him at a small village near the border. He also received a note, seemingly from her. The two were secretly photographed together. The photos were quickly spread around Europe and passed to several newspapers, possibly via Romanian diplomatic bags. It was a very clever set-up intended to discredit von Hötzendorf. It worked. Franz Joseph, the Austrian Emperor, had no choice but to dismiss him. Within a few days the July crisis had been defused. A major war in Europe was avoided.

That, of course, did not happen. Marie *was* a granddaughter of Queen Victoria and queen of Romania; but not until the death of her father-in-law about four months later. Secret services, and secret intelligence services, did not really exist in the 1910s. Or did they? Such James Bond-like entrapment simply didn't happen. Or did it?

Britain responded to the July crisis very firmly. King Christian of Denmark received a letter from his aunt, Queen Alexandra (the widow of King Edward the Seventh) asking him to receive an audience from the British ambassador. The ambassador explained that, in order to maintain peace in Europe, Germany had to be deterred from entering the war. The ambassador requested Danish covert and diplomatic assistance in doing so.

At or about the same time Fisher ordered the British Grand Fleet to demonstrate off Kiel. The German High Seas Fleet was at sea, conducting manoeuvres off Norway. British minelayers practiced laying minefields just outside German territorial waters. British submarines were sighted in the narrow waters between Denmark and Sweden. Naval officers made enquires in the London shipping exchanges about hiring merchant shipping to transport army units to Denmark. Much of the Territorial Army was deployed for annual training. It was mobilised and warned for military operations in Denmark or North Germany. The Army began to advertise contracts for horses, which would be needed by the reserve (Yeomanry) cavalry. Reports quickly circulated around Europe.

There was panic in Berlin. In 1905 a threat by Fisher had resulted in serious concerns about the security of the north German coasts and, perhaps more importantly, Baltic shipping trade. Germany was critically dependent on Baltic trade, not least from Sweden. British submarines operating in the Baltic, supported or protected by a British army in Denmark, might persuade Sweden to stop trading with Germany. It could completely disrupt German war plans. The Danish government invited all parties to a series of discussions about the July Crisis. War was, in fact, avoided.

That, of course, did not happen either. Fisher was no longer the First Sea Lord in July 1914. British strategic planning for war in 1914 was, effectively, non-existent. Even worse, Britain lacked an effective planning *mechanism* by which to respond to war or the threat of war.

What *did* happen? Franz Ferdinand and his wife were assassinated at Sarajevo by Serbian terrorists. It was quite obviously the work of the Serbian secret service. Austria-Hungary understandably demanded satisfaction. The Serbian reply was evasive. Germany appeared, at least to Austria-Hungary, to give the latter a free hand in the matter. Russia acted to protect Serbia, initially by declaring partial mobilisation against Austria-Hungary. That prompted German mobilisation against Russia. Russia and France, which were allied, declared war on Germany and Austria-Hungary. Using its only operational plan, German armies marched into Belgium in order to envelop French border fortifications. Violation of Belgian neutrality brought Britain into the war against Germany, and then also against Austria-Hungary. Italy, the Ottoman Empire, Bulgaria and Romania remained neutral for the time being.

Queen Marie of Romania *was* British, but her husband (King Ferdinand) did not come to the throne until after the death of her father-in-law (King Carol)[2] in October 1914. Both Carol and his wife were German. Importantly, Carol was *pro*-German. Queen Alexandra *was* Danish and was the aunt of King Christian. She was also the aunt of Kaiser Wilhelm the Second, who she disliked intensely. Fisher was a highly accomplished strategist, something many historians overlook. He *did* manipulate a panic in Germany over access to the Narrow Waters in 1905. The First Sea Lord, Prince Louis of Battenberg (a German by birth), retired due to gout in October 1914. Fisher was then recalled by the First Lord of the Admiralty (navy minister), Winston Churchill. We shall probably never know to what extent Battenberg's gout was real or merely diplomatically convenient. What would have happened if Battenberg's gout had become problematic in, say, May 1914? Wilhelm the Second's father (Friedrich the Third) had ruled for less than four months in 1888. He died of cancer of the throat. We shall never know; but it if he had ruled for any reasonable length of time,

---

2   'Karl' in German; 'Charles' in French or English.

the whole history of the Great War, and therefore the 20th century, might well have been very different.

There is a strong tendency to describe the beginnings of the origins of the Great War in structural terms. That is, largely in terms of alliances and their consequences. Structures do have consequences. However, all human structures involve human beings. Human beings are agents, who make decisions, which have consequences. Those human beings might well have made different decisions which would have different consequences. We have also seen the consequences of luck: for example, of Friedrich the Third contracting cancer, or Carol of Romania dying a few months earlier. Luck can be good or bad.

The nations involved had a number of professional, capable officers. For example, British military correspondence shows a perceptive insight into the practical military problems of any forthcoming war. In 1905 Britain wargamed the possibility of deploying an army into Belgium in the event of a German invasion. Such professional expertise was in no way limited to Britain.

What was generally missing, however, were adequate strategies. War plans were typically made in isolation from foreign policy. Germany did not really have a strategy. It had one war plan. It was, essentially, to mobilize first against France, defeat it, and then attack Russia. It did not consider any war aims. The plan would have been totally irrelevant if France had not entered the war. It required the casual violation of Belgian neutrality, which can be seen as politically naive. The Chief of the German Great General Staff, Moltke the Younger, said during the July Crisis that it was impossible for Germany to respect Belgian sovereignty. Regrettably, he was right. The only plan that Germany had to fight a war required the invasion of Belgium.

In a sense the situation in Britain was even worse. There had been no Secretary of State for War since March 1914. Britain went through the July crisis without a war minster (the Prime Minister, Asquith, had carried out the role himself). Britain had created a Committee of Imperial Defence in 1902, as a result of the Boer War. However, the Liberal government, which had been in power for eight years, had failed to produce a strategy for a war in Europe. There were contrasting requirements. One was the need to project the Army on to the Continent; but where, and to do what? There was a plan to deploy the Army to Flanders, but the purpose of doing so was unclear. The other requirement was the need to use the Navy, the most powerful navy in the world, strategically in order to defeat Germany. That might have involved a war on trade. But how would that be done? The War Office and the Admiralty could not agree. The government failed to create a consensus, or impose a decision, and then resource it. Britain knew that France, its major ally, might be defeated by Germany in three weeks (that had, effectively, happened in 1870). Britain needed contingency strategic plans, and it needed a strategic planning mechanism. It had neither.

France had a war plan, or at least an operational plan. It involved a quick mobilisation followed by an attack into Alsace and Lorraine. That is, a strategic offensive regardless of the political circumstances. The President and the Chief of the General Staff concealed the plan from the war minister. It was never discussed in parliament.

However, the key problem was not a lack of parliamentary oversight. France went to war on a plan which was largely independent of government policy.

Russia had technical problems. Mobilisation would be slow, due to Russia's sheer size and lack of resources. The plan was ponderous and inflexible. Germany realised that if Russia mobilised *for any reason* it would inevitably mobilize against Germany. Understandably, Germany saw that as a threat. It was reasonable to respond by mobilising: either before Russia did; or failing that as quickly as possible.

There is always unfinished business in international affairs. In a world society of what is now about 200 actors, there will always be. Structural issues are important. So is human agency. Luck plays some part. Technology plays a part: war, and warfare, in the first decade or so of the 20th century were highly characterized by the technology to hand. Perhaps the biggest problem in 1914, however, was a failure of strategy. It was not a failure knowing of how to conduct planning. It was a failure to have strategic planning bodies in existence, and strategic plans available for contingencies which might reasonably be expected to arise. More importantly still, it was a general failure to link foreign policy goals to military objectives. Nations went to war. But for what goals?

There was also, as ever, a difference between planning and execution. Germany, France, Russia, Austria-Hungary and Britain all had some kind of operational plans for use on mobilisation. In the case of Germany there was a strong expectation that its plan to defeat France, and then Russia at its leisure, would dictate the outcome of the forthcoming war. It did not. It dictated no more than the course of the first phase. War, and warfare, are unpredictable.

2

The Great War

There are several significant misconceptions about the Great War. One of the most common relates to the size of the British Army. It is generally held that it grew from just six divisions on mobilisation to about 70 by 1918. That overlooks the 14 infantry divisions and 14 Yeomanry (militia cavalry) brigades of the Territorial Army. The British Army did enlarge considerably, but not twelve-fold. It was roughly threefold. Many writers have overlooked those 14 divisions and 14 brigades. What else have they overlooked? We should reconsider what we think we know about the Great War.

One highly reputable British historian named the 'four men who won the war' as Lloyd George, Hankey, Milner and Wilson. Many people will only have heard of David Lloyd George, Minister of Munitions and then Prime Minister from December 1916. They may be able to distinguish between Thomas Woodrow Wilson, President of the United States and proponent of the 'Fourteen Points' and (General, later Field Marshal) Sir Henry Wilson, Chief of the (British) Imperial General Staff (CIGS) from February 1918. They may have no idea as to which of the two Wilsons was being referred to; nor who Hankey and Milner were. Was the writer serious; was it a gross exaggeration; or is the history of the Great War seriously misunderstood by many people, writers included?

A number of misconceptions arise from the German official history. It was written to justify and sustain the place of the German Army in society. The three overall commands of the Army were those of Moltke the Younger (until September 1914), General Erich von Falkenhayn (until late August 1916) and then Field Marshal Paul von Hindenburg and General Erich Ludendorff. Under Moltke, the so-called 'Schlieffen Plan' for the defeat of France failed. It was important for the official history to show that that was due to failings on Moltke's part; not that of the plan itself, nor the Army. Under Falkenhayn, the Army failed to defeat France at Verdun. The official history was written to blame Falkenhayn. Hindenburg and Ludendorff were Falkenhayn's arch-rivals. Their subsequent achievements, the eventual outcome of the War, and the so-called 'stab in the back' myth all pivot around a German interpretation of history which was first aired in the 1920s. It persists to this day.

Further misconceptions stem from Lloyd George's memoirs. A post-war rush by ministers, admirals and generals to publish included several accounts which were critical of Lloyd George. A publisher offered him such a large advance for his memoirs that he was widely accused of profiteering from soldiers' deaths. He withdrew his drafts, and eventually published one volume a year from 1933 to 1938. His aim was to record and vindicate his own political achievements. In doing so he almost single-handedly destroyed the reputation of several other people, particularly Field Marshal Sir Douglas Haig. Haig had died in 1928. He never published his diaries, nor any memoirs. When his diaries were published in 1952 they were largely overlooked. Those who read them assumed they had been extensively rewritten for publication. They had not.

If one couples Lloyd George's interpretation with post-war disillusionment, one sees a bad war which must, self-evidently, have been fought by bad generals. Haig was the most senior general, so he must have been the arch-villain. Lloyd George's criticism of Haig, in his memoirs, was vitriolic. Add in Alan Clarke's 1961 book 'The Donkeys', widely seen as anti-Haig, together with the stage show and film of 'Oh! What a Lovely War!' (1963), and one sees a bad war fought by bad men for no purpose; nothing but pointless slaughter.

It was not so.

This chapter looks at the strategy of the Great War. It is too easy to become fixated with the campaigns of the Western Front. To avoid doing so we shall first look at the war at sea, and then consider German strategy. An outline chronology of the Great War is at Figure 2-1.

In 1914 Britain's place in the world, ruling 'the empire on which the sun never set', depended very strongly on maritime trade. Within days of the outbreak of the war German cruisers were sinking British merchantmen around the world. They sank 203,000 tons of shipping in 1914. In turn those cruisers were all sunk by March 1915. The only German naval formation at sea, the Far East squadron, was destroyed off the Falkland Islands in December 1914. 1.14 million tons of German maritime trade was confiscated. 2.87 million tons was trapped in neutral ports. Just 2.16 million tons was available to the Central Powers (initially Germany and Austria-Hungary). A naval blockade was in place which was never lifted. By late 1917 food rationing in Germany was having a serious effect on public health, morale, and political sentiment.

British naval policy depended on a North Sea blockade. It was neither 'close' (blockading German ports) nor 'distant' (mounted by cruisers operating from British home ports), but 'intermediate' (mounted by cruiser patrols at sea). German counter-blockade operations attempted to lure British naval units into ambush by elements of the German High Seas Fleet. In turn, the British attempted to intercept the High Seas Fleet at sea. The Battle of Heligoland Bight in August, the British attack off Dogger Bank in September 1914, and German cruiser raids in November and December 1914 and April 1916 were all inconclusive. In May 1916 the British Grand Fleet caught the High Seas Fleet at sea off Jutland. The British lost a few more ships, but many more German ships were severely damaged. Several were not fit for sea again for weeks.

Western Front	Italy	Eastern Theatres	Turkey
1914 Aug. Germany attacks France through Belgium and Luxembourg		Russian armies invade East Prussia. Defeated at Tannenberg. Austria-Hungary attacks Serbia	German warships arrive in Dardanelles
Sep. 1st battle of the Marne			
Oct. 1st battle of Ypres		Russian offensive in Galicia	Turkey Declares war
Nov.			Royal Navy bombards the Straits. British forces occupy Basrah. Russian invades Caucasus
Dec. 1st battle of Artois		Austria-Hungary defeated in Serbia	
1915 Jan.			Turkey attacks Suez Canal. Turks defeated in Caucasus
Mar. 1st battle of Champagne. Battle of Neuve Chapelle			
Apr. 2nd battle of Ypres			British landings at Gallipoli
May. Second battle of Artois. Battles of Aubers and Festubert	Italy Declares war on Austro-Hungary and Germany 1st Battle of the Isonzo	German Gorlice-Tarnow offensive	Russian summer offensive in the Caucasus opens
Jun.	2nd Battle of the Isonzo		
Jul.			
Sep. 2nd battle of Champagne; battle of Loos			
Oct. Third battle of Artois	3rd Battle of the Isonzo	Bulgaria enters war. German, Austro-Hungarian and Bulgarian forces overrun Serbia (by Dec)	
Nov.	4th Battle of the Isonzo	French and British forces arrive in Salonika	
Dec.			
1916 Jan.			Siege of Kut (until Apr)
Feb. Germans attack at Verdun			Evacuation of Gallipoli. Russian winter offensive in the Caucasus
Mar.	5th Battle of the Isonzo Austro-Hungarian offensive in the Dolomites		
Jun.		Russian Brusilov offensive (until Sep).	
Jul. Somme offensive (until Nov)			
Aug.	6th Battle of the Isonzo	Romania declares war. Invades Transylvania	Turkey attacks Suez Canal

	Western Front	Italy	Eastern Theatres	Turkey
Sep.		7th Battle of the Isonzo	Bulgarian and German forces attack Romania	
Nov.		8th & 9th Battles of the Isonzo	Austro-Hungarian, Bulgarian and German forces overrun Romania	
Dec.	Operations at Verdun closed down			
1917 Feb.	German Army withdraws to the Hindenburg line			
Mar.			February Revolution in Russia	First battle of Gaza. Baghdad occupied by British
Apr.	Nivelle offensive; battle of Arras (to May)			Second battle of Gaza
May		10th Battle of the Isonzo		
Jun.	Battle of Messines			
Jul.	3rd Battle of Ypres (until Nov)		Kerensky offensive. Defeated by German and Austro-Hungarian forces	
Aug.		11th Battle of the Isonzo		
Oct.		12th Battle of the Isonzo (Caporetto). Italian front collapses		
Nov.	Battle of Cambrai		October Revolution in Russia	Third battle of Gaza
Dec.			Russia signs treaty of Brest-Litovsk	British forces enter Jerusalem
1918 Mar.	German spring offensive opens			
Apr.				Turkish forces attack towards Caspian
Jun.		Battle of the Piave		
Jul.	Second battle of the Marne			
Aug.	Battle of Amiens. General allied counteroffensive begins			
Sep.			Bulgaria attacked at Salonika. Surrenders	Battle of Megiddo
Oct.		Battle of Vittorio Veneto. Allied counter-offensive begins		Turkey surrenders
Nov.	Germany seeks armistice	Austria-Hungary surrenders		

Figure 2-1 Outline Chronology of the Great War

The result was a propaganda success for the Germans, who reported the battle much faster than the British. Jutland was, however, operationally decisive for the British. The High Seas Fleet never put to sea against the Grand Fleet again.

German submarines ('*Untersee-*', or 'U-boats') operated against British trade from October 1914. They had considerable success, principally against targets in the North Sea, around Ireland and the western approaches to the English Channel. The sinking of the liner *Lusitania* in May 1915 provoked considerable public and political protest in America, which was still neutral. The U-boats were withdrawn.

In January 1917 Germany declared unrestricted submarine warfare again. It was a calculated gamble which risked bringing America into the war. The Germans believed that the war would be won before America could have a significant impact. America did enter the war, on 6 April 1917. That was a major factor in Germany's defeat. American battleships joined the Grand Fleet. American destroyers operated out of the British port of Queenstown, now Cobh near Cork in Ireland.

Maritime losses to U-boats grew alarmingly. The British Admiralty delayed introducing convoying, concerned about the disruption of trade that would result. Convoying was introduced in April 1917. After May, losses to maritime trade dropped to less than one percent of all ships in convoy. The U-boat threat had been defeated. Allied control of the sea was not challenged again.

Neither Greece, Russia nor Turkey had any Dreadnought battleships at the beginning of the War. Turkey had ordered two in 1911, largely paid for by public subscription. The ships were essentially complete in August 1914. Churchill, who had been the First Lord of the Admiralty for most of that period, ordered their seizure and transfer to the Royal Navy. The arrival of the German battlecruiser *Goeben* and a cruiser (the *Breslau*) at Istanbul that month changed the operational balance in the region significantly. They were transferred to the Turkish navy and interdicted Russian naval operations in the Black Sea.

Austro-Hungarian ships and submarines operated out of ports in the northern Adriatic throughout the war. More than half of all ships sunk by submarines were sunk in the Mediterranean, many of them by German U-boats using Austro-Hungarian ports. Italian, French, British and Japanese naval forces were employed to contain the threat throughout the war. Sea routes to the Far East via the Suez Canal were not significantly affected.

There were virtually no losses to troop movements across the English Channel. Only three ships carrying American soldiers to Europe were torpedoed, and only 63 American soldiers were lost at sea. The uninterrupted movement of armies, and their logistics, without significant loss was one of the most important achievement of the Western navies.

Germany did not have a strategy in August 1914. It had plans for a maritime cruiser campaign. Quite separately, its Army had an operational plan (the 'Schlieffen Plan') to defeat France quickly and then turn east to defeat Russia. It was very sophisticated in terms of 'what to do' and 'how to do it', but critically weak in terms of 'why?' That is, its political purpose. No obvious political ends were linked to the ways and means employed. The 'ways' (particularly the violation of Belgian neutrality) brought Britain into the war and generated considerable American sympathy for Belgium. German naval and military plans were largely unrelated. The offensive in the West broke down somewhere between first contact with the French and British armies (on the Sambre and at Mons from 21 August) and the battle of the Marne (from 6 September). In the east, Germany suffered local reverses before a brilliant operational counterstroke at Tannenberg, which destroyed the Russian Second Army and badly mauled the First.

In 1915 the German Army was principally occupied with supporting Austria-Hungary in the east. Its Gorlice-Tarnow counteroffensive in May 1915 was successful and turned into a general advance eastwards, inflicting significant casualties but failing to achieve any major encirclement. The Russians appear to have learnt from Tannenberg. German operations in the west were largely limited to a local attack at Ypres, involving the first large-scale use of poison gas.

For 1916, Falkenhayn intended to defeat France and thereby bring about strategic success in the West. He planned to attack early in the year at Verdun, which the French would be politically obliged to defend, and to inflict so many casualties that the French Government would collapse and sue for peace. The plan did not work. The battle opened on 21 February. Falkenhayn wished to discontinue the attack as early as 4 April, but was overruled. The battle continued into the summer, at which point the Allies attacked on the Somme. German attacks at Verdun were discontinued, but Germany was forced to defend on the Somme until the end of the year. In the east, Germany supported Austria-Hungary against the Russian Brusilov offensive and provide both troops and leadership against Romania, which entered the war on the side of the Entente ('the Allies').

Falkenhayn was removed in August 1916. His successors, Hindenburg and Ludendorff, had been a senior command team on the Eastern Front. They reorganised the defences of the Western Front. That included the construction of strong rear positions which would become known as the Hindenburg Line.

Hindenburg and Ludendorff did not believe that the war could be won in the west in 1917 with the forces available. Clausewitz wrote that wars could only be won by attacking. Strong German forces were already deployed in the east. The Kaiser, the chancellor and the army and navy commanders held a conference at Pless Castle in Silesia on 6 January 1917. It was the only German conference that explicitly considered strategy in the whole war. The conference is known for the decision to recommence unrestricted submarine warfare.

The records of the conference contain no record of any discussion of what the Army would do. That is clearly an omission and, on reflection, clearly deliberate. It is not reasonable to believe that the German army would do nothing, or that no decision was taken. It is entirely reasonable to believe that Hindenburg and Ludendorff stated their intention to defeat Russia that year. As we shall see, it is also entirely reasonable to believe that the relevant documents were deliberately excluded, or subsequently removed, from the files.

German strategy, formulated at Pless, was therefore as follows. Defeat Russia in the summer of 1917. Cripple Britain with a U-boat campaign at the same time. Shift forces west and defeat France and Britain. The U-boat campaign would probably bring the USA into the war, but America would probably be unable to contribute significantly until well into 1918. However, even if the U-boats failed to defeat Britain, Germany would be able to redeploy and defeat the Western nations before American armies could intervene.

Under those circumstances Hindenburg and Ludendorff would have quite happy to agree to unrestricted submarine warfare at the Pless conference. What harm could it do? At the very least it would probably weaken Britain, which would help the subsequent German attack in the west.

A revolution broke out in Russia a month later. The Tsar abdicated and the Kerensky government took over. The German foreign ministry asked the Army (and the Army agreed) not to attack, so as not to unite the various Russian factions with a common cause. However, Kerensky and his colleagues intended to continue the war. The German foreign ministry had been subsidising subversion in Russia, but had not got the revolution it wanted. It therefore arranged (with Ludendorff's express knowledge) to transport Lenin and his colleagues from Switzerland, across Europe, to bring about a second revolution. German subsidies were immense. Lenin and his Bolsheviks used them to print and distribute one and a half million copies of *Pravda*, free, every week. They also produced a number of other revolutionary publications, including one for soldiers and another for sailors.

Kerensky's government planned and conducted another reasonably successful campaign in the summer of 1917. The German Army did just enough to contain it and prop up the Austro-Hungarians. In November Germany finally got the revolution it wanted and had financed. Lenin took control of much of Russia. That is: Germany bankrolled the Communist takeover of Russia. Russia's armed forces largely stopped fighting. By February 1918 the Germans had imposed the highly punitive treaty of Brest Litovsk on Russia. The Russian Empire broke up. Ukraine, Finland and other provinces declared independence.

Germany could now transfer forces westwards in order to defeat Britain and France in the Spring of 1918. Historians have discussed whether, or how many, divisions were actually sent west. The simple answer is to count them. Examining one standard reference that has been available since 1993, 42 divisions left the eastern front and arrived on the western front between September 1917 and March 1918.[1] It is a mystery why such issues remain matters of historical debate. The work has been done.

The German Army's first attack, against the British Fifth Army, was tactically a huge success. Operationally it achieved nothing important. Subsequent attacks against the French, the British and their Portuguese allies had similar results. Allied

---

1   Ellis, John and Cox, Michael, *The World War One Databook*, (London: Aurum, 2001), pp.119-126. First published by Aurum in 1993.

counterattacks continued into July. The predominantly British counteroffensive, begun on 8 August, defeated the German Army in the West. Germany was forced to sign an armistice early on 11 November 1918.

The German Foreign Office had also engaged in subversion elsewhere. A German intelligence officer ran a sabotage campaign in the United states that caused damage worth about $150 million (over $1 billion today). German money was used to suborn the French press. That was discovered and closed down. Two deputies in the National Assembly (one of whom was a minister) were convicted of treason. German espionage and subversion failed almost completely in Britain. The main exception was support to the Easter Rising in Ireland.

There were several peace initiatives during the war. German initiatives were rejected for several reasons, including the failure of the Entente to find a formula which was acceptable to all of the three major partners (France, Italy and Britain).

In August 1914 Austria-Hungary was dismayed to learn that German had no immediate plan to attack Russia. Thus any pre-war joint, strategic, military planning had been totally ineffective. Austria-Hungary invaded Serbia but failed to defeat it. Austria-Hungary also had to divert forces north to defend Galicia (southern Poland) against Russia. They were heavily defeated. In 1915 Austria-Hungary again failed to defeat Serbia; was again heavily beaten by the Russians in Galicia; and had to improvise a defence when Italy entered the war in May.

In May 1916 Austria-Hungary attacked south through the Dolomites. The thin line of Italian forces broke. Formations panicked. The Italian Fifth Army, the strategic reserve concentrated east of Verona, was surrounded and surrendered. Austro-Hungarian troops reached the Adriatic west of Venice. The bulk of the Italian Army was surrounded on the Isonzo front. The Italian government collapsed and Italy sued for peace (see Figure 2-2).

That did not happen, and it is useful to consider why not. The Austro-Hungarians *did* attack south through the Dolomites. At first they had considerable success. However, the offensive (like many at this stage of the war) began to lose momentum. Critically, the Brusilov offensive opened in Galicia on 4 June 1916. Germany declined to support Austria-Hungary in the Dolomites. The operation there was closed down and forces redeployed to Galicia.

Austria-Hungary successfully defended against 11 Italian attacks on the Isonzo. In October 1917 Germany provided four divisions to support a counteroffensive (the German Army did not, broadly, attack anywhere else that year). Those formations included the German Alpine Corps, a specially-raised division which had fought in the Dolomites, the Vosges and the Carpathians. Spearheaded by the Alpine Corps (including a Major Erwin Rommel), the Germans and Austro-Hungarians broke through the Isonzo front. Rommel was awarded Germany's highest honour, the *Pour le Mérite*, and the armies of the Central Powers exploited as far as the River Piave. Venice very nearly fell. Eleven British and French divisions were rushed to the Piave. Five were still there a year later. A further Austro-Hungarian offensive across the Piave in the summer of 1918 failed. The counteroffensive, led by the British XIV

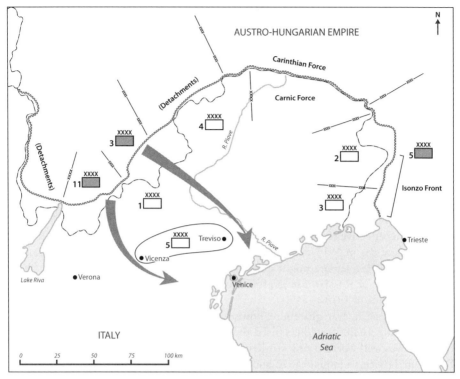

Figure 2-2 North East Italy, 1916.

Corps and specifically the 7th and 23rd Divisions, crossed the Piave. Italian, French and British forces recaptured most of the territory lost in 1917 before Austria-Hungary sued for peace on 29 October 1918. The peace conditions allowed Entente troops to move through Austro-Hungarian territory. Germany would have faced war in 1919 with hostile troops on its borders anywhere from the Swiss border to Poland.

Turkey had lost all of the seven wars it fought against Russia since 1711. It had been fighting on and off since 1910; initially in Kosovo and Albania, and then in the two Balkan Wars. In 1914 it knew that it would not survive a general war without the support of one of the Great Powers. After protracted negotiations, including the offer of five million pounds of gold, it entered the war on the side of Germany and Austria-Hungary in October 1914. More than any other step, Turkey's entry turned the war into a world war. Turkey had planned two offensives: one against Russia in Armenia, the other against Britain in Egypt. Both were major failures.

The Sultan of Turkey was also the Caliph, the spiritual head of the world's 240 million Muslims. Turkey had a population of 21 million, many of whom were non-Muslim. There were 20 million Muslims in the Russian Empire. There were 20 million more in the French colonies. There were about 100 million in the British colonies. That was not lost on the Turks, nor the Germans. They tried a number of measures to suborn British and French Muslim colonial troops, or provoke a revolt in various colonies, with no success.

Winston Churchill, a former junior cavalry officer turned journalist and then politician, was 39 years old. If he had been a naval officer he might have been commanding a cruiser. As it was, he was responsible for Britain's entire naval policy and strategy. Mindful of what had happened to the *Goeben* and the *Breslau*, Churchill ordered an attack on the Dardanelles even before Turkey declared war. We shall look at the Dardanelles (the naval operation) and Gallipoli (the land campaign) later. They failed.

Britain invaded southern Mesopotamia (modern Iraq) in 1914 to protect its oil supply. British forces in Mesopotamia eventually seized Baghdad by late 1917. Turkey was initially focussed on the Caucasus and then, given their proximity to Istanbul, the Dardanelles. Events in the Caucasus see-sawed. Initial Turkish successes in late 1914 were overturned by the Russians in early 1915. Two corps of the Turkish Third Army collapsed; its effective strength fell from 100,000 to about 18,000. There were further Russian successes in 1915 and then 1916. Were it not for the February Revolution in Russia in 1917, Turkey might quite possibly not have survived into 1918. With the withdrawal of Russian forces after Brest-Litovsk, Turkey advanced to seize the Caspian oilfields in 1918.

Turkey's greatest strategic failure, however, occurred in Palestine. 376 British troop ships, carrying 163,000 soldiers, used the Suez Canal in 1914. Strategically, cutting the canal was well worth trying. Turkey attempted to attack across (or at least cut) the Suez Canal twice, in January 1915 and August 1916. Two British counteroffensives at Gaza in early 1917 were defeated. General Sir Edward Allenby, newly arrived from commanding an army in France, led another attack later that year. He succeeded. Allenby entered Jerusalem in December. The Turks, and about 10,000 Germans, constructed a defensive position across central Palestine. British forces broke through that position in September 1918 and advance rapidly as far as Damascus. The advance continued. The British lost 5,660 casualties. They took about 75,000 prisoners. Turkey sued for peace as other British forces advanced on Istanbul from the west (described below). It was effectively the end of the Ottoman empire.

Bulgaria was persuaded to enter the war in September 1915 after extensive negotiations with both the Central Powers and the Entente. Gold, territory and food were all discussed. The Entente's failure to take the Dardanelles helped persuade Bulgaria. Its entry into the war alongside Germany and Austria-Hungary had significant consequences (see Figure 2-3). Serbia and Greece were both threatened.

Bulgaria viewed the war through the perspective of the Second Balkan War. It attacked Serbia from the east. Together with Austro-Hungarian and German successes, that forced the Serbian army to withdraw to the Adriatic. French and British forces, some of them from Gallipoli, landed at Salonika to support the Serbian army. The Serbs were moved by sea to join them. Bulgarian, German and Austro-Hungarian forces contained Entente forces in Salonika until late 1918. The Central Powers could open the railway line through Niş, and then send equipment

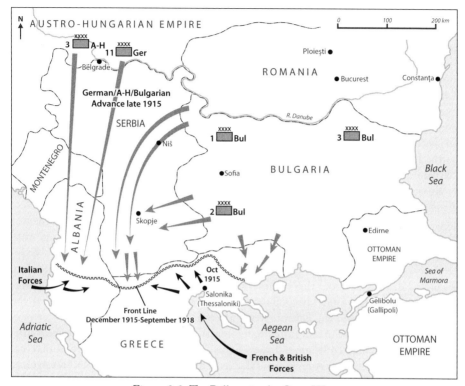

Figure 2-3 The Balkans in the Great War.

(particularly heavy artillery) to Turkey. The British withdrew from Gallipoli before any heavy artillery could arrive. Bulgarian troops also played a significant part in the attack on Romania in late 1916. Almost all German and Austro-Hungarian troops had been withdrawn by the time that the Entente attacked out of Salonika in late 1918. The Bulgarian army, demoralised, poorly fed and poorly clothed, fell apart. French and Serb forces advanced rapidly northwards. They liberated Belgrade on 1 November. British divisions moved eastwards towards Istanbul. Bulgaria capitulated on 29 September, Turkey on 31 October and Austria-Hungary on 3 November.

Serbia had offended Austria-Hungary in June 1914, and started a war, entirely reckless of the consequences. Her army, although not large, was fairly well equipped and highly experienced. It defeated Austro-Hungarian offensives in 1914 and 1915. It was only defeated when Bulgaria attacked from the east in 1916. The Serbian army continued to fight in the sector between Salonika and the Adriatic. It was still fighting as a member of the Entente at the end of the War.

In 1914 Russia felt that it had to be seen to be the protector of the south Slavs. Perhaps more importantly, it did not intend to lose influence in the region to Austria-Hungary. Russia had both historic and more contemporary interests with regard to

Turkey. Historic interests included territory in the Caucasus, including areas popu-lated by (Christian) Armenians. Half of Russia's exports and 80 per cent of its grain harvest were shipped through the Straits. Turkey had closed the Straits in 1912 during the First Balkan War. Russia's balance of payments evaporated. Russia could not afford to have the Straits closed again. That became critical once Turkey joined the Central Powers in October 1914.

A sensationalised report of a Turkish success in the Caucasus prompted the Russian commander in chief, Grand Duke Nikolai, to request British help in reopening the Straits in December 1914. That was the formal issue which prompted the British campaign to the Dardanelles and Gallipoli. The problem in the Caucasus (the Turkish attack on Sarikamiş) had been reversed well before the time the British (and French) landed.

Russian summer offensives in 1915, 1916 and 1917 were described above. The Brusilov offensive of 1916 was timed to take pressure off Verdun. It also had the effect of cancelling Austria-Hungary's offensive in the Dolomites. Romania entered the war the same year; Russia provided the 47th Corps (of two infantry and one cavalry divi-sions) to support Romania in Dobruja (the region east of the Danube bend).

Romania's entry into the war was the outcome of extensive secret negotiation, including discussion about that summer's harvest. Romania needed to sell it, Austria-Hungary needed it to feed its population, and Romania could not export it via the Dardanelles. However, the Entente made a better overall offer.

On 29 September 1916 two Romanian infantry divisions crossed the Danube south-wards near the village of Flamanda (see Figure 2-4). A Bulgarian Army Group, led by the German General August von Mackensen, was operating further east against the Dobruja. Four more Romanian divisions crossed during the next two days. They advanced rapidly south east, enveloping much of von Mackensens's forces. A similarly rapid thrust by the Russian 47th Corps broke up his army group. Romanian forces exploited towards Sofia, prompting the Bulgarian government to seek a ceasefire. The 47th Corps continued southwards. Four days later the (Russian) 3rd Cavalry Division seized a crossing of the Çatalca lines outside Istanbul. Russian reinforcements were pouring south by train.

Meanwhile, Romanian forces had broken through the Carpathians into Transylvania. They advanced rapidly north west. Within two weeks they had seized the undefended southern exits to the Tatar, Uzok and Dukla Passes. Austro-Hungarian and German forces in Galicia were now cut off. The Hungarian Plain lay open to the Romanian Army. As more Russian forces were rushed westwards, Turkey and Austria-Hungary sued for peace. The war was over (see Figure 2-5).

That did not happen, and it is useful to consider why not. The southern operation *was* planned, the forces were assembled, and the leading Romanian divisions crossed the river. Romanian forces *did* break into Transylvania. However, a lack of success in Dobruja (described below) caused Romanian commanders to vacillate and then cancel the Flămânda operation. Several Romanian divisions were transferred to the Carpathian front, but arrived too late to have any impact. Operations in Transylvania were scaled down.

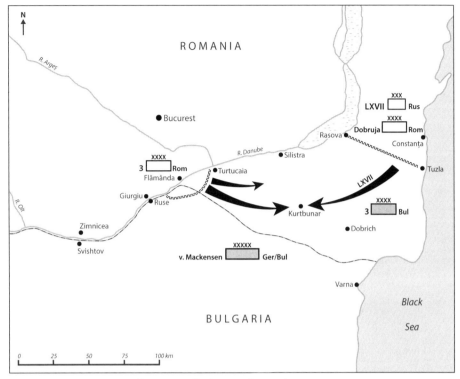

Figure 2-4 Dobruja in September 1916.

At the time Ludendorff was chief of staff to Hindenburg, the German commander in chief in the east. Ludendorff had been extremely worried by the prospect of a Romanian advance against the Carpathian passes into Galicia. If the Romanians had acted quickly, they may well have unravelled the Eastern front. They did not. They had previously overreacted to the loss of a fortified position at Turtucaia on the Danube and withdrawn forces from the Carpathians. Romanian forces spent weeks shuttling north and south. It was strategic indecision. They fought reasonably well, but could be (and were) beaten by German units such as the Alpine Corps.

German-led forces under von Mackensen, Falkenhayn (now commanding the Ninth Army) and others overran most of Romania by early 1917. The remnants of the Romanian Army, and King Ferdinand, withdrew to the northeast. The collapse of the Russian Army in 1917 made their position untenable (despite defensive successes against German and Austro-Hungarian forces). Romania sued for peace. The talks dragged on. Although Romania provided oil and food to the Central Powers in 1918, Ferdinand did not sign the peace treaty. At the end of the war Romania rearmed, threw out its occupiers, and advanced into Transylvania and then Hungary. It earned a place at the Paris Peace Conference in 1919.

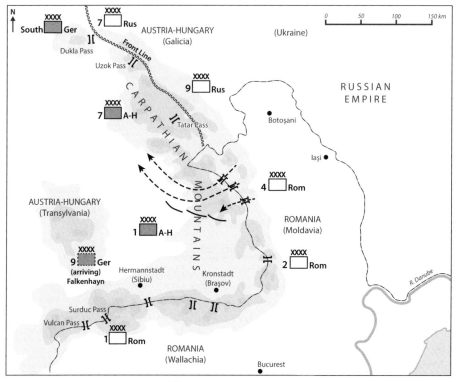

Figure 2-5 The Carpathians in September 1916.

Italy had effectively changed sides. In 1882 it had signed the Triple Alliance with Germany and Austria-Hungary. Naval considerations made it think again. War against the Entente would mean the elimination of Italian coastal and Mediterranean shipping. Italy wanted the south Tyrol, to give it strategic depth against Austria; parts of the Istrian coast; a protectorate over Albania: and some share of the Ottoman, and German overseas, empires. The London Treaty of April 1915 agreed those demands. Italy entered the war on 23 May 1915. Italy's strategy was painfully simple: attack across the Isonzo River into (modern) Slovenia. The Italian army attacked four times in 1915, five times in 1916 and twice in 1917. Then the Germans and Austro-Hungarians then counterattacked, as described above.

Lack of continuity was a problem for French high-level planning. During the War France had four prime ministers, seven defence ministers and three commanders in chief. France's initial war aims were to defeat Germany, recover Alsace-Lorraine, and undo the results of the Franco-Prussian War. Germany attacked in 1914 and was halted. The conduct of that campaign will be considered in Chapter Three. Faced with German occupation of 20% of its territory and 60% of its industry, however, France's immediate strategic goal became much more pragmatic: to eject Germany from France. It fought three battles in Artois (in December 1914, May and October 1915) and one in Champagne (also in October 1915). It encouraged the British Army to fight alongside. The British battles of Aubers Ridge and Festubert took place during the Second battle of Artois. The Battle of Loos was fought at the same time as both the Third Battle of Artois and the battle in Champagne. Although attacked at Verdun in early 1916, France found 12 divisions to attack alongside the British on the Somme that summer.

For 1917 France's main attack, the 'Nivelle Offensive', would take place against the Chemin des Dames in April. The Chemin des Dames is a ridge overlooking the Aisne between Soissons and Reims. The British were to attack at Arras at the same time. The French attack was a bloody disaster. The French appear to have lost 90,000 men on the first day, alone. That is more than the British on the first day on the Somme. Soon afterwards, French units began to refuse to go up to the front line. A mutiny spread quietly across the French Army. It eventually involved 49 divisions: just under half of the army. News of the mutiny was suppressed. Ringleaders were rounded up, many imprisoned, and about 50 shot. The French army could not be relied upon to fight again until 1918.

In 1918 Germany attacked the French Army as part of its Spring offensive, most notably at Chateau Thierry in May. The Second Battle of the Marne, from 18 July, was highly successful for the French. It can be seen as either the last Entente counterattack or the first battle of the Entente's counteroffensive. General Ferdinand Foch had been appointed allied Generalissimo, with poorly-defined responsibility and authority, on 26 March 1918. With a staff of just 26 officers, Foch coordinated a series of Entente offensives which finally forced the German army to seek terms.

Britain's strategic posture in July 1914 was to maintain the peace. After war broke out Britain developed two strategic goals. Firstly, it aimed to preserve its status as a great power. Secondly, it aspired to improve its security in relation to its current enemies and allies. It was never obvious how that was to be achieved.

In the summer of 1914 Britain did not have a war minister nor a body capable of strategic and joint operational planning. Its war minister had resigned in the Spring, and not been replaced. Its cabinet could be described as spineless: a quarter quit on, or over, the declaration of war. The navy minister, Churchill, was more than capable of coming up with imaginative schemes. However he lacked a First Sea Lord who was likely to translate them into action. The government's policy was for peace, but it was not capable of the kind of strategic contingency planning that the July Crisis required.

Herbert Asquith, the British Prime Minister, appointed Field Marshal Herbert Kitchener to be war minister on 3 August 1914. Forceful and a national hero, Kitchener was grossly unsuited to the job. He had almost never served in Britain, and not at all since the Boer War. He was unused to the new staff system. He tended to ignore his staff and never convened the Army Council. He lacked strategic vision as to how to fight a war. In August 1914 he simply decided to deploy the Army to France in accordance with the endorsed war plan. That was an operational deployment plan, not a strategy. Under his guidance the Army was significantly enlarged, and sent to France to fight alongside the French. But to what purpose?

Having deployed to France, the British Expeditionary Force (BEF) moved secretly by rail to Antwerp. On 20 August the German First Army marched through Brussels en route to Paris, bypassing Antwerp. On the 22nd large numbers of 'English' cavalry attacked German rear areas from the north. By the 24th British cavalry reached Liege. The German First and Second Armies hastily turned about. The French Army counterattacked attacked north across the Sambre. After three weeks of bitter fighting the front line stabilised east of Brussels, where it would remain for the next four years.

Clearly that did not happen, either. Why not? Churchill actively planned an operation to protect Antwerp and deployed his newly-formed Royal Naval (infantry) Division (RND) there. The option involved risk. Churchill said that he could not guarantee the safety of transporting the Army direct to Antwerp by sea. In practice it could probably have been done faster via the Channel ports and then by rail. Britain had individuals more than capable of conceiving and planning high level operations. It lacked a strategic planning organisation with the necessary authority.

It was entirely within the remit of the British navy minister to consider strategic options such as the Dardanelles. Churchill did, as early as September 1914. Asquith later said that the potential rewards were enormous. Not least, an attack on the Dardanelles would prevent Turkey sending forces eastwards, either to Armenia or Mesopotamia. Professional advice urged caution. Callwell, now Director of Military Operations, was a former coast-defence artillery officer. He had visited the Dardanelles in 1905 and subsequently written a paper for the Committee of Imperial Defence. It advised against any attempt to force the Straits by sea. If an operation was considered, the forts should be attacked from the land side. Churchill invited Admiral Sir Percy Scott to command an operation to force the Straits. Scott considered that the available ships could not possibly succeed in the task, and declined. Fisher, recalled to be First Sea Lord soon after the outbreak of war, expressed enthusiasm, then changed his mind and eventually resigned over the matter. It should be said that Fisher did not speak out against the operation in the War Cabinet. Kitchener was heavily in favour of the operation, contrary to his staff's advice. His direction to Lieutenant General Sir Ian Hamilton, who he chose to command the operation, was vague and poorly worded.

Nonetheless, having avoided drawing attention to the Straits, a force was dispatched to the Dardanelles. On 16 May 1915 the (regular) 29th Division landed at Suvla Bay. They moved rapidly inland, and cut off the peninsula by noon. Next to land was a squadron of armoured cars, and then Australian light horse. They rapidly overran Turkish rear areas. The British fleet assisted with a diversionary operation further up the Gulf of Saros. Two divisions of the Australian and New Zealand Army Corps (ANZAC) landed in the early afternoon. By nightfall the two Turkish divisions in the lower peninsula were cut off and surrounded. Units began to surrender. By noon on the 17th the Peninsula was in British hands (see Figure 2-6).

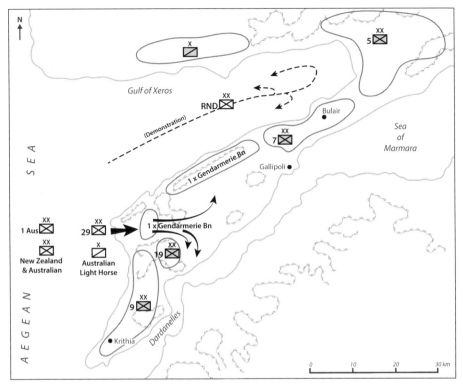

Figure 2-6 The Dardanelles.

Within days a Greek corps was arriving by ship. A second corps was assembling to march through eastern Thrace. The Russian government made representations to neutral Romania and Bulgaria to allow a Russian corps passage down the Black Sea coast. Both countries made token protests and then acceded. A race was on: Istanbul was the prize. In practice the Turks sued for peace soon after British and French warships entered the Sea of Marmora. Bulgaria and Romania joined the Entente soon after. Austria-Hungary then sued for peace. The war was over.

Clearly that did not happen, either. Why not? Firstly, in 1914 and 1915 the British Army was unlikely to conceive of such a sophisticated scheme of manoeuvre. It lacked experience in planning and conducting corps- and army-level operations. Secondly, ANZAC troops were extremely inexperienced (by Regular army standards). Thirdly, Churchill had lost strategic surprise: both months before, when he bombarded the Straits (in November 1914); and then again in March 1915 (when he tried to force the Straits with a naval force). Fourthly, the British troops were thrown in as soon as they were available (the first landing took place on 25 April 1915). Better strategic and operational planning might have indicated that maintaining operational surprise, and a few week's delay to allow for better combined-arms training, was required.

Perhaps more importantly, the British Foreign Minister (Sir Edward Grey) had been completely outmanoeuvred.

Both Russia and Greece had a strong interest in Istanbul. Both *were* approached about the provision of troops. Both could have been led to believe that Istanbul would go to the highest bidder. In practice, however, the Russian foreign minister (Sergei Sasonov) informed Grey that any Greek involvement was completely unthinkable. It was a bluff. Sasonov played a weak hand well, in order to prevent Greece getting Istanbul. Grey, probably too much of a gentlemen, accepted it at face value. By doing so Grey and Sasonov lost an opportunity to take Istanbul.

The second issue is that of a separate peace with Austria-Hungary. The Revolutionary and Napoleonic Wars had dragged on for 23 years because, time after time, one of the partners in the various coalitions would make a separate peace with France. The 'no separate peace' clause in the Pact of London (of 25 September1914) was intended to prevent that. But what about the converse? Entente statesmen tried to arrange a peace with Austria-Hungary. It was unlikely whilst Franz Josef was Emperor. He went to his grave accepting that he, personally, had started the war. However, he died in November 1916. His successor, the Emperor Karl, was far more inclined to seek peace. His main aim was to preserve his empire after the war. However he could not be (or was not) persuaded to make a *separate* peace without Germany

It was entirely reasonable for Britain to consider an operation against the Dardanelles. It might have worked, in some circumstances. But poor strategic and operational planning, and ignoring professional military advice, did not favour a successful outcome.

British failure at the Dardanelles and Gallipoli had far-reaching consequences. It freed up 13 Turkish divisions for use elsewhere. Seven went to Armenia for the 1916 summer campaign against Russia. Four went to Palestine, where they resisted British attacks until late 1917. Two went to Mesopotamia where one, the now-veteran 2nd Infantry Division, made a significant contribution to the fall of Kut (Britain's largest surrender since Yorktown in 1781[2]).

Bulgarian, German and Austro-Hungarian forces attacked Serbia in September 1915. France and Britain rushed forces to Salonika, which lies at the seaward end of a railway line to Skopje (and hence Belgrade). It was too little and too late. The Serbian army was evacuated via Albania and brought back into the line via Salonika. Salonika would become strategically important again in 1918. General Sir William Robertson, the CIGS, advised that the Salonika force be withdrawn at the Chantilly conference in December 1915. However, sustaining the Salonika position maintained a cordon, or barrier, across the lower Balkans. That prevented the German and Austro-Hungarian navies (and especially U-boats) from using the Aegean and north Ionian sea ports, and hence restricted access to rest of the Mediterranean. It kept Greece more-or-less

---

2   More troops surrendered at Kut (about 13,000, versus about 8,000 at Yorktown), but only 3,156 of those who surrendered were British. The remainder were Indian.

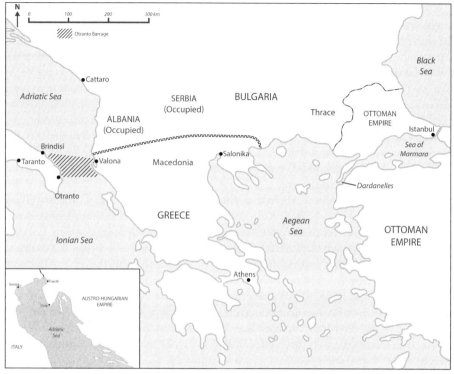

Figure 2-7 Macedonia and Thrace.

on the side of the Entente. Greece did subsequently provide forces. The cordon kept Serbia in the War. It tied down Bulgarian forces. Yet, most curiously, nobody seems to claim credit either for the decision to deploy forces there, nor for the decision to maintain them there. That may well be due to the way in which Lloyd George presented his part in the events in his memoirs.

At the beginning of the war the British government of Asquith, Grey, Kitchener and Churchill repeatedly made poor strategic decisions. Churchill resigned after the Dardanelles. Kitchener died in June 1916. Asquith was manoeuvred out in December 1916. Largely by coincidence, Sir John French had been removed as commander in chief of the BEF in December 1915. Asquith was replaced by Lloyd George, French by Haig, and Kitchener's role was largely filled by Robertson. By that stage Britain had a major and ongoing commitment to France and Belgium, already over 50 divisions strong.

Britain had two main strategic goals for the Western Front. The first was to support France. After 1914 that meant supporting France in the liberation of its territory. From the beginning of 1917 Britain also had to consider the containment, or elimination, of the submarine threat from the Belgian ports.

Unfortunately, Lloyd George was a woeful strategist. He was a great orator; a highly effective parliamentarian; charming, humorous, devious and manipulative; but he could not present any sensible alternative to what he saw as the massive losses and limited gains to date on the Western Front. He tried repeatedly. In December 1917 he urged the French prime minister, Clemenceau, to abandon attempts to seek decision on the Western Front. How naive. No French politician would abandon, or even defer, the liberation of France. Lloyd George never enunciated any practical alternative, beyond a vague hope that defeating Germany's allies would bring about the end of the war. It might have done: but how? Lloyd George repeatedly intrigued against Robertson and Haig, and denied the BEF the resources it needed. Lloyd George failed in all three elements of strategy: the formulation, or agreement, of ends; the articulation of ways; and the provision of means.

British strategy improved slightly during the war. As a result of Machiavellian intrigue by Lloyd George, Robertson was replaced by Henry Wilson. Lord Alfred Milner became Minister of War. Sir Maurice Hankey was the long-standing Cabinet secretary. Between them they arranged what can be described as a competent strategic defence for early 1918. No British troops were withdrawn from the BEF. Divisions were returned to France from Italy. Dozens of British battalions in Palestine were sent back to France and replaced with new units from India. As 1918 progressed Milne, Hankey and Wilson became increasingly involved with post-war strategic issues.

General John Pershing, commanding US armies in France, initially refused to allow American soldiers to fight under British or French commanders (although a few fought at Le Hamel with the Australians on 4 July 1918). The German Spring offensive required him to be more flexible. Whereas the First, and later also the Second, US Armies fought *alongside* the French at St Mihiel and in the Meuse-Argonne offensive, about a third of US divisions (of a total of 32) fought *under* Allied commanders. For example, two divisions fought in the Third Battle of the Aisne as part of the French Sixth Army in early June 1918.

Strategically, however, America's entry into the war was decisive. It ended the war. It forced Germany to seek strategic decision quickly in the west in early 1918. That exposed Germany to operational, and hence strategic, defeat.

Japanese strategy should be seen in light of the Meiji Restoration (the re-establishment of imperial authority in 1868) and all that followed. Japan modernised in many ways. It industrialised. It built a modern army and a seagoing navy. It developed an expansionist foreign policy that brought it into conflict with China and Russia. It annexed Korea after the Russo-Japanese war. Japanese strategy for the Great War was a continuation of all that. For a fairly limited commitment, it gained considerably; largely at the expense of the German overseas empire. Japan became a player on the world stage.

So much for the ends sought, and the ways undertaken, in the strategic conduct of the war. What of the means applied?

There was more maritime shipping in commission, worldwide, at the end of the war than at the beginning: 45.7 million tons against 43.1 million. Some new battleships were completed (the Royal Navy completed 13; the USA and Germany six each). Cruisers and smaller vessels were built in large numbers, not least as convoy escorts. The British Royal Navy, for example, employed up to 193. 125 were typically deployed at any one time. Small numbers of ships were converted, or built, to operate aircraft.

Over 25,000 aircraft were built, but losses were very high. Losses were mostly due to accidents, of which many were in pilot training. The British Royal Air Force (RAF) was created on 1 April 1918 by combining army and navy air services. At the end of the war the RAF had about 2,000 aircraft in operational service. It had 200 squadrons at first line. 100 were on the Western Front and 63 were employed for home defence.

The great measure of effort, however, was in the number of army divisions raised. Figure 2-8 gives an estimate of the number of divisions raised and operated, by nation and theatre of war.

Nation	Total Raised	Deployed: Western Front	Eastern Front	Balkans (1)	Italy	Romania	Dardanelles	Egypt & Palestine	Mesopotamia	Caucasus
Germany	252	204	85	2		12				
Austria-Hungary	88		66	21	54					
Turkey	67 (2)			1		1	15	9	6	12
Bulgaria	16			14		7				
Total Central Powers	423	204	151	38	54	20	15	9	6	12
Russia	296 (3)		170			3				15
Romania	27					27				
Serbia	21			14						
Greece										
Italy	73	2		6	68					
France	152	115		9	5		2			
Portugal	2	2								
Belgium	8	8								
Great Britain: - UK	73	55		4	5		10	6	1	
- Australia	6	5					~2	2		
- Canada	4	4								
- India	13	5						2	9	
- New Zealand	1	1								
US	32	32								
Total Entente	708	241	170	33	78	30	14	10	10	15

Figure 2-8 Divisions Raised and Deployed.

Notes:
(1): Includes Salonika.
(2): Several Turkish divisions were effectively destroyed and replaced, hence the discrepancy in totals.
(3): Of which, 53 cavalry divisions.

The table is approximate, and generally shows the largest number of divisions in a given theatre (and therefore not the average, nor a typical number). Some divisions were destroyed; some of those were reformed. The German and Austro-Hungarian Armies, in particular, moved large forces between theatres.

A broader measure of effort by theatre and nation is given at Figure 2-8. It shows forces in terms of armies, or equivalents, in 1916 or 1917. In general 9-12 divisions constituted an army, but not all forces of that size were called 'armies'. German corps were typically very large, so the number of armies understates the number of divisions. Forces of a corps or so, or less, are not shown. Figure 2-9 is intended to be illustrative only.

Nation	Western Front	Eastern Front	Balkans	Italy	Carpathians	Egypt & Palestine	Mesopotamia	Caucasus
Germany	8	2						
Austria-Hungary		4	2		3			
Turkey						1	⅔	2
Bulgaria								
Russia		17			1			2
Romania					4			
Serbia			3					
Greece			1					
Italy			½	9				
France	9		1					
Britain	5		⅔			1	1	

Figure 2-9 Armies Deployed.

Thus, for example, France committed the great majority of its forces to the Western front. Its other significant contribution was to Salonika. By contrast, only about two thirds of British forces were on the Western Front. After Gallipoli, the remaining third was divided between Palestine, Salonika and Mesopotamia.

The Great War was *not* settled on the basis of Woodrow Wilson's '14 Points', except very loosely. Analysis of the Armistice document signed on 11 November 1918 shows that it meant all but total surrender on the Western Front. The German Army had to leave behind 5,000 guns, 25,000 machine guns, 3,000 mortars and 1,700 aircraft. It marched home with little more than its rifles. The German navy was to be disarmed and several ships surrendered. The document had 34, not 14, clauses. 16 were purely procedural or technical. Six were intended to meet one or more provisions of the 14 Points. 12 were intended to exceed them. Nine of the 14 Points were not addressed at all. The document included war guilt and reparations clauses not present in the original 14 points. (The subsequent Paris Peace conference will be discussed in Chapter Five.)

Forget the 14 Points. Ask who won and who lost. Put simply, if you fought on the side of the Entente, you won. If you fought on the side of the Central Powers, you lost. If you belonged to an ethnic group that was part of the German, Austro-Hungarian or (European) Russian empires, you typically became part of a nation state that may have reflected your ethnic identity. If you lived in an Arab province of the Ottoman Empire, your country became a French or British mandate. If you lived in a German colony outside Europe or the Near East, your country changed hands.

France, Britain and its Dominions gained some protectorates. The most significant were Palestine, Iraq, (Trans)Jordan and Syria (hence subsequently Lebanon). Italy gained the South Tyrol. Serbia became the dominant partner in what became Yugoslavia. Romania gained Transylvania, Bessarabia and Bukovina. Japan gained several small but significant territories in the north Pacific (including the Marshall Islands, the Carolines, the Marianas and the Palau Islands), and Tsingtao on the Chinese mainland.

Germany lost Alsace-Lorraine, parts of Poland, and control of the Rhineland for a few years. Austria lost Hungary, Galicia (to Poland), Czechoslovakia and parts of what became Yugoslavia. Bulgaria lost western Thrace, and some territory to Yugoslavia. The division of the Russian Empire saw Finland, Poland and the Baltic Republics gain independence, as did Ukraine for a few years.

In very few cases did the War's outcome meet any country's pre-war goals. Arguably, they did in the case of France. There was also the issue of reparations, addressed in Chapter Five. Thus the first-order outcomes. Second-order outcomes, in terms of financial cost and casualties, were immense. Casualties will be addressed in Chapter Three.

The Great War was not pointless. Four empires ceased to exist. Eight new countries emerged in Europe. The Arab provinces of the Ottoman empire were divided, roughly, into the countries that exist today. There was a wholesale redistribution of German colonies, not least to Japan (in the northern Pacific).

Britain and France gained territories overseas. Their peer competitor (Germany) lost its fleet, had its army emasculated, returned Alsace-Lorraine to France and had a large region occupied for the foreseeable future.

The benefits were not obvious to the British public. Defensive wars which preserve or improve the *status quo ante* are often not seen as great victories. The Royal Navy's control of the world's oceans was no longer challenged; but that meant little to the man in the street. Neither did, say, independence for Poland or Finland. Britain now controlled some more overseas territories; but what difference did a few more make? Similarly, Britain now had a secure supply of oil for the foreseeable future. Before 1914 many people would not have thought that was important. After 1918 they took it for granted.

In looking at the Great War, many writers have ignored strategic calculus. Unsurprisingly, countries tended to act out of narrow self-interest. Several nations joined the war after a reasonably dispassionate analysis of what they stood to gain and what the potential loss might be. They were quite prepared to negotiate. Some countries, such as Romania, came out of it rather well.

Wars are fought as a series of campaigns, but the outcome is often a result of political wrangling as much as military events. In Romania's case, for example, gaining Transylvania may have been an issue of liberation, or self-determination for ethnic Romanians living there. It was probably more a result of having joined the right side, and not (literally) breaking the Pact of London.

Much of the grand strategy and military strategy of the Great War was poor. Britain's strategy was poor for much of the war. However, it did just enough (by resourcing the Western Front and beating Turkey in the Middle East) to come out of the war moderately well. France, at least, pursued the liberation of its own territory single-mindedly and then sought to avoid a recurrence. Germany does not seem to have balanced ends, ways and means in any meaningful way. In late 1916 and early 1917 she made a decision (or decisions) which effectively lost the war. It translated into two reckless gambles. One was to undertake unrestricted submarine warfare and hence bring America into the war. The other was to bring about a second Russian revolution under a political party over which it had no control. The former *might* not have mattered (in practice it was critical). In the latter, Germany succeeded in the short term. In the long term, it reaped what it had sown. Germany undertook no major offensive in 1917. That is unusual. What would have happened if it had decided to defeat Russia that year is open to conjecture.

At the critical moment, Germany failed to defeat the Western Allies in 1918. That is an operational issue. However, by then the Austro-Hungarian Army was overstretched in Italy. The Bulgarian Army was overstretched at Salonika. Turkey was over-committed in the Caucasus and not strong enough in Palestine to retain its Arab provinces. The Central Powers were grossly over-extended. Austria-Hungary, Bulgaria and Turkey collapsed fairly quickly. However, that might not have happened if the German Army had succeeded on the Western Front six months earlier.

The strategic history of the Great War is also poor. Written history is dominated by the sources. It tends to overlook the gaps. Not much was written down about the strategic choices that nations made, so historians have not really studied them. It is astonishing that they have missed the obvious gap in the records for the Pless conference, and hence the gap in German strategy for 1917. They have not noticed that there is no mention of plans for the Army. Have they not read Clausewitz? Do they really believe that Germany, of all nations, would stake winning (or losing) the greatest war in history to date solely on 105 submarines? Why did Germany not attack, anywhere, in 1917? Why have historians not noticed the issue?

3

Douglas Haig, Master of Manoeuvre Warfare

The separation of warfare into the strategic, operational and tactical levels was not recognised in the Great War. British doctrine didn't really describe an operational level. In other armies it was not recognised with any great clarity. Historians' work reflects that, because the first-hand sources describe what was thought and written at the time. However, analysis has not caught up. This chapter looks at what we can now see as three examples of operational practice. It also looks at some of the broader aspects of military capability, such as raising and training armies, leading them, and commanding them.

The first example looks at the plans for, and execution of, the German attack in the west in 1914. The second considers von Mackensen's operations in southern Romania in the Autumn of 1916. It does so to provide a vignette of large-scale manoeuvre over considerable distances. The third example looks at Haig's command at the operational level on the Western Front from late 1915 to the end of the War.

German official propaganda relating to Moltke the Younger's modification and subsequent execution of the Schlieffen plan does a good job of hiding the truth in plain sight. Reconstructing the events leads to some simple conclusions.

At dawn on 23 August 1914 the situation was as follows. Namur was under siege. It would fall by the 25th. The German First Army was closing up to the Mons-Condé Canal, defended by the BEF. To its east the German Second Army was in contact with the French Fifth Army, which was abreast of Charleroi, then east to Namur and then south along the Meuse. The German Third Army had closed up to the Meuse above Namur. It had attempted to seize a crossing at Dinant on 18 August, but had been repulsed. See Figure 3-1.

On 23 August the German First Army (of five corps and 11 divisions) attacked the BEF, of four infantry and one cavalry divisions. Six German divisions attacked. Another German corps and a cavalry division was advancing around the BEF's left (western) flank, and the First Army still had a corps in reserve. The BEF was heavily outnumbered and would have to withdraw. The French Fifth Army, with 13 divisions, was fairly evenly matched by the German Second Army, with 14 divisions. The Germans made some progress.

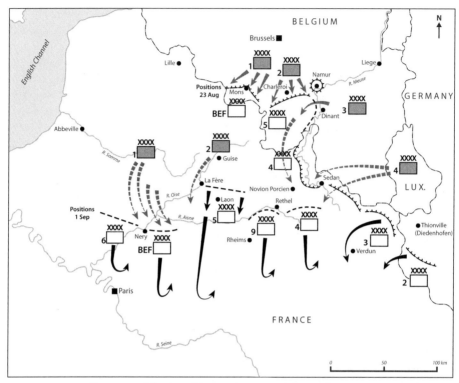

Figure 3-1 Northern France, August and September 1914.

However, a corps of the German Third Army forced a crossing of the Meuse at Dinant. By that evening the bridgehead was about 5km deep. The French Fifth Army's right was exposed. On the 24th it withdrew its flank westwards. That created a gap between it and the Fourth Army, deployed southwards along the Meuse. The Fifth Army, like the BEF, would have to withdraw southwards. It did, all the way beyond the Marne. In passing, remember the importance of the section of the Meuse above Namur.

At this point the Allied left wing (the BEF and the Fifth French Army), with 18 divisions, was facing the German right wing (First and Second Armies) with 25 divisions. On 28 August the commander of the French Fifth Army, faced with the risk of being outflanked to the west as the BEF withdrew, concentrated his Army towards Guise by withdrawing his right-hand corps. That opened another gap between his and the Fourth Army. The German Third Army advanced southwards into that gap, reaching Novion Porcien that evening. The French Fourth Army was pushed further southwards, widening the gap.

The Schlieffen plan called for the German Army to reach the line of Abbeville (at the mouth of the Somme) to La Fère to Diedenhofen by 1 September. The German

First Army *was* at La Fère. However the BEF and the newly-formed French Sixth Army had already fallen back to a line running east to west through Nery. That is about 45km south and west of La Fère. The Schlieffen plan was working. The German right wing was ahead of schedule, and the Allies were being forced to withdraw rapidly.

However, by 15 September the situation had changed radically. The French Commander in Chief, Marshal Joseph Joffre, had ordered a counter-offensive. Another new French Army, the Ninth, had been introduced into the line between the Fourth and the Fifth. The Allied left wing had been reinforced substantially. A further 28 French and two British divisions were committed. Moltke had sent five divisions to East Prussia, three of them from the First and Second Armies. So now the German First and Second armies, with 22 divisions, were facing 48 Allied divisions (in the Fifth, Sixth, Ninth French Armies and the BEF). The so-called 'Miracle of the Marne' was not a miracle. Joffre, his staff and his army commanders had planned and conducted a perfectly respectable operational manoeuvre. It succeeded. The German plan broke down.

On two occasions (23 and 28 August) the German Third Army had found an open flank. If it had attacked west or southwest on either occasion, the French Fifth Army might well have been enveloped and destroyed. But the plan was for Third Army to operate southwards: so it did. In practice the plan, Moltke's handling of it, and the German Army as a whole were not particularly flexible. It was largely a mental and conceptual failure, rather than a physical lack of agility.

18 of the 28 French reinforcing divisions came from operational or strategic reserves. Nine more were moved from the right wing. The last was newly arrived from Morocco. So, in practice, the conceptual basis of the Schlieffen plan did not work. The French advance into Lorraine neither blinded nor fixed them. Joffre could, and did, apply his considerable reserves to halt the German right wing (First and Second Armies). Schlieffen had actually predicted the possibility of the plan breaking down against a temporary (French) defensive position along the general line of the Marne, or perhaps the Seine.

Two particular aspects of the myth can be exposed. Firstly, Moltke is accused of undermining the *concept* of the Schlieffen plan by reducing the ratio of forces between the German right and left wings: from eight to one, to three to one. Given the actual total of divisions deployed (79, plus four reserve (second wave) and two fortress divisions) that is also unlikely to have succeeded. A ratio of eight to one would have meant 71 on the right and eight on the left. But without fixing the French armies in Lorraine, which they did not, the more German divisions marched through Belgium the more French divisions could be moved to face them (operationally, the French were using interior lines). Germany deployed a grand total of 85 divisions in the west. France had 81 and the BEF a further five (at first). Simply marching a proportion of the German Army through Belgium didn't affect the correlation of forces. It did negate the French border fortresses; at the expense of attacking the Belgian forts. But unless the French were fixed in Lorraine, an attack through Belgium was nothing more than a long and tiring march. Nothing in Schlieffen's plan, nor the way it was revised and executed, would or did fix the French in Lorraine.

71 German divisions operating in northern France *might* have been able to defeat a similar number of Allied divisions. It would have required a degree of tactical manoeuvre which the German Army might have been capable of. However, as we have seen, the plan (and the way it was conducted) didn't display that degree of flexibility. Opportunities to envelop French armies were overlooked or ignored. In practice the Germans seem to have demanded adherence to the plan as conceived in advance. It was the opposite of opportunism and flexibility.

If just eight German divisions were left in Alsace and Lorraine, they would have faced the 27 divisions of the French First and Second Armies. That excludes the 11 divisions of the French Third Army and possibly some from the Fourth. The French would have been crossing the Rhine long before the Germans reached the Franco-Belgian border. Germany would have lost Alsace and Lorraine. The Reichstag would have been up in arms. Additionally, the road and rail network in Belgium could not have supported 71 divisions. It was severely overstretched with 27. German officers writing in 1919 or 1920 would have known that.

Moltke is also accused of undermining the *execution* of the Schlieffen plan by removing five divisions from the right wing as the operation was taking place. Moltke *did* remove five divisions from that wing (on 26 August, so after Mons and Charleroi). However it beggars belief to thank that 25, or even 27, German divisions would have succeeded against 48 Allied. That criticism is trivial.

Joffre and his staff had actually done a better job than the Germans. By opposing 22 German divisions with 48 on the Allied left, Joffre was holding off most of the remaining 63 German divisions (in Third, Fourth, Fifth, Sixth and Seventh Armies) with just 40 French divisions on the right. Who was fixed?[1]

The Schlieffen plan was deeply flawed at many levels. Politically (grand strategically) it was naive. Operationally it was conceptually flawed. It might have worked; we cannot know, but it seems unlikely. But post-war German criticism of Moltke was simply wrong. It was politically-motivated official propaganda.

This is not new. The strengths, locations and movements of forces are all available in books published over 25 years ago. Academic historians spent 16 of those years arguing whether there *was* a Schlieffen plan. Ho hum.

The kingdom of Romania was created in 1881 from the former Turkish provinces of Wallachia and Moldavia. Historically, Transylvania had been part of Romania at various times. The majority of its population were ethnically Romanian. Any discussion about Romania entering the war had to consider Transylvania. Earlier disputes with Bulgaria, and particularly the Second Balkan War, had revolved around southern Dobruja. On entering the war in 1916 Romania advanced across the Carpathians into Transylvania. Bulgaria advanced into Dobruja. Most of Bulgaria's forces were committed against Serbia. Von Mackensen's army group initially consisted of four

---

1   The situation quickly changed as both sides move forces into Belgium in the 'race to the sea'; but the point remains.

Bulgarian infantry and one cavalry divisions, one Turkish division, and a few German battalions. See Figure 3-2.

The Danube formed the border from Serbia to just above Turtucaia. It is typically about a mile wide, has a strong current and had marshes on the north bank. Below Silistra the Danube turns northwards. Thus Dobruja is relatively open to the south. One railway ran north into Dobruja; another to Silistra. There were few good roads.

Von Mackensen's forces seized the Romanian positions at Turtucaia and Silistra by 9 September 1916 and then advanced northeast. Romanian forces fell back on a partially fortified line from Rasova to Tuzla. A single German division was brought up with great difficulty, due to the poor condition of the Bulgarian railways. On 19 October it penetrated the Rasova – Tuzla line. Von Mackensen advanced about 40 miles by the end of October. Critically, his forces captured the major coastal port of Constanţa, denying its use to Romania.

Any further advance in Dobruja would be operationally pointless. Ludendorff vetoed it. Meanwhile, German and Austro-Hungarian forces had cleared the Romanian First, Second and Fourth Armies out of Transylvania, but had not managed to force the passes through the Carpathians. In mid-October Falkenhayn's Ninth Army began

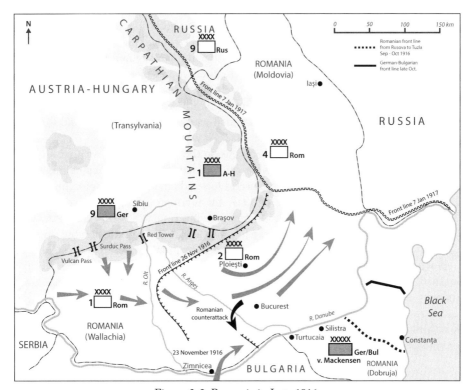

Figure 3-2 Romania in Late 1916.

to force the Vulcan and Surduc Passes, but did not break out until 17 November. It then swept rapidly east, seizing bridges over the River Olt on 23 November.

The Olt is about 180 miles west of Dobruja. Von Mackensen and his staff had planned their crossing of the Danube with great care. Rather than attacking west from Dobruja and approaching Bucurest from the east, Mackensen transferred most of his forces to Zimnicea, 40 miles below the junction of the Olt with the Danube. They started to cross on 23 November. The bulk of his forces had had to march, all the way from northern Dobruja. They then advanced on Bucurest from the south west.

The Romanian First Army had been defending western Wallachia, facing north and north west. Von Mackensen's crossing of the Danube threatened to cut it off. A counterattack by Romanian forces from north of Bucurest on 1 December threatened von Mackensen's left wing. The situation was quite critical. Cavalry divisions from the German Ninth Army linked up with von Mackensen's forces soon after, but much of the Romanian First Army escaped eastwards across the River Argeş. Bucurest fell on 6 December. The Romanian First and Second Armies continued to withdraw north east into Moldavia.

Romanian forces had fought reasonably well. They had fought along a 1600-mile frontier for three months with just 25 divisions. Their commanders had, however, vacillated between the Danube and Carpathian fronts. German forces had broken through in Dobruja and the western Carpathians, but both sides had conducted operational-level manoeuvres. Notably, von Mackensen switched his forces westwards by over 100 miles before crossing the Danube. The Romanians managed to withdraw elements of five or more divisions east across the Olt and then the Argeş. Elements of the Romanian First Army withdrew over 350 miles. Cavalry divisions played a significant role, particularly with the German Ninth Army. We tend to think of the Great War in terms of the stalemate of trench warfare. In some places and for long periods, it was. In other times and other places it was anything but.

When looking at the conduct of operations on the Western Front we are caught in a trap of terminology. Haig fought what can be identified as four major campaigns; three offensive and one defensive. It is useful to see them as the Somme campaign of 1916, the Passchendaele campaign of 1917, the German Spring offensive (from 21 March 1918), and the Hundred Days campaign (from August 8, 1918). Unfortunately, for historical reasons, writers refer to the first two as 'the *Battle* of the Somme' and 'the Third *Battle* of Ypres'. That is not helpful. It is a conceptual barrier to understanding.

Not least, the official historians identified 12 separate, named battles on the Somme in 1916, and eight at Third Ypres. A linked series of battles is a campaign[2]. Haig thought of the Somme and Ypres in terms that we can recognise as campaigns. The 12 battles were fought on substantially the same ground on the Somme, and similarly for Third Ypres. That contributes to the confusion. The relatively limited amount of ground captured strongly supports a perception of pointless slaughter.

---

2   Or a 'major operation'. 'Campaign' is used here for clarity.

Haig had three operational objectives for the Somme. All had strategic significance. None related to terrain features. They were: to relieve pressure on Verdun; to prevent the movement of forces to other theatres; and to contribute to wearing down the German Army to the point where it could be beaten. He achieved all three to some extent, but none of them completely. He explained his rationale, and the events of the campaign, in a dispatch published as a supplement to the London Gazette on 29 December 1916[3]. It is quite a lengthy document, but clearly written, absolutely explicit and available on line. It is curious that some writers criticize Haig's conduct of the Somme campaign without seeming to be aware of his dispatch.

Allied strategic planning for 1917 was underway even before end of the Somme campaign. Germany declared unrestricted submarine warfare in January. Haig was well aware of the difficulties caused by German submarines operating from the Belgian ports. He discussed operations against the U-boat bases with Admiral Sir Reginald Bacon, commanding the Dover Patrol, several times in 1916 and early 1917. Haig wanted to attack in Flanders in the Spring of 1917 with the strategic aim of eliminating the U-boat bases. Allied strategy formulated at the Chantilly conference in November 1916, however, required him to attack in the south in conjunction with the Nivelle offensive on the Chemin des Dames.

In February 1917 the German Army conducted a major withdrawal from the area of the Somme battlefields to what it called the Siegfried Line. It laid waste to the area over which it withdrew. The move released 14 German divisions. Several were transferred to the Chemin des Dames in anticipation of the Nivelle offensive. The withdrawal was a second-order, and hence unforeseen, consequence of the Somme campaign. Haig's offensive would have to take place slightly further north, near Arras. It also meant the cancellation of a subsidiary French attack south of the River Somme. Haig had previously noted that French offensives were often late. This was no exception. The battle of Arras opened on 9 April 1917; the Nivelle Offensive on the 16th. With the exception of the Canadian Corps attack on the Vimy Ridge, Arras progressed only as well as the later stages of the Somme campaign (discussed in Chapter Four). The failure of the Nivelle offensive meant that there was no further operational, hence strategic, purpose to the battle of Arras. It was shut down.

It took some time to shift effort back north for an offensive in Flanders. As that happened, news was received of the French mutinies. Strategically, only Britain and Italy could attack the Central powers in the autumn of 1917. After Caporetto, it was just Britain. The Flanders offensive would be the only major attack on the Western Front in 1917 after the failed Nivelle offensive. It opened with a preliminary operation, the seizure of the Messines Ridge, on 7 June. The main offensive opened with the Battle of Pilckem on 31 July. Pilckem was the first of the eight battles of the Passchendaele campaign.

---

3   Haig, General Sir Douglas, *Dispatch*, 23 December 1916. Published as Supplement to the London Gazette, 29 December 1916.

Passchendaele village is five miles from the railway at Roulers. The U-boats were based inland at Bruges, with sea exits by canal at Zeebrugge and Ostend. In 1917 the only railway to Bruges ran through Roulers. The Roulers railway had operational and hence strategic importance. Additionally, the Dutch border is only 30 miles from Passchendaele. An advance to Roulers, or a longer one as far as the border, would have had considerable benefits. However, Passchendaele was towards the north end of a ridge (the other end is near Messines) from which observers would be able to see Roulers. Gaining observation posts near the village would enable observed artillery fire onto the railway. A breakthrough was not entirely necessary. Capturing a section of the ridge near Passchendaele would be sufficient.

From the north east, the Passchendaele ridge dominates the landscape. From the Allied side it is scarcely noticeable, because the contours are far gentler[4]. Many British soldiers would never have realised its significance. In war, generals and their staff spend hours studying maps. It seems that many historians do not.

We will consider Haig's tactical methods in Chapter Four. It is fair to say here, however, that he had *some* understanding of the operational level. He linked his tactical objectives (such as the Passchendaele ridge) with strategic goals (the elimination of the Belgian U-boat bases). He didn't always succeed as well as he would have liked. He succeeded better than the Germans would have liked. Haig conducted one other operation in 1917: the battle of Cambrai. It seems to be an anomaly. We will consider it in Chapter Four.

The Germans and Russians signed an armistice on 15 December 1917. It led to the treaty of Brest Litovsk. It was obvious to the Entente that Germany would attack in the west, in strength, in Spring 1918. Germany transferred about 40 divisions from the east before mid March 1918. Strategically, and therefore operationally, the French and British armies prepared for a defensive. The Germans attacked on 21 March against the British Fifth (and parts of the Fourth) Army. Operationally, Haig applied reserves to prevent the Germans turning north. Strategically, he persuaded Foch and Clemenceau to order Pétain to attack northwards to contain the Germans, rather than withdrawing to protect Paris. Foch was appointed Allied 'Generalissimo' on 26 March. In practice that gave Haig clearer guidance and better coordination than he had previously enjoyed. He also made it clear to Foch that the latter did not command British troops. These operational-level command arrangements worked well enough for the remainder of the war. As we have seen, the German offensive was halted by mid-1918.

Whatever the definition of the French attack on the Marne on 18 July, Haig's attack on 8 August was the beginning of the BEF's final, offensive, campaign. Ludendorff literally went into shock; albeit briefly. He and his staff telephoned corps HQs, three levels down the chain of command, in person. Ludendorff called it 'the Black Day of the German Army'; for good reason. It was the first time that any army had prepared and opened an army-level attack (with four attacking corps) in complete surprise. (Cambrai

---

4   I am grateful to Dr Nigel Dorrington for that insight.

was also a complete surprise, but involved only two corps). If the Entente, and particularly the British, could now carry out army-level surprise attacks, what chance did the Germans have? In addition, the British (particularly the Canadian and Australian Corps) broke right through the German defensive system at Amiens. It was a major tactical success. The British failed to exploit the breakthrough. No army achieved that on the Western Front. Three days later Ludendorff said that 'this war must be ended'.

The French, Americans and Belgians also attacked (although much of the work done by the King of the Belgians' Army Group was actually done by the British Second Army under General Sir Hubert Plumer). During the 100 Days' Campaign British armies fought 18 separate battles. From 8 August to 11 November they took more prisoners of war than the French, Belgian and American armies combined. The German Army was decisively beaten on the Western Front in 1918.

Most armies grew in size. The US Army was about 200,000 men strong when America entered the war. By the end of 1918 it had 1.98 million men in France. Many more were on the way. The French Army entered the war with 92 divisions but fielded a total of 154. The German Army grew from 103 divisions to 252, but that was partly a result of the reduction of divisional strength, described below. Most armies slimmed down their divisions. Many started the war with divisions of two brigades each of two regiments, each of three or four battalions (a total of 12 or 16 battalions). By the end of the war a pattern of three regiments or brigades, each of three battalions (hence nine in total), was typical. The US Army was the exception. Its divisions were, and remained, huge. Figure 3-3 shows the shape and size of several nations' divisions, on entry into war and by the war's end. Slimming divisions allowed more divisions to be created. Removing a level of command allowed more responsive control. Within reason, smaller divisions are more efficient and more effective. That was realised even before the war by the General Colmar von der Goltz, the German adviser to the Turkish Army. He studied the Russo-Japanese war at length and had reorganised Turkish divisions prior to the war.

Army	On Entry into the War	At the End of the War
German	2 brigades of 2 regiments of 3 battalions (12 in total)	1 brigade of 3 regiments of 3 battalions (9 in total)
French	2 or 3 brigades of 2 regiments of 3 battalions (12 or 18 in total)	3 regiments of 3 battalions (9 in total)
Turkish	3 regiments of 3 battalions (9 in total)	As left
Russian	2 brigades of 2 regiments of 4 battalions (16 in total)	2 brigades of 2 regiments of 3 battalions (12 in total)
American	2 brigades of 2 regiments of 3 battalions (12 in total), with large battalions and large regimental, brigade and divisional troops	As left
British	3 brigades each 4 battalions (12 in total)	3 brigades each 3 battalions (9 in total)

Figure 3-3 Divisional Organisations.

The British Army's enlargement at the beginning of the war was somewhere between the American and the French or German cases. Britain had seven divisions ready for war and put together six more from regular units. It had 14 TA infantry divisions and 14 yeomanry brigades which could potentially be deployed a few months later.[5] The commitment to the Western Front would require far more. In addition, losses mounted rapidly. 23 TA infantry battalions and some yeomanry regiments arrived in time to qualify for the Mons Star (the campaign medal awarded to those serving before 23 November 1914).

Kitchener's only experience of British reservists was from the South African War. He had not been impressed. He wanted to form entirely new armies of volunteers. In practice two things happened. Firstly, TA divisions were split and then doubled. Some of the first-line divisions were sent abroad as soon as possible: the 46th (North Midland) Division arrived in Flanders in February 1915. Secondly, five waves of six 'New Army' divisions were raised. Four of the first wave arrived in June 1915. New Army divisions were integrated into the existing structure of corps and armies, which expanded to accommodate them. The BEF grew to a maximum of five numbered armies and 21 numbered or named corps.[6] Some second-line TA divisions were kept back in the UK. Some were disbanded, and some eventually arrived in France as late as March 1917. 63 British, four Canadian, five Australian, five Indian, two Portuguese and one New Zealand divisions fought on the Western Front.

Training was a massive undertaking. Initial recruit training processed millions of men. In the British Army many under-trained officers commissioned in 1914 and 1915 had to be withdrawn, a few at a time, and sent on courses. Schools were set up behind the front lines for specialists and for entirely new disciplines. They included sniping, gas warfare, trench mortars and even bombing (the tactical use of hand grenades). Armies quickly realised that their tactical doctrine was inadequate. It was either insufficient (it did not cover certain subjects, such as trench warfare), or soon out of date. Doctrine had to be standardised, disseminated, and then taught. One of the most important lessons for the BEF from the Somme was that it did not have standardised ways of doing standard things, such as regular trench-to-trench attacks. It produced dozens of training pamphlets. The two most important, on platoon and on divisional tactics, emerged from the Somme battles.

Intelligence techniques developed rapidly. The British established a dedicated Intelligence Corps in August 1914. Traditional information sources (such as patrol reports, captured enemy documents and prisoner of war questioning) were expanded to include aerial photography, wireless intercept, and specialist artillery techniques such as flash spotting and sound ranging. Techniques of collation, analysis and dissemination were improved.

---

5   The TA was not liable for service overseas and had to volunteer to do so. The great
    majority did.
6   18 numbered corps and the Australian, Canadian, and Cavalry Corps.

One of the biggest problems for the rapidly expanded armies was a shortage of trained staff officers. By the middle of 1916 the British Army had more staff officers than the whole Regular Army officer strength of 1914. They were not just untrained; they were inexperienced. Two of the corps commanders had been commanding brigades just 18 months before. *Every single* division, 11 Corps and three Army HQs were involved in the Somme campaign.[7] By its end, British staffs had planned and conducted far more operations than during the whole of the preceding 23 months of the war combined. At the very least, formation HQs now knew their business from first hand.

Commanders and staff became much more proficient at planning and conducting operations. It was not until the Somme, for example, that commanders came to understand that it took five hours for an order from corps HQs just to reach front-line battalions. One benefit of streamlining divisions would have been to reduce that time. By late 1917, British attack orders were often reduced to not much more than an annotated barrage map, typically produced at corps or divisional level. Attacks became markedly more successful, took less time to plan and execute, and resulted in fewer own-force casualties.

Improvements to communications helped enormously. There was no single solution. Telephone networks, and network maintenance, improved to the point where lines were typically working forward to battalions within about 60 minutes of Zero Hour. Radio was used increasingly. It allowed some operation, in the advance and the withdrawal, down to brigade level. Lamp signals worked, but generally only backwards from the front line. Despatch rider services, using motorcycles, became increasingly regular and efficient. They would typically operate as far forward as the rear trenches. Much has been written about the difficulty of communicating. It was difficult, not least because trench warfare raised novel and difficult problems. But soldiers, and sailors, and airmen, learnt to make it work.

When the 1st Canadian Division arrived in Britain in 1914 it was not impressive. Its militia soldiers were unruly and its officers did not display the authority needed to keep them in check. The Canadians learnt quickly and well. So did the New Zealand contingent. For the Australian Corps, however, the story is somewhat different. Observers repeatedly remarked on what could be described as 'a more relaxed view' of formal discipline, meaning things like saluting officers. The Provost Martial of the BEF assembled statistics which showed that Australian soldiers were far more likely than British, Canadian or New Zealand troops to be jailed for ill-discipline. The great majority of Australian soldiers were jailed by Australian officers. Haig thought that the situation was due to the Australian Army not having the death penalty. We cannot know whether he was right, or wrong.

---

7   One division did not fight *on the Somme*. The 61st Division fought in a supporting attack at Fromelles on 19 July. It suffered heavy casualties. It had only arrived in France in late May (1916).

However, in the Hundred Days' offensive the Australian Corps captured more prisoners than any other corps of the BEF. Some German units apparently refused to fight against Australians.

Most Continental armies had the death penalty. Discipline in the Italian Army was inhumane. The French and Italian armies made little provision for soldiers' leave or canteens. German and British provision was probably better, perhaps because they were operating mostly outside their home territory. The German Army had the death penalty, but only 48 soldiers were executed (against 361 British and 1148 Austro-Hungarian soldiers). German Army discipline was not necessarily effective. By early 1918 tens of thousands of deserters had slipped over the border into the Netherlands. Signs of ill-discipline and poor German morale were detected by both German *and* British commanders as early as the Passchendaele campaign. Conversely in the midst of the Spring Offensive, during major withdrawals, Haig observed that British (meaning BEF) morale had never been higher.

We now know a lot about the men of the British and Dominion armies. Studies have looked in great depth at certain units or divisions. Others have looked at cohorts, such as unit or formation commanders. We know, for example, that 40 British officers commanded corps in the BEF. 10 were promoted to command at army level or higher. 15 were in post at the end of the war. About a dozen had been sacked. The average age of corps commanders was 53½ years, which is just lower than the minimum age of most Army commanders.[8] That suggests that the corps level of command had not been greatly affected by casualties or sackings. Divisional command had been: some commanders were only 38 years old, roughly a dozen years less than the peace-time minimum. Most brigade commanders were not much younger, which suggests genuine competition to command divisions. Most brigade commanders of 1918 had been Regular captains in 1914.

Attrition at battalion level had been significant. By 1918, officers were not appointed to command battalions if they were over 35 years old. Some were as young as 24. Company commanders were typically 22 or 23 years old, against 30 to 32 in peace-time. We should remember, however, that anyone commanding a battalion in 1918 was probably a pre-war Regular or TA officer who had fought on the Western Front for up to four years. They were probably some of the toughest and most experienced commanders their army had ever seen. The same applied in several armies.

A proportion of commanders at all ranks had been sacked. In the BEF it included one Commander in Chief (Sir John French), one Army commander (Lieutenant General Sir Hubert Gough), 10 to 12 corps commanders and dozens of brigade and divisional commanders. It is useful to look at a few. Gough became an *army* commander at the age of 45, hence younger than all other *corps* commanders. He was hugely personable, massively ambitious, and tended to blame subordinates for his own failings. He was the son of one holder of the Victoria Cross and brother of another.

---

8   The exception being Gough; see below.

French had appointed him to command a corps, and Haig an Army. It seems that he was a driven personality, and that he was over-promoted by superiors who had a soft spot, or a blind spot, for him. By the time Gough was removed from command Haig, for one, was quite aware of his failings.

The corps commanders who were sacked typically lost their commands for losing ground during enemy attacks. The cases are not all clear cut. Lieutenant General Sir William Pulteney was removed after the German counterattacks following Cambrai. Or was he? Pulteney was no great star. He was the only officer to command a corps in the BEF 1914 who was still doing so in late 1917. However, he then took command of a home defence corps in the UK. Was he sacked, or had he done enough to deserve a rest after three years in command? Lieutenant General Ivor Maxse was removed from command after the German Spring Offensive. Or was he? His Corps HQ (XVIII) was dissolved. Maxse was appointed to be Inspector General of Training in HQ BEF, where he had an important impact on the BEF as a whole.

Many of the brigade and divisional commanders who were sacked lost their jobs in the summer of 1916. Many had not commanded on operations before the Somme. Some were found wanting. A number were re-employed after a gap of six months. The overall picture is of a massively expanded army which showed growing pains amongst its formation commanders. That is not surprising, nor unique. The biggest personnel problem which the US Army had may well have been in finding good divisional commanders.

The US Army also had other, more basic, problems. After the battle of the St Mihiel Salient it was quickly moved across to the Meuse-Argonne sector. Its transport system broke down. Senior American officers remarked that soldiers did not know how to handle vehicles in order to avoid traffic jams. Junior officers did not display the authority needed to get the traffic moving again. Feeding broke down. Thousands of soldiers went hungry for days. In October 1918 the US Army reported that thousands of 'stragglers' were missing from their units. This is not the picture of a bad army. It is the picture of a very inexperienced army which was capable of great enthusiasm and bravery at the soldier level. It was an army which learnt fast. By European perspectives, it was in many ways an army of 1914 which had not yet learnt the lessons of 1915 and 1916.

Armies were moved by rail and then marched into battle. Almost all of their ammunition, rations and supplies were moved by rail. A small but increasing proportion was carried forward from railheads by truck. The trucks had neither pneumatic tyres nor four-wheel drive. They were road-bound. Thus guns had to be hauled into and out of gun positions by horse, and occasionally by oxen. There were a few steam tractors. The great tonnages of ammunition (2.38 million tons for the initial bombardment on the Somme; 2.08 million tons per week in the Hundred Days;[9] for the BEF alone) were carried forward by standard-gauge or specially-built narrow-gauge railway; by truck; or by horse-drawn wagon. They were then stacked and loaded by hand. All of the

9   Roughly a million tons of HE and a million tons of Shrapnel in each case.

hundreds of thousands of wounded casualties were carried off the battlefield by hand. Logistics was hugely manpower-intensive. It depended to a great extent on the pre-existing railway network, although in 1916 and 1917 light railway networks were built on a massive scale. They were fairly easily visible from the air and therefore a good indicator of a forthcoming offensive.

In the summer of 1916 the BEF's logistic system almost broke down. Sir Eric Geddes, a civilian railway expert, was posted in to reorganise it. The following summer the critical issue was actually the capacity of the railways to bring forward road stone with which to build new railways and repair roads. Railway operation became increasingly efficient. On the first day of the Battle of Arras casualties were being offloaded at Charing Cross Station in London just after noon. Zero Hour had been at 0530 hours. The ambulance trains were built to a special design (which had, for example, double doors wide enough to allow stretchers to be carried on sideways) using lessons from the South African War.

The outbreak of war was *not* met with ecstatic jubilation everywhere. There were protests in several towns and cities across Europe. Nevertheless, men joined up in large numbers. In some countries and in part that was due to recession, and hence unemployment. No country had effective plans for economic mobilisation. Shell shortages were common in 1915. Wartime regulations were brought in to mobilise the economy, protect the currency, and deter or prevent industrial disruption and subversion. Nevertheless, most countries experienced increasing numbers of strikes as the war continued.

Austria suffered badly from food shortages. Germany suffered from large numbers of strikes; protests; naval mutinies; and finally revolution. The British naval blockade had significant effect. Female mortality in Germany rose markedly in 1916 and then even more in 1917. The main cause was malnutrition.[10] In January 1918 over 400,000 people protested over food shortages in Berlin, and possibly four million across Germany. The German Chancellor (Prince Max of Baden) effectively deposed the Kaiser. On 9 November 1918 he declared that the Kaiser had abdicated. The Kaiser was actually at the Army HQ at Spa in Belgium. It was technically treason and, in practice, a coup.

To conclude, one could debate endlessly whether the Schlieffen plan might have worked. Nonetheless, what has been the received wisdom (that the concept and its execution were fatally flawed by Moltke the Younger) is largely the product of German official propaganda.

The Great War is often characterised by the stalemate of the Western Front. For most of the French Army, for most of the war, that was what they experienced. For much of the British Army, that is what they experienced on the Western Front, at Gallipoli and at Salonika. Similarly for about two thirds of the German Army. But it was not always so. In the 100 Days' campaign the BEF advanced over 100 miles. At

---

10   Blockade was not the only reason. A shortage of agricultural labour and the failure of the potato crop in 1916 were also major factors.

about the same time British forces advanced about 340 miles in Palestine and Syria. That was scarcely a stalemate.

There are several reasons why the Great War is misunderstood, especially in Britain. The first, as discussed in Chapter Two, is that its outcomes weren't obvious to the British public. A second is a confusion about the operational level of war. The Somme and Passchendaele weren't battles. They were campaigns. The losses incurred are far more readily understood if seen in those terms. A third reason relates to Haig and, to some extent, his army commanders (men such as Rawlinson, Plumer, Horne, Byng and Birdwood). They were not butchers, nor bunglers. There were no open flanks on the Western Front. They faced an enemy whose commanders had much more experience at corps and army level. The enemy's forces were tactically just as good as their own, and in some respects better. They had no overall numerical superiority. Campaigns fought on the Western Front were bound to be long, hard and bloody.

Haig described what we now call the operational level in terms of 'the break-in', 'wearing out' and then 'exploitation'. It wasn't a sophisticated operational approach. It was the product of his times, his military training, and his experience. He thought, and conducted campaigns, in those terms. That was the proper role of the Commander in Chief of the BEF.

Haig fought four major campaigns or operations. All were successful to some extent, the last two extremely so. On the Somme, Haig could reasonably believe that he had relieved pressure at Verdun. He had restricted the movement of forces elsewhere to a few battered divisions. He could believe that he had contributed materially to wearing the German Army out for its eventual defeat. Wars are won by attacking: at Passchendaele he commanded the only major offensive against the Germans after the failed Nivelle offensive. He could believe that had had further worn down the German Army. He had come agonisingly close to closing down the submarines at Bruges, before winter and Brest-Litovsk had forced him to close his offensive down. In the Spring Offensive he had ensured that German tactical successes were, in practice, an operational failure. Finally, in the 100 Days he broke the German Army and forced Germany to sue for peace.

However, the first two campaigns are referred to as the *Battle* of the Somme and the Third *Battle* of Ypres. That has tended to blind writers to the operational level of war on the Western Front, and its place in British strategy.

Haig did not demonstrate that he was a master of manoeuvre warfare. He showed some understanding of what we now call the operational level. He commanded the largest force that Britain has ever deployed. It was far larger than any British force that Montgomery commanded, and he commanded it for longer.

Haig remained popular in his lifetime. When he returned home immediately after the war he was greeted by a torchlight procession of about 10,000 people, with three bands, which filed past his house. When awarded an honorary doctorate (of a total of at least five), the students carried him shoulder-high into the hall to receive it. When he died in 1928, tens of thousands of mourners lined the route of the funeral procession.

Unlike Montgomery, his forces played the major part in the defeat of the German Army. Haig deserves far more respect than he generally receives.

4

Four Years of Warfare

Soldiers attacking on the Somme were not ordered to walk slowly forward into machinegun fire. There were no battalions of war poets. No British recruiting poster showed Kitchener saying 'Your Country Needs You'. No wartime soldier ever sang 'I Vow to Thee, my Country'. Those are all myths, with some basis in truth. Much of the mythology of the Great War stems from taking its literature, and particularly its poetry, as its history.

The 52 months of the Great War were probably the period of the most concentrated, profound tactical change in the history of warfare. The tactics of many armies in 1914 were almost those of the Crimean War. The tactics of 1918 were radically different. Unsurprisingly, many were still in use at the beginning of the Second World War. Technology was applied to develop weapons which were unimaginable in 1914, yet were in everyday use well before November 1918. This chapter considers the tactics of British, Empire and Dominion forces in order to illustrate those processes, and highlights important variations elsewhere.

In August 1914 airships were possibly more useful than aircraft. The Royal Navy had six airships, rising to 103 by November 1918. Naval airships were mostly used for fleet reconnaissance. They operated both from shore bases and ships at sea. As the war progressed they were increasingly used for anti-submarine reconnaissance and even attack. The Navy was well aware of the threat posed by German airships ('Zeppelins').[1] In 1914 it conducted a small number of bombing raids by aircraft against Zeppelin hangers at Dusseldorf, Cologne, and even Friedrichshafen on Lake Constanz.

A manned aircraft first flew off a ship underway, HMS *Hibernia*, in 1912. The first ship capable of both launching and recovering aircraft was HMS *Furious*, which became operational in 1917. The Navy ordered a torpedo-bomber seaplane in 1913, but it was not successful. The first air-launched torpedo attack was successfully carried out by a Royal Navy aircraft in the Dardanelles in August 1915. By the end of the war

---

1   They were not all built by Ferdinand, Graf von Zeppelin's airship company.

the Navy had ordered 300 purpose-built Sopwith Cuckoo torpedo bombers, although they had not yet entered service.

Armies used balloons extensively for battlefield observation, and particularly for the control of artillery fire. Tethered balloons became very vulnerable once airmen learnt how to destroy them with rockets and phosphorous bombs in 1916. Armies initially used aircraft for reconnaissance and observation. The first British soldiers to sight German forces were Royal Flying Corps (RFC) aircrew. An aircraft located German troops crossing the old Waterloo battlefield whilst the BEF deployed at Mons, 25 miles away, on 22 August 1914.

There was no policy to arm aircraft in August 1914. However, the RFC had some Lewis (light) machineguns available. They were soon mounted on aircraft. Specialisation into observation, bomber and fighter aircraft (and squadrons) developed rapidly. It was generally complete by the summer of 1916. Aerial photography and photographic interpretation became key tools in intelligence, mapmaking, counterbattery location, and artillery fire planning and control. Aircraft performance improved considerably. Much of that improvement was also in place by the summer of 1916.

Control of the air became highly important, principally to allow photographic reconnaissance. Failing to achieve and retain air superiority were significant factors in the outcomes of the battle of Arras and the Nivelle offensive. Bombing airfields and shooting down enemy aircraft in the air became important air superiority tactics.

The operating range of aircraft enabled targets well behind the enemy front lines to be attacked. That became particularly important in delaying the arrival of enemy reinforcements in the early stages of a battle. German post-war analysis showed that RFC attacks on troops advancing across the old Somme battlefields was a significant factor in the failure of the 1918 Spring offensive.

Pre-war Royal Navy plans included the provision of antiaircraft guns and fighter aircraft to protect the Thames. Zeppelins raided both Britain and Paris from the early stages of the war. 53 raids were carried out against Britain (an average of almost exactly one per month). Up to 14 airships were employed on each raid. They killed 556 civilians and did £1.5 million worth of damage to property. Loss of industrial production was appreciable, but typically restored within a few days. It was disruption, rather than destruction.

Counters were developed. The Zeppelins were forced to operate at night, and infrequently, due to losses. 30 of the 84 airships were lost. The Germans conducted 57 air raids with long-range Staaken and Gotha bombers from May 1917. Heavy losses also forced to them operate at night. They were then withdrawn. The RFC, and then the RAF, conducted long-range raids against targets in western Germany, with similar results.

Coal-fired steam turbines had made Dreadnoughts possible, but were also their key limitation. A Dreadnought consumed about a ton of coal per mile at speed, but typically carried about 900 tons in total. Under those conditions their operating range was only about 450 miles. Oil-fired steam turbines were entering service. British 'fast' (oil-fuelled) Dreadnoughts, such as the *Queen Elizabeth* class, were typically four knots faster. In practice they also had a greater operating range.

Limits to range and sea-keeping were critical for destroyers. German destroyers could not reach the main Grand Fleet base at Scapa Flow in the Shetlands. British destroyers could reach German bases near Wilhelmshaven, but would have to return to port if the fleet stayed at sea for a second day.

Conversely cruisers were primarily designed for range and seaworthiness. Their armament varied considerably. Some were armoured, some were not. Battlecruisers had the range and sea-keeping of a cruiser, the armament of a battleship and the speed of a fast battleship. Where they came up against cruisers, as at the Battle of the Falklands in December 1914, they were lethal. However, they had roughly the same protection as cruisers. Where battlecruisers came up against battleships, as at Jutland, the results were catastrophic.

The Royal Navy established a radio listening post on Scarborough Head early in the war. It is still operating today: the oldest continuously-manned electronic warfare station in the world. The Russians captured the German naval code books early in the war and passed them to Britain. German naval communication security procedures were consistently poor. That gave Britain a significant advantage. It enabled the Admiralty to know that the High Seas Fleet was putting to sea on 30 May 1916. That triggered the Battle of Jutland.

Admiral Sir David Beatty commanded the British battlecruiser fleet of six battlecruisers and four fast battleships. He was ordered to put to sea from Rosyth, near Edinburgh, by telegraph. Admiral Sir John Jellicoe, commanding the Grand Fleet at Scapa Flow, was also ordered to sea. Jellicoe had 28 Dreadnoughts. The British had eight armoured and 26 light cruisers, and 79 destroyers. The Germans had 16 Dreadnoughts, six pre-Dreadnought battleships, five battlecruisers, 11 light cruisers and 61 destroyers. The Germans did not know that the Grand Fleet had sailed. Beatty did.

At 1525hrs on 31 August the British battlecruisers sighted the German battlecruiser fleet under Admiral Franz, Ritter von Hipper at a range of about 11 miles. The Grand Fleet was 60 miles to the north. Beatty intended to draw the Germans northwards. Hipper intended to engage Beatty until the rest of the High Seas Fleet under Admiral Reinhard Scheer arrived. The battlecruiser HMS *Indefatigable* sank at 1602hrs, then HMS *Queen Mary* at 1626 hours. Both blew up when hit by shells from German battlecruisers. Hipper lost no ships.

It was not critical. At 1648hrs the British cruiser HMS *Southampton* signalled 'URGENT. PRIORITY. COURSE OF ENEMY BATTLEFLEET N[ORTH]. SINGLE LINE AHEAD. COMPOSITION OF VAN KAISER CLASS. BEARING OF CENTRE E[AST]. DESTROYERS ON BOTH WINGS AND AHEAD. ENEMY'S BATLECRUISERS JOINING BATTLEFLEET FROM NORTHWARD [plus latitude and longitude].[2]' It was the first sighting of Scheer, and exactly what Jellicoe and Beatty needed to know. Beatty led Scheer and Hipper

---

2   Gordon, Andrew, *The Rules of the Game. Jutland and British Naval Command* (London: John Murray, 1996), p127.

northeast. At 1815hrs the Grand Fleet deployed from columns into line astern. Beatty and his battlecruisers slipped into place at the van at 1845hrs, losing HMS *Invincible* at 1835hrs. The Grand Fleet was in a perfect position. Jellicoe's Dreadnoughts were all in line astern. Scheer was sailing in a single column straight towards the middle of Jellicoe's line. Jellicoe's battleships could all engage, with their broadsides. Only Scheer's leading ships could engage; and only with their forward turrets.

The carnage began. Jellicoe ordered his fleet to turn south by south west, into line abreast, and gave the signal for 'general engagement'. In the following 47 minutes 18 German battleships and cruisers blew up or caught fire, for the loss of HMSs *Benbow* and *Superb*. The German pre-dreadnoughts gave the British a three-knot advantage: the Germans could not escape. German destroyers made smoke and launched dozens of torpedoes. Three torpedoes hit, and HMS *Monarch* was seriously damaged. The German destroyers suffered terribly from the British ships' secondary batteries. Scheer ordered his fleet to scatter and make best speed for port. It was a crushing tactical, operational and strategic success.

Clearly that did not happen. It so nearly did. Writers have made much of the fact that Jellicoe could have lost the war in an afternoon. The truth is simple. At Tsushima, in 1905, the Russian fleet had lost several vessels to Japanese torpedoes. Torpedoes had an effective range of about 4,000 yards, which was about the same as that of the Russians' gunnery rangefinders. By 1916 gunnery ranges were much greater. Torpedo ranges were not. It made some sense to turn battleships *away* from destroyers in order to keep outside torpedo range. Jellicoe turned the Grand Fleet away not once, but twice. He was following the Navy's Fighting Instructions. Scheer got his fleet away, substantially intact.

Destroyers carried torpedoes with a 4,000 yard range. Battleships had secondary batteries (typically of four or six inch calibre) which could wreck a destroyer at 10,000 yards. That was, in principle, what secondary batteries were for. It was, of course, not that simple. Not least, a ship crossing at a constant speed was a predictable target for a torpedo. A ship head-on was a far smaller target, and one which could dodge reasonably well. After Jutland, Fighting Instructions were rewritten to instruct commanders to turn *toward* a torpedo threat. At Jutland, the doctrine (Fighting Instructions) was behind the technology.

Most of the naval war was not about fleet actions. It was about the attack on trade. U-boats had a reasonable operating range, but were slow (making perhaps eight knots on the surface and five submerged). They could not remain submerged for long. If submarines could cruise on the surface and pick off merchantmen with gunfire and little fear of reprisal, they could be very successful. Convoying made targets much harder to find, but provided better pickings if the convoys were found. They were, however, also escorted and therefore better protected. Airships or tethered balloons made daylight attack riskier. A four-inch gun on an escort could wreck a submarine with one hit. Convoys sailing with few lights at night would be very hard to spot. In practice, the advent of convoying defeated the U-boat. They continued to put to sea in ever greater numbers, but to ever less effect.

The loss of the three British cruisers (HMSs *Hogue*, *Aboukir* and *Cressy*) to U-boat *U-9* in 65 minutes on 24 September 1914 alerted the British public to the submarine threat. Three British pre-Dreadnought battleships were lost to torpedoes off the Dardanelles in two weeks in May 1915. Those six ships constitute almost half of the 14 battleships and cruisers lost by the Royal Navy to submarines in the whole of the war. The submarine was not yet the threat it would become, but the lesson was learnt. (Only two British battleships were lost to submarines in the six years of the Second World War, and only one of them at sea.)

The German Army crossed the Belgian frontier on 3 August 1914. It came under fire from the forts surrounding Liege the next day. German field artillery made no impression. The German infantry could not penetrate the intervening field defences because of the forts. German 15cm howitzers and 21cm mortars did some damage to the forts. At that stage the Germans could not neutralise Liege, nor bypass it. On 11 August German super-heavy 28cm and 42cm artillery arrived. It opened fire the next day. The defenders raised three tethered observation balloons. The German heavy artillery was soon neutralised by long-range 155mm guns from within the fortress. Unable to reduce Liege and cross the Meuse, the German attack on Belgium broke down.

That did not happen. Why not? All of the elements described were technically possible in August 1914. However, the Liege forts had been designed in the 1880s. Their concrete protection was unreinforced (reinforcement came into use just a few years later). The concrete was badly poured, resulting in structural weakness. The forts were poorly ventilated and their latrines were inadequate. They became uninhabitable after a few days' siege.

'Ring' fortresses, consisting of several small forts surrounding a city, were designed with relatively little protection to the rear faces of each fort. That was intended to prevent a fort which had been captured being held against counterattack by the garrison. Liege was no exception. However, the outer defences had gaps which allowed the Germans to cross the Meuse above and below the city. The inner defences were poorly maintained: attacking infantry could, and did, penetrate between the forts. The Germans then brought their heaviest artillery into the city and engaged several of the forts *from the rear*. The Belgian Army does not appear to have considered an active counterbattery process. (The British 60pdr medium gun of 1905, soon used for counterbattery, was a close copy of the 155mm 'Long Tom' used to good effect by the Boers in the South African War.)

In 1914 Przemysl was just inside Austria-Hungary, on the border with Russia. It was a fairly modern ring fortress. It was besieged by the Russian Army on 16 September 1914. Initial attempts to storm Przemysl cost the Russians 40,000 casualties in three days. The siege was briefly lifted, and then re-imposed through the winter. In March 1915 Russian heavy artillery enabled the northern forts to be stormed. The garrison destroyed everything of military value and surrendered on the 19th. The siege had lasted six months. 117,000 Austro-Hungarian troops went into captivity.

Some of the French forts at Verdun had been modernised, not least with an additional layer of concrete. They were effectively invulnerable to German siege artillery.

Most of the French heavy guns had been removed. In February 1916 Fort Douaumont had a garrison of just 56, against an establishment of 500. Unsurprisingly, a determined infantry assault eventually took Douaumont. Fort Vaux eventually fell with the loss of about 20 French dead and 100 wounded. The attackers lost 2,742 casualties against Vaux alone. Vaux was recaptured by the French with the aid of a 400mm railway gun firing against the rear face of the fort. Engineers then brought the fort back into commission, digging entirely new tunnels 17 metres below the existing galleries, whilst the battle continued outside. The new works strongly influenced the design of the Maginot line in the 1920s and 30s.

In late 1914 German engineers began underground mining against front-line trenches on the Western Front. Ten mines were blown against Indian troops around Ypres on 20 December 1914. Tunnelling and mining became major features of trench warfare. Its epitome was the blowing of 19 mines on the Messines ridge on 7 June 1917. Tunnelling gradually moved away from offensive mining to subterranean construction. For example, an extensive system of deep shelters was built in the Ypres salient after the Passchendaele campaign. Britain formed a total of 28 tunnelling companies, each of 274 officers and men. Infantrymen were also allocated for labouring duties. The BEF deployed up to 15,000 men working on tunnelling projects at any one time.

The German drill regulations of 1906 required a regiment of about 3,200 men to attack in a formation 700m wide and 1,000m deep. The front rank would be spaced one to two meters apart. The leading companies therefore had an effective density of about one man per meter of frontage. A regiment had an effective density of four to five men per meter. Seen by the enemy at ground level, they would look like solid columns. In 1914 the BEF simply shot them flat. The Germans had made some allowance for modern small arms fire, but had overlooked:

- the 'searching' effect of high-velocity long-range, flat-trajectory rifle fire. Bullets hit targets (particularly standing men) over a wide range.
- the British practice of using 'combined sights', right down to section level. They deliberately distributed their fire throughout the depth of an attacking column.
- rapid fire. The 'Mad Minute' practice in the British Musketry Regulations of 1909 required 15 rounds to be fired in one minute. That was routinely exceeded. The record was 36 *hits* at 300 yards.

The German Army quickly abandoned such massed columns. They were relatively inexperienced in the conditions of modern warfare; the British less so. The doctrine of several European armies (including the German) relied greatly on rationalistic logic and aspiration. The British Army relied more heavily on empirical evidence. Few researchers seem to have analysed the German drill regulations and calculated the effective ratio of force to space.

Trench systems were rudimentary at first. The trench system was not completely linked up on the Western Front until the Spring of 1915. The winter of 1914-5 must have been miserable for the soldiers involved. Front-line fire trenches were thickened up with support and reserve trenches, and linked by communication trenches from front to rear. Designs became extremely sophisticated. Traverses in the forward trenches prevented the blast from shell fire travelling along the trench. Communication trenches were zigzagged to protect against long-range machinegun fire.

Troops in trenches are vulnerable to plunging high explosive: whether from hand grenades, rifle grenades, mortar bombs or howitzer shells. All four were quickly developed or procured. British units did not have a good supply of reliable hand grenades until well into 1915. That put the ANZACs at a major disadvantage at Gallipoli, for example. The German army had both grenades and trench mortars, which they initially saw as siege weapons. The biggest trench mortars had very short ranges – perhaps a few hundred yards – but massive bombs that could completely wreck a section of trench. They were largely immobile and vulnerable to counterbattery fire.

The early battles of 1914 showed that it was suicidal for field artillery to fire over open sights. The guns were soon withdrawn behind cover, typically 2-3,000 yards back, and linked to forward observers by telephone. Barbed wire was quickly brought into use to stop infantry attacks against front-line trenches. Dugouts were built into the front faces of trenches, to provide shelter from both artillery fire and the weather. Reinforced concrete was used in some front-line trenches by the Spring of 1915. Machineguns were sited well forward, and fired in enfilade across the front, to form curtains of defensive fire. Commanders soon identified a lethal combination. The barbed wire held up the attackers, who were then cut down by machine guns. Defending artillery wiped out any attackers, and their reserves, caught in the open. The attacker's field artillery could not easily cut barbed wire. The defender's field batteries were relatively safe on reverse slopes to the rear.

In March 1915, at Neuve Chapelle, the BEF found that it was not difficult to storm a single trench line. A short, heavy bombardment followed by a quick assault would clear the position, albeit at some cost. However, surviving machineguns in depth and to the flanks made it impossible for the attackers, or subsequent waves, to penetrate to depth. A breakthrough became a commanders' pipe dream.

German positions developed both in depth and complexity, eventually reaching three separate positions each of three trenches over a total depth of about five kilometres. The second position was explicitly intended to protect the field artillery. It also stopped any attackers who breached the first position, and provided shelter for reserves. Barbed wire was thickened into several belts each 40 yards or more deep.

Attackers rapidly developed tactics of working along trench lines, using hand grenades and bayonets to clear traverses in turn. The same tactics were also used by counterattacking troops. 'Bombing along traverses' became time-consuming and inconclusive.

Medium artillery, typically of four to six inch calibre (105 to 155mm or so) was increasingly used for counterbattery fire to neutralise defending field batteries (of 75mm, 77mm or 18pdr (84mm)). Specialist counterbattery staffs were introduced, typically at corps HQs. Counterbattery fire required a variety of locating techniques, as well as accurate mapping and aerial photographic reconnaissance. That in turn drove the need for control of the air. Antiaircraft artillery developed slowly.

Gas was first used the Germans in the Second Battle of Ypres in 1915. Initially it was released from canisters in the attacker's front line, but increasingly it was delivered by artillery shells. Smoke shells were also developed and brought into use.

The BEF grew rapidly through 1915 and the Spring of 1916, by which point it reached about 56 divisions. Its attacks in 1915 (Neuve Chapelle, Aubers, Festubert, and Loos) were all fought as part of Allied initiatives. They can all be seen as failed attempts to break through increasingly sophisticated German defences. They can also all be seen as part of a process of a new army learning by fighting, and learning in the utterly novel conditions of the modern battlefield. Cavalry was held ready to exploit any breakthrough, but none was achieved. In defence, cavalry formed a screen behind infantry positions as a form of counter-penetration. They were rarely needed.

Wider attack frontages were needed, so that enfilading machineguns (whose fire might be effective for up to 3,000 yards from each flank) would not interrupt the main attack. Rawlinson recognised that after Loos in 1915. Wider sectors meant bigger attacks and more guns. The French Army had entered the war with very few modern medium and heavy guns. Their older guns lacked modern recoil mechanisms. They had to be hauled back into position after each round, and so had a low rate of fire. British planners mistook total *weight* of fire for *rate* of fire (intensity). For both reasons, preparatory bombardments got increasingly longer.

Armies developed their tactics and revised their doctrine. In the early summer of 1916 French tactics were better than British. Neither army had worked out how to break through a thoroughly well-prepared defensive position. That was equally true at Gallipoli and on the Isonzo. The Germans achieved some success in the east against the Russians, the Serbs and the Romanians.

Haig was the operational commander on the Somme. It was entirely right of him to seek a breakthrough, if it was possible,. Why would he not? It was not, however, one of his operational objectives. It was also right of Rawlinson, the relevant Army commander, to seek achievable tactical goals. A so-called argument between Haig and Rawlinson concerned the difference between a depth of 2,500 yards (Haig) or 1250 yards (Rawlinson). They compromised. Neither actually planned to break through the whole position on the first day. The German defences consisted of three separate positions. South of the Albert-Bapaume road the objectives for 'Z Day', 1 July 1916, included the first position and up to the beginning of the second. North of the road, the objective included all of the second position. Orders were written, however, to be able to exploit a breakthrough if it did occur.

Z-Day was not entirely a ghastly failure. South of the road, the French Army and the two British corps took most of their objectives, at reasonable cost. The disaster occurred north of the road.

In some areas in the north the bombardment was planned to lift 10 minutes before the infantry attacked. German trenches, and machineguns, were manned before the attackers left their trenches. Conversely, in some divisions the attacking troops were in no man's land before the artillery lifted. Some got to the enemy front line before the defenders emerged. In one division, however, no officers above company level went forward in the assault. Thus even quite promising successes were quickly defeated by German counterattacks. In other areas attackers were held up by machineguns to their flanks, because the attack there had broken down. Not enough counterbattery work had been done, so the German artillery caused casualties in the supporting waves even behind the British front line. It was the greatest loss of dead and wounded in one day that the British Army has ever suffered.

However, the British continued to attack. 46 minor operations were conducted to prepare the conditions for the next major attack, on 14 July. That morning Rawlinson's troops seized 6,000 yards of the second position, just north of the main road, for modest losses. A warning order was released on 18 July for the next major operation. There were then four separate battles, consisting of 90 local attacks, before the battle of Flers-Courcelette on 15 September. On that occasion 4,500 yards of the third position was seized. Tanks were used, successfully, for the first time. There were then six further battles up to 18 November. Haig could report successes, such as the seizure of Beaumont Hamel, at the Allied conference at Chantilly on 15 and 16 November. Those battles also captured the whole ridge and allowed the preparation of good defensive positions for the winter.

British tactics had developed enormously. Rawlinson had wanted to form up the attacking infantry in no-man's land before dawn on Z Day (1 July). The French vetoed it as being too complicated. It worked spectacularly well on 14 July. Night attacks became common and were often successful. The preliminary bombardment on 14 July was, effectively, 16 or 17 times more concentrated than it had been for Z Day, just two weeks earlier. An artillery officer, Major Alan Brooke (later Field Marshal Viscount Alanbrooke), had studied French artillery methods at Verdun and developed barrage techniques. A barrage was, literally, a moving barrier of fire in front of the attackers. Counterbattery techniques were improved. Machinegun barrages were fired overhead of advancing troops to prevent early counterattacks. The infantry's advance was coordinated with the barrage and the tanks. Tactical objectives were consolidated using 'bite and hold' tactics. A position was seized, consolidated, and held against counterattack. The process was then repeated a few days later. 'Bite and hold' was first identified by Rawlinson after Neuve Chapelle in March 1915.

The British Army did not have enough guns until the end of 1916. An attack needed roughly one field gun per 15 yards of front. It needed one medium battery to neutralise every defending field or medium battery. It needed enough heavy guns for destruction and interdiction targets: possibly several dozen, if not hundreds, of them. The key was then to assemble all of them, undetected, and then register them silently (ie, without being detected). At Arras, the British concentrated 1400 more guns than they had on the Somme, just nine months earlier. Five hundred were medium or heavy. At Cambrai and Amiens the build-up of guns was undetected before Zero Hour.

Ludendorff and Hindenburg oversaw a revision of German defence tactics. The front line was held far more sparsely. It did not rely on the defence of a continuous trench line. The main defence was to be waged as a series of counterattacks in the battle zone which was *behind* the front line. That became the outpost line. Thus German tactics were organised around combinations of outposts, a battle area, and reserves.

The Germans had already formalised a process of stationing reserve divisions to the rear of a threatened front. A process of creating Army Groups was completed. That allowed the roulement (rotation) of divisions to be conducted more effectively. The Somme front was held by eight German divisions on Z Day, but by the end of the battle 42 further divisions had been employed. At the end of August the German high command had only one division available in reserve, anywhere. One of Haig's objectives was to contribute to wearing out the German Army. That was happening. Haig did not prevent divisions being removed elsewhere, although he thought he had. The 15 or so divisions that were sent to other fronts were all exhausted after fighting on the Somme. It was reasonable for Haig to believe that he had relieved pressure at Verdun. Falkenhayn had ordered a stop to attacks there by 11 July.

The German Army formalised the use of reverse slopes in defence. In Flanders, in particular, the reverse slopes were extremely subtle. An elevation of perhaps five meters was enough to conceal a defensive position. Pilckem Ridge, the objective for the first attack in the Passchendaele campaign, is not much more than 15 metres high.

Casualties on the Somme were heavy. The ANZACs lost as many men in six weeks on the Somme as they had in eight months at Gallipoli. The German Army lost more men on the Somme than at Verdun: perhaps 100,000 more. When they assumed command in September 1916, Hindenburg and Ludendorff were not convinced that the German Army was capable of defending successfully in the West. They ordered the construction of strong rear positions (wrongly known by the British as the Hindenburg Line), to which the German army withdrew in February 1917; just 13 weeks after the Somme campaign.

The circumstances of the Arras and Ypres operations in 1917 were described in Chapter Three. The Ypres Campaign did not achieve its main objectives. However, the German Army did not conduct any large offensive, anywhere, in 1917. Thus, in simple terms, all the reserves of the whole German Army could be applied to stop the British attack at Ypres. The Germans were unlikely to run out of troops. They were, however, pushed back. The British were within a few hundred yards of their objectives when the operation was closed down in November. They were so close that a further, limited operation by four brigades was attempted on the night of 1-2 December. Surprise was lost. The attack failed; the British suffered about 1600 casualties. The attempt was not repeated. The Germans and Russians were already negotiating at Brest Litovsk.

On 20 November six British divisions, supported by 476 tanks, attacked near Cambrai. There was no preliminary bombardment. A massive fireplan started the moment that the assaulting troops crossed the start line. The tanks were already moving forward. Surprise was complete. Attacking infantry used Lewis guns to suppress isolated pockets of defenders, and mortars to neutralise surviving machine-guns. By 26 November the British had advanced about six miles on a ten-mile front.

Surprise had been so complete that there were no German reserve divisions stood by to counterattack. A major counterattack started on 30 November. It regained about two miles by 3 December. The British withdrew to a defensive line, which included much of what had been the German third position, on the night of 4-5 December. The battle was closed down.

The BEF conducted a high-level board of enquiry to establish why the ground gained had then been lost so easily. The main conclusion was that the divisions in the front line had not been trained in how to establish a defensive position, rather than just hold one prepared by someone else. Important lessons relating to the layout and conduct of a defensive battle were identified. Doctrine and training for the coming year were amended accordingly.

Why was Cambrai fought? There are very few clues. It may have been an experiment to try out the use of tanks *en masse*. The experiment cost about 44,000 casualties and gained little ground of any significance. Reflection suggests that it was indeed a trial, but of a different scale. Did the BEF now know how to break through German defensive positions in depth? The answer was emphatically 'yes'. Cambrai would be the last chance to confirm that before the German Spring offensive in 1918.

The Western Front represents almost four years of stalemate, but not stasis. A large part of the tactical problem was that the Germans also adapted and developed their tactics. By the end of 1917, the German Army was not just far better at defending than it had been in 1914. It was also far better at attacking. They called their new assault procedures 'stormtroop tactics'. Ironically one German POW referred to them as 'English tactics'.

German successes in the Spring of 1918 were due to several factors. Stormtroop tactics were one. Short, intensive, surprise bombardments with a very high proportion of gas and smoke shells was another. British policy decisions also contributed.

On 3 October 1917 Haig had been told that the Cabinet had agreed that the BEF would take over more of the front line from the French Army. In December he was ordered to reduce each division from 12 battalions to nine, to economise on manpower. Haig also had to send divisions to Italy, although some returned. So, slightly fewer divisions had to hold appreciably more front line; with only three-quarters as much infantry per division. Divisional defensive schemes were now impractical: there were not enough battalions to hold reserves for counterattacks at all levels. Frontages were excessive: one battalion is reported as having to hold 6,000 yards. 1,000 yards would have been typical a year earlier. A German breakthrough on 21 March 1918 was almost inevitable, and much of the reason lay in political direction. 10 British divisions suffered particularly heavily over the next few weeks. Some continued to fight, and were not withdrawn until May. Tens of thousands of reinforcements, previously withheld, were sent out from England between March and June.

On 8 August 1918 the British Fourth Army and part of the First French Army attacked at Amiens. The tactics were largely those of Cambrai. Within hours the Australian and Canadian Corps, in the centre, had broken through the whole depth of the German position. A German corps HQ was overrun, probably for the first and only time on the war. (The commander of the tank which seized it had been explicitly ordered to that location. Its position seem to have been detected by radio intercept, or similar.) British cavalry picked their way across the battlefield and began to exploit. By 3pm they were at Péronne and 5pm St Quentin. The RAF strafed trains and marching columns. French and British divisions poured into the gap. By the end of August the German Army had effectively collapsed. An armistice was agreed on 11 September.

That *did* happen; but only up to the point where the cavalry was committed. In reality tactics for committing cavalry through the front line didn't quite work. British cavalry unit and brigade commanders were perhaps too cautious. The RAF did good work at first. When it switched to battlefield interdiction it was much less successful. It took considerable losses. 8 August was, nonetheless, the 'Black Day of the German Army'. It was the beginning of the 100 Days' Offensive. The German Army was beaten on the Western Front and the War was brought to an end. Germany lost.

By this stage British attack tactics were far more flexible. The leading wave of infantry would follow the barrage closely, right up to their objective. That would typically be a line just within the limit of field artillery range. By doing so they would generally pass right through the Germans' first and second positions. They would bypass any pockets of resistance, which would then be taken from the flank or rear by follow-on forces. They did not waste time bombing along the traverses. In the South African War Kitchener had forbidden frontal attacks; by 1918 flank or even rear attacks were the norm once more, from section to divisional level. Some reserves would be well forward to defeat immediate counterattacks. The area just seized would be thoroughly 'mopped up' by other follow-on forces. When well-planned and executed, such tactics were highly effective. At their best, they could break right through the toughest defences. After Amiens, they often did. The net price was high. The BEF suffered about 412,000 casualties during the 100 Days. But it broke the German Army in the west.

The Germans almost always counterattacked. By mid-1917 or so the British were largely prepared to beat off immediate counterattacks. Nonetheless, those counterattacks had important second-order effects. Anticipating them constrained the British to limited, bite-and-hold attacks. It also severely limited opportunities for exploitation.

For the attack on the Hindenburg Line in September 1918, Rawlinson widened the attack sector of the US 27th and 30th Divisions (attacking as part of the Australian Corps) by committing the British 1st, 12th and 46th Divisions on the flanks. He was applying the lessons of Loos, three years before. Ironically it was only the British 46th Division, on the right, which broke through the Hindenburg Line that day; for just 800 casualties. The 32nd Division then passed through it before midnight. It was one of the greatest feats of arms of the whole war.

On 19 September the British attacked again. After an initial penetration by two infantry corps, three cavalry divisions were committed. By about 11am 88 squadrons of cavalry, with supporting horse artillery, were on the move. Within 36 hours the enemy were in full retreat. The cavalry had overrun an Army HQ 45 miles to the rear. The RAF had done an outstanding job of destroying communication infrastructure, and continued to interdict retreating enemy columns. Within a week, an enemy army group had been defeated. Within a month, the British had advanced 340 miles and the enemy had signed an armistice.

That *did* happen. 'Armageddon' denotes a catastrophe of Biblical proportions. It was a real place. Megiddo, in Palestine, is its modern name. The Battle of Megiddo, from 19 September, was the beginning of the destruction of the Turkish Yilderim Army Group, and hence the Ottoman Empire. Cavalry *could* have operational effect. In Palestine, it did. Writers often denigrate Megiddo, citing this or that reason why it should not be considered to be important. The British Army had thought about its tactics, adapted them to the conditions, and brought about operational and even strategic effect. What more should it do?

Why is Megiddo not better known? The answer is probably quite simple. Not a single Regular cavalry regiment fought there. The cavalry was either British Yeomanry or Australian and New Zealand Light Horse. The first-hand written sources of the Great War contain very little written by Regular cavalrymen in Palestine. There was also very little British Regular infantry. Much of the British infantry had been sent to the BEF, and replaced by Indian battalions which had been doubled. There was therefore little or no Regular institutional memory. The Arab Revolt, which took place more or less simultaneously, might also have been largely forgotten had T E Lawrence not written his memoirs some years later.

Haig was a cavalry officer. As chief of staff to (the later) Sir John French he had witnessed, and may have taken part in, the successful British cavalry charge as Elandslaagte in the South African War. Military men are not stupid about things that they have seen. In January 1916 180 troopers of the Dorset Yeomanry charged and routed about 1,600 Senussi tribesmen, supported by three Turkish machineguns, in Libya. The Yeomanry killed between three and five hundred Senussi. Cavalry charges could, and did, succeed. French and Haig were not reactionaries. Haig was a moderate reformer. He knew exactly how difficult it was to create the right conditions for success. As Commander in Chief of the BEF he was responsible for achieving an operational breakthrough if possible. In the Great War that was only possible using cavalry formations. Haig never threw his cavalry away needlessly. He should not be criticised for trying to use it for best effect.

On the Western Front the Great War was generally four years of stalemate; but not stasis. Elsewhere it was a war of movement in many places. The literature of the War is, understandably, dominated by the major exceptions. That is where most of the fighting took place, and where most of the British experience was gained. The Eastern Front, the Balkans, the Carpathians, the Caucasus, Mesopotamia and Palestine were a mixture of static fighting interspersed with manoeuvre on a grand scale. So were Napoleon's campaigns; and Marlborough's; and Caesar's.

The war saw dramatic changes in the tactics and equipment employed, the techniques of command, and the methods of training. British commanders had no pre-war experience of the operational level of war, and very little of any sort above divisional level. They learnt a lot, and they learnt fast. European commanders had far more prior knowledge, and in some cases experience. In some cases they were hamstrung by doctrines that would result in many unnecessary deaths.

Armies learnt by fighting. So did navies and air forces. War is adversarial and evolutionary. The learning process, in such a large-scale and hard-fought war, was very steep. It wasn't perfect. It was haphazard in some places and also, perhaps, when seen from a distance. Describing it as a learning 'curve' is too prescriptive. But they did learn.

Tactically, the German Army could, and did, defeat almost everybody it came up against: Russians, Serbs, Romanians, Italians; and the French and the British at the beginning of the war. However, the western Allies learnt. By 1915 the French could defeat them in some circumstances. The German attack on the British at Ypres (in 1915) did not succeed. The Germans broadly succeeded in defence, in so far as they contained any breakthroughs in the west until the end of the war.

In June 1914 the Serbs had selected, trained and equipped Franz Ferdinand's assassins, and given them their orders. Germany bankrolled Lenin and the October Revolution. It funded sabotage in America. It supplied arms and ammunition to the Easter Rising in Ireland in 1916. Britain paid an Italian informer named Benito Mussolini. A British intelligence officer ('spy'?) destroyed the Ploieşti oil production facilities in Romania before the Germans overran the area in 1916. Britain bribed the Arabs to revolt in the Near East in 1918 with millions of pounds of gold. Von Hötzendorf and his mistress *were* the centre of scandal – twice; but she was not the main cause of his removal in 1917.

Nations *did* indulge in espionage, subversion and dirty tricks. The spy novels of John Buchan (such as 'The Thirty-Nine Steps' and 'Greenmantle') now seem tame compared to those of Ian Fleming. Buchan worked in British War Propaganda Bureau and then as an army intelligence officer. Fleming worked in naval intelligence in the Second World War. What made Buchan's novels more interesting at the time is that they came out *during* the Great War. James Bond did not appear until 1953.

Apparently the German Army did not fail. The so-called Schlieffen plan would have worked, if not for Moltke the Younger's tinkering. Verdun only failed because of Falkenhayn. The German Army only lost the war, if lose it did, because it was let down by big business; by socialists; by Jews; … . Isn't it odd that the chief individuals who (apparently) failed the German Army, Moltke the Younger and Falkenhayn, were the people in charge of it? In practice, that story was largely a narrative that the post-war German Army created for domestic political purposes. To a large extent, it worked.

The apparent futility of the Great War arose to some extent from war poetry: the work of sensitive young men exposed to horrors which no-one should ever have to live through. 72 published British war poets died in the War. Seven died on the first day of the Somme alone.

The battle of the memoirs was perhaps even more important. Regrettably, Lloyd George won his. Churchill did not forget that. Any British schoolboy learning history in the later twentieth century would have learnt three things: Moltke the Younger fatally compromised the Schlieffen plan; the war on the Western Front was unremitting, pitiless futility; and the British Army consisted of lions led by donkeys. Its generals were all butchers, bunglers, or both.

The issue over the Schlieffen plan resulted from German domestic propaganda. The poetry of the Great War is a significant addition to the canon of English literature, perhaps even on a par with Shakespeare; but it is not history. The 'butchers and bunglers' theory is due in large part to Lloyd George, aided and abetted by Liddell Hart. The narrative becomes hugely important: never more so than in the history of the Great War.

Casualties were horrific. If you assemble large armies and have them fight at close quarters for years, they will be. If your armies aren't very proficient, like the Austro-Hungarians, Italians or Russians, they will be. If your army is too small and its replacements are half-trained at first, like the British and Americans, losses will be horrific. If your operational approach is initially one of all-out attack at all costs, like the French, the cost will be high. If your tactical doctrine is like that, your losses will be high until you learn better. Thus the Germans.

Four empires disappeared. The shape of Central and Eastern Europe changed significantly. There were real winners and real losers. That may not be obvious to the British. Defensive wars can be like that. But if anyone doubts how magnanimous the Germans would have been in victory, they should study the treaty of Brest Litovsk. The Great War was not futile.

Furthermore, the conduct of war had changed radically. To repeat: the 52 months of the Great War were probably the period of the most concentrated, profound tactical change in the history of warfare.

5

Who Is Afraid of Virginia Woolf?

Writing in 1930, the then Brigadier Archibald (later Field Marshal Earl) Wavell remarked, amongst other things, that:

a. The six-wheeled (hence cross-country) truck had only just been invented;
b. 'Strategic' (meaning 'operational') cooperation between aircraft and ground forces had not yet been worked out;
c. Mechanised forces, in armoured vehicles, were not yet a reality;
d. Motorisation (in the sense of the transport of land forces over long distances) had been little practiced in the Great War.
e. Experimentation into mechanisation had only happened quite recently.
g. That there would be technical limits (in armoured vehicle design) due to the well-recognised conflict between gun and armour. There would be a practical upper weight limit on armoured vehicles due to the road infrastructure.
h. Decisive battles would normally take place on the plains. Mountain warfare would be subsidiary. Mechanised forces must be able to cross rivers readily.
i. That independent attack by air forces was the most difficult and controversial to predict:
    1) There were claims that aircraft had made armies redundant.
    2) Aerial bombing had had little effect in the Great War.
    3) The accuracy of antiaircraft fire had improved greatly.
    4) Aircraft were very vulnerable (once hit).
    5) Separate (ie, independent) air forces favoured technical development.
j. A change in the whole nature of warfare had to be recognised.
k. There was a great need to look at civil organisation in war.
l. There was a need to mechanise front-line troops. Armies would get smaller, but there would be some special-purpose troops (for example, for mountains and woodland).
m. Britain currently (in 1930) had a lead (in military capability,) and there was every chance of maintaining it.

n.   The greater part of the British Army would eventually become mechanised.[1]

Wavell's thoughts were remarkably clear-sighted and prescient. He was not entirely right.

The interwar period, from 1918 to 1939, included a number of significant conflicts. It should, however, largely be seen as one of transition, innovation and change between the Great War and the Second World War. Military innovation can be seen to be largely driven by three factors: the strategic context; technology; and the relationship between military and civil authorities.

The new strategic circumstances were confirmed by the outcome of the Paris peace conference, which followed the armistice of November 1918. The conference achieved several things. It dictated peace terms to the five countries on the losing side: Germany, Austria, Hungary, Bulgaria and Turkey. Each was required to sign a separate treaty. The conference also established the concept of a League of Nations, which introduced a form of collective security arrangements on a worldwide scale. Unfortunately, the League was compromised in a number of ways. Not least, Woodrow Wilson could not persuade the US Senate that America should join it. For that and other reasons, the League lacked the authority it needed to enforce its mandates.

The principle of self-determination was used to do two different things. Within Europe, it detached parts of the Russian, German and Austro-Hungarian empires where other races had majorities, and formed new countries. Some of those countries then inherited ethnic minorities of their own. For example, there were German ethnic minorities in Poland, Czechoslovakia and Romania. That created several new problems. Most races outside Europe were not considered to be currently capable of self-government. Turkish provinces and German colonies were placed under mandate. There were more-or-less vague promises of eventual independence.

It has been said that the Versailles Treaty, imposed on Germany, was the principle cause of the Second World War. The poor, benighted Germans were so hard done by that they had no option but to go to war 21 years later. Alternatively they were so aggrieved by the way that they were treated that they gladly rushed off to war (in 1939) as soon as they had found a new, messianic, leader. What rubbish.

Germany signed the Treaty after a large majority vote in the Reichstag. The government, and particularly the foreign office, then took particular exception to two provisions. One was the 'war guilt' clause. That said that Germany took *responsibility* for the outbreak of the war. It did not ascribe *guilt*, and it was similar to clauses in the other four treaties. However, the German Foreign Office established a section whose sole responsibility was to refute the clause. This made 'responsibility' or 'guilt' into a major issue. It would have consequences for decades. (Neither responsibility nor guilt were mentioned in the Fourteen Points.)

---

1   Wavell, Brigadier A P, 'The Army and the Prophets', *RUSI: Royal United Services Institute for Defence Studies Journal*, 75:5 (1930), reprinted in 155:6 (December 2010), pp.86-93.

The second issue was reparations. Put simply, Germany did not want to pay them. The German government engaged the British economist, John Maynard Keynes, to advise them. Keynes rushed out a book ('The Economic Consequences of the Peace') which immediately became a best-seller in Britain and elsewhere. Keynes had developed radical economic theories at Cambridge University just before the Great War. He argued that punitive reparations would beggar Germany and foster massive social, hence political, resentment. Keynes was wrong. In practice Germany paid very little in reparations. The hyperinflation which Germany suffered in the early 1920s was largely a consequence of German mismanagement of the German economy. Nevertheless, the German government took every opportunity to blame Versailles. The British public generally seems to have believed that, not least due to Keynes' book.

German objections to the terms of the Versailles treaty can be seen as disingenuous, to say the least. Can they really have expected better, having imposed the treaty of Brest-Litovsk on the Russians?

There was a genuine international desire for peace in the interwar period. The Washington Naval Treaty of 1922 and the London Naval Treaties of 1930 and 1936 sought to avoid another naval arms race, and particularly the cost of new naval construction. They were largely successful. Virtually no new battleships or aircraft carriers were built until the mid-1930s. The Locarno Pact of 1925 sought to regularise post-war relations between France and Germany. In negotiating for it Britain encouraged Germany to look eastward, to create stability in central and eastern Europe. The Pact should also help to limit Soviet expansionism. Conflict between France and Germany was in practice avoided, although the Pact was not popular further east. Under the Kellogg-Briand Pact of 1928, nations undertook not to use war to resolve disputes or conflicts. It was not particularly successful in the short term, but became a useful aspect of the international political situation after the Second World War. Such treaties were generally quite popular domestically. Most countries' populations did not want to fight another major war.

One aspect of the strategic context was that many countries were seriously short of money. That was not just a security issue, but an aspect of economic management. Lloyd George's post-war coalition government passed 14 acts to improve social welfare. All had a cost. He was still serving as PM in 1921 when the Treasury commissioned a series of reports which resulted in cuts to government spending of over 10%. Cuts to defence spending were included in order to reduce the impact on welfare. Lloyd George had promised to build 'a country fit for heroes to live in', but failed to pay for it.

Keynes was a leading member of the 'Bloomsbury Set', a well-known but poorly-defined group of intellectuals, art theorists, novelists and wife swappers who exerted a strange influence on early to mid-century English society. The description might include 'homosexuals'. The novelist Virginia Woolf was a member. The British population had just been involved in the biggest war in history. It was, by today's standards, highly socially conservative. They might have found it ironic that the Bloomsbury Set were almost exclusively conscientious objectors, medically unfit, female, or worked in reserved occupations. None had fought in the War. Only one had even served. It is remarkable how insidiously an unrepresentative elite can hijack public thought.

There is always unfinished business in international affairs. Italy and Japan had entered the Great War to advance their own strategic goals. They had been on the winning side. Not surprisingly, they continued to advance those goals. Japan had maintained its occupation of parts of Manchuria. From 1931 it expanded slowly into the rest of Manchuria and then China. China had largely collapsed into feudal fiefdoms in the 1910s. Nationalists under Chiang Kai-shek were gradually imposing control, although opposed by the Communists and the remaining warlords. Japan effectively invaded China in 1937. In practice the League did nothing.

Italy suffered massive social unrest after the war. Benito Mussolini was a minor journalist who had been supported financially by the British intelligence service during the Great War. He seized an opportunity to take over as prime minister and create a fascist government under the nominal rule of the King of Italy. Mussolini promoted a vision of a second Italian empire in Africa. He manipulated border skirmishes between Italian Somalia and Ethiopia (known in Europe as Abyssinia). Trouble broke out in 1934; Italy invaded in 1935. Britain and France negotiated, in a misguided attempt to achieve conciliation without recourse to war. However, Hitler re-occupied the Rhineland in March 1936. France wanted to avoid drawing Italy into war in Europe. As a result, France and Britain effectively gave Italy a free hand in Ethiopia. The League, in practice, did nothing.

The Spanish Civil War of 1935-39 also presented problems. The League, and particularly France and Britain, did act to contain the conflict within Spain; not least through a naval blockade. It was a big war. Both the *de facto* Republican government and the counter-revolutionary Nationalist party assembled armies of over 700,000 men. Germany and Italy supported the Nationalists. The USSR supported the Republicans. The Nationalists were organised around regular troops from the Spanish Foreign Legion and Moroccan colonial forces. They were better organised, enjoyed more effective (German) support, and eventually won. The main external effect was what German and Soviet forces learnt in terms of research, field trials and combat experience.

There had been other instances of 'unfinished business' at the end of the Great War. In Ireland the republican community resumed hostilities almost immediately. It was *so* pointless. The British Government was largely preoccupied with Paris, disarmament, and taking up new colonial mandates. It quickly offered southern Ireland the status of a dominion within the Empire. A moderate delegation from the Dail (the republican parliament) negotiated with Lloyd George and Churchill, two of the most experienced international diplomats in the world. Nationalist hype aside, the delegation (under Michael Collins) accepted the offer with few real modifications. After much wrangling, the Dail agreed. The Irish War of Independence was over.

The faction which had proclaimed the Republic at Easter 1916 repudiated the treaty almost immediately. Its main political leader, the Machiavellian Eamon de Valera, initiated a civil war. It lost. De Valera was jailed. (He had only escaped execution in

1916 because he was an American citizen: a peculiar interpretation of natural justice). Regrettably Collins died in the Civil War. De Valera eventually returned to take over as prime minister for about 20 years and then president for a further 14. He cast a long shadow over Ireland for decades. It is fair to say that, with a more moderate regime, perhaps under Collins and his colleagues, the history of Ireland in the 20th century would have been very different.

The end of the Great War found Russia in turmoil. The 'Whites', the counter-revolutionary faction under Admiral Kolchak and General Wrangel, initiated a civil war. It attracted western (mostly French and British) military support. The Bolshevik 'Red' Faction was generally better organised and enjoyed the advantage of a more central position. The Civil War saw large cavalry forces employed over very large distances. That underpinned the writings of General Vladimir Triandafilov and Marshal Mikhail Tuchachevsky, which led to considerable development in operational thought. The civil war ran on until 1923. There had been well over seven million casualties. That formed part of the social, economic and political background to Soviet centralisation of agriculture and industry.

In 1919 Poland attempted to expand eastwards into Ukraine. That brought it into conflict with the Soviets. Poland and the Soviet Union were at war until late 1921. After an initial string of successes, the Soviets were defeated at the battle of Warsaw in August 1920. The outcome of the war was an independent Polish state, but Ukraine had become part of the Soviet Union. The Russian Civil and Russo-Polish Wars fixed the western boundary of the Soviet Union, and limited Soviet expansion, for the next two decades.

The Second World War was the product of many things. The relative ineffectiveness of the League of Nations contributed. Hitler's personality and his interpretation of the legacy of the Great War were also major factors. Hitler personally played a very large part in starting the Second World War. However, two important institutions made the war possible: the German Army (and, in particular, the General Staff) and the German Foreign Office. The Versailles Treaty pruned the German Army down to four thousand officers. However, with any good pruning what survives grows back healthier than before. In the 1920s the German Army underwent the most profound and detailed analysis of recent operations ever undertaken by any army. The German Foreign Ministry, conversely, was untouched by Versailles. Highly professional and effective, it quietly continued to improve Germany's international position from the low point of Versailles right up to the point where it achieved a pact with Stalin just days before the invasion of Poland in September 1939.

Several of interwar Germany's political institutions were, however, quite weak Its handling of its economy in the 1920s was poor. It could not prevent the leader of a parliamentary minority seizing absolute power. Having seized power, Hitler ruthlessly got rid of opponents, including several military leaders: discrediting, sacking, or simply murdering them. Kurt von Schleicher (Chancellor and defence minister), Ferdinand von Bredow (Schleicher's deputy defence minister), Werner von Blomberg (later, head of the German armed forces) and Werner von Fritsch (commander in chief of the army) were all disposed of. The Nazi party took over the running of much of the government. In a very real sense it became the government.

Europe did not sleepwalk into the Second World War. Many people, in many nations, genuinely wished to avoid another war. Neville Chamberlain, British PM from 1937 to 1940, attempted appeasement right up to the Munich Agreement of September 1938. Parliament voted to accept the Munich agreement. Nobody voted against, although Churchill and some other leading Conservatives abstained. For most European countries the options were appeasement or rearmament. Nations tried elements of both. Britain came off its 'Ten Year Rule' (which assumed no major war for that period) in March 1932. It started building capital ships (battleships and aircraft carriers) with its 1936 defence budget.

Apart from genuinely pacifist sentiment, appeasement appealed for two reasons. Firstly, Germany appeared to be powerful militarily, and the western powers had not yet rearmed. Secondly, due to the sheer cost of another war.

Germany invaded Poland on 1 September 1939. France and Britain declared war on Germany. They did not do so in order to defend Poland. That would have been physically impossible, although possibly a long-term strategic goal. They did so because appeasement had failed. Hitler, and Germany, had to be stopped. Poland was the 'line in the sand'. There is good evidence that Hitler did not think that Britain would fight. That resulted from a combination of inconsistent signalling by Britain (which had signed the Munich agreement just a year before) and of Hitler being told only what he wanted to hear. Telling him things he did not want to hear was, by that stage, neither particularly successful nor particularly advisable.

Technology is a human artefact. Inventions do not just happen. Men conduct science, and develop machines and systems, in response to problems whose solutions appear useful. That is particularly true of military technology. People may well then adjust and adapt the results to different purposes. They do so particularly where that produces a warfighting advantage.

Radio developed steadily during the interwar years. Britain, particularly the Royal Navy and RAF, probably held a leading position. It did so in one critical, major application: radar. Britain developed land-based radar in response to a strategic need for early warning of air attack. Its cruisers and battleships were equipped with radar by the outbreak of war. Airborne radar followed soon after.

Warships underwent a number of incremental, but significant, improvements. Oil replaced coal: warships got faster. High-speed long-endurance diesels were introduced for smaller ships. Compartmentalisation, better design, and fire suppression systems improved survivability. Greater elevation for guns led to increases in range. Improved computation led to improved accuracy at longer ranges. Most battleships and cruisers had aircraft for reconnaissance and for gunfire spotting.

Many improvements to military aircraft originated in civil aviation. The biggest change was the development of monocoque construction: the use of lightweight alloy framing and stressed skins, as opposed to wood and fabric. When coupled to developments in engines, aircraft became relatively lighter, stronger, faster and more manoeuvrable. Multiple weapons in aircraft wings, and powered gun turrets, were becoming common by 1939.

The biggest developments in land armament were in tank design, but we should not overstate the results. Best practice in the late 1930s was for single, three-man rotating turrets with a high-velocity main gun of about 37mm; a power-to-weight ratio of perhaps 20 horsepower per ton; and armour about 15mm (half an inch or so) thick. In practice no army had many tanks of that quality. Radio was by no means universal, and in some cases armour was still riveted (as opposed to welded or cast). There were some attempts at much heavier tanks, but they were all grossly underpowered.

High-velocity antiaircraft cannon were making low-level air attack dangerous, both at sea and on land. Cross-country trucks were appearing in numbers. The British replaced six- or eight-horse gun teams with a four-wheel drive truck of 70 horse power. Not perfect, perhaps; but clearly an improvement.

In 1919 the head of the German army, General Hans von Seeckt, initiated a series of detailed studies into the course, conduct and outcome of the Great War. Unsurprisingly, it focused on winning: the conduct of operations and tactics. In choosing his 4,000 officers (and particularly those who led the studies) von Seeckt strongly preferred General Staff officers over experienced front-line commanders or those with political connections. In doing so he ensured thoroughness, honesty, and far-reaching assessments. The studies sought empirical evidence, which contrasted with Germany's somewhat rationalistic pre-war thinking. Von Seeckt then had new army regulations written. They were, effectively high-level conceptual doctrine. With just one major revision they carried the German Army right through the Second World War, and in some aspects through to today. It was a landmark development.

The studies looked into every field of army endeavour and included the operational basis of the Luftwaffe. 400 of the 4000 officers were fliers. Typically every regiment in the army had at least one qualified pilot amongst its officers.

The Germans observed that long-range bombing against infrastructure was inefficient and ineffective. The British Independent Air Force had lost one aircraft for every ton of bombs dropped, and one casualty for every civilian killed. Bombers did not always get through. Conversely the Germans had been very interested in some aspects of RAF performance, such as battlefield air interdiction. As a result, Luftwaffe doctrine almost entirely ignored long-range infrastructure bombing and concentrated on operational and tactical aspects. True to its experience, however, it tended to overlook air support to naval operations.

The German army had more experience of anti-tank defence than any other army. It was initially forbidden to procure tanks. Its officers thought at length about how to restore tactical and operational mobility to the army. They translated articles and books by foreign writers such as the British Colonel (later Major General) J F C Fuller and Captain (later Sir) Basil Liddell Hart. Those works stimulated thinking, but did not have much direct impact. The German army established a secret tank development and training facility at Kazan in Russia in 1929. They did not begin to produce tanks until after Hitler came to power, although they had built prototypes. Development of both tanks and armoured formations was then rapid. The appointment of Colonel Heinz Guderian as chief of staff to the Inspectorate of Motorized Troops in 1933 was significant. He was not a particularly leading thinker. He was a tenacious, pugnacious and effective organiser, and became a highly effective commander.

The German Army did not invent the term 'Blitzkrieg'. What they did, by 1939, was develop and field a highly coherent force which stressed operational envelopment, all-arms cooperation, air liaison and support, rapid decision making, and massive concentration of force at the critical point. That thinking was physically embodied in its Panzer divisions. It was the practical application of the doctrine resulting from von Seeckt's studies.

Given its adversaries and its limited experience in the Great War, the Japanese Army did not innovate very much. By 1939 its forces were tough, capable, highly experienced, devoted to the point of fanaticism, but not particularly modern. Conversely, Japanese admirals had given a lot of thought to a Pacific war. They probably gave more thought to amphibious shipping than any other navy. For example, they pioneered the design of landing ships with internal docks for landing craft. They also gave considerable thought to carrier air operations. They emphasized the importance of pre-emptive strikes against the fleets of larger nations (meaning Britain and America). They also developed long-range bomber aircraft (both carrier- and land-based) to enable them to be able to strike first before the opposition came into range.

Of the three major Axis nations, Italy innovated the least. It produced one of the great early air theorists, General Giulio Douhet. Douhet was perhaps the arch-proponent of the use of long-range bombing against cities and the enemy's population. He was court-martialled during the Great War for insubordination, exonerated, wrote his one classic book and retired. His thinking provoked strong reaction from Italian admirals and generals. He probably had little impact on the development of the Italian armed forces.

One area in which Italy excelled, however, was that of underwater frogmen and submersibles. It was an important niche, and quite significant in the Mediterranean in the Second World War. The battleships HMSs *Queen Elizabeth* and *Valiant* were attacked in harbour and damaged in December 1941. Both were out of action for months. That altered the operational balance in the Mediterranean. It was not, of itself, a war winner.

Triandafilov was the thinker. Tuchachevsky turned the thinking into capability. By the early 1930s the Red Army was conceptually far in front of any other army in terms of long-range, deep operational theory. One consequence was a requirement for 'fast tanks'. 'Fast' meant quick enough to run down horsed cavalry and prevent horse-drawn gun teams from getting away.

The Soviet Union bought British Vickers Medium and Mark 'E' (light) tanks in 1930. They then started to build their own (the Mark 'E' as the T26), and then massively expanded their tank production. Over 11,000 T26s were built. The USSR gave great thought to war production. By 1939 it was probably better prepared than any other nation to move industrial production onto a war footing. That would include the wholesale relocation of factories, if necessary.

The Red Army had the high-level thinking and lots of moderately good tanks. They did not develop low-level tactics nearly as well as the German Army. Training standards and logistics were both poor. Perhaps the Red Army's greatest achievement was to observe, during the Spanish Civil War, that tanks would have to be 'shell proof'. 15mm or so of armour was not enough. Tanks would also need bigger guns, both to combat enemy 'shell proof' tanks and to defeat enemy antitank guns. Fast, shell-proof and large gun: the result was the T34.

Triandafilov died in an air crash in 1931. Tuchachevsky, his wife and brothers were executed on Stalin's orders in 1937. His sisters were sent to the Gulag. Radical operational thinking was not part of the Red Army's repertoire when it entered the Second World War.

At the end of the Great War the French Army knew that methodical, set-piece attacks supported by lots of artillery worked. They knew that properly-designed reinforced concrete fortifications worked. They knew that light tanks – effectively machineguns on tracks – were extremely useful, as were heavier tanks that could destroy field fortifications. Strategically they knew that the next major war would, once again, be fought against Germany. In the air, they were aware of the importance of having large reserves of aircraft available against attrition.

The French realised that antitank guns would be required. They also realised that their cavalry formations would have to be motorised, at least in part. Critically, not least due to the prompting of Colonel Charles de Gaulle, they reasoned that heavily armoured counterattack formations would be needed to stop any breakthrough by German armoured formations. (As armoured theorists went, de Gaulle was even more vain and egotistical than Liddell Hart.)

The French turned those observations into reality (they even appointed de Gaulle to command an armoured division). The cost of their new frontier defences – the Maginot Line – was monumental. The equipment of the field army was mediocre and the standard of training, on mobilisation, was poor. That should not have mattered: in practice it had nine months to train before the Germans attacked. The French had an army and an air force that was well suited to the task in hand: if the task was to fight the last battle of the last war.

It is wrong to say that armies simply prepare to re-fight the last battle of the last war. Some don't even do that don't. If they did, they would not repeat the mistakes of the last war. The French did, largely, avoid such mistakes. *Good* armies (or navies, or air forces) prepare very thoroughly to refight the last battle of the last war. *Excellent* armies think very deeply about the first battle of the next war. Unfortunately for France, that is just what the German Army had done. Put another way: the losers can learn most from a war; if they are professional. The Germans were.

The Reichsheer, and its successor the Wehrnmacht, has been criticized for not concentrating on things that don't win wars, such as intelligence and logistic; but rather on things which do: operations and tactics. Surely that is perverse. Intelligence and logistics are supporting functions. Similarly the Wehrmacht is criticized for poor strategy, over which had practically no control.

The Washington Naval Treaty limited the United States Navy (USN) and Royal Navy to 15 battleships and five aircraft carriers each. Early USN planning revolved around a line of 12 battleships fighting a major fleet action, as at Jutland. Wargames stressed the need to gain air superiority over the enemy fleet. That implied sinking the enemy's carriers, hence massing the greatest possible number of attack aircraft to strike in one wave. Seagoing trials and modifications showed how that could be done. For example, aircraft carriers were expected to launch an aircraft every 15 seconds. To do that, aircraft had to be parked on deck in preparation for a strike. Having achieved air superiority, subsequent waves of aircraft would attack the enemy battle fleet. It was a good, clear example of thinking through a problem from a strategic requirement (for example: to attack Japan, which had a fleet of nine battleships and three carriers), through the operational, to the tactical.

The USN and the Marine Corps (USMC) also thought through the problems of amphibious warfare, which would clearly be required in a Pacific (and possibly an Atlantic) Ocean scenario. The USMC led the way in the development of ramped landing craft ('Higgins Boats') and tracked assault amphibians. They also developed the techniques, procedures and training needed to operate them.

Two differing schools of thought evolved in the United States Army Air Service (later 'Corps', or USAAC) after the Great War. Both schools considered control of the air to be essential. General Billy Mitchell was a key figure in the 'bomber' school. It held that bombers could sink battleships; that the bomber would always get through; and that the best way to win the air war was through bombing. That was extended through a series of questionable assertions in tactical publications, which were used to make a case for an independent air force. Conversely the 'pursuit' (ie, fighter) school held that bombers would not get through. Fighters would always have the advantage, as they had in the Great War. The bomber school countered that with the assertion that sufficiently large formations of fast and heavily armed bombers would be able to fight their way through, despite enemy fighters.

The development of the B17 bomber, which first flew in December 1936, was seen to win the case for the bomber school. The B17 carried 13 machineguns and had a top speed of 250mph. As the in-service pursuit fighter, the P26, had a top speed of just 234mph the case was, seemingly, proven. The bomber school dominated USAAC thinking by the late 1930s.

That was either technically illiterate or disingenuous. When the B17 entered service, the Curtis Hawk fighter was already flying. Its top speed, on entry into service, was 303mph. When the engine from the B17 (the 1200hp Wright Cyclone) was fitted onto Hawk-series aircraft (such as Kittihawks and Warhawks), speeds of 350mph were achieved.

It is hard to believe that USAAC officers were technically illiterate.

Strategy matters. In the 1920s it was not obvious to the US government why its army would need tanks, other than possibly to support the infantry. A very good case could be made for the retention of horsed cavalry, not least because it was often used along the Mexican border. America did not see the need for a large army at all, and did not prioritise the development of new weapons such as tanks. In several other areas the US Army did not develop its thinking, nor its equipment, to the same extent as European armies. For example, it did not develop a section light machinegun, and section ('squad') tactics remained relatively simplistic. In crude terms, the US army did not fight long enough in the Great War to learn some of the things that other armies did.

That cannot be said of the British Army. Two of its best-known military thinkers, Liddell Hart and Fuller both served on the Western Front. Fuller did so for the whole of the War. Hart, a civilian who joined the Army in August 1914, made a major contribution to codifying infantry tactics after the war. The work was continued by others such as Lieutenant Colonel (later Field Marshal Viscount) Bernard Montgomery. The famous 'Bren' section light machinegun was procured in 1936. It was used until the early 1990s.

Hart, an Oxford graduate, never served above battalion level. He was gassed on the Somme and did not see active service again. He had no insight into the practicalities of command. He seems to have considered that all British Generals were incompetent, which is statistically unlikely. He became famous as a writer. His thinking about strategy (the 'British Way of War' and the 'Indirect Approach') borrowed heavily from other, mostly British, writers. He failed to acknowledge that. His thinking was highly rationalistic, opinionated and largely failed when exposed to events.

Fuller was a Regular officer. He was a student at Staff College when the Great War started. He became the chief tactician of the Tank Corps and was, without doubt, a leading figure in the development of armoured warfare. His work contributed significantly to the successes at Cambrai in 1917 and Amiens in 1918. His thinking beyond that ('Plan 1919', etc) was an entirely reasonable rationalistic extrapolation from his experience; but no more than that. He was appointed to command the world's first experimental mechanised force, on Salisbury Plain, in 1927. He refused the appointment. He had no further real involvement in British armoured warfare theory, nor practice.

Nonetheless Fuller and Liddell Hart dominated inter-war military debate, in Britain and elsewhere. Conversely they had very little practical impact. The main British doctrine pamphlets, such as the Tank Corps' 'Purple Primer', were written by serving officers who did not subsequently command tank formations. It was Fuller who suggested that there should be two main tank types; heavy 'Infantry' tanks and fast 'Cruiser' tanks. However, he also ensured that both were armed with high-velocity antitank guns and machineguns. The guns were 2pdr (40mm), and quite effective, but had no HE shell. British tanks therefore entered the war with no weapon with which to neutralize antitank guns and field emplacements.

On the outbreak of war in September 1939 the British Army had five Regular and six TA tank brigades. The TA had 18 tank and 20 armoured car units. Both the Regular and the Territorial Armies still had a few horsed cavalry units as well. What the Army generally lacked, however, was tanks. Very few units were fully equipped.

The Army also lacked good armoured formation doctrine. Any advantage that Wavell had identified in 1930 had been eroded by 1939.

In 1919 Britain was allied to Japan. There was no German Navy until after 1933. The Royal Navy had no obvious enemy, but a large fleet and a massive long-term responsibility. The 'sunk' investment in capital ships was a national issue. The useful life of a hull was a major factor: HMS *Warspite* fought both at Jutland in 1916 and Normandy in 1944. One British aim at the Washington Naval Conference was to maintain naval capability, probably for decades, at minimum cost.

The Royal Navy subsequently developed plans to fight Japan by defending the Malay Barrier (denying access into the Indian Ocean), fighting forward to relieve Hong Kong, and then advancing towards the Japanese mainland. By the late 1930s its plans were modified to fight alongside American forces further forwards, to include the defence of the Philippines. When Germany rearmed, the Royal Navy's plans had focus on the defeat of small numbers of very modern German capital ships (*Tirpitz*, *Bismarck*, *Gneisenau* and *Scharnhorst*; and 'pocket battleships' such as *Graf Spee*). Those plans did not include major fleet-on-fleet engagements. Britain had more experience of carrier warfare than any other country. That emphasized the horrible vulnerability of aircraft on deck, and the need to be able to launch and recover aircraft in rough seas. Aircraft operated from hangers below armoured flight decks. They were designed with low take-off and landing speeds.

On 11 November 1918 Major General Hugh Trenchard, commanding the British Independent Air Force, wrote that 'a greater waste of time there had never been' [sic]. He was referring to the creation of the RAF. Within a few years, as Chief of the Air Staff (CAS), he was a leading exponent of long-range bombing. This apparent 'about face' can be ascribed largely to the need to find an exclusive role for the RAF. If he did not do so, the RAF risked being abolished.

That organisational imperative quickly brought ridiculous consequences. In 1924 the RAF wrote to the Combined Chiefs of Staff saying that is was, in essence, ignoring its own operational history. The newly-established RAF Staff College quickly became a centre for the propagation of the faith in bombing.

The RAF was quick to adopt 'air control' of mandated territories. That is, colonial policing using aircraft. It was widely advertised as being cost effective. It wasn't. It was ineffective, but cheap. In Iraq the RAF bombed villages until the population resented them; and then …? In Palestine the RAF failed to contain the Arab Revolt of 1936. The Army then took back control; the revolt was suppressed within a month or so. Air Control was seen as making the RAF useful: an organisational imperative. But even if one accepts that Air Control was effective, which it wasn't, or cheap, which it was, it was no justification for an independent air force. The RFC could have done it just as well, and probably better (because air-ground cooperation would probably have been better).

The RAF's faith in long-range bombing revolved around the assertion that 'the bomber will always get through'. That assertion was contrary to the evidence of German bombing of Britain in the Great War. It was also contrary to the lessons of the Independent Air Force's operations in 1918, but the RAF never conducted a rigorous survey of the results (despite most of its targets being accessible in the Allied Control Zone in Germany).

The creation of the RAF's Fighter Command was perhaps the only truly revolutionary military development anywhere in the world in the interwar period. It linked radar and other ground-based warning assets, command posts, communications, fighters and antiaircraft guns. It was truly revolutionary, not least in the way it harnessed both science and operational research in its design. Air Chief Marshal Sir Hugh Dowding was its architect and its commander in the Battle of Britain. Fighter Command did everything it was designed to do. But the air defence of Great Britain had been forced on the RAF against its will. The enlargement of Fighter Command from 1937 was largely due to men such as Sir Thomas Inskip, Minister for the Coordination of Defence and Sir Warren Fisher, Under-Secretary to the Treasury. The RAF had wanted to buy more bombers.

RAF doctrine insisted that air superiority was to be gained, and wars won, by bombing. But bombing what? It was not clear whether bombing enemy airfields was the intention, nor whether it would work. Pre-war RAF doctrine wrote that 'it was clearly illegal to bomb built-up areas in the hope of hitting military targets'[2]. In 1939 the RAF did not have any four-engined heavy bombers. It had virtually no overseas bomber bases, but neither did it practice flying over water (nor at night). Bombing accuracy was poor. The RAF resisted calls to support the Army, or the Navy, through doctrinaire assertions about the best use of aircraft.

This reached ridiculous proportions. The RAF refused to strengthen the defences of Malta (a critical Royal Navy base). Since the bomber would always get through, Malta was indefensible. At or about the same time, RAF observers in Spain reported that antiaircraft guns could make an important contribution to air superiority. They defended air bases, and therefore protected the fighters. Fighters attacked the bombers, which therefore *didn't* get through. So, empirical evidence contradicted rationalistic conjecture. The response? Argue away the evidence.

The Luftwaffe changed its fighter tactics as a result of its experience in Spain. The RAF didn't study the lessons closely enough; in 1940 its fighter tactics were crude. Operationally, it didn't matter: the RAF won the Battle of Britain. Tactically, a lot of pilots died unnecessarily.

Maynard Keynes was wrong. However, his thinking had become the accepted truth: Versailles, in some weird, poorly-enunciated way had apparently caused the Second World War. It didn't. The Second World War was not inevitable. It was the consequence of the choices which people made. To think otherwise is to ignore the actions, and choices, made by a whole generation of politicians (including Hitler) over a twenty year period.

2   Overy, Richard, *The Bombing War*, (London: Allen Lane, 2013), p239

Strategy matters. There was a pressing strategic need for Britain to improve its national air defence. It did. Germany foresaw major land-air campaigns against numerically larger enemies. Armoured formations, and an air force optimised for air interdiction, made sense. It was not particularly obvious why Britain needed armoured formations. It was not particularly obvious to Germany why it needed aircraft carriers. Most countries were short of money and had to make hard strategic choices.

British and American air forces fell victim to their own dogma. The evidence of the Great War indicated that the long-range bombing of infrastructure was ineffective and highly inefficient. The Germans recognised that. British and American air forces latched onto long-range bombing, contrary to evidence which they did not bother to analyse, in order to justify or obtain their own independence. It is not clear whether dogma drove organisational imperatives, or the converse. The outcome was the same. Whichever was the case, they entered the next war with equipment and doctrine which would fail when exposed to reality.

What were aircraft carriers for? Japan and America espoused long-range naval aviation strikes, in order to gain air superiority at sea and then attack the enemy's battleships. Britain developed carriers as part of a mixed solution to a relatively small number of powerful German surface units. The key issue was to be able to find, and then attack, single battleships (perhaps escorted by heavy cruisers), in all weathers, in the North Atlantic (but also with an eye to possible operations against Japan). It was an entirely different strategic and operational requirement. Not surprisingly, British carriers were different, too.

Armoured warfare is not just about tanks. The extensive and much-discussed writings of a few British tank theorists were sometimes wrong, sometimes ignored, and did little to affect the course of the next major war. German commanders did read Fuller's and Liddell Hart's writings. They interpreted them in light of their own doctrine. They observed British experimental trials. They also conducted their own. They operated a tank force, and 36 antitank batteries, in Spain and observed the results. By 1939, they may have had better tanks. They certainly had better armoured formations. They were extremely well trained. Their tactical doctrine was a product of what they had learnt.

Empirical experience was much more important than air dogma or the assertions of well-known armour theorists. As the next war would show once again, you can cling to dogma and assertion if you wish. Thousands of young men will die to no good purpose.

Armed forces did innovate between the wars. They did not do so equally, nor symmetrically. Not all did so particularly well. But change was the rule, not the exception.

6

The Proper Application of Overwhelming Force

In the summer of 1939, some months before the outbreak of war, the British Ministry of Agriculture offered farmers £2 an acre to plough up grassland in order to grow food. Their target was 1,285,000 acres. Britain knew that war was coming.

The Ministry also made an agreement with Ford to build a tractor factory (most British agriculture was still horse-powered). It built 136,000 tractors by the end of the war.

For many British and Commonwealth readers the history of the War is, effectively, Churchill's. Thrown out of government in late 1945 and remembering the battle of the memoirs after the Great War, Churchill ensured that his memoirs were published first. 'The Second World War' was published in six volumes between 1948 and 1953. Churchill's version of events still dominates received wisdom. It is in practice an auto-biography cunningly disguised as a history. One half of the English-speaking world has seen the war through Churchill's version of events, complete with suggested false-hoods and suppressed truths, ever since.

American readers would probably be more familiar with General Dwight Eisenhower's 'Crusade in Europe', which was published in 1948; not least because Eisenhower went on to be President for two terms. British and American accounts of events differ. That has flavoured subsequent interpretations.

The state of military technology at the beginning of the War was described in Chapter Five. In the Second World War aerial warfare enabled the conduct of campaigns over great distances. It including bombarding cities with thousands of rockets at ranges of up to 200 miles. Non-visual sensors were used widely for the first time. They included radar, sonar and to a very limited extent infra-red.

Eisenhower ascribed victory to three mundane items of military equipment: the bulldozer, the landing craft and the Dakota transport aircraft. However, perhaps the most iconic piece of military equipment for the Second World War was the half-tracked truck. 'Half tracks' might be armoured or unarmoured. They were produced as personnel carriers, gun tractors or specialist vehicles. Advances to both wheeled and tracked vehicles meant that half tracks would be consigned to history soon after the war.

The Second World War was, in practice, three conflicts in one. The first was a major European war. It started when Germany invaded Poland on 1 September 1939. Given Germany's challenge to the British and French navies, that rapidly spread to the Atlantic and even the Indian oceans. The second conflict resulted from continuing Italian opportunism. Italy entered the war in June 1940, soon after Germany invaded France and the Low Countries. Italian involvement extended the war across the Mediterranean and into Africa. The third conflict emerged from the Sino-Japanese War. In December 1941 Japan extended its operations by attacking American, British and Dutch possessions around the southwest Pacific. Germany had already invaded Russia. The war had become global. This chapter looks at how the major nations developed and executed their strategies. It also considers how national resources were applied to support those campaigns. An outline chronology of the Second World War is at Figure 6-1.

Western Europe	Eastern Europe	Mediterranean	Far East & Pacific
1939 Sep.	Germany and USSR invade Poland		
Oct.	Poland surrenders. Italy attacks Greece		
Nov.	USSR attacks Finland (until Mar 40)		
1940 Apr. Germany invades Denmark and Norway			
May. Germany invades Belgium, France, Netherlands and Luxemburg			
Jun. Allied evacuations from Dunkirk. France surrenders		Italy attacks Kenya and Sudan	
Aug. Battle of Britain (until Oct)		Italy attacks British positions in Egypt	
Oct.	Italy attacks Greece		
Dec.		Italian army defeated in Egypt	
1941 Feb.		German Afrika Korps arrives in North Africa	
Apr.	Germany attacks Yugoslavia & Greece		
May.		Most Italian forces in east Africa defeated	
Jun.	Germany attacks USSR		
Nov.		Italian forces in east Africa surrender	
Dec.	German offensive at Moscow halted		Japan attacks Pearl Harbour.
1942 Feb.			Singapore captured by Japanese

Western Europe	Eastern Europe	Mediterranean	Far East & Pacific
May.			Philippines captured by Japanese
Jun.	German summer offensive begins		Naval battle of Midway
Jul.		1st Battle of El Alamein	
Aug.	Battle of Stalingrad begins		
Oct.		2nd Battle of El Alamein	
Nov.		Allied landings in Morocco and Algeria	
1943 Feb.	German troops in Stalingrad surrender		
May.		German and Italian forces in north Africa surrender	
Jul.	German attack at Kursk	Allied invasion of Sicily (to Aug)	
Sep.		Allied landings in Italy	
Nov.			American landings on Tarawa
1944 Mar.			Battles of Imphal & Kohima (Burma) begin (until Jun)
May.		Operation Diadem (including 4th battle of Cassino)	
Jun. Allied landings in Normandy	Soviet offensive (Operation Bagration) begins	Rome liberated	
Aug. End of Normandy campaign			
Sep. Operation Market Garden			
Oct.			American landings in the Philippines
Dec. Battle of the Bulge (until Jan)			
1945 Mar. Allied forces cross the Rhine			
Apr.	Soviet armies attack Berlin		American landings on Okinawa
May. Germany surrenders		German troops in Italy surrender	
Aug.			Atomic bombs dropped on Japan. Japan surrenders

Figure 6-1 Outline Chronology of the Second Word War.

It is possible that German National Socialist ideology was internally coherent. It might have been possible to construct a national and a military strategy to achieve the goals of that ideology. It is not at all clear whether that strategy would have succeeded. It is entirely clear that Hitler did no such thing.

Hitler was largely self-educated, ideologically fanatic and virulently racist. He had some grasp of the economic aspects of war, but was no strategist. He was not fully in control of the German armed forces until at least December 1941 (when he sacked Field Marshal Walter von Brauchitsch, head of the Army). However, in practice Hitler dominated German strategy and much of its operational planning. He also constructed a moral framework, with no great precision, which his National Socialist subordinates operated under.

Hitler initially had no clear strategic plan. He conducted a series of small wars (against Austria, Czechoslovakia and then Poland) in which the Wehrmacht succeeded easily. France and Britain effectively did nothing. When they attempted operations in Norway in early 1940, they were defeated decisively and at little cost. Germany then overran France and the Low Countries in May and June 1940 for the loss of 43,000 dead. Contrast that with failure, and the loss of 1.7 million dead, after four years of war, from 1914.

It was perfectly reasonable for Germany to believe that it could defeat the Soviet Union. It had beaten the Russian Army time after time in the Great War, for a loss of just 300,000 dead. More importantly, Russia then collapsed. Why should it not do so again? The German Army was quite used to operating in the Russian winter and in the spring and autumn thaws. It had done so from 1914 to 1919. The Finnish Winter War of 1939-40, in which Germany supported Finland, showed just how inept the Red Army was.

Hitler had already decided in principle to attack Russia in late July 1940. The Battle of Britain opened on 13 August, and Hitler cancelled plans to invade Britain in September. Hitler may have been ambivalent about invading Britain. It was worth a try, and if it worked, it worked; but he does seem to have been uncharacteristically irresolute in practice.

The German Army high command (OberKommando des Heeres, OKH) was responsible for operational planning. Differences between Hitler and OKH meant that the 1941 campaign against the USSR had not one, but three aims; no main effort; and three operational objectives (Leningrad, Moscow and Ukraine). OKH's view had been that the destruction of the Russian rail network centred around Moscow, and the Soviet reserves located in front of the city, would allow Germany to then take whatever economic and industrial resources it wished.

Hitler thought that Moscow was unimportant. It was not. On 19 October 1941 Stalin ordered it to be defended to the last. It is entirely possible that a campaign designed to destroy the Red Army in 1941, with Moscow as its operational objective, would have succeeded. Forced to stand and fight in front of Moscow, the Red Army might well have been fixed for just the sort of operational envelopments at which the Wehrmacht excelled.

The Wehrmacht failed in 1941. In 1942 it struck south. Bypassing Stalingrad, it quickly reached Astrakhan and cut off the Caspian oil supply. The Red Army was forced to fight to reopen the oil supply, and was then defeated. Clearly that did not happen. Germany's actual operational plan for 1942 had two goals: the capture of both the Caspian oilfields and Stalingrad. By splitting its forces, it achieved neither. Neither would have been decisive of itself. If the oilfields had been seized, the Red Army would still have been at liberty to take them back. Stalingrad was of no more than tactical, and perhaps totemic, significance.

By 1943 Germany also faced an invasion of southern or western Europe by the western Allies. Germany did not have the resources for a major campaign in Russia: the Kursk operation had no obvious strategic goal. From the summer of 1943 Germany was strategically on the defensive. Even at that stage, it need not have lost. A mobile defensive posture in the east might have negated the Soviet threat long enough to beat any western invasion and bring about a stalemate peace. Hitler refused to accept that option. The German Army Group Centre was effectively destroyed by the Soviet Operation Bagration. It lost perhaps 400,000 men. Many divisions were destroyed or badly damaged. At the same time the Anglo-American Normandy operation succeeded. Germany was overrun ten months later.

German lost, and lost badly. Its territory was occupied and divided. 12 million ethnic Germans were forced to flee westwards. Well over a million German women were raped. About 20% of German children lost their fathers. Most German cities had been heavily bombed. 593,000 German civilians died in the bombing.

For much of the war Germany deployed about 170 divisions on the Eastern front. By late 1944 there were also 20-25 German divisions in Italy, about a dozen in the Balkans and 60-70 facing the American and British armies in the west.

In 1940 Italy attacked British colonies in east Africa. It also invaded Egypt from Libya, and Greece from Albania. That had some merit as an opportunist strategy to profit from British preoccupation with Germany. However, Britain fairly easily overran Italy's territories in east Africa (Eritrea, Ethiopia and Italian Somaliland). It used mostly Dominion, Indian and African troops.

Greece fought back and halted the Italian offensive. It earned a rare vote of respect in the German Reichstag. Britain quickly garrisoned Crete and Lemnos. The strategic logic for doing that is questionable. It prompted Germany to intervene in the Balkans. Germany overran Yugoslavia and Greece in a few weeks in the spring of 1941. That had consequences. Firstly, the German invasion of Russia was delayed for several weeks. Secondly, Britain had diverted troops to Greece from Egypt. Many of them were lost. One Indian division had also been diverted from Egypt to Ethiopia. Italy's invasion of Egypt from Libya was defeated just inside the border at great loss, prompting Germany to send the Afrika Korps to reinforce it.

After the eventual defeat of German and Italian ('Axis') forces in North Africa in May 1943, the western Allies invaded Sicily and then the Italian mainland. Italy signed an armistice with the Allies in September 1943. Italian losses were considerable: a total of about 300,000 dead; roughly 230,000 prisoners of war (POWs) in East

Africa; over a quarter of a million POWs in North Africa; 64,000 in Russia; and 650,000 interned by the Germans after the armistice. Perhaps the main thing that the Italians achieved was to divert German, and British, resources from elsewhere. Italy mobilised almost 100 divisions at various stages.

Japan had signed a Tripartite Pact with Germany and Italy in September 1940. Japan's and Germany's war efforts were largely uncoordinated. Their interests actually clashed, in a number of unimportant areas. Their relations were characterised by mutual distrust, self-overestimation and racial bias on both sides. There was no joint strategic planning. Their capabilities were asymmetric: the German Navy played a relatively small part, whereas the Imperial Japanese Navy (IJN) was at the least a coequal partner with its army. Emperor Hirohito had fairly little impact on Japanese strategy, which was dominated by a small group of generals and admirals, including the prime minister (General Hideki Tojo).

The fall of France in June 1940 allowed Japan to occupy French Indochina. That concerned the United States, which increased diplomatic pressure. Steel was embargoed and an oil ban was considered. At the time 80% of Japan's oil was imported from the USA. Japan had aspirations, but no clear strategic plan. It had a very sober view of the importance of strategic materials such as oil and rubber. It was aware of strategic geography, and (for example) the implications of the Royal Navy base at Singapore and the US Navy base at Pearl Harbor. Japan had a brilliant *operational* plan to destroy the US Pacific fleet, overrun much of the British, American and Dutch territories in south east Asia, and then defend a strategic perimeter. However that plan did not describe how to *defeat* the United States or Britain. The attack on Pearl Harbor might have destroyed the entire Pacific fleet. That, however, was only half of the US Navy.

The initial offensive swept Japanese forces into Burma and the Indian Ocean. Doing so placed the French colonies at risk. Britain therefore occupied Madagascar. Japan bombed Darwin in northern Australia. The Philippines were captured after a short campaign. Thereafter Japan largely went over to the strategic defensive. In 1944 Japan conducted two linked offensives. One was in southern China. It aimed to open a land route to Indochina, and also in part to push American bombers back out of range of the Japanese mainland. The other offensive was in Burma. It was intended to cut the strategic supply links from India to China. The Chinese operation was broadly successful, although American aircraft could already reach Japan from Saipan in the Pacific. The Burma operation was defeated by the British. It took the Allies just under four years to defeat Japan. Nagasaki and Hiroshima were destroyed with atomic bombs. 67 other cities were burnt out by firestorm attacks. Over two million Japanese soldiers and sailors died, as did 580,000 civilians. Japan had deployed up to 10 divisions in Burma, 20 in the Pacific, 15 in Manchuria and 25 or so in China.

France and Britain entered the war to stop Germany. The problem was 'how?' They both believed that it would be a long war, that they needed to build up their strength first, and that a naval blockade would defeat Germany eventually. They agreed on a strategic defensive. Both they, and Hitler, believed that time was on their side. In the winter of 1939-40 issues of iron ore and possibly helping Finland suggested an operation to Norway. France contributed about a division of troops, the British slightly more. Germany moved first. The Allied operation was a fiasco, but Germany attacked the Low Countries through the Ardennes before the Norway campaign was over. Six weeks later France had capitulated and de Gaulle was on his way to becoming the leader of the French forces in exile.

De Gaulle has been described as extraordinarily rude and ungrateful. That was apparently a form of political genius, since it was the only approach available to him to counter his country's weakness. Oh, really? Wasn't he just extraordinarily rude and ungrateful?

America re-armed France from 1942 onwards. It was a difficult and bad-tempered process. France contributed a corps to Italy in time for the Cassino battles. After the Allied landings in southern France in 1944 the French Army rose to a strength of ten divisions.

Churchill had no peer as a hatcher and dispatcher of inspired but poorly-considered amphibious operations. He was largely responsible for the Norway disaster. In a Commons debate on 7 and 8 May 1940 he accepted his share of the blame; but avoided explaining what that might be. It was Chamberlain who lost the confidence of the House and resigned. Churchill became Prime Minister on 10 May. Germany invaded the Low Countries the same day. British grand strategy can be divided into three periods: before the fall of France; up to Pearl Harbor; and thereafter.

In the first period, strategic planning was woeful, largely because it lacked leadership. After the fall of France and Norway, Germany gained access to Atlantic ports from North Cape to the Bay of Biscay. Britain developed an Atlantic defence strategy, of which the defence of the United Kingdom was the core. Britain garrisoned Iceland, earmarked up to an army corps for deployment at short notice, significantly strengthened the garrison of Gibraltar, stationed two Royal Marine brigades in Sierra Leone (Britain's only possession on the Atlantic coast of North Africa), and invoked the Anglo-Portuguese treaty of 1373 (the world's longest-standing treaty). Britain started to ship an average of 1000 men a day Egypt in order to defend sea communications to the Empire. 20,000 men were *en route* at any one time.

Throughout the war, shipping and manpower were Britain's most critical resources. The shipping needed for the Atlantic operations reduced the flow to the Middle East by 3,000 men per month, and the food supply to Britain by 17,000 tons. The Royal Navy was opposed by both the German and Italian navies. It simply could not afford to allow Germany to take over the somewhat French fleet as well. French naval forces at Mers el Kebir in Algeria were therefore attacked and neutralised in July 1940.

The term 'strategic bombing' is, not least, a claim that such operations were entitled to a place of their own in strategic planning. Churchill effectively ordered the bombing of Germany. Not least, that demonstrated to the home population that Britain was fighting back: a form of political signalling. The proportion of national resources then allocated to bombing was probably the biggest British strategic mistake of the war. 1,5673,000 civilians were employed building aircraft, most of them bombers. At its peak in June and July 1943 the Air Ministry and Ministry of Aircraft Production had

3,619,500 civilians working for them, which was 20% of the entire national workforce. The RAF grew to 1,012,000 men and women. Many Bomber Command squadrons were at double establishments (hence up to 36 aircraft, as opposed to 12 in a fighter squadron). There is a strong suggestion that that was done to conceal the real size of Bomber Command from domestic audiences.

There is a tendency to accept the Allied bombing campaigns as a 'given' or somehow inevitable. They were not. There was considerable debate in British and American war cabinets. The public was generally kept out of the debate. Important decisions and policies were deliberately concealed. As we shall see in the next chapter, the bombing was a gross waste of resources which were needed elsewhere.

The key issue for Britain's grand strategy after the fall of France was to bring America into the war. The Tizard Mission, from September 1940, was the most important science and technology transfer of all time. It included giving most of Britain's secret wartime research, free, to a country which had not yet entered the war. In August 1941 Churchill and Roosevelt met in Placentia Bay, Newfoundland. They issued a joint statement. It would become the North Atlantic Charter on 1st January 1942, just 25 days after the attack on Pearl Harbor.

Regarding the Japanese attack on Pearl Harbor, Churchill later wrote 'we had won, then!' America's entry into the war had not been guaranteed; but now the war's outcome became virtually inevitable. America had been supporting the nationalist Chinese Kuomintang against Japan, but slowly came to realise that no amount of American aid would create an independent China grateful to America.

Roosevelt had ordered the development of an industrial mobilisation plan (the Victory Programme) in July 1941. He faced internal opposition to war, not least from the 'America First' committee (Gerald Ford, a student at Yale, was a member). Pearl Harbor was, politically, a gift to Roosevelt. Hitler presented another gift by declaring war on America on 11th December 1941. The key strategic decision was whether to focus on Japan or Germany first. Operationally the biggest problem was that America's army was, at the time, simply not capable of fighting Germany; and probably not Japan either.

America's first strategic response was 'hemisphere defence'. US Marines took over the garrison of Iceland from the British Army. Shipping convoys were initiated. Airbases were built on Bermuda and then the Azores. Guns from battleships sunk at Pearl Harbor were mounted in coastal batteries in California.

After Pearl Harbor, Anglo-American strategy was directed chiefly through high-level conferences and the creation of the Combined Chiefs of Staff (CCS). There were three conferences in Washington, two in Quebec and one in Casablanca. The Casablanca conference took place after Operation Torch, the Allied landings in North Africa in November 1942. The decisions for Torch, the subsequent Sicily and Italian campaigns, and for a second front in northwest Europe in 1944 were all made at those conferences. Operations in the Mediterranean provided a strategic entry into Europe for America, gave its forces valuable experience, and bled German forces from other theatres.

The policy of demanding the unconditional surrender of Germany was also agreed at Casablanca. That was useful to Roosevelt in silencing internal critics. Internationally it helped convince Stalin that the Western allies were fully committed to the war.

The CCS was probably the most important Anglo-American organisation of the war. The two allies had differences over goals and approaches. The CCS allowed those differences to be aired, and agreement reached, fairly effectively. Churchill repeatedly sought further landings in the Balkans. Admiral Ernest King, US Chief of Naval Operations, continued the press for a 'Japan first', hence 'Pacific first' (and so 'Navy first') policy as late as the Casablanca conference. The composition of the CCS was remarkably stable throughout the war.

America quickly built up bomber forces in Britain and North Africa. A Combined Bomber Offensive was agreed at Casablanca. The first coordinated raids took place in July 1943. Significantly, Air Chief Marshal Sir Charles Portal (the British CAS) said at Casablanca that 'air bombardment alone was not sufficient'. Bombing was not intended to win the war. British bombing had previously been useful in convincing Americans that Britain was actually fighting the war: another instance of political signalling. America poured vast resources into bombing: the USAAF cost about $50 billion during the war. That was about 30% of all the money spent on the US Army.

Britain became aware of the German flying bomb ('V-bomb') threat during 1943. 10,923 V-bombs were fired at Britain from September 1944 onwards. Britain would need to clear the French and Belgian coasts: that became a strategic planning factor.

After the Normandy landings the British 21st Army Group grew to 15 divisions: three Canadian, one Polish and 11 British. The US Army continued to grow, reaching 13 armoured and 40 infantry divisions in north-west Europe by May 1945. There were a further two British, four American and one multinational airborn divisions.

The British have typically been well aware of the Burma campaigns but largely unaware of those in the Pacific. The fighting in Burma was fierce but smaller in scale. Eventually 12 Allied divisions fought there: British, Indian and West African. Up to 28 Allied divisions fought in the Pacific: six USMC, 15 American Army, six Australian and one New Zealand.

In 1939 Albert Einstein had written to Roosevelt on the subject of an atomic bomb. At the Quebec conference in August 1943 Britain agreed to send all of its atom bomb scientists to join the American Manhattan project. After the defeat of Germany in May 1944 the Allies focussed on Japan. Roosevelt had died on 12 April 1945. Harry Truman succeeded him as President. The casualty estimate for an invasion of Japan was up to one million Allied dead. Unsurprisingly, Truman decided to use atom bombs against Japan. Japan surrendered, after the second bomb, on 10th August.

It is not clear what Stalin was planning between overrunning eastern Poland in October 1939 and the German invasion of the Soviet Union in June 1941. The Red Army was mobilised and deployed forward, but broadly in defensive positions. Stalin received accurate warning of the German attack, but did not act. Stalin's strategic goals were then clear: to liberate the territory of the USSR; to defeat Germany; and, increasingly, to establish a sphere of influence in central and eastern Europe.

Defeat followed defeat for the Soviets in 1941. Limited successes that winter were followed by more defeats in early 1942. Later that year the German attacks at Stalingrad allowed the Red Army to do something that it was good at. Its units could defend doggedly when they had their backs against a wall (in this case the River Volga). That gave it time to plan and organise a major counteroffensive, Operation Uranus. The success of Uranus gave the Red Army the confidence that German armies could be defeated. Thereafter the balance slowly swung in favour of the Soviet Union and its western allies.

Pre-war economic planning allowed the Soviets to preserve and then develop their military industrial capacity. Its management was repressive and highly coercive, but actually quite inefficient. A massive backlog of cases in the labour courts developed, and factory managers developed a habit of non-enforcement against absenteeism. That is not the official nor the commonly-held view. It was in stark contrast to military discipline, which was draconian. The Red Army and NKVD executed over 16,000 soldiers in Stalingrad alone.

By mid 1942 the Red Army had largely learnt to withdraw its forces when faced with German envelopments. It also benefitted from having, typically, several million more men at the front than the Germans and their allies. From late 1943 the Red Army outnumbered its opponents by at least two to one. It was not, however, just a matter of force ratios. The Red Army was increasingly able to make massive troop concentrations in times and at places of its choosing; especially as the proportion of armoured forces grew. See Figure 6-2 (all strengths in millions of men):

Date	German and Axis Forces	Soviet Forces	Soviet Numerical Superiority
July 1941	3.96	2.74	-1.22
December 1941	3.36	4.97	1.61
July 1942	3.76	5.65	1.89
February 1943	3.00	6.10	3.10
July 1943	3.67	6.9	3.23
March 1944	2.77	6.39	3.62
July 1944	3.18	6.80	3.62
January 1945	2.53	6.75	4.22
May 1945	1.51	5.70	4.19

Figure 6-2 Soviet and Axis Manpower Strengths on the Eastern Front.

The Soviet Union and the western Allies made strange bedfellows. It was not a marriage of convenience but of necessity. It was characterised by mutual suspicion under a public veneer of geniality.

Germany did not prevent American forces reaching Europe. Once the western Allies had successfully gained a lodgement in France (Operation Overlord, the Normandy landings and campaign in July and August 1944), the Germans would lose. Allied strategy was extended to include the Soviet Union through another series of conferences. At Moscow, in August 1942, Stalin was briefed on western plans. The intention and proposed date for Overlord was agreed at Teheran in November and December 1943. Plans for post-war Europe were agreed at Yalta in February 1945. Stalin agreed to enter the war against Japan in due course. The division of Germany was agreed at Potsdam in July and August 1945, as was the call for the unconditional surrender of Japan.

Contrary to the spirit of Yalta, the Soviets began to impose their will on the newly-liberated countries of central and eastern Europe. In May 1945 Eisenhower refused to withdraw Western forces to the line agreed at Yalta. Tension escalated rapidly. After some sabre-rattling (not least by Patton) and carefully-leaked talk about atom bombs, Stalin gave way. The Red Army withdrew to the pre-war boundaries of the Soviet Union.

Clearly that did not happen. Roosevelt had been well aware of Soviet intentions, but was dead. Churchill had never met Truman, who had not been fully party to Roosevelt's views. Truman was strongly influenced by Joseph Davies, a pro-Soviet pre-war US ambassador to Moscow. Truman was persuaded to be more accommodating towards the USSR and attempted to convince Churchill. Churchill accepted the reality of the situation. The atmosphere at the Potsdam conference was decidedly that of 'possession is nine parts of the law'. An iron curtain descended across Europe.

Other nations had had to choose their own courses. Historically, Finns have slain Russians without number, but not found peace. Russia invaded Finland in November 1939. Once again, Finns slew huge numbers of Russians. Finland reputedly made Russia pay for every snowflake its soldiers trod on. Russia accepted a negotiated peace in which Finland ceded some territory. After Germany attacked Russia, Finland chose the lesser of two evils and joined forces with Germany. However, Finland was not too adventurous. It made no real attempt to cut the railway line from Murmansk, which would have cut off the material from Britain's Atlantic convoys. In September 1944 Finland accepted a ceasefire with the Soviet Union. German troops in Finland began to withdraw northwards, around Sweden and into Norway. Finnish troops pursued them doggedly enough to make the Germans keep moving, whilst avoiding taking too many casualties.

The irregular Polish Home Army had risen up as the Red Army approached Warsaw on 1 August 1944. The Soviets may have acted in bad faith by not pushing forward to link up with the Poles. However, four German panzer divisions completed the encirclement and destruction of the Soviet 3rd Tank Corps just east of Warsaw on 3 August. Two other Russian tank corps were severely damaged. That caused the Red Army significant problems, but does not entirely explain the failure of the Red Army to link up with the Poles. The Warsaw uprising was brutally suppressed by SS troops by 5 October. The situation in Poland remained confused into the spring of 1945. 15

Home Army officers were abducted and murdered by the Red Army as they tried to negotiate. Moscow denied responsibility.

Romania had been run by a fascist dictator, General Ion Antonescu, since September 1940. It fought on the side of the Axis until the Red Army broke through near Iaşi in Moldavia in August 1944. The young king, Mihai (Michael), staged a counter-revolution against Antonescu. Romanian troops fought against the Wehrmacht and liberated both Bucurest and the Ploieşti oilfields. Within a few days the Soviets occupied Bucurest and forced Mihai to install a pro-Soviet government. (Mihai was forced to abdicate and go into exile in 1947. He returned to Romania after the end of the Cold War and died in December 2017.)

The British Dominions declared war on Germany, along with Britain, in September 1939. They were not formally represented on the CCS nor the British Chiefs of Staff Committee. Their forces acted under British or (in the Pacific) American command. However, national interests were well represented. For example, Britain indicated to Australia in December 1941 that it intended to abandon Singapore. Britain had long realised that it could not fight Germany and Japan at the same time; let alone Italy as well. Australia's response was couched in somewhat inflammatory language. Britain relented. Nevertheless, Singapore fell. The newly-arrived 8th Australian Division surrendered with the rest of the garrison.

After America's entry into the war, Churchill wrote that 'all the rest was merely the proper application of overwhelming force.' It is clearly not possible to describe the whole of the strategic course of the war here.

Like the Great War, the Second World War was short. The Napoleonic Wars had lasted for 23 years. After the fall of France in 1940, Britain continued to fight. Hitler attacked Russia. Japan attacked America. Those countries, and their allies, then fought continually to the finish. That took more than three years of hard fighting. Germany and Japan were hard to beat.

One consequence of unconditional surrender was the enforced political reorganisation of Germany and Japan. One could, and people did, call that 're-education'. The moral and legal bases for that are unclear. Those countries have since declined to play a leading part in world affairs. That is unlikely to last forever. Another consequence of the war was that several ethnic minorities in central and eastern Europe were eliminated. For the Germans in central and eastern European countries, it was through enforced migration. For many Jews, and others, it was genocide.

The cost of winning was considerable. For the USA much of the cost was financial, but it was a good investment in the long term. For the USSR the cost was massive in human, social and economic terms. Its total loss of life was about 39 million people, including births foregone. The cost to Britain was much nearer to America's than the Soviet Union's. Relatively more British servicemen were lost, and far more civilians, but there was nothing like the human loss of the USSR.

German strategic planning was inadequate. Like Japan, it had no coherent plan to beat the nations it engaged. It increasingly lived off the resources and the labour of the territories it overran. That worked; until those territories were taken back.

Germany was beaten when its territory was overrun. That happened because it could not defeat the Red Army *and* the armies of the western Allies together. In 1944 it might have beaten the Red Army if it had not had to commit 60-70 divisions, including ten panzer divisions, in the west. It had to face the western Allies because America entered the war. America might, or might not, have done so if not for Pearl Harbor. The Japanese decision to attack America was foolish and decisive. All the rest was merely 'the proper application of overwhelming force'. It was sometimes messy and sometimes bad tempered. Thus in war.

The resources which Britain committed to the long-range bombing of Germany was a major strategic mistake. In 1940 Britain was chronically short of antiaircraft guns to protect its cities. It was short of tanks. It did not have enough fighters to protect Malta, nor Singapore the following year. As bomber production ramped up it remained short of maritime patrol aircraft for anti-submarine defence and maritime strike aircraft to attack shipping. The consequences of those shortages, and other uses to which those resources could have been put, will be considered in later chapters.

Britain and America generally mobilised their home fronts better than Germany and Japan. That probably resulted from better application of the lessons of the Great War. Almost all protagonist nations suffered conscription, rationing and increased taxation. America avoided having to direct its labour; Britain did not. People in occupied countries typically had to choose between collaboration, resistance, and trying to live one's life quietly and survive. America, Britain, its dominions and colonies are lucky that they never had to make that choice.

Mobilisation of the home front extended to the use made of science. Despite Germany's formidable scientific assets, the Western allies won that campaign. It was largely won by better cooperation between governments, research laboratories and industry.

Germany was beaten when its territory was overrun. It was not defeated by bombing. The use of air forces was without doubt a significant factor in *how* the Allies won. That will be discussed in Chapter Seven. The use of atomic weapons did convince Japan to surrender. Bombing was decisive in that specific issue.

The greatest failing of any side was moral. Nations and individuals were drawn into massively unethical actions, and the Allies were not blameless. Racial violence and genocide were not 'additional to' the conduct of the war. They were integral to the way in which the German and Japanese leadership waged war. Barbarism and bestiality were never far below the surface, and often above it. There could be no more obvious example of the need for a more comprehensive framework of international humanitarian law.

Notwithstanding his faults, of which there were several, Churchill was a great man. Despite some notable disagreements, he generally listened to his service chiefs. After the appointment of Alanbrooke as CIGS, Churchill rarely if ever acted contrary to their advice. Churchill's oratory will remain some of the finest in the English language. He was not perfect: no-one is. He was greatly idolised during and after the War. Some of that was deserved, some of it not. If that is true of Churchill, then also of Roosevelt.

Both were generally very well served by their service chiefs, once the right ones had been found. Marshall, Alanbrooke and Cunningham (the British First Sea Lord in the later stages of the war) were particularly effective; others less so.

In looking at the literature of the Second World War it is clear that 'victory' is a much over-used and under-defined term. 'Total War' is another such term. Its main value seems to be to give historians and political scientists something to debate. All major wars involve the use of large-scale violence and civil mobilisation to some extent. Neither are ever actually 'total'.

The War raises big issues. What happens when a major element of strategy, in this case bombing, gets stuck? How does it happen? What should the relationship between military effort and the home front be? The war demonstrated that in most cases the home front was not the weak link. Moral escalation (of violence) or decline (of ethical standing): how are humans, and human institutions, drawn into moral hazard? How can it be avoided?

The most important observation, however, is simple. The political issues involved in the Great War were not obvious nor clear, neither at the time nor subsequently. That is not true of the Second World War. For the Allies, it was necessary. Indeed, it was essential.

7

'If You Do Not Destroy Them …'

The basis of much of the British operational history of the Second World War comes to British and Commonwealth readers from Montgomery's memoirs. Americans are more likely to have read General Omar Bradley's or George Patton's. The differences are, not surprisingly, considerable. On balance it seems that American writers are more critical of British commanders than *vice versa*. Montgomery, in particular, seems to come across to American writers as arrogant and a 'stuffed shirt'. He may well have appeared that way to American contemporaries. American commanders, however, also had their faults.

Conceptually, the operational level did not really exist during the Second World War. The Red Army had an advanced understanding of major operations. The Luftwaffe had a sound grasp of the 'air operation' and the Wehrmacht was beginning to differentiate between tactics and operations. The British Field Service Regulations of 1935 outlined the sequence of a campaign. Beyond that, commanders and staffs often worked quite adequately; but without an explicit schema for what they did. This chapter looks at the Second World War from the operational level. It does not consider every campaign and every theatre. Instead, it considers the subject by domain, looking at air campaigns first.

The events of the Battle of Britain are well known. What the Luftwaffe intended to do is less well known. Its orders were to achieve air superiority, to support army landings and parachute drops, and to attack ports, docks and warehouses. Initially the Luftwaffe conducted a counter-force operation to gain air superiority. It under-estimated the RAF, and assumed it was defeated before it was. Hence the switch to attacking ports and docks in September 1940. The nearest were in London. As the invasion was cancelled, and bomber losses mounted, the Luftwaffe increasingly focussed on port, dock and warehouse targets; further afield, and largely by night. Its targets also included aircraft factories, hence cities such as Manchester, Birmingham, Coventry and Bristol.

The Luftwaffe wasn't really aware of fighting a 'Battle of Britain'. After September 1940 it thought it was conducting an air operation as a form of economic blockade, in conjunction with the Kriegsmarine. There was always a major discrepancy between what the Luftwaffe set out to do and the way it was reported in the western media. That had started with the bombing of Guernica in 1937. The Luftwaffe had been ordered to attack communications and troop concentrations. It was *reported* as conducting 'terror raids'. The Luftwaffe's bombing was not particularly accurate, and it may not have been too concerned about civilian casualties. Similarly in 1939 against Warsaw, and in 1940 against Rotterdam.

The Luftwaffe conducted one further air operation, '*Steinbock*' (the 'Little Blitz' to the British), against British cities from January to May 1944. There was some loss of industrial production. Faced with efficient RAF night fighter forces, the Germans lost 60 to 70% of their bombers. The main effect was that those bombers were not available against Operation Overlord a few months later.

The RAF started bombing Germany on 10 May 1940. Its first raids were on targets near the Rhine. On 15 May Churchill chaired a meeting of the War Cabinet which decided to bomb the Ruhr. The decision was largely made on operational grounds; that is, to support the operations in France and Belgium. The scope of the bombing was widened into a campaign through a combination of the RAF wishing to expand its mandate and politicians wishing to be seen to be doing something.

Initial efforts and results were disappointing, but the effort increased steadily through 1941 and 1942. Churchill personally ordered the bombing of Berlin in late August 1940 in retaliation for the bombing of London. Bombing was highly inaccurate. In 1941 only 5% of British bombs fell within five miles of the target. The great majority fell in open countryside. Scientists estimated that it was taking five tons of bombs to kill each German civilian. Cities such as Rostock and Lübeck were attacked simply because they could be (they could be found easily at night because they were close to the coast). Planners resorted to euphemisms such as 'dehousing' to disguise the deliberate targeting of civilian industrial workers. The RAF invented, and perfected, the tactics of creating firestorms.

The USAAF started bombing Germany in earnest in 1943. The Combined Bomber Offensive helped convince Stalin that the western Allies were actually fighting in 1943. That was not easy, since they also told him that there would be no second front that year. The USAAF's policy of unescorted precision daylight raids did not work. Bombing was inaccurate and losses too high. The USAAF increasingly resorted to 'non-visual' bombing (area bombing under a different name). It developed long-range single-engined escort fighters, and losses dropped. In April 1944 both bomber forces were ordered to concentrate on support to Overlord (the 'Transportation Plan'). Compliance was grudging and partial. They were also ordered to attack oil targets. American attacks on Ploiești had little effect. Air attacks on German synthetic oil factories did suppress production, and effectively stopped it: at the end of the war.

The effort was immense. 1,927,000 tons of bombs were dropped on Germany. The British built 7,317 Lancaster bombers. Almost all went to Bomber Command. The number of Lancasters at front line doubled between March 1944 and April 1945. The main German synthetic oil plant, the Leuna works near Leipzig absorbed 6,552 sorties in 22 raids. Just 301 oil workers were killed, of whom 126 on the first raid. The Germans closed the plant on 4 April 1945.

The British Army lost 55,000 officers in the Great War. By comparison, Bomber Command lost 56,000 aircrew in the Second World War. In the Battle of Berlin, from November 1943 to March 1944, it lost 5.1% casualties per raid. At that rate, only 20% of aircrew would survive a 30-mission tour of duty. In 1944 the US Air Forces in Europe were losing 220 men per day, most of them killed. The USAAF lost 4,754 B17s and 2,112 B24s over Europe. 593,000 German civilians were killed by bombing; effectively one for every 3 ¼ tons of bombs dropped. The bomber offensive cost Britain £2.78 billion at 1945 prices.

Air Chief Marshal Sir Arthur Harris took over command of RAF Bomber Command in February 1942. To make a sensible comparison of effort and effect, we will take German military industrial production in January 1942 as 100%, and similarly for Allied bombing effort (in terms of tons of bombs dropped). Figure 7-1 shows German production from 1943 to 1945 to that scale.

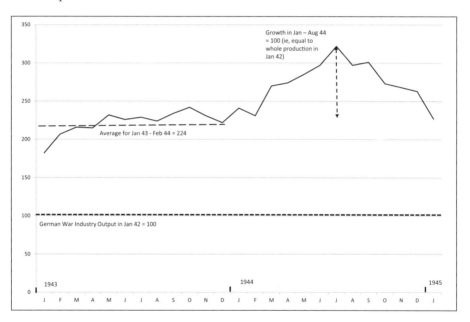

Figure 7-1 German Military Industrial Production, 1943-5.

By February of 1943 Harris had been bombing Germany for a year, but war production had *doubled*. In fact average production for 1943 was about 224%. However, in 1944 production rose by another 100%. That rise alone equals the whole of German production in January 1942. After September 1944 production fell, but only back to 220% or so. Bombing did not stop German war production. It was contained at well above the 1942 level. Bombing did not destroy factories: continuous re-attack was required to curtail production. Figure 7-2 shows Allied bombing effort against war production and, specifically, tank production. Figures are not shown after January 1945, because Allied land forces were overrunning German factories (hence production was being lost to causes other than bombing).

Year	Month	Bombs Dropped[1] (Jan 42 = 100)	Military Production[2] (Jan 42 = 100)	Tank Production[2] (Jan 42 = 100)
1943	Jan	215	182	154
	Feb	503	207	169
	Mar	527	216	210
	Apr	538	215	289
	May	648	232	465
	Jun	768	226	340
	Jul	886	229	367
	Aug	1,054	224	328
	Sep	970	234	495
	Oct	839	242	454
	Nov	1,119	231	364
	Dec	1,318	222	415
1944	Jan	1,746	241	438
	Feb	1,539	231	480
	Mar	2,520	270	498
	Apr	2,455	274	527
	May	3,452	285	567
	Jun	5,148	297	580
	Jul	4,789	322	589
	Aug	5,112	297	558
	Sep	4,810	301	527
	Oct	5,098	273	516
	Nov	4,658	268	571
	Dec	4,598	263	598
1945	Jan	3,272	227	557

Figure 7-2 Germany: Bombing Effort and Effect, 1943-5.

1   Ellis, John, The World War Two Databook, (London: Aurum, 1993), Table 22.
2   Tooze, Adam, The Wages of Destruction. The Making and Breaking of the Nazi War Economy, (London: Allen Lane, 2006), Table A6.

The Germans were selective: tank production rose to 598%, as late as December 1944. Production could not have grown any further: Germany was at the limit of its manpower and raw materials. And note that bombing effort (in terms of bombs dropped) had peaked at 5,112%. The effort applied was grossly disproportional to the results achieved. The allied air forces dropped over 50 times more bombs on Germany in October 1944 than it had in January 1942; but war production was still 2.7 times higher, and tank production five times.

Bomber Command bombed 23 smallish towns for the first time from late September 1944 onwards. They were obviously so unimportant that they had not been attacked in over four years of bombing. Four of them weren't even bombed until March or April 1945. Only two of the 23 were bombed more than twice. The Combined Bomber Offensive had run out of targets. The air forces were bombing small towns in Germany because they could.

Nor did bombing stop the oil supply. In 1943, between domestic, synthetic and imported oil, Germany had a considerable surplus of fuel. In 1944 Germany received 467,000 metric tons less oil, overall, than it had used in 1943. It produced 1,786,000 tons less synthetic oil: bombing had had some effect. But in 1944 Germany also lost 1,805,000 tons from Romania, almost entirely because the oilfields were lost. Germany would thereafter receive *no* oil from Romania. Germany could have withstood the loss of synthetic oil. Going into 1945, it could not withstand the loss of Romanian oil *as well*. As with industrial production, oil losses become significant well after the point at which Germany had effectively lost the war. The eventual failure of the German economy was largely due to the loss of raw materials: chiefly iron ore from Sweden and the Donbass and oil from Romania. Industry was still functioning, albeit damaged and at reduced capacity, when the factories were overrun. In late 1944 the key problem was possibly not production but distribution, due to air interdiction of the fuel supply.

Critically, in the summer of 1944 the USAAF destroyed the Luftwaffe day fighter force. German fighters had to attack American bomber formations, but were then shot down in large numbers by American fighters. That was partly related to attacks on Germany. It was also, in large part, a result of Transportation Plan attacks. The USAAF then committed large numbers lot of medium bomber and fighter-bomber sorties to keeping the Luftwaffe neutralised.

That had a useful and unpredicted benefit. By March there were only 500 German fighters on the Eastern Front, as against 13,000 Soviet aircraft. As we shall see, the Russians still lost thousands of aircraft. The consequences of having, say, a thousand Luftwaffe fighters is hard to imagine.

The diversion of German resources to air defence was unimportant. There were about 25-30,000 antiaircraft guns protecting Germany in 1944. However only about 100-105,000 men in the antiaircraft units were adults of military age. That was enough for just five or six more army divisions. Germany built 70,700 guns of all types in 1944 (24,600 more than the previous year). Antiaircraft production was a small proportion, and the field army was not short of guns.

The diversion of Allied resources to bomb Germany is rarely considered. More British aircraft might have been used to support the Army in France in 1940. More aircraft might have been used to defend Malta or Singapore. The RAF did not sink a single submarine until November 1941. A few more long-range aircraft over the Atlantic would have made a major impact.

Less aircraft production could have meant more, and better, tanks; or more antiaircraft guns (Britain was critically short until 1943 or so). A smaller RAF might easily have meant five more armoured divisions, and appropriate logistic support, in north west Europe. That would have made a major difference. (Britain only deployed three armoured divisions to north-west Europe in 1944-5.)

At the beginning of the war long-range bombing was, to the RAF, a doctrinal and an existential necessity. If it didn't bomb, it wasn't needed as an independent force. Therefore it needed to bomb. The RAF then won the early battles for strategic resources. The priority which it gained was never rescinded. The strategic task did not merit doubling the Lancaster force from March 1944. For the USAAF, the argument was slightly different. If it could win the war by bombing, it could become an independent force. In practice, it was not technically capable of meeting the doctrine it had written for itself. But it got plentiful resources and proceeded anyway. Thus also the RAF.

Both air forces were drawn into a web of deceit, euphemism, concealment and downright lies. The details were different in each case. Both forces deliberately attacked civilians under euphemisms such as 'industrial production', 'dehousing', etc. Raids were designed to kill fire, rescue and medical workers as an integral part of the plan. The USAAF displayed little, if any, practical concern for the lives of German civilians; but neither did the RAF.

It was commonly felt to be morally acceptable to bomb German cities because 'Hitler bombed our chippy' [fish and chip shop], or similar. That is no excuse. The commission of one offence does not excuse another, either morally nor legally. In practice senior commanders were slowly drawn into moral hazard. Many of their aircrews honestly believed that what they were doing was right: Hitler *had* bombed their chippy. That does not mean that what they were told to do was right.

Churchill's attitude was politically opportunistic. He initially expressed enthusiasm. But as early as September 1941 he wrote to Portal that '[i]t is very disputable whether bombing by itself will be decisive in the present war. On the contrary, all that we have learnt since the war began shows that its effects, both physical and moral, are greatly exaggerated.'[1] Despite having effectively ordered the bombing of Germany in person in 1940 and having seen Bomber Command grow steadily, Churchill made virtually no mention of Allied bombing in his memoirs.

The USAAF air campaign against Japan started badly. The B29 bomber had been procured specifically to bomb Japan, in daylight, from high level. The B29 programme

---

1   Hastings, Max, *Bomber Command*, (London: Pan Books,1999) p.120.

cost \$3 billion; 50% more than the Manhattan project. In early 1945 Arnold sent Major General Curtis LeMay to take charge of the Japan bombing campaign. On the night of 9 March 1945, B29s dropped 1665 tons of incendiaries on Tokyo (at night; from low level). The result was a firestorm. About 100,000 civilians died.

Arnold had previously said that the 'use of incendiaries against cities is contrary to our national policy of attacking only military objectives.'[2] Later he told the US Secretary of Defence that 'they were trying to keep civilian casualties to a minimum.'[3] Operational research had indicated that only about five or six firebomb raids on Japanese cities would be effective. There were 67. In practice, firestorm attacks made very for good newspaper photographs. Arnold repeatedly talked about an independent air force being a strategic objective: for the USAAF. The (American) domestic benefits of firebombing were too spectacular to halt.

After Dresden, in February 1945, the USAAF was well aware of the casualties caused by firebombing. Over 300,000 Japanese died in conventional (non-atomic) bombing raids. Most were burnt to death. LeMay later said '[t]o worry about the *morality* of what we were doing – Nuts.'[4]

In June 1944 the Luftwaffe opened another bombardment campaign against Britain. 9,521 V1 flying bombs and 1,402 V2 ballistic missiles were launched. Up to 100 V1s were launched every day in the summer of 1944. About half of them were shot down. Only a quarter reached London. V2s were, in practice, unstoppable once launched. Over 500 hit London. 8,938 Britons were killed by V-bombs. As German land forces were pushed away from the Channel coast, the Luftwaffe switched targets. 2,448 V1s and 1,664 V2s were fired at Antwerp. 211 V1s and 590 V2s hit the city. The biggest loss of life in Europe to a single weapon occurred when a V2 hit a cinema in Antwerp, killing 576 people.

V1s were relatively cheap; V2s horrendously expensive. The V-weapon programme cost Germany about 50% more than the Manhattan project. The strategic effect was almost nil. The last V2, launched in the Netherlands, fell on London on 27 March 1945. The British had obviously decided not to clear the Dutch coast as a strategic priority. That is obvious in retrospect. It was obviously not made public. Historians have not remarked on it.

The scale of naval operations is best gained by looking at fleet sizes at the outbreak of war, and then at British and American wartime construction and losses. Figure 7-3 shows fleet size by class for Britain, France and Germany in September 1939. For Japan and the USA the figures are for December 1941. Numbers shown are 'in commission

2   Arnold, quoted in Chennault, C L, *Way of a Fighter: The Memoirs of Claire Lee Chennault*, New York, 1949, p.97.
3   Ralph, William W, 'Improvised Destruction: Arnold, LeMay, and the Firebombing of Japan', *War in History* 13:4 (October 2006), p.519.
4   LeMay, C with Kantor, M, *Mission with LeMay*, (New York, 1949), p.383. Italics in original.

+ in building'; hence (for example) 15 British (RN) battleships in commission and five under construction.

Class	RN	France	Germany	Italy	USN	IJN
Battleships and Battlecruisers	15+5	7+4	5+11(a)	6+?	17+15	10+3
Aircraft Carriers	7+6	1+2	0+2 (b)	0+2 (b)	7+11	12+7
Cruisers	66+23	19+3	8+9 (c)	19+?	41+42	38+6
Destroyers	184+52	78+27	22+12	59+?	171+188	126+43
Frigates and Corvettes (d)	45+56					
Submarines	60+9	81+38	57+?	116+?	114+79	68+?

Figure 7-3 Fleet Size at the Outbreak of War.

Notes:
(a) Only 2 (*Bismarck* and *Tirpitz*) completed. (b) None completed. (c) Only 1 completed. (d) ie, purpose-built maritime convoy escorts.

Put simply, Britain narrowly replaced its losses for battleships, cruisers and destroyers. Otherwise, Britain and America built far more ships than they lost during the war. See Figure 7-4:

Type	Britain		America	
	Built	Lost	Built	Lost
Battleship	5	5	12	2
Aircraft Carrier	52	8	98	11
Cruiser	39	30	87	10
Destroyer	120	110	368	71
Convoy Escort	473	58	578 (a)	10
Submarine	152	77	87	53
Cargo ship	Built about 4,300. Lost 5156			

Figure 7-4 British and American Construction and Losses.

Note: (a) Of which, 108 for Britain.

The Atlantic was strategically important for two reasons. It allowed food and raw materials to reach Britain, and it allowed the movement of Canadian and American forces to North Africa and Europe.

Germany had 57 submarines in 1939. It built 871 new boats and lost 785. Graphs show the progress of the German submarine campaign quite clearly. Figure 7-5 shows Allied shipping losses by quarter.

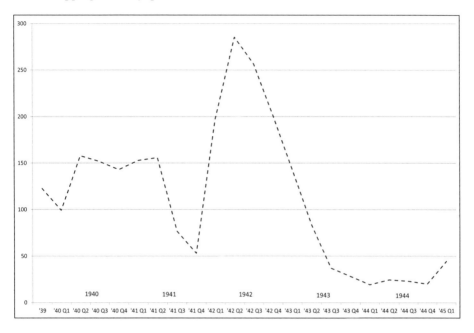

Figure 7-5 Allied Merchant Shipping Losses by Quarter.

Losses fell in late 1941, mostly due to convoying and simply having enough escorts. Losses rose dramatically in 1942 when U-boats attacked unprotected American shipping. They fell over the next year as the US Navy introduced convoying. By October 1943 losses were relatively small. Figure 7-6 shows U-boat losses over the same period.

Losses of U-boats rose significantly from mid-1942 to mid-1943, but from a very low level. However, Figure 7-7 shows U-boats launched, sunk and available against merchant ships sunk.

After 1942 there were plenty of U-boats: but they simply couldn't sink merchantmen. Better sensors, such as airborne radar, contributed. So did better weapons, such as forward-firing salvo mortars on ships. Aircraft, either shore-based or from escort carriers, were highly important. More than half of all U-boats were sunk by aircraft. However deterrence, and better intelligence, saved ships; not sinking U-boats. Perhaps the most significant loss to the Allies was that of ship's masters (captains): one master

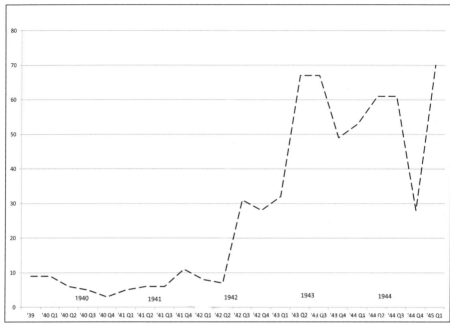

Figure 7-6 U-Boat Losses, by Quarter.

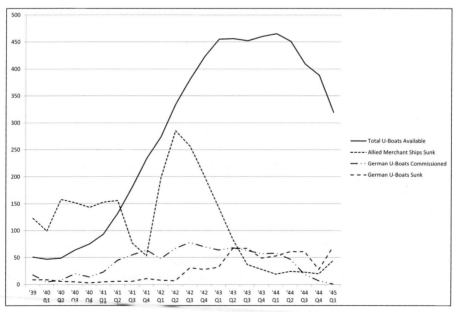

Figure 7-7 U-Boats Launched, Sunk and Available, by Quarter.

was lost for every three or four British merchantmen.[5] That would have been unsustainable in the longer run.

At the beginning of the war Germany had four battleships, three 'pocket battleships' and three heavy cruisers. No more were launched. They were lethal to merchant ships. They disrupted shipping over a wide area. In Operation Berlin, from January to March 1941, the battleships *Scharnhorst* and *Gneisenau* sank 22 merchantmen. However, after the failure of the *Hipper* and *Lützow* to damage Convoy JW 51b in December 1942, all German warships were returned to port. They rarely operated in the Atlantic again. Construction of new ships was halted. The Allies did not know that. Considerable allied forces, including battleships and aircraft carriers, were committed against the threat they posed.

Three of the ten German warships were sunk in fleet actions. One was sunk by a Norwegian coastal battery. Four were sunk in harbour by the RAF. Two survived. Unfortunately the RAF only sank the Tirpitz in November 1944, and the other three in the last month of the war. British submarines had damaged seven of the eight still at sea after May 1941, forcing them to undergo lengthy repairs.

Air support was highly effective. Luftwaffe Condor long-range aircraft sank 52 merchantmen for the loss of four aircraft between August 1940 and February 1941. Overall, however, the Luftwaffe's support to the Kriegsmarine was as meagre as the RAF's to the Royal Navy. For most of the War the RAF committed less than 50 aircraft capable of patrolling the whole of the north Atlantic (compared with, say, 1,000 bombers over Cologne in May 1942). The RAF did not commit as many aircraft to the submarine threat in the Second World War as it had in the Great War. In 1918 788 aircraft were assigned to ASW duties. The highest figure for the Second World War was 785.

Harris said that it was better to destroy U-boats in port than at sea. However, the RAF and USAAF did not, in practice, stop the construction of giant U-boat shelters in Norway and France, despite thousands of sorties. From June 1944 five-ton 'Tallboy' and ten-ton 'Grand Slam' bombs were used against the shelters and the remaining warships. Such weapons could have been developed two or three years earlier; it was simply a matter of priority.

In late 1943 Harris said that the Tirpitz was beyond effective range. So the Altafjord, in Norway, was out of range of Lancaster bombers in 1943; but in range of the same Lancasters, carrying ten-ton bombs, in 1944? Did Harris lie?

For Britain, the Mediterranean was a much shorter sea route to Egypt than sailing round the Cape. For the Axis it was the sea route to north Africa. For the Allies it was the invasion route to Sicily, Italy and southern France. Unsurprisingly it was the scene of considerable fighting. British naval and air forces struggled to achieve superiority. However, British submarines from Malta sank 185 ships between January 1941 and December 1942. By sinking two troopships they killed

5   Merchant Navy Memorial, Tower Hill, London.

more enemy soldiers (about 5,000) than died at El Alamein. The siege of Malta was lifted in late 1942. In the first week of October Malta-based aircraft shot down 114 aircraft for the loss of 27.

Malta-based air and naval forces then sank 230 ships in 164 days. During the war Italy had, or obtained, 983 merchant ships. 565 were sunk or captured. By comparison the 35 British convoys to Malta lost a total of 31 merchant ships. The Royal Navy and RAF clearly conducted a protracted, effective and largely unannounced anti-shipping campaign. Why is it nor more widely known? Is it because it does not appear in any widely-published source, and so historians have not noticed it?

The Royal Navy and RAF had not been able to prevent Italy maintaining a force of about 10 divisions in North Africa for two years. They had not managed to prevent the Germans sending four more under Rommel, sustaining them, and then sending four more to Tunisia. The last division arrived in March 1943. However, the Allies then prevented almost any of these forces being evacuated. The great majority were trapped, and surrendered, in Tunisia. The ability to use harbours and airbases along the north African coast, after El Alamein and Torch, appear to have had a significant impact.

Most of the US Navy's warships were employed in the Pacific. Japan built 77 new submarines, of which only four survived. Japan also built 17 new aircraft carriers (all but three were sunk); four cruisers (three sunk) and 62 destroyers (47 sunk). The outcome was, eventually, massively one-sided.

Japan lost nearly 10 million tons of merchant shipping, of which over five million to US submarines and 2.33 million to carrier aircraft. Many of the major naval engagements, such as the Coral Sea, Midway, Santa Cruz islands, the Philippine Sea and Leyte Gulf were carrier battles. They involved up to 1,400 US and 970 Japanese aircraft. Conversely in December 1941 the British battleships HMSs *Prince of Wales* and *Repulse* had been lost off Singapore due to inadequate RAF air cover. So were the aircraft carrier HMS *Hermes*, cruisers *Cornwall* and *Dorsetshire* and destroyer *Vampire*, all sunk in the Indian Ocean in early 1942.

The Second World War was unusual in being characterised by large numbers of amphibious operations; and in that most of them were successful. The Norway campaign, however, was a clear Allied failure. The problems stemmed from the planning. There was no-one in command. The plan was formed in a British committee of three one-star officers (a commodore, a brigadier and an air commodore) working for the Joint Chiefs of Staff. There were separate air, sea and land commanders, and different commanders at different landing areas.

The German operation was planned and commanded by Lieutenant General Nicolaus von Falkenhorst. He was a corps commander. His staff had served with him in Poland. Naval and air force experts were attached as required, and the basic plan had Hitler's authority. Not surprisingly, the German plan was more coherent and worked much better.

Operation 'Torch', in November 1942, was rare in that it was partly a trans-oceanic operation. The subsequent Sicilian campaign was characterised by both parachute landings and four further amphibious landings along the island's coasts. To invade Italy, landings were conducted by the British Eighth Army at Messina and then Taranto, and the US Fifth Army at Salerno. To break the deadlock at Cassino, the US VI Corps (initially of four Allied divisions) landed at Anzio. In August 1944 the US Seventh Army landed in southern France. There were problems, not least due to inexperienced American corps commanders. Overall, however, the Mediterranean theatre was good example of a coordinated series of major opposed amphibious landings. Most of them were conducted in range of land-based aircraft, but they also relied on significant carrier air support, antisubmarine operations, and amphibious shipping.

Operation 'Overlord' was the largest amphibious operation in history. Apart from the D-Day landings, it included the commitment of heavy bomber forces for five months, an invasion fleet of more than 8,000 ships, a ten-week land campaign, and over-the-beach logistics which continued until February 1945.

'Overlord' benefitted enormously, and at many levels, from the disastrous Dieppe raid of August 1942. The first American soldier to die in Europe lost his life there. The Allies learnt not to attempt direct assaults on ports from the sea. Requirements for fire support to the landings, to neutralise shore batteries, for tanks in the assault, and methods of getting vehicles across the beach were all learnt or reinforced. It resulted in the creation of a dedicated armoured engineer force, the British 79th Armoured Engineer Division (79 AED).

The purpose of Overlord was to gain a lodgement on the continent of Europe. The planned lodgement area included Normandy and Brittany, the latter for its Atlantic ports. Eisenhower and Montgomery had only a rudimentary plan for the land campaign. The (bomber) Transportation Plan did a good job of isolating the landing area, and Operation Fortitude (the deception plan) worked well at the strategic level. OKW appears to have believed in a second landing in the Pas de Calais until about 4 August.

Fighting was bitter. Caen and St Lô were captured by 19 July. At that point almost all of the German armoured divisions were facing the British in the east. On 25 July the Americans started to break out in the west with Operation Cobra. Within days, four US armoured divisions were advancing in parallel southwards: an almost unequalled achievement. After six more days the US Army broke out of Normandy through Avranches. Patton took charge of Third US Army.

Detailed analysis of what follows demonstrates the limits of Allied operational thinking. On 9 August Montgomery gave orders for an encirclement on the line of the River Orne, which would become the Falaise pocket. On the 11th he gave further and ambiguous instructions. Bradley, by this stage commanding Twelfth US Amy Group, does not seem to have understood Montgomery's intentions. There was a suggestion of an encirclement on the River Seine. By the 14th Patton, now Bradley's subordinate, ordered three of his corps to head east for the Seine, leaving less than one corps in the Falaise area. Polish and Canadian forces formed the northern arm of the encirclement on 19 August; Patton had already reached the Seine. There were not enough Allied forces to stop Germans escaping the Falaise pocket. The climax of the battle was from 19 to 21 August. About 50,000

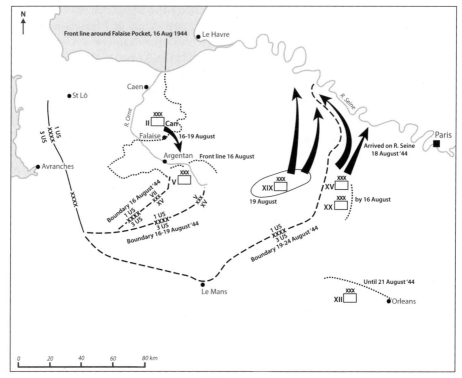

Figure 7-8 Normandy, August 1944.

Germans were trapped in the pocket. Ten to twenty thousand escaped. Between 20 and 23 August tens of thousands of Germans, and 23,000 vehicles, were evacuated across the Seine. Allied encirclements succeeded neither on the Orne nor on the Seine.

Normandy was a major strategic success. It unquestionably gained a lodgement on the continent of Europe. It effectively destroyed two German armies and forced a withdrawal across most of France and Belgium. Yet the Falaise operation was flawed. It allowed the escape of tens of thousands of German soldiers and, importantly, the cadres of several divisions. The Allies would have to fight those same divisions again at Arnhem and in the Battle of the Bulge.

Japanese amphibious operations in late 1941 and early 1942 were highly successful against poor or weak opposition. In Malaya, for example, they concentrated two aircraft for every one British. The Japanese were tough, experienced, and continued to mount amphibious operations long after the tide had turned against them. In Malaya they took over what they described as rather plush 'Churchill aerodromes', but they did not generally make forward airfield construction a priority. That was a key failing. The same cannot be said of America. US Naval Construction Battalions, employed building airfields, found themselves fighting in the front line on a number Pacific islands.

The USMC's landings at Tarawa in November 1943 were, in part, the birth of a legend. They were also, in part, hell in a very small place. Losses were grievous and any number of important tactical lessons were learnt. At the operational level it was the beginning of a campaign that was not just island-hopping but also island-bypassing. Operation Cartwheel, against Japanese forces in the Bismarck Archipelago, included ten separate landings. The last major American operation, against Okinawa, was the conclusion of a hard-fought series of operations which had bypassed and isolated tens of thousands of Japanese on islands from which they could not escape.

Turning to land (as opposed to amphibious) campaigns, the fall of France in 1940 was strategically decisive: for France. It was knocked out of the war. In wargames in 1939 the Wehrmacht had discovered France's key weakness: the fear of operating without secure flanks. In 1940 the Germans did not allow the French to have any. After the Polish campaign they had converted four 'light' divisions to armoured. They also restructured existing panzer divisions to make them smaller and more mobile.

Detailed analysis shows that it was not Guderian's attack at Sedan, nor Rommel's crossing of the River Meuse at Dinant, that unhinged the French Army. It was the crossing of the Meuse and 55km advance to Moncornet on 15 May by Major

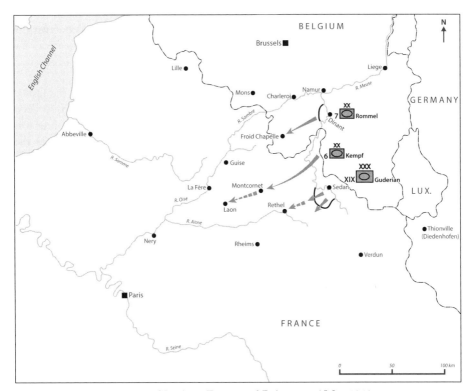

Figure 7-9 Northern France and Belgium, 15 May 1940.

General Werner Kempf's 6th Panzer Division. That evening, panzers were reported approaching Rethel and Laon, sending the French government into panic. Guderian was 20km east of Rethel but Kempf, at Moncornet, was 30 km from Laon. Their leading troops probably were near Rethel and Laon. It is quite possible that the French did not actually know where those tanks had come from.

The dominant narrative for this operation comes from Guderian's memoirs. Rommel's activities also attract historians' attention. Studying the map displays a different picture.

Just as in 1914, it was the defense of the middle Meuse between Namur and Sedan which gave the French such problems. The northern section of the river is in Belgium. Perhaps its significance is not obvious on French maps.

The following day the Sixth French Army counterattacked northeast from Reims. Two French armoured divisions, followed by five infantry divisions (rising to ten by 18 May), cut the German armoured columns off. Von Rundstedt, German Commander in Chief in the West, ordered a halt and withdrawal. The front stabilised. The campaign ground to a halt.

Clearly that did not happen. *There was no French operational reserve.* The French Seventh Army had been sent north, to the Dutch border near the coast, on 10 May. In effect, the French fell for the Wehrmacht's theatre-level deception. No subsequent reserve was created. French armoured divisions were not concentrated. Whatever the truth, half truth and legend about the campaign, the French failure to create a new operational reserve was critical. The issue stands in stark contrast to 1914. Historians have not remarked on that.

The Germans advanced to the sea at about 43km per day. It was one of the fastest armoured advances of all time. After Dunkirk the French Army still had 60 divisions. They formed a defensive line east-west across France. The Maginot line was still intact. The second phase of the campaign was even quicker than the first. The Wehrmacht attacked on 5 June. France surrendered on the 22nd.

The French and British had both, in their own way, held their air forces back. The Germans did not. They concentrated 1500 aircraft over Sedan on 14 May. The RAF had detected German armour moving through the Ardennes on 12 May, but the French instructed them not to attack. The RAF's real failing was not that identified later in the Bartholomew report, of not enough close air support to the Army. It was a failure to conduct an integrated land-air campaign.

The following year Britain formed nine more armoured brigades. It combined several of them into armoured divisions. Wavell had anticipated such developments 11 years before. Britain's greatest concentration of armoured divisions was in the Western Desert, where five British and one South African armoured divisions were deployed.

In the first four days of Operation Barbarossa, the German invasion of the Soviet Union, the Red Army lost 8,000 aircraft, many of them on the ground. In the second half of 1943 it lost another 20,000. It lost 20,000 more in the second half of 1944, from a front-line force of 13,000. It was opposed by only 500 German fighters. Soviet air force losses were colossal. Its pilots and commanders were inept.

'A tiny proportion of the German Army was armoured'? Germany formed 39 panzer divisions, of which up to 30 operated on the Eastern front at any one time. As we shall see, it also formed 29 motorised divisions. The Wehrmacht created more than 90 battalions of assault guns. Most active infantry divisions which needed one, had one. By contrast the British Army only fielded 34 divisions in total. Only seven were armoured.

'The Soviets were the masters of the operational level of war'? The Red Army made mistakes and kept on making them. Even after 1943 it suffered many setbacks. Many of them were significant. The Soviets either covered them up, explained them away as diversions or demonstrations, or downplayed their significance. In the offensive after Operation Uranus (around Stalingrad) they pushed more and more men into a pocket at Kharkov and lost 86,000 men. The Germans lost about 11,500. Slightly earlier the Soviets had lost 215,000 in Operation Mars, west of Moscow. Mars was a larger operation than Uranus. It failed totally. The Soviets airbrushed it from history.

In the Kursk operation in the summer of 1943 the Red Army lost about 863,000 men and about 9,200 tanks. The Germans lost 203,000 and fewer than 1300 tanks. Who won?

In practice the Red Army could afford the losses; the Germans less so. The initiative passed to the Soviets. The Germans could no longer dictate the operational course of events.

The average rate of advance for German armoured forces in major offensives was about 10-20km per day. Infantry formations can, and did, march faster than that. The problem facing German operational planners was that, at the beginning of an operation, armoured formations might advance 40 or 50km per day for a few days and open up a gap in front of the marching infantry divisions. That gap could typically be covered by a few motorised divisions. Some Soviet troops inevitably escaped. The Wehrmacht created 29 motorised or 'panzer grenadier' divisions. Not surprisingly, most of them fought on the eastern front. This was not, in practice, a major operational problem.

The Germans fought well at what became known as the operational level. At times they were excellent. Their biggest single problem was Hitler. Hitler was not always wrong, and his generals were not always right. However, his interference down to divisional level was a constant constraint on his army's freedom of operation. The Germans' use of large-scale manoeuvre often allowed them to win when outnumbered. However Hitler did not believe that successful manoeuvre in defence changed the overall ratio of forces, contrary to the evidence. After 1943 he generally refused to allow it. That seems to have been a major factor in the destruction of Army Group Centre in the summer of 1944.

The Wehrmacht had a deliberate process for rebuilding divisions. Reinforcements, and replacement equipment, were generally not sent to divisions in combat. Divisions were allowed to run down to perhaps 20% strength, then pulled out and refurbished over about six weeks. The process contributed significantly to their combat effectiveness. It has been mistaken for an aspect of poor logistics. German formations generally had just enough equipment and supply to keep the forces actually in contact moving and fighting. The Wehrmacht did not pay as much attention to logistics as the western Allies. That, however, made it less dependant on supply and less tied to lines of communication. 'Sufficiency' is a principle of logistics. 'Excess' is not.

In North Africa the British were more than good enough to defeat the Italians. However they were completely unused to mobile, armoured warfare. Right up to Alamein Axis divisions outnumbered the British, often by four or five divisions against a British force that never exceeded ten. Rommel, however, generally outmanoeuvred the British using his three or four German divisions. The British had an unfortunate mixture of indifferent commanders and some who were good but unlucky. They had five different army commanders and two theatre commanders in the 20 months between the initial Italian invasion and Montgomery's arrival. Lieutenant Generals Richard O'Connor and Philip Neame VC were captured. William ('Strafer') Gott[6] died in an air crash, which created the vacancy for Montgomery. Montgomery inherited Eighth Army in a position where its southern flank could not be turned; with time to train; and with fresh formations and equipment *en route*. Montgomery had known that Operation Torch would start on 8 November 1942. He had been under pressure for a victory at El Alamein before the Western Desert became overtaken by events.

After winning at El Alamein, Montgomery tried to outflank the retreating Panzer Army Afrika six times. There were several reasons for his failure. One was the general ability of a force of equivalent mobility to withdraw faster than its opponents. Other reasons included poor logistic planning, bad weather and Rommel's skill. The result was one of the longest successful withdrawals in history, by Rommel, to Tunisia. Germany and Italy had already reinforced Tunisia. The Axis armies were defeated in a matter of weeks, despite some embarrassment to American forces. Operationally the result was the loss of the remnants of both Panzer Army Afrika and Fifth Panzer Army. About 200,000 troops, including over 100,000 Germans, were captured.

After Sicily and Salerno the Allied 15th Army Group, commanded by General Sir Harold Alexander, advanced up the leg of Italy. By early January 1944 it had closed up to the German Gustav Line which ran through Cassino, 60 miles south east of Anzio. After two unsuccessful battles at Cassino and the Germans had contained VI Corps at Anzio, Alexander's chief of staff (Lieutenant General John Harding) planned Operation Diadem. It had two parts. At Cassino, a major offensive would break through the Gustav Line and advance up the Liri Valley. At the right moment VI Corps, reinforced to seven divisions, would break out *to the north east*, to cut the Liri Valley. That would encircle the bulk of the German Tenth Army against the Apennines (see Figure 7-10).

---

6   A pun on the German Great War expression 'Gott strafe England' ('may God punish England').

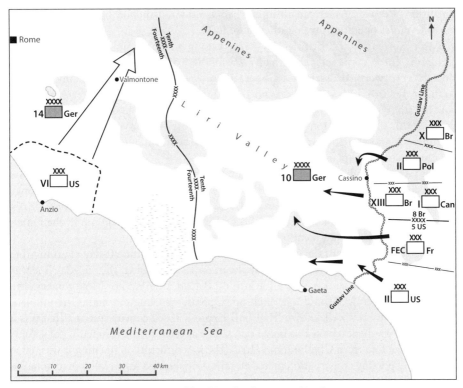

Figure 7-10 The Plan for Operation Diadem.

The third battle of Cassino was fought in March, largely to relieve pressure on VI Corps. Diadem opened on 11 May. After hard fighting, the French and Canadians broke into the Liri Valley. Cassino Abbey fell to the Poles. On 25 May Major General Lucian Truscott, commanding VI Corps, was ordered by Lieutenant General Mark Clark, commanding Fifth US Army, to turn *north* from Anzio and attack towards Rome. Truscott's account makes it clear that the timing was deliberate. By the time the change had been discovered, it was too late. Rome was liberated on 4 June, in time to make the headlines in New York and London before Overlord. More importantly, the German Tenth Army escaped to fight again north of Rome.

If Alexander had been American, Clark would have been sacked. If Clark had been British, he would have been sacked. It seems that, for Clark, a moment's fame was more important than the elimination of an enemy army.

Moltke the Elder wrote that '[a]n offensive without a main effort is like a man without character.' The western Allies' campaign in north west Europe after Normandy was characterless. The British Army's, that is Montgomery's, approach was pedestrian. It conducted deliberate operations and then moved, deliberately, to the next deliberate operation. Pre-war American thinking had considered mobile operations at up to corps level. Its operations were rather more fluid.

After Normandy the British 21st Army Group advanced unimaginatively across Belgium. Three corps led. Each had an armoured division leading. Each captured one city: Antwerp, Brussels and Ghent. There was no focus on the enemy. The US 12th Army Group advanced across northern France on a broad front, reaching a line roughly from Maastricht to Nancy (both on the River Meuse) by 10 September. It was at about this time that Montgomery, Bradley and Eisenhower were debating whether to approach and attack German on a broad or narrow front. Clearly they had no pre-existing operational plan.

The German high command had attempted to form a defence on the line of the Seine, above and below Paris. That failed, largely because Patton had seized crossings of the river before the Germans arrived. The German high command then clearly ordered the evacuation of France west of the Vosges, as well as Belgium to the Dutch border. Historians do not mention that. Why is that?

Logistics broke down. On 25 August the armies crossed the 90-day planning line for Overlord, two days early. Just 18 days later, on 12 September, the 350-day line was crossed. The problem was not with the armies, Patton, Bradley, nor Montgomery. The theatre supply services could not catch up. Operations came to a halt. The problem was not fixed by the well-known 'Red Ball Express' truck convoy system. That was a temporary expedient which also broke down. It was fixed by the re-opening of a dual-track railway line from Cherbourg to Paris. The key difficulty in opening it was, once again, transporting construction material: rails, sleepers and (especially) roadstone for the track bed.

Lieutenant General Vyvyan Pope, commanding the British XXX Corps, led a daring thrust northwards from the Dutch-Belgian border on 17 September. With three armoured divisions abreast and strongly supported by 79 AED, XXX Corps punched a hole through the German defences, crossed the Rhine at Arnhem on the 21st, and reached the Zuider Zee on the 22nd. Allied parachute divisions had been dropped at Eindhoven, Nijmegen and Arnhem to capture the key bridges. The German Fifteenth Army in the Netherlands was cut off, and the Allies had crossed the Rhine. Hitler cancelled a planned counteroffensive through the Ardennes and threw all his reserves north. Patton then had a relatively uncontested advance to the Rhine. The German Army began to collapse. The war in the West was over in December.

Clearly that did not happen. Pope was one of the few Royal Tank Corps officers to achieve high rank. He took over XXX Corps in the Western Desert in 1941 but was killed in a plane crash soon after.

Planners had had seven days to organise Operation Market Garden, the Arnhem operation. It would have been quite possible to gather three armoured divisions (they did) and 79 AED (which they did not. It was conducting operations against the Channel ports). The Guards Armoured Division, on the main effort, was lackadaisical. Its commander, Major General Alan Adair, was probably the only divisional commander who Montgomery was not allowed to sack. The 11th, or perhaps the 7th, Armoured Division would probably have done better.

Figure 7-11 shows the advance of XXX Corps, which reached the Rhein at Driel on the evening of D+5. It is clear that some criticism is misplaced. The Guards Armoured Division might, possibly, have advanced faster to Nijmegen. The real issue, however, would appear to be that having linked up with the 82nd US Airborne Division there at about 1000hrs on 19 September (D+2), neither it nor the 82nd achieved a crossing until 1830hrs the next day. That gave the defenders an extra day. Thereafter the operation got further and further behind schedule.

There were bigger problems with the airborne operation. It is not clear who was in charge. The First Allied Airborne Army had made 18 plans for airborne operations since June. All had been cancelled. Any airborne operation would have to go ahead before the front line moved out of Dakota range from England. If not, the Army would be unable to conduct operations and risked being broken up. It is a clear case of an organisational imperative. Market Garden's planning has been described as 'an airborne picnic with the enemy added to the menu like pepper and salt.' Montgomery might, or might not, have been in charge. Eisenhower had to agree the operation. The First Allied Airborne Army was not under Montgomery's command (although I Airborne Corps was placed under the British Second Army for the operation), and it did not command all the aircraft.

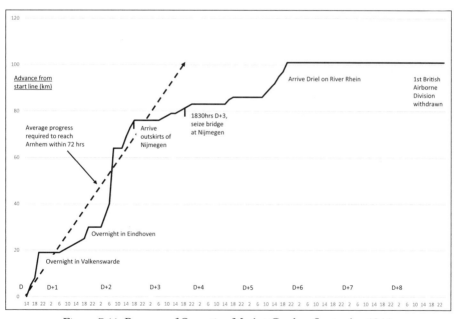

Figure 7-11 Progress of Operation Market Garden, September 1944.

The RAF did not have enough aircraft to drop a division in one lift. Nor did they at Normandy, and nor would they for the Rhine Crossings in March 1945.

Market Garden resulted in a long salient which became the basis for 21st Army Group's attacks eastwards along the Rhine. The Netherlands was not liberated until the Spring of 1945. The German counteroffensive *did* take place: in the Ardennes.

It was not actually necessary to use airborne troops for the operation. Bridges could be seized without them; some were. Infantry could conduct assault river crossings: they did. Engineers could bridge those rivers. However Market Garden would probably not have been conceived without the airborne forces. It is a sad reflection on the pedestrian approach displayed by western army planners.

The Allies had fewer divisions in North West Europe than the Germans until January 1945. The Allies' front line was stretched thin. The Germans attacked on 16 December where the line was thinnest and the divisions amongst the least experienced. The Germans made good progress but were unable to capture Bastogne, which was encircled. Patton turned Third Army north in 36 hours, relieved Bastogne, and linked up with the First US Army on the north side of the bulge. That is, it achieved complete operational success. Unusually for the campaign, Third US Army caused more casualties than it suffered. It moved remarkably quickly. The 'Battle of the Bulge' was a big operation. The US Army lost 19,000 dead; almost as many as in Normandy.

The western Allies had had no operational reserve. That was appropriate for a pursuit, such as in September. It was now December. The Allies were overstretched, but were also not very good operational planners.

Little encapsulates the Allies' poor understanding of the operational level more than the capture of the bridge at Remagen. The 9th US Armored Division seized it on 7 March 1945. However, there was then high-level disagreement. The bridge wasn't part of the current plan. Eventually Eisenhower overruled his chief of operations and the bridgehead was expanded.

Any American or British second lieutenant coming ashore at Normandy would have known that, sooner or later, the Allies would have to cross the Rhine. He wouldn't have been able to call it an 'operational objective'. Unfortunately, neither could most of his superiors.

The Allies had achieved air superiority, and maintained it. Air support to the campaign was good and kept getting better. Indeed much of the campaign's success lay in the fact that it was a well-conducted air-land campaign. Air forces did not, however, detect the buildup for the Battle of the Bulge. Nor did they prevent the movement of German forces against Market Garden. On 1 January 1945 almost the whole of what remained of the Luftwaffe in the west conducted a surprise attack. It destroyed 224 Allied aircraft on the ground and damaged another 84 beyond repair. It was one of the biggest single losses of aircraft in one day, ever. However, very few Allied aircrew were in their aircraft, so very few were killed. More importantly, by that stage the Allies could afford the loss. German losses were also high; they could not afford the loss.

The campaign, and the war, was not over when the Rhine was crossed. That took about another six weeks of fighting. I and II SS Panzer Corps were transferred to defend Hungary in January and February. By that stage Hungary was Germany's only remaining ally. By late February 1944 67 German divisions were facing 83 Allied divisions in the west. Importantly, Germany had the remnants of just six battered armoured divisions in the west. The Allies had 23. One or two American armoured divisions, and up to six infantry divisions, were arriving in theatre every month. The Third US Army reached Czechoslovakia. It was the proper application of over-whelming force.

The Japanese Army invaded New Guinea in January 1942. Fighting against American and Australian troops continued there until the end of the war. The prin-ciple operations against Rabaul later in the war were described above.

In 1941 the Philippines were defended by poorly equipped and poorly trained American and Filipino troops. The Japanese conquest was completed in May 1942, by which time 89,000 American and Filipino soldiers had surrendered. The reconquest started in October 1944. The Sixth and Eighth US Armies, with up to 14 divisions, were still fighting at the end of the war. By that time 16,000 American and 419,000 Japanese soldiers had died. Many of the latter died of disease and starvation. The US armies had conducted a highly effective campaign of isolation and bypass.

Poorly equipped and poorly trained British and Indian forces were driven out of southern Burma in early 1942. Northern Burma was strategically significant as the area from which the Kuomintang was supplied. With the loss of Rangoon, supplies had to be flown over the mountains into China. Work began on a new road from northern India in December 1942.

Strategically, Britain did not have the resources to conduct an offensive in Burma on any scale until 1944. Early that year the Japanese Fifteenth Army, of three divi-sions, advanced into northern Burma in order to cut strategic communications with China. They pushed the British and Indians back to Imphal and Kohima, where they were stopped. In the subsequent counterattack the Fifteenth Army was heavily defeated. British forces had lost about 20,000 dead; the Japanese about 30,000. In early 1945 the British Fourteenth Army captured Meiktila and Mandalay in a bril-liant manoeuvre and then forced the Japanese out of Burma.

The Second World War was also characterised by irregular warfare, on a large scale and in several countries. In south east Asia it often took the form of indigenous villagers and tribesmen run by organisations such as Britain's Special Operations Executive (SOE) (founded in 1940) or the US Office of Strategic Services (OSS) (from June 1942). However, indigenous Communist organisations were also active; in coun-tries such as China, Korea and French Indochina. They were often Soviet-sponsored. A different form of irregular warfare was developed in Burma. Britain's Chindits (of up to divisional size) and the American Merrill's Marauders (of brigade size) were conventional army units which conducted long-range, long-duration raiding opera-tions sabotage in Japanese rear areas.

Yugoslavia became the scene of protracted partisan warfare and German anti-partisan operations. Britain originally supported the pro-royalist Chetniks, but came to realise that Tito's Communists were more credible. The Germans supported the anti-Serb Croat Ustaše and raised a Croat SS mountain division, in a classic 'divide and rule' policy. Similar methods were used in the Baltic republics and parts of the USSR.

Soviet partisans were controlled reasonably effectively by the Red Army, which airdropped supplies, leaders and equipment. Many partisans were soldiers who had escaped captivity in German encirclements. By the end of 1941 there were over 2,000 Soviet partisan detachments, with a total of over 90,000 men. Partisan bands operated until their territories were liberated by the Red Army. Soviet partisans were not always popular: some had a tendency to banditry, rape and murder. They also clashed with anti-Soviet Ukrainian partisans and the Polish Home Army.

The Home Army, Czech resistance, and all western resistance forces were coordinated and equipped from London. Details varied from country to country. Several had their 'governments in exile' in London. France did not. In France there were Gaullist Free French groups, pro-communist resistance groups, and others. Navigating internal politics was a considerable problem for the SOE and OSS in several countries.

In western Europe the main activities were espionage and reconnaissance, with some sabotage. That changed on D-Day. On the night of 5-6 June 1944 French Resistance forces cut railway lines throughout France. Railway lines were cut in 486 places in June. By 7 July 26 main lines were unusable. That probably had more effect on the movement of German armoured divisions to Normandy than Allied bombing. It is generally overlooked. (Those divisions were forced to move by road. Accounts tend to mention the subsequent air attacks which they did experience, rather than the rail journeys which they did not.) Resistance groups were closely coordinated by Supreme HQ, Allied Expeditionary Forces (SHAEF). Allied 'Jedburgh' liaison teams were inserted. Uniformed British, French and Belgian Special Air Service (SAS) units conducted long-range reconnaissance, raiding, and liaison. Resistance groups were not encouraged to engage in open warfare until Allied forces reached their general area. Where they did, German countermeasures could be swift, effective and ruthless.

The Italian partisan movement grew to about 230,000 men. About 35,000 Italian partisans died, and about 10,000 civilians were killed in German reprisals. As with most partisan forces, its members could be brave and dedicated, but were often poorly trained and equipped. Italian partisans leaders were sometimes exceptional but often inexperienced. Several partisan units were infiltrated by collaborators or the Gestapo.

At the operational level, the key personnel issues relate to senior commanders and the flow of manpower. Personality issues were important; often reflect one-sided bias; but are possibly over-reported.

German commanders were generally more technically proficient than their Allied counterparts. The real extent to which Nazi ideology did, or did not, affect their character and their actions is still not understood. One issue is that senior officers who did complain about SS atrocities tended to be sacked. That did not stop the atrocities; they could no longer influence events; and they lost their jobs. Similarly the high turnover of senior German commanders in the Normandy campaign is not widely known nor appreciated. Hitler executed 89 generals in total.

Eisenhower seems to have been Marshall's second choice as Supreme Allied Commander. Montgomery was not a particularly nice man, but thorough and professional.[7] He fought the way he taught, and had been taught. He had both attended, and instructed, at staff colleges *twice*. In North Africa, US forces were inexperienced and the junior partner in the Alliance. Patton was sufficiently insensitive not to appreciate that. American failings at corps command in 1942-43 were just as significant as British failings at corps and army level between 1940 and 1942.

Many British commanders had attended the Imperial Defence College, created in 1927. It was intended to train the future senior officers of all three Services. A selected list of its alumni is illuminating. See Figure 7-12. Not all were successful. Some commanders, such as Newall, were too old to have attended. However, the list is notable for who it does not include.

Year	Rank	Name	Subsequent Wartime Appointment
1927	Lt Col	CJE Auchinleck DSO OBE	CinC Middle East
	Lt Col	AF Brooke DSO	CIGS
	Wg Cdr	WS Douglas MC DFC	AOCinC Fighter Command
	Brig	AGL McNaughton CMG DSO	Chief of the Canadian General Staff
	Wg Cdr	REC Peirse DSO AFC	AOCinC Bomber Command
	Capt	JC Tovey DSO	CinC Home Fleet
1928	Wg Cdr	AW Tedder	Deputy Supreme Commander, Allied Expeditionary Force
1929	Capt	AB Cunningham DSO	First Sea Lord
	Sqn Ldr	CEH Medhurst OBE MC	Vice CAS
	Wg Cdr	CWH Pulford OBE AFC	AOCinC Far East
1930	Col	Hon HRLG Alexander DSO MC	Supreme Allied Commander, Mediterranean
	Wg Cdr	NH Bottomley AFC	Deputy CAS
	Lt Col	P Neame VC DSO	Lieutenant general, captured 1941

---

7   Marshall's first choice may have been Lieutenant General Frank Andrews, USAAF. He was selected to be Commander, (US) European Theatre of Operations at Casablanca. He died in an air crash some weeks later.

Year	Rank	Name	Subsequent Wartime Appointment
1931	Lt Col	Sir RF Adam DSO OBE	Adjutant General (1941-45)
	Lt Col	GJ Giffard	GOCinC 11th Army Group (India and Burma)
	Capt	H Harwood OBE	CinC Mediterranean Fleet
	Lt Col	FE Hotblack DSO MC	Tank corps officer. Appointed to command 2nd Armoured Division, 1939; suffered a stroke and invalidated.
1934	Lt Col	HDG Crerar DSO	GOCinC 1st Canadian Army
	Gp Capt	TL Leigh-Mallory DSO	CinC, Allied Expeditionary Air Forces
	Lt Col	VV Pope DSO MC	Tank Corps officer. Appointed to command XXX Corps; died in an air crash
1935	Wg Cdr	Hon R A Cochrane AFC	AOC Nos 7, 3 and 5 Groups, Bomber Command
	Lt Col	RN O'Connor DSO MC	Corps commander, North Africa (captured) and North West Europe
	Lt Col	AE Percival DSO OBE MC	GOC Malaya
1936	Lt Col	NMS Irwin DSO MC	GOCinC Eastern Army, India (responsible for Burma)
	Mr	A Rowlands MBE	Civil servant. Private Secretary to 3 ministers and, separately, Permanent Secretary to 3 ministries
1937	Lt Col	AG Cunningham DSO MC	GOCinC 8th Army
	Gp Capt	KR Park MC DFC	AOC Malta then AOCinC Middle East
	Lt Col	WJ Slim MC	GOCinC 14th Army
1938	Gp Capt	RD Oxland OBE	Senior Air Staff Officer (ie, chief of staff), Bomber Command
	Lt Col	GAP Scoones DSO OBE MC	GOCinC IV Corps (Burma)

Figure 7-12 Selected Students at the Imperial Defence College.

Portal and Harris are obvious omissions. Newall and Peirse were sacked (effectively by Churchill) because they were insufficiently committed to bombing. A number of senior RAF officers were university graduates, whilst their Army and Navy counterparts were generally not. A surprising number of them were unfit for Army service (including Park, Tedder and Slessor). That is ironic, because they were all aircrew. They would not have passed an aircrew medical. The RAF Official History makes it quite clear that Harris was a seriously unpleasant character. He tendered his resignation often enough to know that Portal would not sack him. The Official History also states quite clearly that the Battle of Berlin was a defeat; but Harris was not sacked. Generals and admirals tended to get sacked when they lost battles. Air force 'reassignments' seem to have been more about political issues, many of them internal.

Britain was very aware that its manpower was limited. Three of the divisions which fought in Normandy were broken up to reinforce the others. America seriously mismanaged its army manpower. The main effect was that several divisions arriving in Europe after Normandy were effectively untrained as formations. That did not go unpunished (witness the Battle of the Bulge).

Intelligence and deception had significant impact. Hitler had read a telegram from Churchill to Eisenhower about the planned landings in Sicily. However the Germans did not know in advance about the Anzio landings, nor the location and date of Overlord.

Signals intelligence (SIGINT) played a major part. The role of Enigma and the resulting intelligence, Ultra, are well known. On reflection it is perhaps surprising that Enigma was made public only 30 years later. The Kriegsmarine could read Royal Navy codes, sometimes within minutes, until late 1943. That, coupled with good analysis, allowed it to direct its U-boat operations almost in real time. Italy intercepted US diplomatic traffic, including some military content. America broke Japanese diplomatic and, less successfully, naval codes. Gott's death in August 1942 resulted from to a communication security (COMSEC) breach. So did the death of Admiral Isoruku Yamomoto, commander of the Japanese Combined Fleet, in April 1943. In both cases the aircraft they were travelling in were intercepted and destroyed.

Poland, and later Britain, had spies in OKW. The Soviet Union had spies in the British Foreign Office and secret intelligence service (MI6). There were numerous double agents. Security services, such as the Gestapo, MI5 and the FBI, generally did a good job of rounding up agents. However, for example, the Gestapo generally did *not* know that the British *did* know that the Gestapo had compromised some SOE radio stations in France and Belgium. Tragically, in other instances SOE ignored similar evidence.

The Battle of the Bulge represented a clear failure of intelligence. The operation was in the sector of First US Army, IX US Tactical Air Command, 12th US Army Group, and SHAEF. The intelligence branches of all of those HQs had significant intelligence but did not predict the attack. Patton's intelligence branch did, which allowed his staff to undertake contingency planning.

Intelligence was subject to organisational and ideological battles in all countries. The most important question is what use was made of it. German intercepts told them of the dates and details of the Norway campaign of 1940. In 1941 Stalin was told that Germany would attack Russia, and the exact date. Freyberg, commanding British forces in Crete, ignored Ultra intelligence about the German attack. The RAF deliberately ignored evidence that bombing was not working. Churchill's scientific advisor did not, but Churchill did not then reduce Bomber Command's role nor resource allocation.

The Second World War was won strategically because America entered the war. Operationally, the war against Germany was won when Germany was overrun. That happened because of the destruction of Army Group Centre and Overlord, both in 1944. It was not won, nor appreciably shortened, by bombing. Japan was not defeated by atomic bombs. They merely hastened its end. Operationally, Japan was largely defeated by a highly effective series of amphibious campaigns.

Neither Japan nor Germany effectively interrupted the western Allies' use of the sea. The Allies could, effectively, make such use of it as they wished. Russia apart, after 1940 most major campaigns depended on amphibious operations, which in turn depended on naval operations; not least to retain command of the sea. Where they did not depend on amphibious operations (such as in North Africa and Burma), they did depend on control of the sea to deliver and sustain the forces. The Russian front benefitted significantly from supply by the Arctic convoys.

Bombing was wrong. It did not achieve its operational objectives. It was a major diversion of resources which could have been put to better use. As late as December 1944 bombing industrial targets did not prevent the re-equipment of two Panzer Armies for the Ardennes operation. German and Japanese civilian morale did not collapse. Evidence of failure had long existed, but was deliberately ignored in order to progress irrelevant organisational goals. Decent and well-intentioned men were drawn through moral hazard into immoral actions. Others did not need much prompting. The bombing was, effectively, raiding against logistic infrastructure. Bombing *was* useful for political signalling. That did not require a thousand bombers over Berlin, night after night.

All the most effective campaigns were joint undertakings in which air forces were the junior component. The Battle of Britain should not be seen as an air campaign. It was a major air operation which was intended to be the *opening stage* of a campaign: the German invasion of Britain. The RAF's Fighter Command was successful, so the campaign (the invasion) did not proceed. In general, the more effective the cooperation with surface forces, the more effective the campaign overall. Achieving and retaining air superiority was, literally, essential.

The most effective land campaigns generally included the envelopment, or encirclement, of significant enemy forces and their elimination. Failure to do so typically required fighting those forces which escaped again. Campaigns where the enemy escaped might well be operationally successful, but not strategically decisive. That was a particular problem when fighting the Wehrmacht, but also (for example) applied to the Red Army after 1942. If you do not destroy them, you will have to fight them again. Put another way, armoured warfare works: if it is conducted at the operational level.

The Soviets were not masters of the operational level of war. Before the war, they had thought about large-scale manoeuvres over large distances. They could be quite proficient. They made several mistakes and were often beaten operationally by inferior

German forces. Their key successes came when they had an overall superiority of over two to one. It is, surely, not difficult to appear good if your army has four million men more than the opposition. The Red Army's alleged mastery of the operational level also disguises the fact that that it was, generally, woefully bad at the tactical level.

The Western Allies had no clear understanding of the operational level. They won in western Europe not by superior numbers but by fighting a very competent air-land campaign. The Normandy campaign created an unassailable lodgement on the continent of Europe. The Battle of the Bulge, mostly thanks to Patton, destroyed Germany's last operational reserves in the west.

Armed forces are human institutions. They have organisational dynamics and imperatives. Problems will arise where those imperatives are inconsistent with strategic and operational goals. That applied to the RAF and the USAAF. It also applied to the First Allied Airborne Army.

Several senior commanders were idolised. Some of them still are. They were, however, human. They had strengths but also weaknesses. It is probably more fruitful to understand those strengths and weaknesses, and the relations between those commanders, than to idolise or demonize them. Several were, truly, great men in great times. But they were human.

Allied commanders were sometimes drawn into actions that were unattractive. At times some lost their moral compass. Their memoirs rarely admit that: men are human. One reason why there is no consensus over the Combined Bomber Offensive is probably that airmen would rather avoid defending the indefensible.

On 8 May 1945 Churchill declared victory over Germany. Victory is a declaratory political act. The victory happened on Truman's 61st birthday. Fittingly, Truman dedicated the victory to the memory of his predecessor, Roosevelt.

8

Blood, Toil, Tears and Sweat

Chapter Eight considers the tactics of the Second World War. It is at the tactical level where technology has the most direct impact. Technology is tangible in vehicles, weapons and communications systems; hence in tanks, ships, and aircraft. The jet engine played relatively little part, radio more so. Radio was typically to be found on every ship and aircraft. Initially not all armies had radios in every tank, and perhaps only down to infantry company level.

In what follows it is useful to make comparisons using one tank or aircraft engine as the unit of measure. Consider, for example, an RAF squadron of Whitley bombers in 1940. It had 18 aircraft, hence 36 aircraft engines. It had 35 officers and a total of 395 all ranks. Conversely a British armoured regiment of 1944 had 79 tank engines, 36 officers (44% fewer per engine) and (proportionately) 30% *less* manpower per engine.

In 1940 a Spitfire with a Rolls Royce Merlin engine cost £9,850. A Panzer IV cost £9,740. In 1944 prices an M4 Sherman cost £9,660. A British Cromwell tank, with a Meteor engine, cost about the same: £10,000. A Meteor was, essentially, a Merlin. A Lancaster with four Merlins cost £42,000: four times as much. A twin-engined Mosquito cost only a third (rather than half) that of a Lancaster, but that was partly because it used very little aluminium.[1] Aluminium was expensive to buy and manufacture. There was far more steel in a tank than aluminium in an aircraft, but the costs speak for themselves. Aircrew cost about £10,000 each to train. That was roughly the cost of sending ten students to Oxford or Cambridge Universities for three years. A new tank cost the same as a fighter, or the training an airman. So using one tank or aircraft engine as the unit of force comparison is usefully indicative.

On 10 May 1940 the Luftwaffe lost 308 aircraft over France and the Low Countries. The following day it lost 387, mostly to RFC Hawker Hurricanes. Losses continued to mount. Luftwaffe commanders began to realise that the RFC had some form of Ground Control of Intercept (GCI), linked to radio-frequency direction finding (ie, radar).

---

1 The Mosquito was wooden-framed.

On 13 May 71 and 76 Wings of RFC Hawker Henleys started dive-bombing German tank columns in the Ardennes. Pilots attacked targets near bridges, causing traffic jams. That led to more and better targets. Luftwaffe fighters tried to intervene, but were repeatedly intercepted by superior numbers of Hurricanes. 59 and 75 Wings continued dive-bombing at night, using parachute flares and the light of burning vehicles. More and more RFC units were committed. German aircraft losses continued to mount. Traffic jams stretched back into Germany. On 19 May the Germans abandoned the attack through the Ardennes. The German offensive broke down. Dunkirk and the Battle of Britain didn't happen.

Clearly that did not happen. All of the elements required to make it happen, however, existed. Britain had transportable radar sets. Several were sent to France. It would have been quite possible to construct a deployable GCI system. The Henley single-engined dive bomber was in service. It had the same Merlin engine as the Hurricane. It was almost as fast as the current Messerschmitt Me 109, and 60mph faster than the Fairey Battle light bomber. The RAF had rejected dive-bombers and invested in the Battle. Battles were slow and vulnerable. They have been described as 'obsolete in 1939', but had in fact only been in service for four years.

The RAF had apparently proven that dive-bombers were ineffective. Curiously, the German Junkers Ju 87 'Stuka' was highly effective in that campaign. Dive bombing was far more accurate than level bombing. A few months later, in the Battle of Britain, Stukas suffered proportionately fewer losses than conventional ('level') bombers and single- and double-engined fighters. The RAF had clearly made a wrong choice. Its evidence seems to have been that dive-bombing *on the battlefield* in the Great War led to high losses. The RAF did not wish to indulge in close air support *at all*, and therefore did not get involved in dive-bombing. Dive-bombing as interdiction, however, might have been an entirely different issue.

In 1939 the RAF had 25 squadrons of twin-engined medium bombers (Whitleys, Hampdens and Wellingtons), so nominally 900 engines. Just 10 squadrons of Hurricanes and 9 of Battles were deployed to France. Instead of the Whitleys and Hampdens, the RAF might have invested the same number of engines in single-engined aircraft. It could then have had, say, 35 squadrons of Hurricanes and 34 squadrons of Henleys in France, whilst keeping an unchanged number of fighters back, in Britain, for home defence. It was a matter of choice. The choice reflected the doctrine.

Alternatively, instead of those extra Hurricanes and Henleys, Britain might have enough tanks for two armoured divisions. In May 1940 the British Army did not have a single armoured division in France. On 21 May 4th and 7th Battalions, Royal Tank Regiment attacked the flank of Rommel's 7th Panzer Division near Arras. The attack was beaten off, but resulted in Hitler's (or possibly General Gerd von Rundstedt's) famous 'halt order'. The panzers were ordered to stop. Imagine what might have happened if two armoured divisions had attacked, rather than two tank battalions.

In practice the Army did not have the doctrine nor the training to handle all-arms armoured formations, and would not for some time. There was no-one to teach them. There is, however, a degree of 'cart before horse' here. Britain had invested in the RAF bomber force. It had not invested in an armoured force, nor an 'RFC' capable of joint air-land operations, nor a transportable GCI system.

The Luftwaffe *did* lose 308 aircraft on 10 May 1940. That was its biggest loss of the war, and far bigger than on any day of the Battle of Britain.

Level bombing with single-engined light bombers, such as Battles, did not work. The Battle was the first aircraft to use the Merlin engine. It was rapidly standardised. It was used on Henleys, Hurricanes, Spitfires, Mosquitoes, Lancasters and several other types. Packard built Merlins under license for the American P51 Mustang. The Mosquito was probably the most successful British aircraft of the War. By 1944 the RAF could destroy individual factories with absolute precision, using a few Mosquitoes and 10-15 tons of bombs. However the RAF typically continued to use hundreds of Lancasters, and hundreds of tons of bombs, and miss. The RAF had had no stated requirement for the Mosquito.

On the night of 16-17 May 1943, 19 Lancasters of 617 Squadron RAF attacked four targets in Germany using special 'dam busting' bouncing bombs. Two dams were destroyed. Eight aircraft (42%) were lost, and the operation was never repeated. The undoubted heroism of the crews should not be used to cloud objective assessment.

In June 1942 a small force of USAAF Liberators attacked the Ploiești oilfield from north Africa. The oilfield was poorly defended but damage was light. The next attack was 14 months later. 162 Liberators attacked the target at low level. In the interim the Luftwaffe and the Romanian air force had reinforced the air defences with three fighter groups, several hundred antiaircraft guns, and radar. Surprise was lost due to poor navigation and COMSEC. Only 88 aircraft returned to Libya, of which 55 were damaged. Surprise is a principle of war. In this case it was lost both operationally (by attacking in 1942) and tactically. With surprise lost, attacking at low level in daylight resulted in horrendous losses. Damage to the oilfield was negligible.

Bombing is a raiding tactic. Surprise is a key feature in the success of raids. Air forces are not exempt from adherence to the principles of war.

On 4 April 1944, 40 carrier-based Royal Navy dive-bombers attacked the *Tirpitz* in Altafjord in northern Norway. Surprise was complete. Watertight compartments were not closed and antiaircraft guns were not manned. *Tirpitz* was hit 15 times and heavily damaged, but not sunk. Two RN fleet and four escort carriers had launched the sorties. The Navy made several more attacks that summer, and scored some hits. However the bombs were not heavy enough sink a properly-protected battleship. The RAF sank *Tirpitz*, on the third attempt, with 32 Lancasters with Tallboy bombs on 12 November.

In February 1942 *Scharnhorst, Gneisenau, Prinz Eugen* and escorts had made a dash from Brest in Brittany through the English Channel, aiming for the German North Sea ports. German EW units jammed many British radar and radio frequencies in a surprise electronic attack. Nevertheless, at about 9.30am on 12 February British operators detected the ships. 67 Wing RNAS, a naval strike group of two torpedo bomber and one dive bomber squadrons, was scrambled from airfields between Havant and Hastings. By noon *Gneisenau* had been sunk, *Prinz Eugen* was heavily damaged (and sank that night), and *Scharnhorst* turned back to Brest.

Clearly that did not happen. The few RAF anti-shipping aircraft had recently been sent to North Africa. RAF naval strike wings *were* assembled, but not until months after the German ships had reached Germany.

In May 1941 *Bismarck* had been torpedoed by carrier-based aircraft which had located their target using airborne radar. *Bismarck's* steering was damaged. That led to her being destroyed by gunfire the following day. Airborne torpedo attacks were not easy. In December 1941 HMS *Repulse* dodged 19 Japanese torpedoes before being hit. In the same attack HMS *Prince of Wales* was hit by just one of nine torpedoes launched at her. It made her lose power and list to port. Her starboard antiaircraft battery could no longer depress to sea level. That left her vulnerable to further attacks from the starboard, which sank her.

Airborne torpedoes had a range of perhaps 1500 yards. Surface- or submarine-launched torpedoes had a range of about 4,000 yards, with a run time of about four minutes. Japanese 'Long Lance' torpedoes could reach 44,000 yards. However, with a run time of maybe 30 minutes to that range, the target had to be careless or unlucky. In the Great War destroyers typically had perhaps two or three tubes. By the end of the Second World War they had eight or ten. By 1944 British destroyers were jamming the guidance signals to German anti-ship guided bombs. They were usually, but not always, successfully.

Naval gunfire became deadly once linked to radar fire control systems. In 1942 Japanese battleships could hit another ship with perhaps the fourth salvo. US battleships could soon hit with the first salvo. On 15 November 1942 the US battleship *Washington* engaged and sank the Japanese battleship *Kirishima* off Guadalcanal, at night, at ranges from 8,400 to 4,800 yards, firing 62 rounds within seven minutes (and despite having to cease fire for 90 seconds).

Montgomery's attack at El Alamein opened on the night of 23-24 October 1942. It could be described as 'Arras 1917, with sand'. Four British divisions attacked on a frontage of 12,000 yards, widening to 18,000. The British had just over 1,000 tanks; the Germans and Italians about 540. It had been planned to take 12 days. It took 19.

Only 456 field guns, and just 48 mediums, fired on the attacking sector. All of the mediums were used in one group, which neutralised one enemy battery at a time. The field guns fired a preliminary 15-minute counterbattery fireplan in which the 72 guns of each division's artillery concentrated on one enemy battery every three minutes. The main fireplan launched the infantry onto the objective, 6-8,000 yards distant. Return fire was described as 'feeble'. The initial attack was broadly successful. The 'Blue Line' objective, also called 'Oxalic', was reached in most places.

However most of the British armour was held not just in different divisions, but in a different Corps. It was difficult to clear minefield lanes during the night, so very few tanks got through before dawn. German and Italian armoured forces were held in depth behind Oxalic. Hence, from the first day, the British were trying to fight through a salient between enemy infantry positions, and into Axis armoured forces deployed in depth. The British had a total of 860 guns, but had great difficulty in bringing them all to bear through the salient.

For each of the next several days the pattern was broadly the same. A few enemy machineguns, mortars or antitank guns which survived the British fireplan would hold up the advance. It took until perhaps 1 November for Montgomery to refine his methods. On the night of 1-2 November, for Operation Supercharge, 192 guns fired a barrage. 168 fired in counterbattery, and two New Zealand infantry brigades cleared a gap about 6,000 yards deep. However 9th Armoured Brigade, attacking at dawn, was then held up on an antitank screen. A similar attack on the morning of 4 November broke through; but largely because Rommel had started to withdraw.

Once an initial fireplan had been fired, British artillery was too inflexible to neutralise those remaining pockets of resistance. It should have been easy to neutralise antitank guns – even the feared 88mm antiaircraft guns – with artillery or, particularly, mortars. That, however, rarely happened. Sherman tanks, with 75mm guns which fired HE, had just arrived in theatre. They could neutralise antitank guns. Rommel lost all of his 88s at El Alamein: a significant, but largely unnoticed, occurrence.

British forces would typically do what they were ordered, if they could. They would then expect to be told what to do next. That applied right up to corps level. British tactics remained pedestrian, throughout the Army. Command was over-centralised. It worked, but not well.

In Burma the Japanese held an initial advantage in jungle fighting. They were tough, highly disciplined, able to survive with a minimum of supplies, obedient, unimaginative and inflexible. They excelled at meeting engagements which they developed into envelopments. By doing so they cut the trails behind their enemies, causing them to panic and fall back.

Initially both the Japanese and the British tended to operate with their forces widely dispersed. That was an advantage to the Japanese whilst they held the initiative. When they lost it, their formations and units could be isolated and defeated in detail. That is broadly what happened in the Kohima-Imphal campaign.

The British did not really consider jungle fighting until forced to, in late 1941 and 1942. It took them until 1944 to adapt to jungle conditions and gain the confidence to take on the Japanese. British tactics in the first Arakan campaign of 1942-3 were often unimaginative, frontal, and often failed.

By early 1944 the British had the tactical and then operational initiative. Japanese tactics were frequently predictable. Artillery was often ineffective through the jungle canopy. The situation required the coordinated use of small arms, occasionally tanks, and well-executed minor unit tactics. British, Indian and West African units learned how to beat the Japanese through hard experience.

Much the same applied to American forces in the Pacific. There was little sharing of tactical lessons between the Allies. American learnt to avoid frontal attacks and exploit flanks. In defence they learnt to encourage the Japanese to attack frontally, and then destroy them with massed firepower.

Aircraft became highly important for resupply, casualty evacuation and interdiction. Casualties could sometimes be collected by light aircraft from battalion aid posts and taken straight to field hospitals, considerably shortening evacuation times.

Similarly, aerial resupply was not so much a question of capacity as of getting relatively limited quantities of ammunition and rations quickly to units relatively deep in the jungle. The alternatives, of manpack or mule transport, could take days or even weeks.

It is difficult to appreciate just how bad Red Army tactics were. Russia had entered the Great War with 19th century tactical methods. It had never learnt better. It fought the Second World War with the same methods but 1940s equipment. It lost commanders so quickly that there was virtually no-one to teach it how to fight better.

Near Gusevo in November 1942, during Operation Mars, the German 110th Infantry Division had to defend a 30km sector. That meant just a single platoon in reserve per battalion; a company per regiment; and possibly one battalion for the division. Every front-line company (21 out of 27) would have a sector of almost 1,500m. The Soviets failed to break through. A few days later four Soviet rifle divisions and two tank corps attacked near Osuga on a 4km sector. They were supported by 2,500 guns, mortars and rocket launchers. They were faced by elements of two German regiments. The Soviets attacked for three days and gained less than 1,000m. They didn't capture a single village. Casualties, of both tanks and infantry, were over half of the whole force. In Operation Mars German casualties were typically one or two hundred per division per week: not particularly high.

At or about the same time the German General Gotthard Heinrici commanded the 4th Army. He had ten divisions to defend a 200km front astride the Minsk-Moscow highway. The Red Army attacked five times on the 20km sector nearest the road, for five or six days at a time, and typically at three predictable times per day. The Red Army deployed between 20 and 38 divisions on each occasion. Most of them were fresh for each battle. The Russians typically had 1,000 guns to the Germans' 380. Heinrici defended that sector with roughly three and a half divisions. The crisis of each battle typically came on the fourth or fifth day. German casualties were typically equivalent to about one battalion per day of battle. The Red Army did not get through. Soviet losses were often 12 times, and sometimes 18 times, that of the Germans.

German assault gun battalions would typically destroy about 10-15 Soviet tanks for each assault gun lost. In poor battalions it would be six or seven to one; in good battalions up to 22 to one. Individual assault gun commanders knew that they could safely attack if four enemy tanks were visible. Five would be tricky, but possible.

At Kursk the German armies were outnumbered by about 2.45:1 in men and 3.12:1 in tanks; but attacked. They inflicted about 4.25 times as many casualties on the Russians as they suffered, and 7.07 times as many tanks.

Red Army units could be dogged in defence at low level. In general their artillery fire was heavy but inaccurate and ineffective. It was often predicted, not observed, and based on poor intelligence. Soviet units' tactical reporting was often non-existent or poor, resulting in bad decision-making. COMSEC was frequently appalling. Yes: the Soviets sometimes managed to deceive the Germans. Their officers were often poorly trained. Attempts to motivate, normally based on Soviet ideology, were often ineffective. Draconian punishments did not prevent ill-discipline, but resulted in poor morale.

Clearly those are generalisations. The statistics given above tend to emphasize the best and overlook the worst German performances. There was some Soviet improvement later in the war, and the overall quality of German forces declined. Yet even at the Seelow Heights east of Berlin in April 1945, and then within the city itself, German units often repeatedly outperformed their opponents by a large margin. But, in the end, the Red Army's quantity had a quality all of its own.

Anyone who thinks that a T34 was a good tank has not seen a T34. It had a reasonably powerful, reliable engine and a fairly good gun. The early models also had a two-man turret, no turret basket and no turret crew seats. Initially few had radios. The optics and fire control system were appalling. Its main advantages when it entered service was that it weighed 26 tons and had sloped armour. It was therefore well-protected. The best German tank, the Panzer IV, weighed just 21 tons.

The T34 was service when Germany invaded Russia in 1941. The German Army produced the Panzer V (Panther), specifically to counter the T34, in time for Kursk two years later. They had examined captured T34s. Why did they not simply reverse-engineer them? The T34 later carried an 85mm gun. Its recoil energy was greater than that of the (much higher velocity) 75mm of the Panther. The gun travel, in recoil, was about the same. Hence the turret ring was about the same size. The T34's engine was powerful but crude. The Panther's engine was more powerful but was, effectively, smaller. The Panther's turret had a basket, a three-man crew, crew seats, and excellent optics and fire control equipment. German engineers could fairly have easily made a much-improved T34, with the Panther's gun and engine.

Germans engineers prefer to design their own solutions. They rarely copy. The Panther was an extremely good tank once production issues (such as oil seals and gaskets) were overcome. That took a few months. The Panther was considerably better than early T34s and was never upgraded. However it was, if anything, too heavy. It entered service at 44 tons.

British tank design and production was woeful for several years. Thousands of tanks, of several different makes, were built just in time to be found inadequate and scrapped. They including over 1700 A13 Mk III Covenanters, 500 A24 Cavaliers and 900 A27L Centaurs. The situation changed after late 1941 when W A Robotham, a Rolls Royce design engineer with no experience of tanks, was put in charge of tank design. Robotham had proposed the use of Merlin engines for tanks. They were very powerful, yet compact. The Merlin was redesigned as the Meteor and fitted into three tank projects. They were essentially a 30-ton, a 40-ton and a 50-ton model. They appeared in 1943, 1944 and 1945 respectively. The first, the Cromwell, was remarkably fast and could mount a 75mm gun; but only just. The 40-ton Comet was a very respectable late-war tank, but could not quite carry the required gun (its '77mm' gun was a down-rated version of the 17pdr). The third was the Centurion. It entered service, with the 17pdr, days before the end of the war. Its last battle was in 1991.

In looking at tanks one has to consider numbers and equipment schedules. The US Army standardised on M4 Shermans until they could start to replace them with M26 Pershings. The German Army wanted as many Panthers as it could get. It never got enough. Late in the war half the fleet (one battalion of the two in most panzer divisions) still had Panzer IVs. There were only ever 15 battalions of Panzer VI 'Tigers'. In practice that meant perhaps half a dozen in the east, typically one or two in western Europe, and perhaps one in Italy at any one time. Germany built 5,976 Panthers but only 1,843 Tigers.

At the end of the war there were more assault guns in German service than any type of tank. Similarly there were 52 tank battalions in US armoured divisions, but 65 for use with infantry divisions. The British 21st Army Group had five armoured brigades in armoured divisions, but eight armoured or tank brigades for use with infantry divisions.

Terrain can be a problem if forces are not trained for it. That was especially true in southern Italy. Typically, the mountains drop rapidly to the sea. The rivers can be narrow, but deep and very fast.

German and western defensive tactics were based on a covering force, a main line of resistance and counterattacks. The skill lies in the relation between the three elements, and between them and the terrain. In December 1943 the Bernhardt Line marked the covering force area for the main Gustav Line at Cassino. At San Pietro Infine the reinforced US 36th Infantry Division committed 12 American battalions and an Italian regiment, and fought for seven days, to drive back three German battalions in the covering force area.

Several commentators remarked that American minor unit tactics were poor. More generally one (British) Indian Army general described the first *three* battles of Cassino as 'military sins'. His experience of the Indian North-West Frontier probably informed his opinion. The Polish Corps studied the terrain at Cassino in great detail, albeit learning from the experience of three previous failed attacks. They concluded that the key terrain was not the Abbey, nor Castle Hill below it, nor the town below that (see Figure 8-1). It was the narrow ridge behind the Abbey. Again, it is possible that experience in the Carpathians gave the Poles a different perspective (their senior division was the 3rd Carpathian Infantry Division).

The German infantry positions on the ridge were the main line of resistance for the Gustav Line. Section outposts were sited on the forward slope, and re-occupied whenever possible. The ridge is steep but narrow. Reserves on the reverse slope were effectively immune to indirect fire, but close enough to counterattack quickly. It was a hugely strong position.

The Germans used assault guns. The Americans, Canadians, British, New Zealanders, Poles and French used Shermans. All had 75mm guns which could fire HE. However, the terrain made it very difficult to use more than a few tanks at any one time. Due to the knife-edged ridges behind the Abbey, it was technically very difficult to use artillery effectively. The Poles therefore used most of their antiaircraft gunners to man mortars. The Germans had moved the elite 1st Parachute Division into Cassino. It had fought the Canadian 1st Infantry Division at Ortona ('Hell's Courtyard') on the east coast the previous December. One reason why the fighting at Cassino was so bitter was that the defenders were highly experienced in urban warfare.

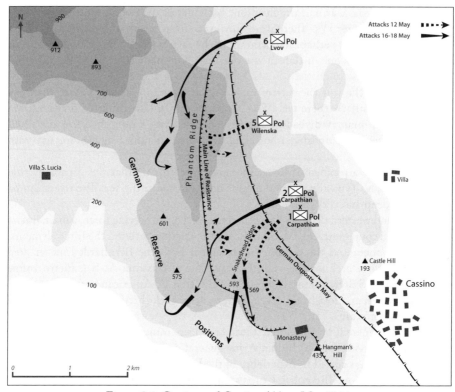

Figure 8-1 Cassino and Cassino Abbey, May 1944.

In January 1944 a senior New Zealand officer remarked that American front-line GIs at Cassino were in bad shape. However, he said, American senior officers didn't know that because they didn't go forward often enough. US forces suffered badly from trench foot; other armies much less so. Trench foot is largely preventable. French and British troops had learnt how to prevent it in the Great War. It is not good enough to blame poor-quality issue socks. Poor socks reflect an army that hadn't learnt that lesson. These are not reflections on poor soldiers, nor a poor army, They reflect an army had not yet learnt certain lessons.

The 4th Indian Division fought in the 2nd and 3rd Battles of Cassino. The 4th / 6th Battalion of the Rajput Regiment lost perhaps 200 casualties in two days; 'the battalion was never the same again'. Other battalions lost about 100; in one case 149 including almost all its officers. Overall this was apparently a 'grievous blow to what had been an elite division.'

We should not take remarks like that at face value.

The French corps commander, General Alphonse Juin, executed a number of his North African colonial soldiers for raping Italian women.

After Cassino and Anzio, western attention shifted to Normandy. Montgomery's hand-written one-page concept for the landing has its last word in capitals, underlined three times: SIMPLICITY. Yet the landing plan for each of the seven American assault battalions on Omaha beach was different. One very experienced amphibious commander has described the plan as 'the work of a drunken spider' and referred to 'the seductive appeal of complexity'. The landing forces on Omaha became hopelessly intermingled. Amphibious ('DD') tanks were poorly handled. There were no armoured engineer tanks: obstacles had to be cleared by hand, on foot, under fire. Boat handling and seamanship was poor. Of the seven or eight main reasons for the high casualties on Omaha, perhaps two were beyond the US Army's gift.

Casualties were light elsewhere, but deserve analysis. 79 AED lost 379 engineer tanks on Gold, Sword and Juno beaches on D-Day. 452 crewmen were killed: roughly the same as all infantry killed on those beaches. Comparison with Omaha beach suggests that a few hundred armoured engineer casualties saved thousands of infantry casualties.

The early fighting north of Caen and in the hedgerows further west was bitter. The hedgerows were described as 'the graduate school of the US Infantry'. German machineguns were highly effective and their mortars a constant hazard. Almost every attack, British and American, needed tanks. Artillery alone rarely got the infantry onto the objective. British doctrine had stressed that 'it is the platoon commander's duty to lead the assault.' That had to be modified. Battalions could simply not afford the losses. Forty years later, infantry subalterns were told that their place in the assault was 'between and slightly behind the assault sections'. It didn't stop them getting Military Crosses. It did stop them dying in such large numbers.

The Goodwood and Cobra battles deserve comparison. By late July 1944 seven, and elements of an eighth, panzer divisions were facing the British (the rest of the eighth was facing the Americans). It may have been the highest concentration of panzer divisions on one sector ever. Heavy bombers were used at both Goodwood and Cobra. At Goodwood, south east of Caen, a railway line marked the end of the bomb line and, effectively, the limit of artillery range. It is normally forgotten that the attacking divisions completely overran the front-line (Luftwaffe Field) division: Arras, 1917 yet again. Three panzer divisions were deployed behind it. In broad terms the British armoured divisions did not get beyond the railway line on the first day. They had not yet learnt how to conduct all-arms tactics on the move.

After Cobra it took six days of attacking before the US armoured divisions broke out. They did break out. British armoured divisions never did. On several occasions in Normandy, and later, British reconnaissance units found undefended bridges in the enemy's rear. However their parent formations simply did not exploit the opportunity in time. German formations were adept at establishing ad-hoc defensive screens in depth, and strengthening them before the following morning. Allied forces were not good at realising that there was little, and sometimes nothing, in front of them. The British were the more pedestrian.

Throughout the 10 weeks of the Normandy campaign, the largest tank battle involved 28 tanks on both sides. Lots of tanks were needed. Large armoured forces were not. What was needed were integrated all-arms groups that fought well together. They emerged, as the campaign progressed.

German antitank units were generally very well handled. That was a major factor in the Germans' ability to assemble defensive screens quickly. British antitank units worked well once a deliberate defensive position had been established; less well before that. Conversely American tank destroyer units were highly variable. Some were outstanding. Many were mediocre or poor. The problem seems to have been their doctrine. Some COs adapted their tactics. They exploited terrain and mobility in order to engage the enemy repeatedly from flanking positions. It could be very effective. It was not common.

On 13 June the veteran British 7th Armoured Division was mauled by a few Tigers of 101st SS Heavy Panzer Battalion at Villers Bocage. The 17pdr antitank guns of the divisional antitank battalion were quite capable of destroying Tigers. Infantry battalion 6 pdrs could do as well, if used properly. Villers Bocage is a clear example of poor unit and formation tactics. The divisional reconnaissance battalion failed to give warning. The antitank battalion failed to protect the armoured units. The leading tank and infantry units were caught halted in column of route. Caution characterised British handling of armour for a long time afterwards. Villers Bocage became an SS propaganda victory. The Anglo-Saxon description should be rather more vulgar.

Allied artillery improved as the campaign progressed. The British had formed and employed Army Groups, Royal Artillery from Alamein onwards. They were large brigades of medium and heavy artillery which could be switched to support corps as required. They provided not only more medium and heavy guns but also more flexible control of indirect fire. The record appears to have been a Canadian call for fire on an impromptu (unregistered) target which was answered by just over 1,000 guns within 33 minutes. A hundred guns in 12 minutes was fairly typical. In November 1944 185 tons of artillery ammunition was fired in 3 ½ hours to support a British battalion attack on the village of Bauchem in the Netherlands. Of the 150 or so defenders, 10-15% were killed or wounded. All of them were captured. The attackers suffered three casualties. The village was taken.

79 AED had no flamethrower tanks on D-Day. Ten weeks later it had a brigade of them. Every infantry battalion soon had tracked, carrier-mounted flamethrowers and some manpack equipments. British forces developed highly successful combined tank, infantry and flamethrower attack tactics. Typically, relatively few Germans were killed. 30 times as many surrendered. Curiously, British accounts (and history books) rarely mention the subject.

As the campaign developed, independent American Armored Cavalry Groups (small brigades) were brought into the line. They simply didn't work as intended. The Germans had effectively no corps or army reconnaissance forces. They operated entirely effectively without them.

At Cassino there had been two good examples of British infantry battalions infiltrating in the advance and attack, seizing objectives surreptitiously and for little loss. Some junior officers in Normandy stumbled onto the tactic. There are few good examples of it being done deliberately. One was Canadian. Conversely the Germans were quite good at it. It didn't generally succeed against a well-integrated defensive position.

Allied defensive tactics were good. There were virtually no instances of German attacks penetrating beyond British forward companies. German attacks rarely prompted Allied divisional-level, let alone corps-level, counterattacks. That was partly due to massive artillery fire support, but also to good minor unit tactics. Arcs of fire *were* interlocked. Antitank weapons *did* cover likely tank approaches. Mortars and artillery were available when needed. Reserves, with tanks, were on hand. Allied defences were generally more deeply echeloned than German: effective, but less efficient (more troops were required for a given frontage).

German units were generally tactically more effective than Allied units. Some were poor. As the campaign progressed German quality tended to drop. British infantry fighting a German parachute regiment in December were surprised to find that the Germans surrendered fairly quickly. They then discovered that the regiment had only been formed in September.

Normandy was, essentially, a joint land-air campaign. The air component could have significant effect. The German armoured counterattack at Mortain on 7 August included much of the remaining panzer forces. Ordered to move in daylight, it was mauled by rocket-firing fighter bombers. Few tanks were destroyed. Whole columns, however, were wrecked. The counterattack ground to a halt. The use of heavy bombers was generally less successful.

Training and experience matter. The British 3rd Division had practiced amphibious landings about a dozen times, some of them in the ships it would use on D-Day. Its landing plan was simple. Its landing went very well. Most British divisions had not fought since 1940, but had been training for four years or more. By the end of the campaign, most had fought for several weeks. So had many American divisions. One British brigade conducted an assault river crossing on each of three successive nights. One engineer company built five bridges, on five different rivers, in seven days. Given so much experience, units and formations became quite proficient. Only two more British divisions were sent to north west Europe thereafter. One of them came from Italy. Allied divisions that had fought through Normandy generally went on to fight well. American divisions which came ashore after Normandy could be less good.

Casualty rates in Normandy, per division per day, were about as high as on the Somme. However, there were fewer divisions, fewer days, and no First of July. Tactically Normandy was a 'school of hard knocks', but it stood the armies in good stead.

There were atrocities. The 12th SS Panzer Reconnaissance Battalion executed 66 Canadian and two British PW in the Chateau d'Audrieu in early June. That provoked a deep bitterness amongst Canadian soldiers. It has entered the mythology. Many SS soldiers were tough and well trained. Some were vicious. They were not supermen. Waffen SS units could be, and were, beaten. The mythology is partly due to German propaganda and partly due to western accounts, not all of which are reliable.

One in 8.01 soldiers in the German Army died in the war. Of those sent abroad, the figure for the British Army was one in 14.85. For the US Army it was one in 29.85. Oddly, nearly the same number of American soldiers died as did British. The figures were 177,800 British and 165,800 American, rising to 185,800 when US Marines are included.

Roughly one third of those Germans died in the first 53 months of the war, one third in the next ten months (including Operations Bagration and Overlord), and one third in the last five. That tells us that the Red Army did not significantly damage the Wehrmacht before Operation Bagration. Neither did the western Allies before Normandy.

British and American infantry casualties in north west Europe show a persistent pattern: 100-120% casualties per battalion over the campaign, representing 65-70% of all army casualties. Typically that would mean about 20-25% of the original battalion still present at the end of the war. A study of a British infantry company of 120 all ranks shows 16 still with the colours, but not necessarily the company, at the end. Infantry officers were twice as likely to die as their soldiers. In British tank battalions about 30% of all ranks became casualties. 100-120% of the tanks were damaged by enemy action. About 90% of the officers were killed or wounded.

Medical statistics show a remarkably consistent ratio of about three wounded to one killed in action. In Europe and North Africa one British or American soldier was admitted to hospital as a psychiatric case per 2.4 – 2.7 wounded; except for the British Army in north west Europe. There, the rate was less than half that. Personal accounts ascribe the reasons to what were, essentially, the lessons of the Great War. Psychiatric casualty rates for western armies in the Far East were generally much higher.

RAF Bomber Command medical statistics show a different pattern. Officer aircrew hospitalization rates for all medical (as opposed to surgical) conditions mirror the rate of wounding quite closely. Wounding almost invariably happened whilst flying, so wounding rates can be taken to be a good measure of combat activity. The pattern for NCO aircrew is different. Respiratory tract and, to some extent, alimentary tract hospitalizations do not mirror the rate of wounding. They grew rapidly after 1940. Station-level evidence suggests that respiratory disorders were being used as a cover for apparent exhaustion. If that is so, why were officers not so prone to exhaustion? They flew the same missions in the same aircraft.

Another piece of evidence comes from disciplinary evidence. RAF senior officers decried the practice of unit and station commanders simply giving aircrew time off when they were not flying; rather than training, organised sport and so on. The evidence suggests large numbers of undertrained, under-employed NCOs losing their motivation from 1941 onwards and increasingly reporting sick. It is related to a wider debate about 'lack of moral fibre' in aircrew. It suggests weak leadership.

Some army unit and formation commanders failed, generally the first time they fought. Others rose very rapidly and successfully through the ranks. Possibly a larger number rose rapidly and then failed. A review of British armoured division commanders suggests that the failures tended to come from socially selective regiments: Guards, cavalry and rifle regiments.

There has been considerable, and often sensational, discussion of poor morale in various forces at various times. In Autumn 1944 Eisenhower reported to Marshall that there were about 100,000 American 'stragglers' absent from their units in north west Europe. The important question, however, is brutally simple. Did such 'poor morale' result in units being below strength; combat refusal; desertion; or unauthorised surrender? If not, the issue is perhaps historically or sociologically interesting. Tactically it is relatively unimportant.

Dummy tanks and aircraft were commonly deployed as decoys. The Luftwaffe simulated burning cities to decoy RAF night bombers. The RAF and the Kriegsmarine had been intercepting tactical radio traffic since the mid-1930s. British naval units monitored enemy radio communications to giver early warning of air raids. By the middle of the war they could detect large raids, using radar, out to about 60 nautical miles. Radio intercept was generally better than the opposition's COMSEC. Communications discipline was quite poor in many armed forces. In the Western Desert, the officers of 4th Indian Infantry Division were confident that Rommel's SIGINT service could not analyse radio traffic in Urdu. They were right. However, the ability to identify and locate that one division quickly and repeatedly, and place it in the order of battle, was a gift to the Germans. Similarly the Japanese Army did not believe that US forces could read Japanese writing. They were wrong. The Japanese were careless about document security, which was a considerable advantage to the Americans.

Failures could have serious consequences. The British aircraft carrier HMS *Glorious* was sunk off Norway in 1940 due to a SIGINT failure. It was not a failure of detection, interception, nor analysis; but of dissemination. *Glorious* was not told that enemy warships were known to be in the area. At roughly the same time 'Ultra' failed for the critical first ten days of the French campaign.

Successes were also valuable. SIGINT allowed RN planners to predict which deep water passages would be used during the 'channel dash' of 1942. The channels were quickly mined. Both *Scharnhorst* and *Gneisenau* were damaged as a result. On 17 May 1944 the German 1st Parachute Division declined to withdraw from Cassino. It had to be ordered to do so, by radio, by Kesselring. The Poles intercepted the order.

At about 9.30am the following morning a Polish patrol entered the abandoned Abbey from the ridge behind. A hastily-assembled red and white pennant was raised at about 9.50am. A bugler played the medieval '*Hejnal Mariacki*' ('St Mary's Dawn'). The battle was over.

In a sense, not much changed between 1939 and 1945. Many of the Allied warships fought throughout the war. Messerschmitt Me 109s and Spitfires flew both at the beginning and at the end. Panzer IV tanks, 25pdr field guns and Bren guns equipped their armies throughout the war. Most British and German soldiers wore the same uniforms and helmets throughout. Tactics were generally the same in many cases.

The main change to tactics was, effectively, that they were much better done. By 1945 western armies integrated their tactics down to platoon level for tanks and infantry; to company level for mortars, artillery and engineers; and brigade or perhaps battalion level for air support. They were, typically, less likely to attack frontally. They used indirect fire support better. Units and formations could (and did) plan and execute quite sophisticated operations, such as night assault river crossings, in a few hours. British infantry platoons were expected to be attacking within five minutes of the enemy being located. Battalions were expected to be 100% successful in an attack if given four hour's notice. Similar considerations applied to naval and air forces. Integration went up as well as down. Tactical air forces were integrated right up to theatre level. The USMC deployed integrated amphibious *corps* in the Pacific.

The weapons and platforms had actually changed significantly. Spitfires and Me 109s were no longer 'state of the art'. Many aircraft now carried electromechanical or electronic equipment: radars, gunsights, bombsights, sensors, jammers, receivers and radios. Ships had started to bristle with antennae: communicating, navigating, detecting, sensing, directing, jamming. Some of the smallest landing craft had navigation radar. Even the humble antiaircraft shell could now be radar-fused. Much of this was secret, not discussed openly, and was neither obvious nor remarked upon.

Tanks had roughly doubled in weight, from typically 15-20 tons to 30-45. Tank guns' calibres were generally 75mm or larger, double the 37 or 40mm of 1939. They could penetrate armour about six times thicker. Aircraft were not much faster, but bomb loads for heavy bombers had more than tripled.

Some weapons and equipment had not changed. As in the Great War, the principal field guns had not. But, writ large, there had been considerable development. It was not so much in look, or name, as in performance. Similarly with tactics. In 1939, or 1941 most armed forces had a broad idea of what to do. Some were much better than others at actually doing it. By 1945, they had all become better at 'actually doing it'. What the Red Army was 'actually doing' was still quite crude. It had, however, become good at doing simple things well, quite quickly, and taking huge casualties in the process. It was still doing so when it captured Berlin.

In six years of warfare there had been considerable tactical adaptation, evolution and development. There was also much continuity from the Great War. British Army attack tactics slowly adapted from being simultaneous (leading units advancing straight to their final objective, then consolidating) to sequential (clearing each objective in turn). The change was gradual, not explicit, possibly not well considered, and was never likely to achieve a breakthrough. German defences were more elastic in front line units, and far more flexible with reserves. British tactics were unspectacular but rarely resulted in high losses. American tactics were more flamboyant at the formation level; less good at the minor unit level. Allied air-land tactics were far more effective than German by 1944. That was in large part due to the destruction of the Luftwaffe day fighter force by US air forces during Overlord. From June 1944 German Army formations could not safely move in daylight: a considerable constraint.

Navies had been well aware of the threat from aircraft. The Royal Navy had started to order dedicated antiaircraft cruisers in 1937, largely for convoy and carrier escort.

The antiaircraft armament of virtually all classes of warships increased considerably through the war. Escort carriers were built in large numbers, largely to provide fleet and convoy air defence. It was all symptomatic of the continuing integration of air and naval forces, and of tactics at sea.

9

The New World Order

Much of the course of post-war history resulted from the events and outcome of the Second World War. That stood on previously unfinished business, and also produced some of its own. This chapter considers the period from 1945 to 1975, but overlaps with Chapter 10 in some areas.

The three most important developments of the period were the beginnings of the Cold War, the creation of functioning international organisations (such as the UN, NATO and the Warsaw Pact), and decolonisation. They were, inevitably, interlinked.

The Second World War probably resulted in more tanks, aircraft or warships built than in all subsequent conflicts combined. Similarly for numbers of wartime flying sorties. It also resulted in vast amounts of operational experience and huge numbers of veterans. Demobilising servicemen, and settling others in the right places (such as American, British and Canadians in Germany), was sometimes problematic. Many countries were short of money. Britain finally paid off its wartime debt to America on 31 December 2006 with a payment of $83m (£45.5m).

Jet aircraft quickly replaced older models. American soldiers had worked out how to weld (rather than rivet) aluminium in 1944. That revolutionised aircraft design, as did advances in casting. British Spitfires were replaced by jet-engined Meteors from 1946. The B29, produced at such cost, was redundant by the end of the Korea War in 1953. It was simply too vulnerable to Russian MiGs. The first transistor was developed in 1947, leading to major developments in electronics. By the mid-1970s the supersonic jet aircraft, packed with advanced solid-state electronics, had come of age.

The most obvious characteristic of the Cold War was the threat of the use of nuclear weapons. Other than the use of atomic bombs to end the Second World War, nuclear warfighting has never happened. All the analysis, research, development, discussion and hype remains untested. There is no evidence as to how, or even if, nuclear warfighting works. There is considerable evidence as to how the weapons work.

Free-fall atomic bombs were available from 1945; nuclear bombs from 1952. Battlefield nuclear rockets were deployed from 1954. They were soon followed by nuclear artillery shells. Inter-Continental Ballistic Missiles (ICBMs), Submarine-Launched

Ballistic Missiles (SLBMs) and short-ranged air-launched (nuclear) cruise missiles followed in the early 1960s.

'Strategic' refers to the conduct of wars. The conduct of a nuclear missile or bomb attack is a tactical issue. A plan to conduct of series of such attacks would be an operational issue. Labelling nuclear weapons as 'strategic' or 'sub-strategic' is potentially misleading, as discussed below.

Similarly, deterrence which aims to prevent wars is strategic. Deterrence aimed at preventing a given campaign is operational. Deterring the use of particular weapons is tactical. It is entirely accurate to talk of 'nuclear deterrence'. That is not necessarily the same as 'strategic deterrence'.

Strategic nuclear questions include decisions as to which nuclear campaigns or major operations to conduct; and decisions relating to investment in research, development and procurement of nuclear weapons and delivery systems. These became major national and international issues. They include the sharing of nuclear know-how, exporting such weapons, and basing them overseas.

The stakes were high. The Soviet Union had recently suffered well over 25 million deaths in order to win a war. It was reasonable to believe that deterring it from fighting another war might require it to consider losing, say, 30 million people in the process. Governments and their armed forces were obliged to consider what 'winning' a nuclear war meant. It was not irrational. Presumably it meant more than simply 'not losing'.

The costs were also high. Very few nations (the USA, USSR, France, Britain and China) had a nuclear warfighting capability. They were also the permanent members of the UN Security Council. A few other nations had a capability to worry or threaten their neighbours with nuclear weapons.

A huge amount of thought was given to the conduct of long-range nuclear exchanges. In the absence of empirical evidence, such thinking remains largely rationalistic and theoretical. As with long-range bombing during the Second World War, it is inaccurate to call it 'strategic nuclear exchange'. It would have been long-range nuclear bombardment.

Initially it focussed on devastating cities. British readers will be broadly familiar with the development of the V-Bomber force (employing Vulcan, Victor and Valiant aircraft) in the 1950s. They may not know of the development of the American prototype Mach 3 XB70 Valkyrie, cancelled in 1962. Early plans for the British V-Bomber force of the late 1950s involved sending just one raid by 100 bombers, at high level and high subsonic speed, to 100 cities in the Soviet Union. Each bomber had one free-fall nuclear bomb. 100 aircraft, 100 bombs, 100 cities. After the aircraft took off there was *one* 'go/no go' confirmation signal. There was *no* 'recall', by design. American and, presumably, Soviet plans were similar. It would be Armageddon.

Developments in Surface-to-Air Missiles (SAMs) in the early 1960s required new weapons (such as the Hound Dog and Blue Steel stand-off missiles), tactics (such as low-level attack) and, eventually, entirely new operational approaches (principally the use of ICBMs and SLBMs). France and Britain chose an entirely submarine-based deterrent. That required both nuclear ballistic missile submarines ('SSBNs') and nuclear-powered 'attack' submarines ('SSNs') to defend them against other submarines.

Operational plans were developed to include (nuclear) attacks on air bases, air defence sites, missile silos, submarine bases and command centres. That might be intended to deny the enemy the use of nuclear weapons, in a pre-emptive attack. It might also be to enhance the chances of success of the main attack. Sophisticated theories of counter-value (bombing cities) or counter-force (attacking enemy nuclear warfighting installations) approaches, game theory, and the psychology of deterrence were developed

Mobile nuclear ballistic missiles gave land forces the option of theatre-level nuclear bombardment as part of joint air-land campaigns. One option, for example, might have been to attack the rail and road crossings of the major rivers in western Soviet Union, in order to hinder the deployment of operational reserves to the Central Front.

The execution of an attack by nuclear-armed bombers, ICBMs or SLBMs would be a tactical issue. So would be the patrols of SSBNs; their defence; detecting them; or attacking them. It took some time for the Soviet Navy to realise that their surveillance 'trawlers', towing long antisubmarine sensor arrays, were quite conspicuous. Unlike real trawlers, they were rarely surrounded by seagulls. The 'diesel sniffer' (ie, exhaust sensor) on a RAF maritime patrol aircraft followed a trace upwind for well over 100 nautical miles. It eventually found not a Soviet diesel-electric attack boat, but a peat fire in a Scottish croft.

Putting a nuclear warhead on a battlefield rocket was not difficult. Making the rocket accurate was. Finding a worthwhile target before it had moved, at a worthwhile range, could also be hard. The 'Corporal' system entered US and then British service with a maximum range of about 130km. Hitting an airfield in East Germany might have been be a reasonable target.

Eight-inch (203mm), seven-inch (175mm) and eventually six-inch (155mm) nuclear artillery shells might have significantly changed warfighting. The M107 175mm gun was very accurate and had a range of about 30km. At that range an enemy divisional or Army (corps) HQ might be a useful target. The M109 155mm howitzer had about half the range, but was fielded in large numbers. At El Alamein it had taken a brigade of medium guns to neutralise each enemy battery. That could now be done with one round.

The USSR had similar weapons. Typical counters to enemy nuclear weapons included dispersion, concealment, and digging in everything (men, tanks, trucks, HQs, airbases, logistic stocks) as far as time and resources allowed. Concealing and dispersing forces made them harder to find, but harder to operate and potentially easier to infiltrate around. Naturally, Warsaw Pact forces developed similar measures to protect their own forces.

Weapons and tactics developed continually. The Corporal's eventual successor, 'Lance', had broadly the same range but was much more mobile, faster into and out of action, and far more accurate. So were its Soviet equivalents. The use of such weapons was practiced many times, but never carried out in a real war. That was the virtual war that didn't happen, whilst the real wars of the period were being fought.

Korea and Vietnam were both, effectively, former colonial territories. Korea had been occupied by Japan. At the end of the Second World War it was divided into American and Soviet zones. Vietnam was one part of French Indo-China (the others were Laos and Cambodia). It had been occupied by the Japanese, liberated itself, and was then re-occupied by the French. The fact that both the Korean and (Second) Vietnam Wars were largely fought by the United States clouds their origins as former colonial territories.

In China the Kuomintang had been fatally weakened by the Japanese. The third Chinese Revolutionary War of 1945-9 was won by Mao's Chinese Communist Army; or perhaps lost by the Kuomintang. In the Liaoshen campaign of 1948 it lost 470,000 men. Of those, 109,000 deserted and 306,000 were taken prisoner. Just as in the Soviet Union in the 1920s and 30s, the Chinese Communists then murdered millions of their subjects and saw many millions more starve to death in the 1950s and 60s.

South Korea had a moderately effective army of 200,000 men, trained as border guards and for counter-insurgency. By the summer of 1950 it had reduced communist insurgents in the south from 5,000 to about 1,000. The USSR had appointed Kim Il-sung to lead the (north) Korean Communist Party in 1945. In late 1949 Mao, Kim and Stalin had held extensive talks in Moscow. The Chinese Army returned 50-70,000 Korean soldiers, who had been fighting the Kuomintang, to North Korea. The North Korean People's Army reached a strength of ten infantry and one tank divisions, reasonably well-equipped with Russian (and some former Japanese) equipment.

The initial North Korean attack in June 1950 decimated the South Korean army. 85% of the country was overrun within a month. American air forces slowed the advance, creating time for the formation of a perimeter around the southern city of Pusan. MacArthur planned and executed an inspired amphibious counterattack at Inchon which threatened to cut the North Korean Army off. American-led UN forces exploited rapidly north towards the Chinese border (see Figure 9-1).

China then intervened. An initial force of about 150,000 Chinese soldiers crossed the Yalu River southwards in November. Much of their air support was Soviet. After considerable fighting the front line stabilised roughly on the 39th Parallel in July 1951. There was more fighting but, in essence, the war came to an end in 1953.

Air forces had initially been critical to holding back the North Korean Army and then the Chinese Army. However they soon switched to attacking targets in northern Korea. By the end of the war practically every town in the north had been severely damaged. US air forces dropped 503,000 tons of bombs in the Pacific during the Second World War. They dropped 653,000 tons in Korea. That included 32,000 tons of Napalm, twice as much as in 1944-5. The USAF, which had become independent in 1947, was justifying its existence.

36,574 American servicemen died in Korea: about 70% more than in the Battle of the Bulge. Over 1100 British, 500 Canadians and 300 Australians also died there, as did servicemen from several other nations. Estimates of Korean and Chinese dead are unreliable but certainly number hundreds of thousands.

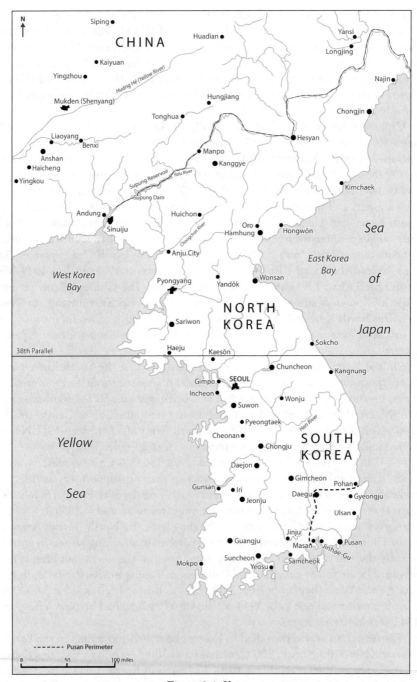

Figure 9-1 Korea.

After nine years of fighting, several governments and several commanders-in-chief, the French General Henri Navarre developed an operational plan to bring the North Vietnamese Army (NVA) to battle in northern Vietnam in 1954. The tactical plan was to drop a division of paratroops, and then build an airfield, at Dien Bien Phu in northern Vietnam. That would, effectively, challenge the NVA to attack. Every one of Navarre's immediate subordinates objected to the plan. After five months of preparation and seven weeks' fighting, the French force at Dien Bien Phu surrendered. Tactically, they had been beaten. Operationally, the Navarre plan did not fix the NVA for destruction by the French. It fixed the French for destruction by the NVA. Strategically, the French could no longer defend northern Vietnam, despite massive American financial support. Vietnam was divided along the 17th Parallel.

By the early 1960s communist irregulars were operating in south Vietnam in large numbers. The Strategic Hamlet Program, initiated in 1963, was inspired by similar policies in Malaya and Kenya. It was very poorly done and abandoned in late 1963. It had alienated much of the rural south Vietnamese population. In a sense, American forces were committed to reinforce failure. To that extent, they were set up to fail.

In 1964 the Gulf of Tonkin incident brought America into the war. It is not clear who misinformed and manipulated who in President Lyndon Johnson's administration over the affair. It is clear that a massive American troop build-up got under way. Force levels increased from about 16,000 men to 549,000 by 1969.

America's war aims were limited to defending South Vietnam. Could America have done that? Of course it could. It did not. It failed. Johnson tacitly admitted that, when he ordered a halt to the bombing and declined to run for re-election in 1968. His successor, President Richard Nixon, withdrew American forces. South Vietnam was overrun in 1975. However, at much the same time, Nixon managed to engage with Communist China for the first time, and to persuade the USSR to sign the first Strategic Arms Limitation Treaty. It might reasonably be said that Nixon accepted one strategic failure in the process of achieving two major strategic successes. The cost to America was about 58,000 dead.

That analysis overlooks the part played by the North Vietnamese Communists. Well aware that they could not match American forces in battle, they developed a long-term delaying strategy linked to an information campaign in America and elsewhere. The war dragged on. Dramatic images were brought into American homes on TV, almost live, for the first time. The White House was at times inclined to believe the TV more than its armed forces' reports. American public opinion was sharply divided. Support for involvement in Vietnam fell. Put simply, North Vietnamese strategy was successful.

The US operational approach was based on attrition. If you try to boil a frog in a pan of water, the frog will sometimes stay in the water long after it should have jumped out. The American gradualist approach of psychological and strategic persuasion, linked to bombing, tried to 'boil the frog' through attrition. America wanted the frog to jump out of the pan; that is, for North Vietnam to quit the south. Unfortunately there was nothing stopping the North Vietnamese from turning the heat down; that is, staying in the south but choosing to avoid contact when they wished to. Operational approaches based on attrition do not work unless the enemy is forced to accept unsustainable losses. That did not happen in Vietnam.

It has been claimed that America won every battle in Vietnam. That might be true, but it was irrelevant. There was a failure of operational planning. America was, largely, fighting battles that would not contribute to strategic success.

Initially the most common American low-level tactic was to 'search and destroy'. At first that meant searching for, and then destroying, the enemy. It developed into searching villages for the enemy and then destroying the village. In defence, American trenches were too shallow, too wide, poorly revetted, and lacked traverses. In the advance and attack fieldcraft (camouflage and concealment) and minor unit tactics were poor. Skill at arms was patchy. That will not beat an experienced light infantry force on ground of its own choosing. According to American statistics, the enemy was attacked and destroyed in 9% of infantry engagements. So, in 91% of cases, it was not. Such statistics will not result in effective attrition. So, what did 'winning every battle' actually mean?

In 1968, with a new theatre commander, tactics changed and the emphaisis switched to building up the South Vietnamese armed forces. Clearly the US armed forces cannot be blamed for the fact that South Vietnam was subsequently overrun. However, between poor strategy, poor campaign planning and poor tactics, America failed to win a war which it should have been able to win.

The air campaign was initially a controlled escalation which soon ran out of targets. Thereafter several thousand armed reconnaissance (that is, airborne 'search and destroy') sorties were conducted every month. 864,000 tons of bombs were dropped, including 388,000 tons of Napalm. 20 *million* gallons of defoliants were sprayed, much of it for crop destruction (rather than deforestation). More than 20% of the crop-growing area of Vietnam was sprayed every year for nine years. In December 1972 about half of all the B52 bombers in the USAF were used to bomb Hanoi and 'force' North Vietnam to sign an agreement which it had agreed to sign several months before. The North Vietnamese exercised patience, and overran South Vietnam three years later.

The US Navy ended the Second World War with dozens of aircraft carriers. Many were unsuitable for jets. A fleet of about a dozen large, jet-capable carriers was developed. Carrier aviation played a major role in both Korea and Vietnam. Both were peninsulas and the US Navy had control of the sea. The US Navy and the Royal Navy operated carriers world-wide in a number of conflicts. Converted carriers were very useful for operating amphibious forces, increasingly by helicopter. In the early 1960s the Royal Navy operated about a dozen carriers of various types, but they were a wasting asset. HMS Hermes, for example, was laid down in 1944; commissioned in 1959, and was in and out of service until 1987. It was the last carrier still in service when the smaller '*Invincible*' class of three ships joined the fleet, just in time for the Falklands conflict in 1982.

The Korean and then Vietnam Wars took place against a backdrop of decolonisation. By signing the United Nations Charter, all colonial and mandated powers had endorsed the principle of self-determination. They *were* going to decolonise. Some did not quite realise what that implied. Others knew what it meant but deliberately underplayed it presentationally. Many writers overlook it. America was seen by some as just another colonial power. Its involvement in post-war France, and in Egypt, tend to be forgotten.

It is difficult to separate wars of decolonisation from the resulting secondary struggles. Most of the former were insurgencies. Some of the latter were major conventional wars. Not all wars were related to decolonization, but many were. See Figure 9-2:

Former Colonial or Mandated Power	Modern Name	Year Granted Independence	Remarks
France	Vietnam	1954	a. North and South Vietnamese independence in 1954. b. South Vietnam overrun in 1975. c. Invaded by China in 1979.
	Cambodia	1954	Invaded by Vietnam in 1978.
	Laos	1953	Civil war related to Vietnam 1953-75 (see above).
	Algeria	1962	Resulted in the Algiers Putsch of 1961, then independence in 1962.
Japan	Korea	(1945)	Resulted in the Korean War.
Netherlands	Indonesia	1949	Insurgency 1945-9. See Timor-Leste.
Portugal	Angola	1975	Angolan civil war from 1975 to 1990. Cuban, South African, US and Soviet support.
	Mozambique	1975	Independence led to removal of support to Rhodesia (see below), and contributed to Zimbabwean independence.
	Guinea-Bissau	1973-4	Insurrection from 1956.
	Timor-Leste	1975 & 1999	Occupied by Indonesia in 1975. Independence from Indonesia in 1999.
(Rhodesia)	Zimbabwe	1980	Britain had refused to grant Rhodesia independence until majority rule was agreed. Subsequent black African insurgency against the white Rhodesian government.
South Africa	Namibia	1990	Independence granted once Angolan conflict resolved (see above).
United Kingdom	Aden	1968	Subversion and then insurgency from 1956.

Former Colonial or Mandated Power	Modern Name	Year Granted Independence	Remarks
United Kingdom	Cyprus	1960	a. Insurgency by EOKA from 1955. b. Continued inter-factional conflict until 1974.
	India, Pakistan and Bangladesh	1947	Indo-Pakistani wars in 1965, 1971 and 1999. See also Sri Lanka.
	Egypt	1952	Then Arab-Israeli wars (see Israel).
	Israel	1948	Arab-Israeli wars 1948, 1956, 1967, 1973, 1982 (and conflict continues).
	Kenya	1963	Mau Mau insurgency from 1952 to 1960.
	Malaya	1957	a. Communist insurgency from 1947. b. Further separation of North Borneo, Brunei and Singapore in 1963.
	Northern Ireland	(1922)	Republican insurgency from 1969 to 1976. Then terrorist campaign to 2006.
	Sri Lanka	1947	Subsequent Tamil insurgency (from 1983).

Figure 9-2 Selected Conflicts Arising from Decolonisation

The legislation to grant independence to India (hence Pakistan, Burma, Sri Lanka and Bangladesh) had been in place since 1935. Indigenous politics and the Second World War prevented independence being granted until 1947 and shaped the resulting conflicts. A draft constitution for Cyprus, which would create a federal solution between Greek- and Turkish-speaking Cypriots, was not adopted. The actual settlement led to inter-factional violence and renewed intervention a few years later.

Writers tend to forget that Britain's strategic end-state for Malaya was independence. Similarly for Aden, Cyprus and Kenya. So talk of 'victory' for the indigenous factions is meaningless. In each case Britain's intention was to leave; but to leave in place a regime which was pro-Western and (if possible) pro-British. The issues, however, were never clear-cut.

It is not obvious how France viewed the strategic end-state for Algeria in the 1950s. Algeria was legally part of France. It had a large white settler population; but so had the British dominions, where that issue had been resolved 50 years earlier. French strategy over Algeria, like that of all other colonial powers, has to be seen as part of its wider post-war strategic situation. That cannot be separated from domestic political issues in the home country.

Jomo Kenyatta achieved independence for Kenya after the Mau Mau insurgency had been defeated. He was not a member of the Mau Mau. Was Mau Mau a nationalist insurgency, or an old-fashioned tribal uprising? Britain could not reasonably have granted independence until the uprising was defeated. It not at all clear whether the Mau Mau campaign contributed to independence at all.

More broadly, did Communism inspire, support, or merely fund indigenous nationalist movements? In many ways, Communism was useful. To the insurgents it could be a source of support. To the colonial power it could be a useful public distraction.

The colonial powers owned the infrastructure: colonial political, social and economic institutions were generally in place, to a greater or lesser extent. In all colonies, counterinsurgency operated around the functioning of the civil government. The key question was how well the two aspects were integrated. British colonies had had police Special Branches, tasked to prevent subversion against the colonial authorities, since the 1920s.

Aden was an interesting case. The workforce in its sole urban area was heavily unionised. The rural areas were tribal or perhaps medieval. Egyptian agents organised and supported unrest in both areas from 1956. They murdered locally-recruited Special Branch officers and attacked their British colleagues. Britain was slow to recognise the threat, and only created a unified intelligence structure in 1965. In 1966 the British Government declared that independence would be granted in 1968, and effectively reneged on previous undertakings. Indigenous politicians were, effectively, undermined. They withdrew support for the colonial authorities. Law and order began to break down. British armed forces protected the expatriate community and then withdrew as ordered. It was not a proud moment for Britain, but scarcely a victory for the insurgents. The mutiny by RAF Police over working hours at Khormaksar, in 1967, was nothing to be proud of. It was, however, not on the same scale as the 1946 mutiny by 50,000 RAF airmen across 60 bases in India (who had protested over what they saw as the slow pace of demobilisation).

Egyptian nationalists had overthrown King Farouk in 1952, leaving the British in a difficult situation. British advisers were ejected in 1954, but British troops remained in the Suez Canal Zone. The nationalists were possibly supported by the CIA. US policy in the region had often been pro-Egyptian. One US ambassador was described as malevolently anti-British. Eisenhower's support to Egypt was a significant issue in the Suez crisis of 1956 (described below). That changed after Johnson's election in 1964, opening the way for Soviet intervention and then the Six-Day War.

Well-trained and well-led armies should have had no difficulty going into towns, cities or the hinterland and capturing or neutralising insurgents. That was not particularly difficult. Knowing who, and where, the insurgents were was hugely difficult. Finding that out risked alienating peaceable and well-disposed members of the population. Good COIN tactics therefore required the generation of intelligence, restraint in the use of force, and retaining the support of the majority of the population. That called for an integrated approach. It could work well.

It did not require 'minimum use of force'. It required discrimination. France was quite capable of using punitive and repressive force from the earliest skirmishes in Algeria. Using a cruiser stationed offshore to shell villages in May 1945 was scarcely 'restraint'. Poor tactics could also include a brutal and naive approach to interrogation.

If you beat someone up, he may well tell you what you want him to tell you. That is not the same as telling you what you need to know.

There was an understandable but frequently misplaced urge to use parachute forces. Yes, they could be dropped out of aircraft fairly quickly, but what then? Helicopters made it increasingly easy to insert and extract forces and redeploy them. That does not require paratroopers. Part of a British parachute battalion was dropped near Suez, to seize and airfield that had already been bombed for five days. It was scarcely necessary. Several parachute forces came to see themselves as an elite, requiring special training, weapons and equipment which would be better shared across the force. They sometimes also tended towards ill-discipline and even mutiny due to the perception of their self-importance. The Algiers Putsch of 1961 was effectively an attempted *coup d'etat* which failed. It was not France's oldest infantry regiments that were involved in it. It was the newest (the paratroop units).

By 1975 almost all former colonies around the world had been granted independence if they wanted it. Britain had decolonised about 45 territories, most of them peacefully. Most are still members of the Commonwealth. (The United States, Israel and Ireland would be eligible to join if they wished.)

In 1975 British GDP per head was roughly twice that of 1935 in real terms. Its national debt was about half, as a proportion of GDP. Despite decolonisation and a major war, Britain was materially richer. The same is broadly true of other former colonial powers. Many other factors confuse the picture; but, financially, decolonisation was not negative. Many former colonies also benefitted financially in the long run. If they did not, it is generally hard to blame the former colonial power. The nations involved probably prefer independence to the alternative.

What did 'victory' mean? That the colonial power achieved its intended strategic outcome? That the indigenous population did? So, can victory include 'win-win' situations? It is not difficult to recognise circumstances where the colonial power clearly achieved its aims, but publicly did not make an issue of it.

From the liberation of the first concentration camps in Germany in 1945 it was inevitable that a homeland would be created for the Jews. There was no realistic alternative to Palestine. That is not to suggest that the history of the state of Israel has been straightforward; that there have not been significant problems; nor that all of the most important of those problems have been resolved.

Israel's military strategy has always been defensive. Its grand strategy has been to cultivate powerful allies, notably the United States. Mrs Golda Meir, a future prime minister, raised a staggering $48 million in a fundraising tour of America just prior to independence in 1948.

Given its small size, Israel's strategy and its campaign planning must be closely linked. The Mediterranean is visible from the crest of the Golan Heights (see Figure 9-3). Excluding the West Bank territories, Israel is only 14 km wide at its narrowest. What would be minor tactical reverses elsewhere could be strategically catastrophic for Israel. At times Israel's operational stance has been offensive (for example, to occupy part of southern Lebanon).

Figure 9-3 Israel.

Colonel Gamal Nasser became president of Egypt in June 1956. He nationalised the Suez Canal almost immediately. Later that year Britain, France and Israel collaborated to seize the Canal back. Britain and France were forced to withdraw through pressure from America and the UN. Nasser's pan-Arab ambitions then extended to exterminating Israel.

In the two years before the Six Day War of 1967, Egyptian-sponsored Palestinian Fatah irregulars carried out 122 raids against Israeli settlements. On 23 May 1967 Egypt closed the Straits of Tiran to Israeli shipping. Israel mobilised, and attacked on 5 June. The Israeli Air Force (IAF) destroyed 393 Arab aircraft on the ground, most of them on the first morning. Three Israeli armoured divisions struck into the Sinai, breaking through the Egyptian army. It began to withdraw, rapidly, within 48 hours. On the 6th, eight Israeli brigades attacked into the West Bank, driving the Jordanian Army out in two days. The 8th Israeli Armoured Brigade drove 350kms from the Sinai to the Golan. On 9 June it took part in the assault on the Golan Heights. It was joined by two other armoured brigades which had just fought in the West Bank. A ceasefire was declared on 10 June. The Israeli Defence Forces (IDF) were in possession of the West Bank, the Golan Heights and all of the Sinai.

It was a crushing defeat for the Arab armies. It was a brilliant example of high-tempo combined-arms operations. Destroying much of the Arab air forces on the ground gained air superiority. That allowed the IAF to support ground forces almost wherever required. Israeli armoured forces conducted daring, high-speed manoeuvres deep into enemy positions. That created confusion, panic, retreat and rout. Israeli infantry forces attacked fast, hard, and often at night; with similar results.

Egypt and its allies were re-trained and re-equipped by the Soviet Union. Nasser's successor, Anwar Sadat, ejected his Soviet advisors in 1972. Arab strategic and operational goals for war in October 1973 were modest. The Egyptian Army intended to seize crossings of the Canal and occupy a deep zone in the Sinai. Syria intended to seize the Golan Heights and down to the Jordan River. Both would provoke Israeli counterattacks, which would be beaten off, forcing Israel to make political and territorial concessions.

Israel was largely, but not completely, taken by surprise. Front-line troops were at high alert, but reservists were not mobilised. 40 Egyptian engineer battalions created 60 crossings of the Canal in the first 12 hours. Five Egyptian infantry divisions, followed by several armoured formations, crossed the Canal and advanced into the Sinai. Israeli armoured counterattacks were beaten off by massed antitank guided weapons (ATGW). The IAF was driven off by surface-to-air guided missiles (SAMs). The IDF went over to defence in the Sinai whilst dealing with the greater threat on the Golan.

Three Syrian mechanised divisions, three tank brigades and two armoured brigades had attacked. They were initially met by one armoured brigade and two infantry battalions. The IDF's defence was nothing but epic: one tank in the Israeli 53rd Tank Battalion destroyed 35 Syrian tanks. The Syrians did not create enough crossings of the main antitank ditch. No BMP infantry fighting vehicles penetrated beyond the forward IDF infantry strongpoints. Unsupported Syrian tank units were destroyed by Israeli counterattacks. The IDF then went over to the offensive. Iraqi and Jordanian formations were committed. The Jordanians were well led. The Iraqis were cut up badly. Both were defeated.

The subsequent Israeli counteroffensive in the Sinai broke through Egyptian defences, defeated their armoured reserves and crossed the Canal. Soviet officials showed Sadat satellite photos of IDF tanks on the west bank. The Egyptian Army hurriedly withdrew from the Sinai. In 17 days the IDF had defeated the Syrian Army and its Iraqi and Jordanian allies, recovered the Golan, and thrown the Egyptian Army back out of the Sinai.

With few exceptions, the tactics used were those of the Second World War. Israeli M48s, upgunned Shermans and Centurions had fought post-war Soviet tanks, and occasionally Jordanian Centurions. Success generally went to better gunnery, not better tanks. Little that the Israelis or Arabs did would have surprised Guderian; nor Patton, Bradley or Montgomery.

In early 1973 the commander of the IDF Northern Command had seen Syrians using ATGW in skirmishes. He began to develop countermeasures. Not least, he began to increase the provision of mortars in armoured units. It was too late. Similarly, the IAF had difficulty in countering Soviet-built SAMs at first. Within a few days Arab SAM sites were being destroyed through a combination of cluster bombs dropped from very low level, EW, anti-radiation missiles, and long-range artillery fire.

IDF successes resulted from aggression and daring; rapid decision making and high-speed manoeuvre; concentration of force; and vigorous exploitation of success. Arab generals were often competent and their soldiers brave. Their junior and middle-ranking officers, however, followed orders slavishly, misrepresented events, and lacked initiative. Israeli armoured formations were, genuinely, commanded on the move. Arab forces had to be commanded to move.

About 23,000 Israeli soldiers died in the Arab-Israeli conflicts of the 20th century. They killed about 81,000 Arab soldiers. Loss exchange ratios of about 3.5:1 were typical for those wars and battles, and about 2.5:1 in tanks. The IDF has consistently fought successfully, quickly, and at relatively low cost. The IAF has consistently shot down far more aircraft than it has lost. Over the same period at least 357,000 Arabs were killed by other Arabs. If you are an Arab, you are far more likely to be killed by an Arab than by an Israeli. Who is your enemy?

Many of the commanders of the period were veterans of the Second World War, but that was not necessarily obvious. The North Vietnamese commander, General Vo Nguyen Giap, had fought against the Japanese in Vietnam. Kim Il-sung fought the Japanese in Korea and then served in the Red Army for four years. Colonel Pierre Jeanpierre died commanding the 1st Foreign Legion Parachute Regiment in Algeria in 1958. He served in Syria early in the Second World War, then returned to France and joined the Resistance. He was captured and imprisoned in Mauthausen. After the Second World War he fought in Indochina before being captured by the Viet Minh and held for four years. His father, an infantry company commander, had died at Verdun.

Personnel issues are as much about regulations and processes as about commanders and heroes. The US Army got its call-up for Korea wrong. That resulted in too many service troops, not enough infantrymen, and key shortages in specific trades. Basic training was cut short, resulting in poorly-trained replacements. Vietnam saw other problems: officers rotated in and out too quickly, and 'shake and bake' sergeants with no experience leading soldiers in combat. Drug-taking became epidemic. About a thousand instances of throwing grenades at officers ('fragging') were recorded. For the army of a developed nation, it was ill-discipline on a huge scale. The US Army's personnel (G-1) system is run by personnel management specialists. Perhaps that is a mistake.

There was considerable continuity from the Second World War in the areas of intelligence and security. A senior Chinese liaison officer handed Giap a copy of the Navarre Plan, which led to Dien Bien Phu. Intercepts of Vietnamese military radio traffic played a part in the Gulf of Tonkin incident. The North Vietnamese moni-tored USAF radio traffic. They could predict major air raids about 80-90 minutes in advance. Israel attacked, and nearly sank, a US SIGINT ship during the Six Day War, apparently by mistake. The targets may have been different. The methods were generally similar.

Just as after the Great War, intelligence officers sought re-employment. Many former members of OSS joined the CIA after its formation in 1947. Similarly, some SOE personnel moved into MI6 and related organisations.

The Cold War was not a nice time to be involved in intelligence. The East German security service erected a guillotine in a cellar in East Berlin. Several agents were beheaded. At least one was British. The CIA ran an operation to discredit eastern European security agencies to the KGB. Several thousand men, and some women, were killed at very little cost to the West. Gritty spy novels, such as John le Carré's and Ian Fleming's, sometimes come close to the truth. When the James Bond film 'Doctor No' was shown in a cinema in Aden in 1964, a young British colonial civil servant recognised about 15 (British) intelligence officers in the audience.

By 1975 supersonic jet aircraft were the state of the art. On land, however, relatively little had changed. A new generation of tanks was being produced which were obvi-ously the linear descendants of their wartime predecessors. Guided weapons were beginning to appear. Basic night sights were becoming common. They were typically either active (rather than passive), or not very effective. A number of ships from the Second World War were still in service: hull life is a key driver for navies. Ships were upgraded at each refit and new ships entered service with ever more capable sensors and weapon systems. The last (Second World War) cruisers left Royal Navy service in 1978 and 1979. Tactics evolved to accommodate new weapons, but quite gradually. The appearance of the ATGW in 1973 started a reappraisal of tactics on land.

It would be an exaggeration to claim that all of the wars from 1945 to 1975 resulted from decolonisation, but many did. Almost all wars of decolonisation achieved the intended strategic goal for the colonial powers: independence. Many writers have not noticed, or chosen not to notice, that. Communist expansionism and opportunism was also a factor. It was not particularly successful. Few former colonies adopted communist governments.

Governments and their armed forces were quite right to consider both how to win nuclear wars and what winning meant. There was no point in planning to lose.

Airborne forces were rarely used for airborne operations, but continued to press to be used. Any parachute operation was likely to be risky. Dien Bien Phu showed the possible strategic consequences of a failed airborne operation.

Some things, however, do not change. Human nature is one of them. There is a strong parallel between Navarre in Indochina and Nivelle in the Great War. Experienced, charismatic, opinionated: it is ironic that Henri Navarre was also the name of a famous French king. Commanders may be right when they over-rule the advice of their subordinates: MacArthur was, when planning the Inchon landing. Commanders who make a habit of it risk over-reaching themselves. Nivelle and Navarre went almost immediately; MacArthur was sacked eight months later. The ancient Greeks were thoroughly familiar with Hubris (overweening pride) and Nemesis (divine vengeance).

10

99 Red Balloons

By 1975 the Cold War was almost 30 years old, but in some ways its later years are the most interesting. The total number of sovereign states worldwide had grown from about 70 in 1950 to about 160 in 1975, much of it due to decolonisation. The total grew again to over 190 by 1999. That was driven largely by the collapse of the Soviet Union (adding 14 new states) and Yugoslavia (five).

'99 Red Balloons', a 1984 German pop song by Nena, protested against the threat of nuclear war. It reached No 1 in the Charts in 14 countries (and No 2 on the US Billboard 100). Today it is easy to forget that the threat of nuclear war hung over Europe and North America for over 40 years. The two parts of Germany were, in effect, re-arranged to host the biggest land war that never happened.

It is not entirely clear why the Cold War ended. Mikhail Gorbachev was the first General Secretary of the Soviet Union since Stalin who had *not* been an apparatchik during the pre-war Purges. He was also the first since Lenin to be a university graduate. Gorbachev withdrew Soviet forces from Afghanistan. He developed a close relationship with American President Ronald Reagan. Reagan had previously increased US defence spending, introduced medium-range ballistic missiles to Europe, and overseen a more offensive posture by the US Navy (for example, in the North Atlantic). Gorbachev oversaw the demise of the Soviet Union after 1989.

The armed peace of the 1970s and 80s in Europe was not matched in the Middle East. The Iranian Revolution of 1979 led to the Iran-Iraq War of 1980-88. The Soviet intervention in Afghanistan of 1979 lasted until in 1989. It was a conflict which the Soviet Army could not understand, because it did not conform to Marxist-Leninist theory; so it was unlikely to win.

Solid-state electronics had led to reliable and affordable guided weapons, available in their thousands. The US 'TOW' ATGM entered service in 1970; the Franco-German 'Milan' in 1972, and the smaller US 'Dragon' in 1975. The US Phantom jet served in the air forces of many Western countries. Their tanks were generally armed with the British L7 105mm tank gun. Many of the their soldiers were equipped with the Belgian FN FAL rifle and the MAG machinegun[1]. Soviet equipment equipped almost all Warsaw Pact armed forces. It, or license-built copies, could be found around the world in most places where NATO equipment was not. Computers were appearing on the battlefield by the time of the Gulf War in 1991.

International military attention was initially focussed on NATO's Central Front: a war that never happened. Although the Cold War was generally a stand-off, there was significant development of concepts; especially as the US Army recovered from Vietnam. The most important development was AirLand [sic] Battle, introduced in 1982 by the US Army. It was adapted and adopted as NATO's Follow-On Forces Attack (FOFA) in 1985. AirLand Battle was, essentially, a conceptual and tactical refinement of long-range interdiction to shape the contact battle. Amongst other things it sought to improve the ratio of forces in contact by delaying, or causing attrition to, reserves and echelon forces. It was a rationalistic but reasonable conjecture about the best use of emerging weapons systems. They included the Multiple Launch Rocket System (MLRS), Apache attack helicopter and A-10 attack aircraft. Air-Land Battle introduced consideration of 'deep', 'close' and 'rear' operations. Its key enabling technologies were those of surveillance, target acquisition and reconnaissance. At the theatre level it was complemented by the introduction of medium-range ballistic missiles and enhanced-radiation nuclear weapons.

The proceedings of post-war US Army infantry and armour conferences show that it was entirely aware of the tactical lessons of the Second World War. However, it was greatly hampered by failing to develop a good scout vehicle and a workable section machinegun. It was also hampered by its affinity to 'cavalry'. The evidence strongly suggested that armoured formations *were* the new cavalry. Providing further armoured cavalry formations *as well* was unique to the US Army. On balance, it was mistaken.

American infantry persisted with 'fireteam' tactics at section ('squad') level. If a good, reliable section light machinegun had ever been fielded, it might have driven development in the direction indicated at the 1946 infantry conference: one machinegun and one grenade launcher per section.

American training pamphlets for the defence dwelled at length on the planning and coordination of direct fire, and its integration with indirect fire. Use of Dragon drove the deployments of infantry sections to 300-400m apart in defence. That provided good mutual support: Dragon had a 1,000m range. Using TOW was far more problematic. Its range suggested long-range, head-on shoots, but doctrine suggested flanking shots from concealed and protected positions. It is not clear that that was ever resolved. It was made worse by the development of the Bradley Infantry Fighting Vehicle (IFV) in the 1980s. The Bradley mounts a medium-range 25mm cannon and a TOW launcher. Separate TOW (antitank) companies were abolished. Siting Bradleys near to their sections, yet engaging at long, medium and close ranges,

---

1   Known as the SLR and GPMG in the British Army.

remains a problem. Bradley is also too big and too well-armed to be used as a quiet, stealthy scout vehicle.

American doctrine for the advance strongly favoured flanking attacks and envelopment. It was clearly a better approach than the British Army's, particularly as it evolved in the 1980s. Another wartime legacy was the concept of the air-land team. It was adapted after Vietnam to include attack helicopters. Other western armies had antitank, but not attack, helicopters from about the same date. There were typically several dozen such helicopters per division.

British tactics also reflected wartime experience, adapted for new weapons. Long-range ATGW were sited for long, head-on shoots to engage the enemy early. At shorter ranges, reverse slope defensive positions were strongly recommended. Medium-range ATGW and machineguns were sited for crossfire from positions behind cover, providing mutual support and a complex network of defensive positions to halt or delay the enemy. Analysis of tactical doctrine indicates that British doctrine for the defence was more sophisticated than American. US teaching seems to have stressed massing fire. British teaching stressed the subtleties of siting weapons (for fields of fire, and for protection behind cover).

British tactics stressed blocking moves or counterattacks at higher levels, right up to corps. However, advance and attack tactics were plodding and deliberate. An American observer in the late 1970s noted that one had to 'engrave an invitation and wait for their recon'. A 'quick' (battalion) battlegroup attack was expected to take about an hour to mount. The evidence suggests that American forces were considerably more agile, at least until the early 1990s. The British had no drill for the march: only techniques for a planned road moved followed by occupying a concentration area.

The Yom Kippur war prompted a study of logistic demand. British 155mm artillery ammunition scalings were increased from 70 to 360 rounds per gun, per day; mortar ammunition from 70 to 240. Armoured vehicle fuel stocks were increased from 40 miles (64km) per vehicle per day to 100km.

There was a tendency for British armoured battalions, who spent ten to twelve years at a time in Germany, to 'play the game' on major field exercises. Infantry battalions spent only five years in the mechanised role in Germany in every 20. They took some time to adapt, and often remained somewhat plodding in their approach to armoured warfare.

West German tactics were well-considered, simple, and very well executed. There was obvious linkage from Wehrmacht concepts. Tasks and responsibilities for reconnaissance were clearly spelt out, which is conceptually not simple. In defence there was a clear and explicit requirement for outposts, and guidance as to how to provide them. Platoons were cross-attached between companies, and there was little or no formal battalion-level reserve. Strong reserves were held at higher levels. Battalions were expected to attack off the line of march in 15-20 minutes from first contact. It was recognised that frontal attacks are only decisive if they break through the whole depth of the enemy position. The Bundeswehr had clear doctrine for operating with open flanks. It had explicit drills for deployment, so as to link road marches to subsequent operations.

Soviet minor unit tactics remained grossly simplistic. The drill for a company attack was a single skirmish line[2]. Western companies had manoeuvred within *platoons* in 1918, and within *sections* by 1939. Soviet defensive tactics showed little counterattack below divisional level. The Soviet Army clung to simplistic, outdated tactics and attempted to make them work by brute force. The Arab-Israeli wars had shown precisely what happened when those tactics were exposed to a competent enemy. They failed.

At higher levels the Soviets were aware of the potential problems of penetrating NATO defences. In the 1980s they proposed to counter that with 'Operational Manoeuvre Groups' (OMGs). OMGs were probably of divisional size, operating fast and independently. They were intended to strike deep into NATO's defences. They would disrupt defensive preparations, seize objectives in depth, and create confusion. OMGs were conceptually a reasonable response to the problem of a well-planned, coherent NATO defence. They were not without problems. An OMG identified before committal would provide a good target for FOFA. If committed too late against a coherent defence, they ran the same risk as any other uncoordinated, independent attack.

Western doctrine published in the 1970s repeated and often re-emphasized lessons of the Second World War. Unfortunately, armed forces forget. In 1975, British doctrine gave firm guidance to use reverse slopes in defence. In the 1980s that had become ambivalent (it described advantages and disadvantages). By the 1990s it was often overlooked. In 1986 one brigadier criticised a battlegroup commander for even considering a flanking attack. That would have been entirely normal in 1918. Platoon attacks had become more and more frontal. The use of one of a platoon's machineguns to cut off enemy attempting to withdraw from the objective was entirely forgotten. The use of outposts in defence to prevent identification of the main position had largely disappeared.

The (American) Pentomic and (British) Wide Horizon trials of the 1960s and early 1970s tried to delete brigade HQs and increase the span of command from three to five within the division (hence fewer, bigger battlegroups). They failed, not least because span, rank and level of command are behavioural issues, which are still not well understood.

General Donn Starry had served in the Second World War, commanded a cavalry regiment in Vietnam, and was the architect of AirLand Battle. His near-contemporary, Field Marshal Sir Nigel Bagnall, had just missed the Second World War. He commanded an armoured division for the Wide Horizon trial. Bagnall should be remembered for two main things. In the early 1980s he reorganised the 1st British Corps in Germany from small, wartime armoured divisions to fewer, larger formations. That was a reasonable response to the particular battle to be fought on the Central Front. Bagnall also inculcated a process of conceptual thought which began

---

2   It is not clear whether the attached SAM teams should join in, or advance 15m behind.

to incorporate deep, close and rear operations; the meaning of manoeuvre; and the implications of decentralised command.

Subsequent analysis shows that the 1st British Corps was only just big enough for its task on the Central Front. Strategically, that reflects reasonably good planning. The Army had enough tanks and infantry. The problem was the number of battalions, and hence probably the number of barracks, located in Germany. Once reinforced by Regular units from Britain, the Corps might just have been large enough. Once reinforced with TA brigades (only available on mobilisation), the problem was probably solved. Corps can be too big; the usual result is poor army-level performance (discussed later). Some organisational changes were made at corps level, typically the inclusion of specialist units not normally found in divisions. An example was covert stay-behind parties to target deep attack.

Bagnall correctly refined the need for reserves at various levels of command. However, the resulting formations were too large, and insufficiently flexible for anything other than the one task at hand. Ironically, in Operation Granby (in Iraq in 1990-91) the 1st British Armoured Division was roughly the size of a smaller, Second World War division.

Those remarks result from a detailed review of army formations, which is summarised in Appendix I. It considers the divisions of the US and major European nations from the Second World War to the end of the century. Such investigation can show whether a divisional structure is too big or to small. It can also show, quite separately, whether it is overmanned or undermanned.

A key finding is that the fighting power of a division is only weakly correlated with its size. It is more closely correlated with its mobility. Thus smaller is better, within reason. Large divisions hold their reserves in the wrong place. They hold a high proportion of their troops as high-level reserves where they are historically unlikely to be needed.

The analysis strongly suggests that armies should have organised more, smaller divisions. That would allow a slight increase in the overall ratio of combat support (artillery and engineers) to line companies; and to match the provision of logistic support to demand. In round terms each NATO Cold War division might sensibly have produced about 1.7 more effective, smaller divisions. The analysis also indicated that more, smaller corps should have been organised.

In practice, however, the organisation of divisions (and probably armies, and armed forces in general) is not an issue of objective, rational design. It is a matter of political, social and cultural issues which can, and do, override empirical evidence.

A similar analysis of the development of tanks and Infantry Fighting Vehicles (IFVs) is considered at Appendix II. It looks at the evolution of those vehicles over the 55 years from the end of the Second World War. In terms of tanks, its findings can be illustrated by two surprising questions. Firstly, why did the US Army produce 8736 M47 tanks, and then discard them within five years? Secondly, why have historians not noticed that? The key finding for IFVs is somewhat different: that the IFV concept is a rationalistic experiment that has consumed vast resources on the basis of poor thinking and no good historical justification.

It would be possible to conduct similar analyses for, say, bomber aircraft, or submarines, or frigates. The same sorts of lessons (about human behaviour and interaction) would probably have emerged. Army formations were analysed in Appendix I because the focus of land warfare depends more on units and formations, and less on platforms, than do air or naval warfare.

In August 1969 conflict erupted between native Americans and rednecks along the Arkansas – Oklahoma state border. Federal troops were brought in as the violence escalated. The conflict rapidly assumed national, and even international, importance. It was finally brought to an end in 2006, by which time over 18,000 Americans had died. It was the biggest domestic loss of life in the United States since the American Civil War.

Clearly that did not happen, but as an analogy with the Troubles in Northern Ireland it is useful. The figure for loss of life is *pro rata* to the British and American populations (about 3,600 people died in the Troubles).

One of the key differences between the situation just described and Northern Ireland is the presence of an international border which is just a few miles, and in some places yards, from the conflict zone. The early, insurgent phase of the Troubles was defeated by a troop surge (Operation Motorman) in mid-1972. Insurgent Republican leaders fled across the border into Ireland, regrouped, and changed their tactics. By 1976 the Provisional IRA (PIRA) had become a largely terrorist group with up to 16 cells. They were called 'Active Service Units' for reasons of historical legitimacy. From then onwards there were rarely more than 300 active members of PIRA. There was also a confusing number of splinter groups and several Loyalist (pro-British) paramilitary organisations. None were neither as professional, nor so well disciplined, as PIRA.

PIRA then conducted a terrorist campaign coupled with attacks on security forces. It conducted a spectacularly sophisticated and successful attack at Warrenpoint, on the border, in 1979. 18 British soldiers were killed. The British Army developed its tactics and, particularly, its tactical EW capability. Thereafter PIRA never managed to kill as many as 10 soldiers in any one year. PIRA's political counterparts, Sinn Fein, became increasingly adroit. Violence was increasingly linked to political action, but had little or no political effect.

John Major became the British PM in 1989. He instigated political development: not least, through the (second) Downing Street Declaration. That led to a ceasefire, and eventually to the Good Friday Agreement of 1998. His predecessor, Margaret Thatcher, had had a very interesting involvement with Northern Ireland. Her friend and mentor, Airey Neave, had been murdered by PIRA five weeks before she became PM. The Warrenpoint attack took place soon afterwards. She quickly, and very publicly, visited Crossmaglen in 'bandit country' in south Armagh. Mrs Thatcher then made a point of visiting Northern Ireland every year. She did not introduce any political initiative towards a settlement in almost 12 years as PM. She participated in the Hillsborough peace process of 1985. That, however, was an initiative by Garret Fitzgerald, the Irish Taoiseach (PM). Hillsborough failed, due to a failure to include Unionist politicians in the agreement.

Operationally, the British Army and the Royal Ulster Constabulary (RUC) defeated the insurgency. They contained the terrorist campaign at a level which allowed political development to take place. It did take place: eventually.

Terrorists commit terrorist acts. Tactically, the Army and the RUC prevented PIRA from committing terrorist acts at anything more than a nuisance level (although that 'nuisance' involved many civilian deaths and significant damage). On balance, that should be seen as operational and tactical success. The security forces did not destroy PIRA. But PIRA was unable to commit sufficient violence, to create enough fear, to achieve political change. It failed. To that extent, it was defeated. PIRA's violence did contribute to keeping the underlying social, economic and political issues visible as matters of public and governmental concern. It is far from obvious that violence was the best way to do that.

After the introduction of interment without trial in August 1971, the security forces had an extremely good intelligence picture of exactly who the key Republican terrorists were. That picture was maintained for decades, although internment was abolished in 1975. For example, in the mid 1990s the security forces knew exactly who the head of South Armagh PIRA was; where he lived and worked; who his associates were; and how many times he had bombed the Dublin-Belfast railway. He would have been a boy in 1971. However, he was not prosecuted for terrorist offences because the security forces could not assemble enough evidence to convict him. He, and dozens like him, operated within a legal niche. That phenomenon will be explored later.

A very different war broke out in 1982. The Argentinians and the British fighting over the Falkland Islands was described as 'two bald men fighting over a comb'. Argentinian political claims for the ownership of the Falklands always indicate that the Argentinian government of the day is trying to divert domestic political attention from internal issues. For Britain in 1982 the issues were straightforward. They were: the wishes of British subjects (the Falkland Islanders) to remain British; and the defence of sovereign territory.

The Falklands are just over 7,000 nautical miles (nm) from Britain. The nearest British territory was Ascension Island, 3,200nm from the Falklands. Major General Edward Fursdon, the long-serving defence correspondent of the Daily Telegraph, wrote that nobody who has not visited the Falklands can really understand the Conflict.[3] The Islands are roughly the size of Wales, or the State of Massachusetts, had a population of about 1,800 (and several million sheep), and virtually no trees. The Falklands were invaded on 2 April 1982. South Georgia, 840nm further east, was invaded the next day. Britain despatched an amphibious task force to recapture the Islands under Operation 'Corporate' on the 5th. The first landings were made on 21 May. Argentinian forces surrendered on 14 June.

---

3   I served on the staff of Headquarters British Forces, Falklands Islands from March to October 1990.

Britain has repeatedly been accused of 'punching above its weight', over the Falklands and elsewhere. That is to misunderstand strategic capability. It should be measured primarily by GDP, not population or land mass. In the late 20th century Britain's GDP was generally the fifth to seventh largest in the world. Excluding China, Germany and Japan placed Britain in third or fourth place. Who was it trying to out-punch?

Britain's national intelligence system did not predict the Argentinian invasion. It was shaken up after the Falklands Conflict. Then, as in the 2002 'dodgy dossier' affair over Iraq's NBC capabilities, the issue was not intelligence collection but assessment. The Secret Intelligence Service (MI6) had become too closely involved in the policy consequences of its assessments.

What is a navy for, if it can't protect an island colony? Both operational British aircraft carriers and about half of the surface Navy were sent to the Falklands, as were six submarines. The Argentinian six-inch gun cruiser *General Belgrano* was an early casualty, sunk by HM Submarine *Conqueror* on 2 May. *Conqueror* had detected the civilian tanker escorting the *Belgrano*, by sonar, at a range of about 100nm. Sinking the *Belgrano* was unquestionably a legitimate act of war. British forces had already bombed the airfield at Stanley on East Falklands, shelled Argentinian positions, and recaptured South Georgia. A state of war existed. The Argentinian Navy has always accepted that the sinking was lawful. Controversy over the sinking arose largely because British politicians publicly fudged the issue.

The naval campaign saw the first major use of guided weapons at sea. All British ship losses were caused by air attack. Three warships, one fleet auxiliary and one landing craft were sunk by bombs. Five more warships and three auxiliaries were hit by bombs, but not sunk. One warship and one merchantman were sunk by Exocet missiles. Another warship was hit, but not sunk, by a missile. Unfortunately the merchantman, SS *Atlantic Conveyor*, was carrying all the heavy-lift Chinook helicopters. Only one survived the attack.

The RAF's most visible contribution to Operation Corporate was the bombing of Stanley airfield by V-Bombers. Seven separate attacks were mounted, each by a single aircraft, flying from Ascension. They were, at the time, the longest bombing missions ever flown. Damage was negligible. The runway was damaged. However Argentinian fast jet aircraft had already been withdrawn to the mainland, as a result of naval bombardment. At best, the bombing was a piece of signalling. The intended recipients of the message were the policy makers in the MOD. The message was that the RAF was still relevant. It was generally received with a hearty dose of cynicism.

Otherwise the British air campaign was largely conducted by 28 RN Sea Harriers operating off the two carriers. Six further RAF Harriers arrived slightly later, with the *Atlantic Conveyor*. Ten Harriers were lost, of which five were shot down (two Navy and three RAF). All five were hit by ground-based air defences. 12 helicopters were lost, of which five were shot down. The Argentinians lost 91 aircraft due to enemy action. 30 were shot down by Harriers. Seventeen were shot down by SAMs from warships. Eleven were destroyed on the ground in a Special Forces raid. Twenty-nine were captured on the ground at the end of the conflict.

In total, RAF pilots appear to have shot down 10 enemy aircraft since the Second World War. 12 RAF aircraft appear have been shot down. The actual numbers do not seem to have been published. 4,305 members of the RAF have been killed on active service. The great majority were aircrew. Very few died in war. Most died in flying accidents.

The landing force commander was Brigadier Julian Thompson, Royal Marines (RM). His initial orders for the landing ran to just 11 pages and seven annexes. His main difficulty in planning the landing was the sheer number of possible landing sites. Planning the ship-to-shore movement was relatively straightforward. He had an experienced amphibious planning staff, and all of his four infantry battalions had done at least one practice landing. Thompson did not make a campaign plan. He described a concept of operations to his subordinates, which was to be followed by a fragmentary order in due course. The initial order had to be scrapped when the Chinooks were destroyed. The battalions then had to march across East Falkland in order to attack Stanley. That took several days. One (parachute) battalion conducted an attack to clear a flanking position at Goose Green on the night of 27-28 May. The battalion's CO was killed.

Thompson issued one further order, for the attack on Stanley. The plan was simple. Each of five hilltop defensive positions, typically of battalion strength, would be attacked by a British battalion. Attacks were to be silent (ie, without preliminary bombardment) and at night, due to the shortage of artillery. Three attacks were made on the night of 11-12 June. Two further attacks were made on the night of 13-14 June. The Argentinians surrendered the next day.

The British attacks were all characterised by some degree of surprise, insufficient fire support, defensive weaknesses, and the effectiveness of professional soldiers fighting conscripts. All six attacks were against positions of roughly battalion size. All six objectives were taken.

A detailed analysis of the six battles is revealing. Between two and 39 British soldiers died in each attack. The loss exchange ratio in four battles was similar, but there were two cases where the British took significantly fewer losses. They were Mount Longdon (2nd Battalion, the Parachute Regiment's second battle), demonstrating the benefit of experience and a different CO. The second was Mount Harriet, where 42 Commando RM achieved complete surprise. Harriet was the battle in which only two British soldiers were killed.

There was no strong relationship between the enemy's strength (in terms of platoons engaged) and either the duration of the battle or British casualties. Thus, within reason, the size of the enemy force did not significantly affect the outcome.

Defender's casualties were between 80 and 160, a ratio of two to one. The attackers' casualties (killed *and* wounded) varied from 13 to 63, a ratio of about five to one. There was a strong inverse relationship between attackers' casualties and duration. That is: if the attackers attacked quickly, they took fewer casualties. What the attackers did to the enemy (in terms of casualties inflicted) was far less significant. Taken with other observations, the key finding is a need to achieve surprise and then fight quickly through the enemy's position, maintaining the momentum of the attack. That will achieve success for fewer casualties to the attackers, and do it quicker. That outcome largely resulted from the attackers' plan and how they executed it.

Six battles is a small sample. Nevertheless, Operation Corporate provides a rare opportunity to compare a reasonable selection of similar battles and draw numerical observations. One post operation report stressed that there were few new lessons, just old lessons re-learnt. In other words, tactical doctrine based on the Second World War was still valid. One particular observation related to projected high explosive. Stocks of light mortar bombs had recently run out. None were available. A new light mortar was procured soon after. 20 years later, stocks of bombs were quickly expended in Iraq and Afghanistan. Another light mortar then had to be procured. ...

British casualties for Operation Corporate were 255 dead and 777 wounded. The Argentinians lost 649 killed, 323 of them on the *Belgrano*. They also lost 1657 wounded and 11,313 POW. The British landing force never exceeded seven infantry battalions. Mrs Thatcher, soon to be nicknamed 'the Iron Lady', cried for about three quarters of an hour (in private) on hearing of the losses from one engagement.

The Iran-Iraq war cost about $1190bn. There were over a million casualties. Iraq became heavily indebted. It depended on oil revenues in order to pay off debt and rebuild. A drop in the price of oil, and Kuwaiti exploitation of reserves along the Iraqi border, prompted Iraq to demand $10bn in reparations from Kuwait. Kuwait offered $9bn. Iraq invaded Kuwait on 2 August 1990.

UN condemnation was almost unanimous. A US-led coalition force began to deploy to Saudi Arabia within days. The force included one French and one British division, and roughly five divisions from Arab countries. The UN mandate called for the liberation of Kuwait, to include attacks on Iraqi territory if necessary. Iraq launched Scud missiles at Israel, hoping to provoke Israeli retaliation. That might have broken the coalition politically. Israel showed restraint.

USAF planners in the Pentagon, led by Colonel John Warden, had developed an air operation called 'Checkmate'. It was handed to the theatre commander (General Norman Schwarzkopf) for refinement and execution. Army planners developed a land force plan. The USMC rejected its part in it and developed a corps-level plan of its own. Schwarzkopf therefore had little opportunity to create a coherent operational plan.

The Iraqi Army deployed 43 divisions. 24 were in Kuwait, 10 were along the Saudi-Iraq border and 9 were in reserve around Basra (including the Republican Guard Forces Command, (RGFC)). The Coalition campaign was highly successful, but its course and outcome showed some shortcomings. Some of them resulted from the lack of coherence of the initial plan.

A 39-day preliminary Coalition air operation began on 17 January 1991. Over 100,000 sorties were flown by about 2,250 aircraft. About 1,800 of them were American. That included the air wings of six aircraft carriers. Some 88,000 tons of ordnance was delivered. Roughly 10% was 'precision', ie guided to some extent.

The USAF conducted what became the longest bombing raid in history, with an operation from Missouri to Baghdad and back. It was totally unnecessary (many nearer bases were available). One could call it inter-service 'one-upmanship'[4]: 'willy waving'. One could call it immature.

The Iraqi Air Force started the war with 934 aircraft, of which about 550 were operational. At the end of the war it had about 300-370 aircraft. The Coalition lost 75 aircraft (52 fixed-wing and 23 helicopters), 44 of them due to enemy action. The Coalition's loss rate to SAMs was about one loss per 1,800 missiles launched.

About 15% of Coalition air sorties were aimed at so-called 'strategic' targets. 535 such targets were engaged. However, many were transport infrastructure, power generation and oil production installations. Very few were national command and communications targets. A local Iraqi advance at Khafji from 29 January was severely mauled by air attack

By the end of the campaign the Iraqi Army had lost (for example) about 76% of its tanks. However, a sample showed that 10-20% had been struck from the air; 50% had not been hit at all; and 30-40% had been hit by ground fire. That sample was, admittedly, small. The Iraqi withdrawal north from Kuwait city led to over 1,400 vehicles being shot up from the air. That is not a small sample. Only 14 were tanks and 14 were other armoured vehicles.

On 24 February, US Marine and Arab forces attacked Kuwait from the south and west. Seven American, one French and one British armoured divisions struck north and north east across the Saudi border. Most of the Iraqi Army was enveloped. The main effort was the attack of US VII Corps against the RGFC. After 100 hours' fighting the Iraqi Army was retreating rapidly from Kuwait. The RGFC was retreating north from the Basra area. The US 24th Infantry Division (Mechanized) had moved about 370km in one of the fastest advances in history.

The two US Armoured Cavalry Regiments (ACRs) had fought well. However it is far from clear that their missions were necessary, or could not have been conducted better in other ways. The two US Army Corps (VII and XVIII Airborne) contained nine divisions and two ACRs. VII Corps was attempting to execute two separate manoeuvres with two division each, and another with the fifth. Its ACR was doing something else. The corps were clearly too large. Appendix I suggests that the 11 US, French and British divisions could have provided troops for 19 smaller divisions in four or even five corps. There was plenty of corps-level artillery and engineers.

The Fire Support Coordination Line (FSCL) was, doctrinally, the forward limit of land force responsibility and the rear limit of air force responsibility. Doctrine required it to be set by army (or marine) corps HQs. Theatre orders required three hours' notice for a move of the FSCL, in order to give air forces time to react. On 27 February the air component declined an army request to attack a target short of the FSCL, and invited VII Corps to move the FSCL back. The resulting argument prompted

---

4   Actually international: USAF versus RAF.

Schwarzkopf to take personal control of the location of the FSCL. The issue reportedly slowed the forward progress of the corps. It probably also resulted in reducing Iraqi losses significantly, particularly those of the RGFC. It is a clear example of poor mutual coordination and subsequent over-control, leading to sub-optimal results.

Studying the operations of the HQ of 1st (UK) Armoured Division showed that it did not quite command on the move. Its command post operated from short halts. Two divisional attacks (on Objectives Tungsten and Varsity) were mounted in 5hrs 32 minutes and 7hrs 10 minutes respectively, from warning order to H-Hour. The commander (Major General Rupert Smith) had only taken command of the division in December the previous year: he deployed to the Gulf that same month. Whilst in Saudi Arabia he issued two written directives and conducted five study periods (of one afternoon each) down to battlegroup level. His division (and the 1st US Infantry Division (Mechanised)) cut the Basra Highway.

After the war, the US Secretary of the Air Force ordered a study into the course and conduct of the air campaign. It became the Gulf War Air Power Survey (GWAPS). The GWAPS report is contentious. Factually, is it often honest and seemingly accurate. For example, about 1,500 sorties were flown against Scud sites, but GWAPS states that it is impossible to confirm whether *any* mobile Scud launchers were destroyed by air attack. However, GWAPS sometimes uses throwaway lines, such as 'common sense' dictating that such-and-such 'must have' had significant effect. Rigorous analysis shows that common sense is often mistaken, because its findings are often counter-intuitive. Apparently the Survey did determine, however, that 'air power rendered resistance by ground forces disorganised and totally ineffective'.

That is not true. Iraqi ground forces were not totally ineffective. Several of the objectives were assaulted from the flank or even the rear; they were not sited for all-round defence. That both disorganised and disconcerted the defenders. Well-organised all-arms ground attacks are shocking and stunning. They make the defenders give up quickly, so resistance *was* often slight. Unsubstantiated generalisations like the one above are scattered through the GWAPS report. One can almost see the editorial battles between the analysts and the air warfare exponents, line by line. There is evidence that the USAF tried to have the GWAPS report buried.

The Gulf War did not demonstrate the unparalleled effectiveness of air forces. A Norwegian Air Force officer later wrote that the USAF had become the dominant arm in the Gulf War. It had not. GWAPS did not say what the USAF wanted it to say. The same officer also wrote that the USAF was 'bureaucratically self-serving almost beyond belief'. He provided good evidence of that.

Overall, Desert Storm was a very successful land-air campaign. It was not perfect. The Iraqi Army had been reduced from about 360,000 to 200-220,000 men before the beginning of the land attack. However, just as in the Falklands, its soldiers had been deployed in forward positions for lengthy periods. It is not surprising that during five weeks of bombing they drifted away. They *were* demoralised. But if demoralisation and desertion had been tactical objectives, the air forces would have done better bombing trenches and dugouts, rather than trying to pick off individual tanks. There was some carpet bombing by B-52s. One suspects that it was done for the benefit of the camera (how else would a TV camera just happen to be filming when the bombing occurred?)

The Iraqi Army did not fight well against Western land forces. The previous discussion about the Falklands strongly suggests that air attack was just one factor among several. It was mostly an issue of better western equipment, training, tactics, and leadership.

Talk of 'strategic' air attack is just talk. Damage is tactical; even when it is to a power station in Baghdad. Nonetheless, air attack *was* important. It disrupted operational movement and command. It prevented large-scale movement by day. It devastated broken, retreating enemy forces: just as in Normandy in 1944. But no more than that. The air offensive was grossly disproportionate to the operational effect achieved.

There were errors in Coalition planning and execution. Overall, however, it was hugely reassuring to see what US arms could achieve after the shadow of Vietnam. Nonetheless, much of the RGFC escaped: 'if you do not destroy them, …' (They were eventually destroyed in 2003.)

The world changed dramatically with the end of the Cold War. The collapse of the Soviet Union changed the political situation in, and relationships between, many countries. Western countries were more inclined to get involved in places where they previously could not. NATO began to enlarge eastwards. Some years later a Polish general and a Danish businesswoman were chatting at a conference. They discovered that during the Cold War his war role had been to seize Copenhagen Airport. Hers was to command an air defence platoon there.

The Marxist republic in Somalia fell apart in the late 1980s. By 1993 Western humanitarian aid was buttressed by American peacekeepers. They quickly found themselves fighting the forces of local warlords. The 'Black Hawk Down' incident brought the operation to the world's TV screens. US forces were quickly withdrawn. It raised significant issues of the west's willingness, and capability, to intervene in failed states.

On 18 June 2015 Prince William of Wales and his wife, Princess Kate, were assassinated during a royal visit to Edinburgh. The French killers were quickly arrested. On questioning they said that the visit was highly provocative, for two reasons. Firstly, it was the 200th anniversary of the Battle of Waterloo. Secondly, Scotland had once been an ally of France.

Clearly that did not happen. Not long afterwards a Serb tour guide in Belgrade was describing the assassination of Franz Ferdinand in Sarajevo in 1914. That visit had been highly provocative, he said, for two reasons. Firstly, because the date was the anniversary of the (first) battle of Kosovo Polye (in 1389). Secondly, Bosnia (hence Sarajevo) had once been part of Greater Serbia. It was factually correct (regarding dates and locations), but arrant nonsense. The tour guide obviously believed it. Rabid nationalism lives on in Serbia. (Some) Serbs are quite happy to tell foreigners their version of the story.

Post-war Yugoslavia had been held together by Tito, who died in 1980. During the 1980s Slobodan Milosevic came to power on a platform of Serb nationalism; or out of personal conviction; or blatant self-interest; or some combination of those. He had previously been an ardent Communist. Milosevic had deliberately manipulated the electoral college. The other Yugoslav republics objected. Yugoslavia fell apart. War broke out in April 1991.

Atrocities don't just happen. The Republika Srpska (a Serb enclave in Bosnia) would have no territorial integrity unless certain Muslim villages were cleared out. 296 Muslim villages were destroyed, starting in 1992. The biggest atrocity was the mass murder at Srebenica in 1993. It was deliberate, and coldly political. At or about the same time, mass murder was being committed in Burundi. Hundred of thousands of people were killed. Massacres took place in Burundi or Rwanda in 1959, 1963, 1972, 1988, 1993 and 1994, all for political reasons. In Rwanda in 1994 the objective was to prevent a national power-sharing agreement. Yes, the atrocities mobilised ethnic hatred. However they were all planned coldly, cynically and brutally for political gain by the organisers.

Atrocities present several problems. They include: whether there is an international consensus to intervene; how to do so; doing so early enough to prevent massacres; and then how to bring the perpetrators to justice. Operations in the former Yugoslavia demonstrated all of those problems. They also forced western nations, and NATO, to develop their procedures to address interoperability. During the Cold War interoperability had largely concerned technical and logistic issues, such as the allocation of radio frequencies or having the same calibre artillery shells. Tactical interoperability had largely been achieved by having national corps sectors on the Central Front. Clearly that cannot work when, for example, a Danish company is working with a Canadian battalion.

At the same time formation HQs became bigger, for several reasons. Firstly, they became semi-static during extended operations. Secondly, all NATO nations wanted to contribute staff officers. New NATO members (initially Hungary, Poland and the Czech Republic) wanted to post staff in to gain experience. Planning timescales grew longer. Political and national direction reached down to individual battalions, and in some cases companies. Western armed forces generally lost the ability to plan quickly and effectively. The benefit, if any, was the ability to sustain international consensus.

It proved very difficult to limit Serbian irredentism. Albanian Kosovars had been waging an increasingly successful insurgency from about 1997. Serbian responses resulted in a humanitarian crisis. The UN and NATO resolved to intervene. NATO began air operations against Serbian forces on 24 March 1999. The air campaign lasted 100 days. NATO land forces were gradually assembled to attack, but no substantive plan nor force was in place when the operation ended.

The campaign revealed a major difference of opinion. NATO's Supreme Allied Commander, Europe, General Wesley Clark, believed that the Serb's Clausewitzian centre of gravity was the Yugoslav Army. The air commander, General Mike Short, believed (once again) that the war could be won by airpower alone and that this was the best-ever chance to justify independent air forces. Both were wrong. Milosevic didn't give a fig for his army. What was critical to him was his retention of power. The war was never likely to be won from the air, not least because Yugoslav ground forces were widely dispersed in mountainous and wooded country. They were very hard to attack. The war ended for two reasons. Firstly, Milosevic was presented with conditions under which he could afford to lose. He remained in power until October 2000, when he lost a presidential election. Secondly, NATO continued to demonstrate resolve, not least through continued bombing. Air attack as political signalling, once again.

100 days of air attack by the most powerful alliance on earth were needed as part of a campaign to persuade a nation of just 7.5 million people to desist. That doesn't seem very effective. The air campaign highlighted several difficulties. NATO aircraft were not allowed to operate under 15,000 feet. That was due to the SAM threat, hence fear of losses in what was demonstrably a politically weak coalition. The NATO 72hr air targeting cycle was inflexible and difficult to coordinate with political decision making. There are good reasons for the 72hr cycle, but it must be responsive. In practice it was the cause of several problems, not the answer to them.

As the campaign continued, NATO ran out of targets. The same had happened in the Second World War, Korea and Vietnam. Running out of targets should tell commanders that, operationally, air attack isn't working. In practice it prompts them to invent more. Ironically, subsequent analysis revealed that the air campaign had not destroyed many of the targets which it thought it had.

A Russian air assault battalion had been based in Bosnia as part of peacekeeping forces. As the air campaign came to an end the battalion moved rapidly to seize Pristina airport in Kosovo. That gave Russia a presentational advantage over NATO. (Russia had been generally supportive of Milosevic, not least for domestic political reasons.) The situation was defused. However, it was the operational motive underlying the creation of US Stryker brigades. The 'Race to Pristina' had created the perception of a need for very mobile, rapidly-deployable formations. Sometimes armed forces get good things for bad reasons. Sometimes they get bad things for bad reasons.

The order for the Russian air assault battalion to deploy to Bosnia was a one-page graphic. Brigadier Thompson's order for the Falklands landing was 11 pages long with seven annexes. The American infantry battalion which rescued the downed aircrew at Mogadishu in 1993 had previously attended the Battle Command Training Program at Fort Irwin, California. Its operation order for the deployment to California ran to 214 pages. Why such differences, and what are the consequences?

At the end of the 'Balkan Decade' the world lacked a good way of imposing acceptable behaviour on small, recalcitrant nations. Air attack was not the answer. It had taken three months of bombing to get Milosevic to desist. It then took 20 years to bring the guilty to justice. The Serbian general Radko Mladic was finally convicted on 22 November 2017. Why should the dictator of a small state be particularly worried about a vague threat of retribution 20 years from now?

The outcome of the 1990s was not all bad. In sub-Saharan African countries, democratically-elected governments or presidents came to power for the first time in six countries in the 1990s (but not a single Arab country). There were virtually no international conflicts in South America. South-east Asia was almost entirely at peace, after the Chinese invasion of Vietnam in 1979. GDP per person rose, and poverty and famine fell, through much of the world.

The long years of 'peace' after 1945 revealed a number of personnel issues. Long-term patterns and problem arose due to human resource management issues. For example, the Bundeswehr, created in 1956, suffered a log-jam at sergeant major level: in the 1980s there were cases of senior NCOs holding (and hence blocking) the same post for 12 years or more. The British Army lived with what were termed 'passed over' majors (ie, passed over for promotion) from the mid-1960s. In the 1990s it detected a pattern of officers being appointed to the rank of Brigadier too early and failing in post. For structural reasons, the main group of failures were artillery officers.

It was a pleasure and a privilege for me to serve with a generation of officers, and to watch some of their (and more senior officers') careers develop. Some were men (there were very few women), of all services, of undoubted and exceptional capability. Some commanded with great distinction. Some would doubtless have done so, if the opportunity had arisen. Most were competent. Some were not. What was more obvious was the tendency for some to look, and act, the part. 'The part' varies from service to service, and nation to nation. A USN admiral does not look and act like a USMC colonel who had been an F18 pilot. Neither look or act like a British cavalry (armoured corps) general.

Looking and acting a given part appears to be far more closely correlated with incompetence than with extreme competence. It also seems far more prevalent in some nations than others. When commentators talk of the 'theatre of war' they do not typically think of the way its actors look and act. If this seemed true of the generations commissioned after 1945, it was probably true of any generation of officers whose careers were formed in long periods of peace. It is still happening.

In March 1993 soldiers of the Canadian Airborne Regiment (CAR) beat and murdered a Somali man in the town of Belet Huen in Somalia. The subsequent investigation exposed a number of issues, not least the culture inside what had been considered by some to be an elite unit. The issue highlights a wider problem of units which are accorded some form of special status. Put simply, the units' members can begin to believe that they are special and that normal rules and regulations do not apply to them. In the later 20th century they were typically parachute units. Such self-belief can cause significant problems both in barracks and on operations, but can also be excused because of their assumed operational effectiveness. The CAR was disbanded.

Armed forces can forget important lessons after long periods of peace. The issue of reverse slope positions in the British Army was described above. The 1975 infantry pamphlet was quite categoric about the advantages of reverse slopes. In 1999 two lieutenant colonels were given a defensive scenario on which to plan a battalion defence, as part of an exercise. They chose a forward slope. Their force was then devastated when exposed to a computer simulation, for exactly the reasons described in the 1975 pamphlet. One of the officers became a major general, the other a colonel. Both would have been taught from the 1975 pamphlet as officer cadets and junior officers. If individuals can forget or ignore their teaching after about 20 years, how likely is it that the army (or navy, or air force) in which they serve will remember?

Comparing Operation Desert Storm with the Falklands Conflict and Kosovo exposes something that is so obvious that it often goes unsaid. Theatre-level armoured operations, as part of an integrated air-land campaign, can be utterly decisive. They resolve or settle the strategic issue categorically. Sometimes armoured operations may not be possible, as in the Falklands, but the issue *can* be resolved. Desert Storm resolved the issue of the Iraqi occupation of Kuwait in 100 hours. It took 24 days to resolve the Falklands Conflict, once the land force was ashore. A few Chinooks might have shortened it by about a week. Operations in Grenada (in 1983) and Panama (in 1990) were conducted very quickly using light, airmobile ground forces. Conversely it took 100 *days* to address the situation in Kosovo. If politicians want a conflict settled, they should commit a ground force; armoured if possible. If they want to undertake political signalling in the hope of a favourable outcome eventually, they should order an air operation. They should not confuse the two. Just as importantly, their military advisers should not over-promise.

11

March and Fight

Major, conventional land warfare does not happen very often. When it does it, can change the fate of nations, and indeed continents. To that, for the 20th century, we should add 'rapidly': perhaps within days, or even hours.

But how are battles and engagements won? And how should those tactical events be linked, in order to achieve success in campaigns? How should ground forces move from one battle to another in a conceptual and physical whole? That is, not just how should armies fight, but how should they march and fight until the campaign is won? We lack a good, simple, clear understanding of how violence can be used to obtain tactical success; and then how tactical success can be used to obtain operational success.

The power of the rifled bullet was apparent at beginning of the century. Western armies achieved working, low-level tactical solutions to the problems that caused by the later years of the Great War. However, connecting that up across the battlefield to the operational level remained elusive. Even at the end of the 20th century it was still very difficult to incapacitate enemy infantry, successfully and reliably, at more than a few yard's range. Defenders had long since learnt the lessons of dispersion, conceal-ment and protection; as events in Iraq and Afghanistan would show. Partial solutions could be, and were, obtained. The overall solution to the problem lay not just with the adoption of tank, but (more generally) the integration of mechanisation.

This chapter describes the overall process. It starts with a concept which is basically simple, brutal and primal. It is that success in a violent and adversarial struggle such as war largely concerns the will to participate. Both sides seek to break the enemy's will, in order to impose their own. The key tactical and operational target, therefore, is the enemy's participation. If the enemy no longer fights, he no longer resists. His adversary can then do what he wants.

In trying to understand how collective violence can be used to achieve military success, one can consider the issue in several different ways. They may be abstract or concrete. In abstract terms the problem can be looked at conceptually, doctrinally or empirically. It can also be considered in terms of the effects of violence, physiological and behavioural issues, or complexity theory.

Land warfare, however, is not abstract. It is helpful to cross-check those abstract views with real elements of military capability: movement, direct fire, indirect fire, close assault and air attack. So, for example, what does Liddell Hart's concept of 'find, fix, strike and exploit' actually mean? What do the terms imply? How important are surprise and shock? What impact does air support have on the outcome of land-air campaigns? It is difficult answer those questions and unify the results into a simple model.

Statistical analysis of battlefield activities reveals some unexpected results. For example, surprise is both a battle winner and *the* campaign winner. Surprise is hundreds of times more effective than any likely force ratio, advantage in command systems, weapons, or anything else. Nothing else correlates so strongly with tactical or campaign success. The next most significant phenomenon in the land battle is shock. Shock is shorthand for both shock action and shock effect. Shock action is the sudden, concentrated application of violence. Put simply, it is far more effective to have (say) 100 field guns firing on a target for six minutes than six guns firing for 100 minutes. Shock effect is observed where the defenders are rendered numb, lifeless and unresponsive; or perhaps acting irrationally. It can be an individual or a collective effect. Combinations of shock and surprise can be devastating.[1]

In terms of operational and tactical success, the strongest logical and statistical correlations between battlefield phenomena are *not* those between weapons effect and damage (surprisingly); *but those between movement and changing behaviour.* That is hugely important. It suggests that the role of movement in relation to the enemy, namely manoeuvre, is underplayed in much of land force practice.

Several conclusions can be identified for the practitioner:

- *First and foremost*, do things which create and exploit surprise. That has major consequences for forms and methods of manoeuvre.
- When violence is applied, do it in a sudden, concentrated and unexpected manner in order to achieve shock effect. Then exploit that immediately.
- Exploit at every opportunity. Ground combat is confusing and chaotic. Any success will probably be local, partial and transient. Tactics, and operational methods, should be designed around the ability to exploit opportunistically. That has significant implications for the conduct of command.
- The thread of purpose should be obvious and explicit. Each and every tactical action should clearly relate to the goals of the higher commander ordering it, and so on all the way up to the theatre commander.
- The perception of dismounted combat as being slow and indecisive suggests that a capability is missing. Shock effect is rare in dismounted combat. Using tanks, to

---

1   Statistical analysis of these issues is described in *The Human Face of War*, Jim Storr, London (Continuum, 2009), pp83-106. The original statistics are in the references to that work.

provide direct-fire HE, can work well; when tanks are present. However, without tanks and therefore without direct-fire HE, dismounted combat remains slow and indecisive. Expressed that way, the problem is obvious.

The key target is the enemies' participation and, to that extent, their will. Little of the above discussion relates to 'will' in any obvious way. 'Will' is seen to be as the strength of determination. It appears to be an amalgam of individual participation, social cohesion, and the effect of commanders' actions. Individual participation is directly affected by death, incapacitation and demoralisation. Social cohesion is a broad topic but, is obviously linked to the behaviour of individuals. There are no other actors, other than human beings. Individual commanders make decisions and motivate and inspire their subordinates. That can have negative consequences. If, for example, a senior and effective commander wrongly decides to retreat or surrender, his subordinates may well do what he tells them to do. That would have significant effect. The key to battlefield (and hence operational) success appears to be to apply violence in such a way as to convince senior enemy commanders to desist. That is scarcely profound. The foregoing discussion, however, suggests how it is done.

If the thread of purpose is obvious, from the highest to the lowest, there is a reasonable chance of operational success. If that linkage is missing or tenuous then the actions of some or all of the forces will be purposeless. That is, pointless; or futile. The resulting casualties will also be futile. The processes by which strategic goals are turned into operational and then tactical goals down the chain of command are a critically important aspect of land operations. The effective and efficient command of land forces depends to a significant extent on a golden thread of purpose which links tactical activity simply, clearly and unambiguously with operational and then strategic outcome. If that thread is missing, or broken, bad things will happen.

So much for consideration of the abstract. What about the concrete? What follows will start with one important low-level engagement. It will then consider what should happen before and after that, and then work upwards to theatre level.

Take a marker pen and draw a small mark on a piece of paper or your thumbnail, about 1.3mm wide and 1.1mm high. Hold it out at arm's length and look at it. That is roughly the size that a triple NATO small arms target appears at 600m. Take a section machinegun out onto a 600m firing range and have the gunner fire at such a target. The target should pop up for a few seconds, fall if hit, and then go down if not. Repeat that every three to five seconds. A competent machinegun team should be able to hit it something like seven times out ten. The gunner will probably fire about 30 rounds per minute.

That is a reasonably good representation of a section machinegun suppressing a single trench with two or three enemy soldiers in it. Now imagine that it is not a firing range but a battlefield. Whilst the machinegun suppresses the trench, have the rest of the section move forward using a covered route until they can get close enough to throw in grenades; then rush in and bayonet anyone surviving. They may have to use rifle fire to cover any movement in the open.

It was a single enemy position which had been *found* before the machinegun opened fire. The enemy was *fixed* with machinegun fire, and *struck* with bayonets and grenades. On a real battlefield the gunner might need to fire more frequently to suppress the enemy. However, the machinegun team leader is a trained NCO who controls the rate of fire appropriately. The keys to success are: accurate location of the enemy, probably using binoculars; good fire control, to get the gunner firing accurately at the target; and controlled, effective shooting. Rate of fire has little to do with it. It does not take many rounds striking near the target to suppress. High rates of fire are wasteful. The machinegun team must remain unsuppressed. If not, its fire will be ineffective and the attack will fail: the defenders can either engage the rest of the section, or move away.

That would be a typical section attack according to the British doctrine for the 1950s to the 1970s. It is perhaps an unlikely scenario, but was used as a training device and considered to be the basis of tactical training. German tactics were similar. The US Army identified the need for an effective section machinegun (such as the German MG 42), but never procured one. There is real doubt that its fireteam tactics would suppress an enemy position as effectively. The same applies to the variant which the British Army adopted after it procured the SA 80 weapon system.

Go up the scale. The objective is now an enemy section of 8-10 men with one or more machineguns. The attackers will employ a rifle section to suppress it. The remainder of the platoon will move to a flank, and then work their way forward along a covered approach to assault the position. They probably won't do that in a rush, but rather work forward in short bounds. One machinegun in the platoon will get to somewhere where it is firing along the enemy position from the flank. The third machinegun will be beyond the enemy position. From there it can do three things. It can engage the enemy from the rear. It can shoot any enemy who try to withdraw. It can also engage any other enemy in depth who are located as the platoon moves forward.

Described like that, it clearly won't work. The chances of an attacking section suppressing an enemy section, which may well be dug in, is very low. The chances of success grow significantly if the attacker can engage the enemy with HE. A light mortar that throws bombs about the size of a hand grenade a few hundred metres might be sufficient. It could be used to neutralise the defenders' machinegun(s), and then the other slit trenches. Grenade launchers might have similar effect.

Scale up again to a company attacking a platoon. The attackers can attempt variants of what was described above, but the evidence is that it just won't work, even with the platoons' light mortars. The problem of rifled bullets is just too great.

Go back to the attacking section. Instead of a machinegun, use a section of two or three medium mortars. If the mortar fire controller can see the enemy position, it should be relatively easy to neutralise it with a few bombs from each mortar. Suppression is good; neutralisation is normally better.

The same applies at platoon level. Coordinating the fire with the movement of the attacking sections requires some thought. At the company level the process may not work. A section, or even a platoon, of medium mortars probably won't cover enough of the enemy position. So, use field artillery. Put another way, most attacks from platoon upwards will need indirect fire support.

Go back to the section again. Instead of medium mortars, use a tank. Once the infantry has located the enemy position and can indicate it to the tank, it is fairly easy for the tank to neutralise or destroy it. Add in artillery as well. Such 'all arms' assaults can be highly successful.

However, defenders have deployed antitank weapons since 1917. If the defending force is anything bigger than one isolated platoon, the position will be a complex and extensive network of machineguns, section positions and antitank weapons. Tanks and dismounted soldiers attacking one position can be engaged by defending machine-guns and antitank weapons from over a thousand metres away. By the 1980s defenders typically had both shoulder-fired Light Antitank Weapons (LAWs) and ATGW. All of the longer-range weapons have to be neutralised, or at least suppressed, to allow the attacking tanks and infantry to move forward. So must the shorter-ranged weapons nearest to the attackers. It is a very complex problem.

It can succeed. There will probably not enough artillery to conduct a Great War rolling barrage, right across the position and into depth. But the guns are now far more powerful (typically 155mm versus 75mm). They will destroy more, and neutralise for longer. But they will probably not neutralise every defending weapon. As the tanks and infantry work forward they will detect the remaining weapons, not least when they fire. Using all the techniques above, including mortar and artillery fire, they can engage them and break into a defensive position. Progress will be uneven and unpredictable.

Consider one attacking infantry company. By this stage it is advancing with two platoons forward, each with two sections forward. One platoon makes no progress. In the other, one section makes some progress. At that stage its platoon commander orders a halt whilst he attempts to bring the other section up into line. At that stage the company commander orders that platoon to halt, whilst he attempts to bring the other platoon up into line.

That may sound stupid. It is. Consider a different scenario. When one section makes progress, the platoon commander feeds his reserve section in behind it. As the leading section encounters another enemy position and starts to engage it, the third section continues to advance. As this platoon continues to make progress the company commander feeds his reserve platoon in behind. Soon the rest of the leading platoon has found the flank of the enemy's nearest position and is attacking it. Soon the flank of the enemy holding up the other platoon has also been rolled up. The penetration is being widened. Superimpose the action of the tanks, which destroy positions revealed by the advancing infantry. Move the tanks forward when enough antitank weapons have been destroyed or neutralised. Add in APCs or IFVs to deliver the infantry to the forward positions, and then into depth when opportunities arise. Above all, do it rapidly. Soon there will be cracks in the enemy's defensive position. The enemy begins to withdraw, break or surrender.

That is a modern interpretation of Liddell Hart's 'expanding torrent'. The evidence suggests very strongly that it can work very well. But as the Bundeswehr observed in the 1950s, a frontal attack is only decisive when it breaks completely through a defensive position. In the Second World War the British do not seem to have managed that. In part, they probably did not manage to neutralise enough of the longer-range enemy weapons in depth and to the flanks. But, probably more importantly, neither do they seem to have learnt about opportunistic exploitation and reinforcing success, no matter how small and how local. Wherever one man can go, a section and then a platoon can follow. Once a section or a platoon has bypassed, the penetration can, and should, be both widened and deepened.

Statistically, surprise is both a battle winner and *the* campaign winner. Nothing else correlates so strongly with campaign success. For example, surprise is hundreds of times more effective than any likely force ratio. That does not just mean surprise at H-Hour, but throughout a battle and no matter how local. The section or platoon that found a flank probably created and exploited surprise, through the use of an unexpected direction of attack (and possibly by attacking before those defenders expected it: unexpected timing). Night attacks can be devastating where they achieve surprise. Modern night vision devices make that harder, but not impossible, to achieve.

Should attacks be addressed against enemy forces or terrain features? At low level the identity of the enemy force may not be significant. The feature should be attacked if its possession creates and advantage. But the enemy platoon or section holding it might be reinforced, or replaced. At higher levels the converse may be true: the destruction of a given enemy formation (such as, for example, the Iraqi RGCF) might be desirable. The terrain features involved might simply be the means to the end of destroying that formation.

The defence is the converse of the attack. Discussion of the defence can also start at low tactical levels. By 1939 most western armies had procured effective section machineguns. A network of section positions, each with a machinegun that covered its neighbour's front, was a particularly difficult position to attack. It hadn't really existed in the Great War. It was typically thickened up with the fire of medium machineguns reaching across from company to company. A typical company with nine rifle sections might place four sections in that network (two from each of two platoons). We shall call that the main line of resistance (MLR). It was generally not the 'front line'.

In the Second World War most infantry defensive positions were a network of section positions (the MLR), outposts, and reserves. Section positions typically consisted of one machinegun (firing to a flank, in well-organised defences) and a group of riflemen. In practice, their main job was to protect the machinegun (see Figure 11-1).

Outposts were normally sections, but occasionally platoons, deployed forwards from the MLR. They had several functions. They provided warning of the enemy's approach. They prevented enemy interference in the preparation of the rest of the position. They caused attrition. Critically, however, they also concealed the location of the MLR. Outposts had to be given reasonable orders as to when to withdraw: their job was not to die to the last man. They would be needed, as reserves, later in the battle.

Just as in the Great War, it was not difficult to neutralise an MLR, once located. That was a typical artillery task. But the outposts made it difficult to identify the

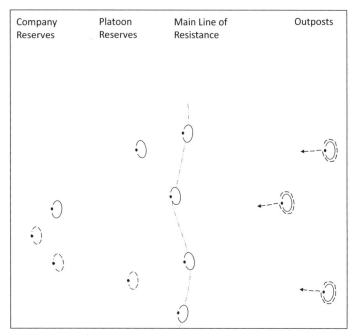

Company Reserves	Platoon Reserves	Main Line of Resistance	Outposts

Figure 11-1 Outposts, the Main Line of Resistance and Reserves.

MLR. The enemy might believe that the outposts were the MLR. Outposts might be moved, once the attackers had been engaged from them, creating uncertainty and ambiguity. By 1944 the Germans appear to have gone one step further. If necessary, they would thin out the MLR to become a new outpost line, thicken up previous depth positions to form a new MLR, and then withdraw some or all of the original outposts. See Figure 11-2.

That could be hard to detect. It might cause the next attack to fail in front of the new MLR. It is probably one of several tactics which allowed to Wehrmacht to hold thin defensive lines very effectively.

Doctrinally, reserves in defence are typically used either: to provide depth to a position (by occupying prepared defences in depth); for counter-penetration (by occupying hasty positions in depth); or counterattack. Counter-penetration does not seem to have existed in most armies' low-level tactical doctrine until the later stages of the Cold War. Earlier doctrine stressed counterattacks, either immediate or deliberate. That was not just an emotional attachment to the retention of ground.

A counterattack allows the defender to inflict surprise and shock on the attacker. Counterpenetration does not inflict shock. It does little, if anything, to create surprise. Doctrine writers seem to have overlooked something that Great and Second World War commanders just knew: that counterattacks were more likely to be decisive in prompting the attacker to break off the attack.

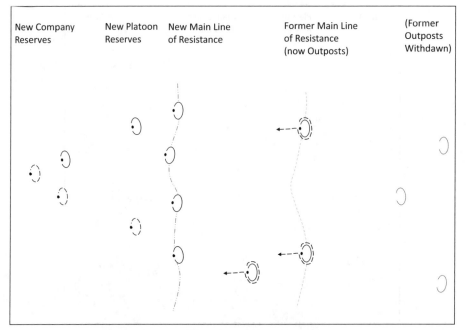

| New Company Reserves | New Platoon Reserves | New Main Line of Resistance | Former Main Line of Resistance (now Outposts) | (Former Outposts Withdawn) |

Figure 11-2 Forming a New Main Line of Resistance in Depth.

Historically, antitank guns have been far more effective than tanks in defence at destroying enemy tanks. That is in large part due to the selection of good fire positions, the coordination of the fire of several weapons, and concealment of the guns. Once dug in, antitank guns (either towed or self-propelled) presented a very small target. ATGW are even smaller, and have longer effective ranges. From the Second World War onwards, most antitank weapons were deployed in or near the MLR. Some were held in depth or to support counterpenetration. The most effective form of defensive countermove appears to have consisted of antitank weapons with alternative positions sited to counter any penetration, linked to counterattacks by tanks and infantry supported by indirect fire.

A well-sited defensive position could be very difficult to overcome. Figure 11-3 illustrates a typical deployment of four Milan ATGW within a British battalion position on the Central Front in the 1980s. Each of a pair of launchers is sited more than 150m from its neighbour. That meant that a single enemy artillery battery would be unlikely to neutralise both launchers. The pairs are about 1,500m from each other, and sited to engage enemy tanks from their flanks. If enemy tanks tried to turn towards one pair of launchers, they would expose their flank or rear to the other. All four launchers are protected against direct fire from their fronts. Neither German, Soviet nor American defences appear to have reached that degree of sophistication. It did, however, take significant coordination and could be slow to deploy.

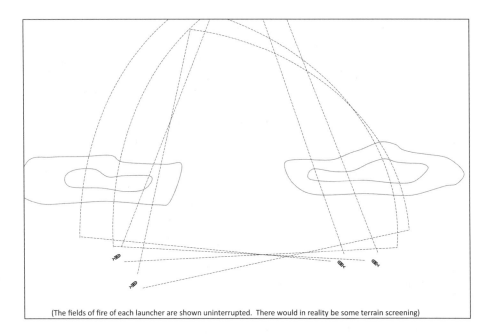

(The fields of fire of each launcher are shown uninterrupted. There would in reality be some terrain screening)

Figure 11-3 ATGW in Enfilade and Defilade.

Troops in forward defences were typically divided between outposts, the MLR and reserves. The proportion could vary significantly. Assuming four sections per infantry company in the MLR, there could be perhaps four section outposts and just one section in reserve; or no outposts and all remaining five sections in reserve. By the late 1980s the British Army had largely forgotten about outposts. It remembered the generally equivalent term of 'standing patrols', but rarely deployed them.

The security zone, forward of the MLR, was a further element of the defence. It was not provided by the companies which manned the MLR, but by a separate covering force. In British doctrine that could be composed of a screen force, a guard force, or both. A screen force provided early warning. It detected and reported the approach of the enemy. Screen forces were not intended to fight. Guard forces were. A guard force might fight to cause delay; for example, to allow for the preparation of the main defensive position. In a sophisticated three-dimensional battle the guard force might seek to halt the attackers for attack by aircraft, helicopters or indirect fire. In the Cold War it might quite explicitly allow for time for political decision making (for example, concerning nuclear weapons release). Where it was deep enough, it might be designed to force the attacker to move his artillery forward, making it vulnerable to attack as it did so.

However the guard force should also have another important function. It should prevent enemy reconnaissance. By doing so it further prevented detection and iden-tification of the MLR. That had been largely forgotten in some armies by the 1980s.

In BAOR there was much discussion as to the wisdom of engaging Soviet reconnaissance forces. It was considered perhaps wiser to hide and allow them to pass. That was naive. Guided by EW units and sensible judgement, Soviet reconnaissance units *would* identify and then locate the MLR, and other key locations such as CPs, if they were allowed to reach them. That would have been a mistake. The power of Soviet artillery was well known.

By the 1980s there was considerable confusion. Outposts had been forgotten in some armies. Covering forces did not necessarily prevent reconnaissance. So-called screen forces, armed with powerfully-armed scout vehicles, might engage enemy reconnaissance vehicles: a guard force task. 'Armoured reconnaissance' or 'armoured cavalry' units with no infantry were expected carry out the tasks of all-arms guard forces, which would inevitably need some infantry. The Bundeswehr was the exception. Their divisional armoured reconnaissance battalions always had some infantry. The proportion of tanks was increased to allow them to act as all-arms guard forces. Scout vehicles were not armed, nor expected, to fight. The Wehrmacht had typically employed line battalions (tanks and infantry) to provide divisional guard forces. The Germans, at least, clearly understood the difference between guard forces, screen forces and outposts.

Field defences strengthened the MLR and provided defence against shock and surprise. Trenches and dugouts reduced the effects of indirect fire. The main use of barbed wire was to prevent grenade attacks on trenches. Antipersonnel minefields slowed and halted attacks, and could prevent or at least reduce the likelihood of surprise. Antitank minefields further out might break up tank attacks or funnel them into pre-planned killing areas. Indirect fire was used to break up enemy attacks and support counterattacks. Outposts prevented or reduced surprise and acted as a buffer to absorb shock. Screen forces were the primary defence against surprise. Reconnaissance forces were withdrawn once attackers had closed up to a main defensive position. One subsequent function might be to form a screen to the rear, so that if the enemy did break through they could at least report their movements.

This discussion started with consideration of the mechanics of the attack, and continued by looking at how to defend. But what happened before the attack?

The attacker might have to march from some distance, or cross an international border, before engaging the enemy. Scout vehicles would generally lead. The main reason for reconnoitring by stealth is now obvious. Surprise is a battle winner and *the* campaign winner. Reconnaissance by stealth allows opportunities for surprise to be identified; without disclosing what those opportunities are, nor the attacker's intentions. Some armies have a predisposition to reconnaissance by fire. We can now see that is simply a predisposition to systematically giving away opportunities for surprise. Experience counts: if they almost never achieve surprise, they will not value it nor seek to create it.

In this context, finding out where the enemy *is* is perhaps less important than finding where he is *not*. Such places may be gaps or flanks. They may provide covered routes to the enemy's flanks and rear. They may reveal undefended crossing places. That may offer opportunities for bypass and envelopment. In the Second World War it was not uncommon for German reconnaissance patrols, typically of two armoured cars, to operate 20-40km ahead of the main body.

The defender will typically employ a screen and possibly a guard force. It may be possible to slip past a screen, and to remain undetected. It should not be possible to slip past a guard force. To do so would require some fighting. Enabling the scouts to get past guard forces is the task of either the heavy patrols of reconnaissance battalions, or forward detachments from line units. Whatever their composition, they both enable scouts to penetrate guard forces and also support the uninterrupted advance of the main body. The defender will try to prevent any attack on the main position in less than, say, battalion strength. He will also try to ensure that the attacker's objectives have not been adequately reconnoitred. The attacker is trying to identify defended positions without committing significant forces. He might be trying to bypass enemy delaying positions.

There is clearly a significant preliminary battle to be fought. The advantage would probably go to the side which best understood the nature of that battle. In the mid and late 20th century that seems to have generally been the Germans. In north west Europe in the Second World War the Polish Army seem to have understood it better than the British.

Air reconnaissance, and preventing enemy air reconnaissance, are the most important roles of aircraft in this process. Air attack could also delay advancing columns, so one of the primary roles of air defence was not to shoot down aircraft but to maintain the freedom of operation of ground forces.

The 20th century was the first to see the military use of large quantities of relatively cheap blasting explosive. It became much easier for sappers to conduct demolitions. Widespread demolition schemes, intended to hinder the enemy's advance, became common. Engineers and armoured engineer vehicles supported the advance and then the attack, not least by bridging gaps caused by demolitions. They also breached minefields. In some cases they demolished fortifications (such as bunkers) and obstacles, using specialist demolition guns.

The object was not solely to attack. Bypassing, leading to encirclement and envelopment, offered a better balance between movement and weapons effect. Covert bypassing on one or several routes to reach objectives in depth is infiltration. It can be highly successful, especially where surprise is maintained. The attack by 42 Commando RM in the Falklands followed from a two-company infiltration on a single route. After a presentation about infiltration by (and within) rifle companies at a conference in 2008, one member of the audience remarked that '[t]hat's the only way to do it.' He had commanded an Israeli parachute brigade. He spoke from experience.

Even the most successful attack is simply a tactical success. What happens once success is achieved is perhaps more important.

Local, low-level success should be reinforced. It will result in some form of penetration or advance. Such initial success will be partial, local, and may be unexpected.

It will typically leave some enemy elements bypassed. They should be left, wherever possible, to be dealt with by reserves. That is not irresponsible. Given time, the enemy will probably be able to gather its own reserves and attempt a counterattack. Continuing the attack rapidly presents him with a dynamic problem. It makes it very difficult to understand *where* to counterattack, and difficult to actually conduct it. Conversely a slow, methodical process of 'mopping up' simply tells the defender where to counterattack. It also gives him time to do so.

Different armies came to this in different ways. The British process of organising an attack 'in depth' was a very thorough and methodical way of making relatively deep penetration at little cost. But the British very rarely managed to exploit beyond the initial objective without reorganisation. So, in the German view, such attacks were rarely decisive in themselves.

The key seems to be organising and training to act quickly. Once an objective is gained the attackers should continue the advance if they can. They may not be able to. If no reserve or echelon force is available to continue the advance, the attackers should push out patrols. They should find out where the enemy is, where he is not, and how to bypass him. Mounted patrols (in scout vehicles or tanks) will be quicker than foot patrols. If an echelon force is to be committed, it should be triggered by events (tactical success) rather than by time. Programmed attacks planned in advance rarely maintain the momentum of the advance.

Patrols, or echelon forces, should be able to detect any gaps or weaknesses that exist. That should help overcome the weakness, displayed by Allied forces in Normandy and elsewhere, of not realising that there was no enemy (or practically no enemy) in front of them. A gap should prompt infiltration or bypassing, followed by an attack from the flank or rear to widen the gap. 'No enemy' should prompt an advance. Reconnaissance elements should be inserted as early as possible to continue the advance.

That could easily fail if leading elements are not supported. Avoiding that requires superior commanders to be well forward. It requires good tactical reporting. It requires reserves to be available, so that they can be committed quickly. It requires all commanders to have an understanding of the higher commander's overall intent. It requires all commanders to display initiative, and to be commended when they do. More than anything else, it requires a determination to continue the attack, turn it into an advance, and then pursue.

Air support in this phase can be devastating. In 1944 Montgomery wrote:

- That of the basic fundamentals in war, the first was the requirement to gain control of the air.
- That a retreating enemy offers the most favourable targets to air attack. In such conditions, action by the air forces can turn retreat into rout. It may be decisive.
- Critically, that the moral effect of air action is very great and is out of proportion to the material damage inflicted.

Engineers should be available to support the advance, primarily by breaching or removing obstacles. Behind the leading elements, engineers improve routes to support the advance of the main body.

Indirect fire controllers should accompany the advancing force. They, and reconnaissance units, should occupy observation posts from where they can see well in advance of the leading elements. Guns and mortars should be moved forward to keep in range.

The logistic chain should extend. Some logistic demands can be quite modest: the immediate resupply for an infantry company might be less than a ton of ammunition. The problem is typically getting it to where it is needed. The last hill taken by the Indian Army in the Kashmir in 1999 was 18,000ft (5,500m) above sea level. Every advance of 10km means that resupply stocks, and the trucks carrying them, have to be moved 10km forward. The trucks then have a replenishment route 20km longer. Medical and repair installations should also move forward.

To be truly able to march and fight, formations should have everything they need carried on vehicles. That typically includes a number of days' stock of ammunition, fuel and rations. About 95% of the weight and bulk carried will be artillery ammunition, and will require hundreds of trucks per division.

Individual reinforcements are almost always a problem. That is ridiculous. Armies often have plenty of soldiers; yet infantry units, in particular, are often understrength at the front line. They are often understrength even on peace support operations in peacetime. The problem lies with personnel systems that do not work effectively. No infantry section should be understrength for more than a few hours – and certainly not overnight – where replacements are available. If the system can deliver bullets, why can it not supply soldiers? That applies in any phase of the campaign.

This description has focussed on the infantry. That can be misleading. Tanks have been a major part of the mix since 1917. The discussion has focussed on the infantry because it forms the framework for the positional defence, its operations are often overlooked, and because infantry operations often dictate the pace of the force as a whole. Nevertheless: of itself, infantry combat is often slow and indecisive.

The picture painted above could be interpreted as a single advance followed by a single battle and then a single exploitation. That its not typical. Battles and campaigns are far more complex. Multiple strands of operation occur simultaneously. The previous discussion was intended only to outline what the building blocks of a campaign should look like. The next section looks at the campaign as a whole.

To win *battles*, armies need a mechanism that they can apply right across the battlefield. In the Great War that was based on the rolling barrage. To win *campaigns*, armies need to be able to move that process, or system, across a theatre; winning battles, and creating opportunities to fight further battles at an advantage. Militarily, 'the initiative' is the ability to dictate the course of events. Operationally, once the initiative is seized it should never willingly be given up. That places great value on being able to move quickly from one battle to the next. That is the ability to march and fight. It require a focus not on the battles but the campaign. Battles are just one part of the means by which campaigns or major operations are won.

The British Army had no process for long marches; just a series of planned moves. German tactical doctrine described the march at length. It requires drills that are practiced and exercised at divisional level. Distances of many tens of kilometres per day are easy to achieve if the march is unopposed.

Two things link the march to the fight. One is the deployment: from the march directly into battle. Again, the British had no process for it. Hence the British Army could be described as a mobile siege train. Ironically, British horsed cavalry seemed to have been quite capable of marching and fighting. The US Army seems to have retained the concept rather better. The second thing armies need in order to march and fight is drills for turning local, tactical exploitation into pursuit; from section level to army group.

Marching and fighting requires some understanding of what operation is likely to come next, after the first battle. That is likely to be unpredictable in detail, but can be refined as the march progresses. That requires the ability to command formations more-or-less on the move. It also requires considerable flexibility, not least in attitude.

It seems genuinely difficult to conduct truly mobile, formation-level operations. The Israelis demonstrated considerable expertise, albeit in relatively limited theatres of operations and against a largely predictable threat. Truly mobile operations requires formations, particularly divisions, which are structured, trained and drilled to conduct them. Those formations should be able to create shock and surprise, exploit the results, and then march seamlessly and purposely to the next engagement. In the 1920s, British trials called for armoured formations to manoeuvre under the control, by radio, of one voice. They never quite achieved that. Few armies have.

Part of the difficulty is the habit of conducting operations with continuous flanks. After 1914 the British Army generally operated in situations where every division operated with another division (or, for example, the sea) on each flank. Long moves were ordered from above, with designated objectives at which flank liaison would be re-established. That eroded any requirement for securing open flanks. Unfortunately the Western Front, much of the Western Desert, Italy in 1943-5 and then North West Europe can be seen as aberrations. However, they describe most of the British Army's wartime experience. Other armies have operated perfectly adequately with discontinuous fronts and open flanks. It should be seen as an opportunity, not a problem.

The German Army knew better. The Red Army could, and did achieve breakthroughs; at grievous cost and typically when the Germans were heavily outnumbered. When the Red Army did break through, its formations' flanks were often left exposed to German counterattack. The Red Army often simply did not fight well enough.

The thread of purpose was described above. Operationally, it should connect the strategic goals for the campaign to the tactical objectives assigned to formations and units. As before, the thread of purpose should be simple and clear. As before, the consequence of it being broken is that the resulting activities would be purposeless. However, the consequences of that happening at the operational level are proportionately greater.

Operations need to be synchronised. That is a clear lesson from the late 1980s and the 1990s. But they should be largely self-synchronised. Subordinates should be required to coordinate their actions with those of their peers. Attempting to impose close synchronisation from higher levels imposes the kind of lockstep which, at best, misses opportunities. At worst, it leads to defeat.

In the 100 Days' Campaign of 1918 armies lacked a mechanism for deep operations. Not least, it meant that the German Army could always withdraw to fight again. Deep operations have typically been the domain of indirect fire, aviation and air forces. That has implications. At corps level the FSCL should be more or less at the limit of range of corps artillery, and similarly for the division level. That may have implications for the structure of divisions. Where, for example, should long-range rocket launchers sit? Should corps aspire to long-range attack helicopter raids? Are such discussions in practice a matter of inter-service turf wars, rather than appeals to historic evidence and rational thought?

Empirical evidence points very strongly to the effectiveness of air forces in joint land-air campaigns.[2] Control of the air is statistically the third most important factor in achieving campaign success, after surprise and shock. It is the fifth most important in achieving operational breakthrough. Within that, air reconnaissance (and denying enemy air reconnaissance) is the single most important role. Close air support after a battle (eg, harassing a broken enemy) is the next; then close air support to an attacker. Air interdiction and armed reconnaissance (search and destroy) is less significant. Gaining air superiority is clearly a critical precondition to conducting such missions.

The analysis discussed at the beginning of this chapter indicated the importance of a form of exploitation. We can now understand what that form should be. It should be opportunistic. It should be widespread: troops right across the theatre should be looking for those opportunities. It should be stealthy: it should create, and allow the further exploitation of, surprise and then shock. Surprise is *the* campaign winner. Exploitation should be rapid: opportunities, like surprise, are transient. And exploitation should guide both marching and fighting. It should lead forces to where they can bypass, envelop and encircle. The battles which follow can then be fought at an advantage.

Little of that can be done on foot. Mechanisation is the key. Entirely motorised forces, with armoured elements in the lead, are the tools of operational success. The 20th century gives little evidence of decisive campaigns fought by largely infantry forces, except where the terrain prevented the use of armour.

Breakthrough battles may be necessary. But battles are costly, unpredictable and (perhaps worst of all) time-consuming. Alamein took 19 days; Cobra took ten. Better, by far, to drive a hundred kilometres than fight a battle. Best of all, drive a hundred kilometres in order to win and avoid having to fight another battle. Operational success is to be gained in the enemy's flanks and rear.

2   See Note 1 above.

The contents of this chapter may appear to be a prescription as to how to fight land battles and campaigns. That is not the intention, and is subtly misleading. What this chapter has tried to describe is what the twentieth century tells us was the best way to fight land battles and campaigns. The analysis considered in the first part of this chapter is based, explicitly or implicitly, entirely or mostly, on evidence from the twentieth century. History *is* our best guide to how to fight, but it is an imperfect mirror.

Would it work today? We cannot be sure. IFVs have never really been tested in the sort of wars they were designed for. Nobody, except perhaps the Israelis, has ever tried to fight through a well-designed modern defensive position based around ATGW. We cannot be entirely sure. But war is ever thus.

Which was the better tank, the M4 Sherman tank or the Panther? That and similar questions lead to frequent but silly arguments. Firstly, how do you compare a 30 ton tank with a 40 ton tank? All things being equal, a heavier tank will be better protected. The Americans could, and did, produce a 40 ton tank (the M26). Without a 700hp engine (which the Panther had), it would never be a good tank. But, secondly, the question assumes that land warfare is a series of one-on-one fights. They do sometimes happen; but analysing them isn't particularly insightful. What was more effective: a US armoured division with Shermans, or a panzer division with Panthers and Panzer IVs? That is an entirely different question. What can we learn from looking at warfare in North West Europe in 1944-5? That is possibly even more insightful. The insights include the observation that large-scale tank battles rarely happened.

The discussion at the beginning of this chapter started from an analysis of section tactics and an integration upwards from there. That could be a fallacy. It might be better to conduct the analysis from the performance of the force as a whole, and work downwards. However, all the earliest lessons of the 20th century point towards the need for greater low-level articulation, in order to overcome the problems caused by the rifled bullet. On balance, a bottom-up approach seems appropriate in the first case.

The French Army invented the divisional system in the 1770s and 80s in order to march and fight as a conceptual whole. In the 20th century many armies knew how to fight, well enough. Some knew how to march. Few, if any, demonstrated the ability to march *and* fight. That is, how to switch fluidly between marching and fighting, and back again. The German Army generally understood, although in the Great War it could not find the mobility need to move across the battlefield, nor from one battlefield to the next. Russian armies demonstrated the theory well enough, but fell badly short in the fighting; then resorted to mass and taking mass casualties. That did not always work.

Fighting may make tactical commanders desist. The Great War showed that it rarely made *operational* commanders desist. The key insight from the Second World War and subsequent conflicts is that decisive operational success comes from a judicious balance of fighting and marching. The emphasis should be on the marching.

Physically, motorisation was the key. However, it is not clear that the conceptual integration of long, motorised (road) marches with fighting has yet been achieved by many armies.

12

The Evolutionary Niche

The reader may think he or she knows a lot about irregular warfare, and may be right. Much of that perception may be a 21st century phenomenon. Before the 'Global War on Terror', and military operations in Afghanistan and Iraq, irregular warfare was generally poorly understood.

A related matter is that of 'not the war I saw'. There are now hundreds of thousands of veterans of those campaigns. People are generally not stupid about things they have seen. They will, however, typically have seen a segment of just one, or two, of the 30 or so relevant conflicts since 1990. And recent experience from Iraq and Afghanistan is not relevant to a study of the 20th century.

Terms such as 'Disarmament, Demobilisation and Reintegration' (DDR) are now part of the military lexicon. They were not common in the 20th century. By 2008 there were 15 concurrent DDR programmes, with an annual budget of about $1.6bn. However the first recognisable programme was only started in 1989.

Irregular warfare is grossly understudied. Of the 911 articles related to the 20th century in 'War in History', just 10 referred to irregular warfare in any general way. The subject is studied elsewhere, but not generally by military historians. The Oxford Companion to Military History does not mention either civil war or insurgency. COIN was described in just one of the thousand or so pages. That is as much as 'conquistadors', or 'military chaplains'.

Until the 1930s much of what is now called irregular warfare could be described as tribal uprisings. Dealing with that was seen as a matter of colonial policing. Irregular warfare has been far more common than its regular counterpart. For example, the British Army lost soldiers killed in every single year of the 20th century except 1969. Yet it was 'at war' for not even 20 years. Irregular war was typically far less consequential on a regional or global scale. It may, or may not, have had significant outcome in any one country; but only after several years, and rarely more widely. Unfortunately, domestic casualties were at times significant.

Irregular warfare occurs on land. Naval operations can make an important contribution, not least through blockade. Air force involvement has been far more visible. Its impact has generally been minimal, but highly overstated.

Definitions are hugely important. Definitions are human artefacts and can be used for political purposes. Since conflict is fundamentally human and there is a wide spectrum of human behaviour, we should not expect definitions in this area to be categoric nor exclusive. They will, and do, overlap. Similarly, definitions that seek to tie categories with political purpose or aspirations are unhelpful, because exceptions abound. Furthermore there is no 'definition police': we cannot oblige different writers to abide by the same meanings. We can, at best, state a set of definitions and then be consistent in using them.

The simplest differentiation is between regular and irregular *forces*. That is fairly simple. Irregular *tactics* are mostly those of raiding and sabotage, by light infantry-like forces. Guerrilla warfare is an operational approach based on that, typically involving the creation (and possibly defence) of enclaves. Tactics may expand to include the use of civilian vehicles, with or without weapons mounted on them, and locally-produced weapons.

Irregular forces are often created in an uprising: a collective resort to armed violence, hence an insurgency. Insurgents normally adopt guerrilla warfare techniques. The use of government forces, foreign armed forces, or both to suppress an insurgency is COIN. It is generally an operational approach. The relevant tactics are considered below.

A militia is an irregular armed force. Militias can be pro- or anti-government. So some of them are insurgent militias. Some of them are no more than criminal gangs.

The general definition of war used in this book is 'collective armed violence for the purposes of the state'. Collective armed violence for the *control* of the state often includes both insurgent and pro-government forces. Regular armed forces may fight on one or both sides. Another term for such a conflict is 'civil war'. By that definition civil war is not a subset of (international) war, but a parallel phenomenon. Civil wars typically involve much of the country's armed forces fighting on the side of the *de facto* government. That may also be called COIN. Definitions are neither categoric nor exclusive.

Terrorism is a tactic. It is the use of violence, to create fear, for political purposes *by non-state actors*. It is generally a tactic of weak organisations. Some of them may be exclusively terrorist. The Red Army Faction (or Baader-Meinhof Gang) in West Germany was an example. Many insurgent groups employ terrorism as well as raiding, light infantry tactics.

The use of violence to create fear for political purposes *by state actors* is not 'terrorism'. It is either 'repression' (if perpetrated against the state's own population), or 'state-sponsored terrorism' if perpetrated in other countries. Writers tend to equate repression with terrorism out of a sense of moral equivalence. That is to overlook the difference of purpose and to understate the immorality of repression. Surely, to a liberal conscience, the first duty of a state is to *protect* its population?

Subversion is the covert, illicit or illegal manipulation of political processes. Methods may include intimidation, bribery, infiltration, secret subsidies, false-front propaganda and deniable paramilitary operations. Subversion may be conducted on its own, or as part of other operational approaches.

Collective armed violence *for financial gain* is gangsterism. It is often conducted by 'warlords' or 'drug barons' with their gangs or militias. Insurgent or terrorist organisations can seek financial gain in order to fund their other activities. There is often a blurred line between criminality and sub-state warfare.

Gangsterism, or gang warfare, can only persist in states where law and order is weak. The most effective recourse is generally adequate law enforcement. That also applies to terrorism and subversion. Indigenous police forces may, however, be inadequate to the task. They may require support from national domestic intelligence agencies, and possibly also from the country's armed forces. Legislative action may be needed to properly criminalise terrorism and subversion. For example, it can be argued that Britain did not have a comprehensive legal framework to criminalise terrorism until 2005, despite (by then) 26 years of anti-terrorist operations in Northern Ireland.

All conflicts are asymmetric. But how much, and in what respects? It is doubtful whether the nature of 'asymmetry' *per se* is a useful subject of academic debate. Analysis which investigates disparities of ends, ways and means might be more productive

We can identify two thresholds among the above definitions. The first is the choice to resort to armed violence: that is, to take up arms (for political purposes). That, of itself, tends to result in terrorism. The second, higher, threshold is the organisation of *collective* armed violence (fighting in groups). That is the point at which an insurgency can be identified.

There is rarely a sharp divide between regular and irregular warfare. Even the most 'regular' wars can have significant irregular aspects. We can consider irregular aspects of regular warfare quite quickly.

It is not clear how effective irregular units have been overall. The evidence is ambiguous. Specially-trained regular forces conducting covert intelligence gathering, or raids, in regular warfare have had important successes. Examples include USMC Raider battalions in the Pacific, or the British Long Range Desert Group and SAS in the Western Desert. In the latter case they were part of a process of pushing the Luftwaffe back from its forward airfields, an important operational effect.

The impact of the Chindits in Burma is far less clear. The operational impact of the 1943 and 1944 expeditions was modest. There were second- or third-order benefits. Some were nebulous, such as 'moral ascendancy over the Japanese' (felt by who?) The Chindits were formed from 14 British infantry battalions, three other British units operating as infantry, four Gurkha and three West African battalions. That amounts to more than two divisions. There were never more than 10 other British and Empire divisions in Burma. It seems highly doubtful that the Chindits represented the best use of the available manpower.

The irregular (mostly American and British special forces) 'Scud hunting' operations in Western Iraq in 1991 had an important strategic effect: they helped prevent Israeli involvement. In the right circumstances the use of 'special' forces can have an impact out of proportion to the numbers involved.

Irregular warfare has often been strategically indecisive. One study suggests that, about eight years after a civil war, a country has about a 40% chance of returning to conflict. The fighting did not definitively resolve the issue. The figure decreases by only 1% or so per year.

War is the extension of politics with other means. In most irregular warfare, resolution will be political and not military. Where such political resolution is ineffective or insufficient, the country will revert to violence in a few years.

That sentence could usefully be repeated, in block capitals.

Insurgent and terrorist organisations were often strategically naive. They had little idea how to apply collective armed violence purposefully. But the question has sometimes been unimportant. They seek to gain political power in a single, albeit protracted, campaign. They may conduct that campaign very well. Sometimes the campaign is poorly planned, or executed, or both. Insurgency can be a good way for a weak faction to gain power, particularly against an occupying power. Conversely terrorism rarely worked of itself. Terrorism often seeks attention, acknowledgment and recognition. Those goals were often achieved. However, where they extended to authority and governance, they were almost never successful. That typically required a transition to insurgency.

COIN strategies falls into two broad categories: those of indigenous and non-indigenous governments. The more significant case is the non-indigenous, namely intervention. Interventionist governments, and their armed forces, often believed that 'this one will work', despite good evidence to the contrary. They tended to overestimate the ability of armed forces to pacify, but underestimate the importance of other, non-military activities. They also tended to underestimate the duration and the social, economic and financial costs. In practice interventionist governments can rarely separate the conduct of the intervention from domestic political issues in the homeland. Similarly for issues of prestige, credibility and international standing. Success is doubtful. Years of occupation are likely, regardless of the eventual outcome.

The organisational response to failure can be enlightening. The case of Vietnam suggests, firstly 'let's not do this'; secondly, an aversion to casualties in subsequent conflicts and a dislike of media attention. Thirdly, it suggests an organisational rejection in which armed forces delete the 'lessons learnt' from their files. Regrettably, those who ignore the lessons of history are fated to repeat them. Perhaps that in part explains the enthusiasm described above.

The wars of decolonisation present a different case: one where the colonial government may have been quite capable of achieving its intended strategic objectives. Regrettably the lessons may be irrelevant (now that decolonisation is substantially complete) and hubristic (where the country, and its armed forces, think they can apply those lessons in different circumstances, some decades later).

Uprisings, seen here as typically being a single (if protracted) insurgent campaign, have succeeded in about 30% of cases. The insurgents achieved some degree of success in a further 29% of cases. Thus the insurgent had at least some success about 59% of the time. However, the government achieved complete success in 41%, and at least *some* success in 70%, of cases.

Insurgent groups have often been naive, poorly organised, prone to dissent, and easy to infiltrate at first. They may well not be particularly representative of the bulk of the population. They are often taken over by determined (and perhaps ruthless) leaders: witness Lenin. Those leaders' sense of self-importance sometimes develops into a sense of personal, national and even divine destiny.

Insurgent leaders have often been relatively well-educated, charismatic and middle class. Ironically their education was often provided by the colonial or occupying power. Those leaders may previously have been members of indigenous armed forces. Those armed forces were often established by the former colonial power and may be the only strong institutions in the country. After decolonisation, those armed forces were organisationally more effective than the country's political institutions. The resulting coups were often successful and relatively bloodless, but generally did not lead to good governance. Why should a Sandhurst-trained second lieutenant make a good president?

Typically only a small proportion of a population have been committed insurgents: say 10%. Another 10% or so might have been committed to the government. The real struggle in an insurgency is for the support of the middle 80% or so. That 'trapped middle' will understandably tend to side with strength, not moral virtue. Individuals tend to be influenced by the real issues of the moment: perhaps duress, poverty, unemployment or injustice. Any support to the insurgents, or the government, may not be widespread and may be coerced.

The presence of identifiable minorities sways the statistics considerably. An insurgent organisation may quite easily mobilise the support of much of an ethnic, religious or social minority. Specific cases (such as Turkish Cypriots or Tamils) often reflected the failure (or, more commonly, the rejection) of a constitution designed by the withdrawing colonial power to balance the powers and rights of majority and minority communities. The existence of minorities was sometimes obscured by the names of political parties which were largely delineated on tribal lines. Alternatively, the insurgent community may have arisen from a grossly disenfranchised majority, as in Rhodesia or South Africa.

Religion is never a cause. Theology is never the issue. For example, almost the only fundamental theological difference between Irish Catholics and Ulster Protestants was the nature of the Miracle of Transubstantiation. Does the host represent the body of Christ during the Mass, or does it actually become it? The Miracle of Transubstantiation did not cause a single death in the Troubles. Theology was at times mobilised to justify political positions. Where a conflict had apparent religious motivation the real issue was power, hence politics. It was typically the politics of identity, and perhaps perceived discrimination. Northern Ireland is a case in point. So were Cyprus and the Palestinian uprisings. If one examines ideology which seems to be religiously motivated, one generally finds expressions of out-group identity: 'they are not like us'.

Insurgent groups often suffer from ill-discipline. They are frequently plagued with factions and splinter groups, who can dilute the effectiveness of the uprising and may allow government forces to divide and overcome. Individuals may act as informers or betray the organisation. Insurgent groups do not have police forces, courts nor prisons. Imposing or maintaining discipline will therefore be illicit and typically involve violence. It will often be intentionally brutal and exemplary. To a liberal conscience, it may well be revolting.

For the government, military success occurs when the insurgent can no longer take recourse to violence. That is unlikely to be clear-cut. The insurgents will typically just drift away. COIN forces erode support, deny success, prevent recruitment, reduce the insurgents' freedom of action, interdict operations, capture arms and kill or capture insurgents. That will not tend to be dramatic

It has typically been very difficult to fix an insurgent force in order to strike it sufficiently hard to persuade it to desist through force alone. Where local military success occurred, it was difficult to exploit. Finding, fixing and exploitation were all difficult. Military operations are most unlikely to be decisive. They will not resolve or settle the issues which drove the insurgents to violence. COIN forces can persuade insurgents to desist because it is no longer effective, or cost-effective, to continue. Ideally the insurgent should be given no hope for a better future through violence. Reducing the general level of violence is critical to allowing political, social and economic development.

An insurgency occurs where political issues have persuaded a faction or factions to resort to violence. If government forces succeed in suppressing an insurgency solely through military means, the insurgency will recur. Only two things will stop that happening: repression, or political change sufficient to remove the grievance that caused the uprising. The resolution of an insurgency will be political.

COIN is not, primarily, a battle of ideas. It is a struggle for the support of the uncommitted middle. If the insurgents win, it will be because they have captured the support of that group. Resolving an insurgency will always require political change. (If the insurgents succeed, they will take power. That is political change.) Cynically, such change might be largely presentational. It will often involve new legislation and changes to systems of governance. It will typically require economic development and social change, such as the provision of education and health care.

Although *some* change, short of regime change, occurred in 29% of insurgencies, that may be a good thing. For example, the goals of the Northern Ireland Civil Rights Association (which motivated the emergence of PIRA) in the late 1960s now seem almost entirely unobjectionable. They have all been achieved.

We know what wins. In 2010 analysts at Rand identified a series of positive and negative factors in achieving success in COIN[1]. There are 15 'good' and 12 'bad' factors, paraphrased in Figure 12-1:

1   Paul, Christopher; Clarke, Colin; and Grill, Beth, *Victory has a Thousand Fathers*, (Santa Monica: The Rand Corporation, 2010), pp 88-88.

Good COIN Practices	Bad COIN Practices
Good strategic communications.	Collective punishment and escalating repression.
Significantly reduce tangible support to the insurgents.	The COIN force was an external occupier.
Establish or maintain legitimacy in the area of the conflict.	Security force or governments actions contributed to new grievances claimed by the insurgents.
The government was at least partially a democracy.	Militias worked at cross-purposes to the security force or governments.
Adequate intelligence.	Resettlement or removal of civilians for population control.
Security forces of sufficient strength to force the insurgents to fight as guerrillas.	Collateral damage by the security forces was perceived as worse than the insurgents'.
The government was competent.	The security forces were perceived locally as being worse than the insurgents.
Avoidance of excessive collateral damage, disproportionate use of force, or other illegitimate use of force.	The security forces failed to adapt their tactics, operations or strategy.
The security force sought to engage and establish positive relations with the local population.	The security forces engaged in more intimidation or coercion than the insurgents.
Short-term investment, infrastructure or development, or property reform, in the local area.	The insurgent force was individually more professional or better motivated than the security forces.
The majority of the local population supported the security forces.	The security forces relied on looting for sustainment.
The security force established and then expanded secure areas.	The security forces and government had different goals or levels of commitment.
The security force had, and then used, uncontested air superiority.	
The security force provided or ensured the provision of basic services.	
The security forces created or maintained a perception of security.	

Figure 12-1 Positive and Negative Factors for Success in COIN.

The factors were identified in a study of 30 insurgencies from 1978 onwards. Success depends on the arithmetical sum of positive and negative factors. That is: do more good things than bad, and you will succeed. In those 30 cases a positive sum (more good factors than bad) perfectly predicted success for the government side. A negative sum perfectly predicted failure. It is that simple. Simple, however, is not the same as easy.

This is not new. In the late 1890s the French General Hubert Lyautey practised policies based on 'politics, force and economic development' in Madagascar. He went on to practice COIN, and then command, in Morocco until 1925. Political, social and economic change can be decisive if done well. If an economy grows by just 4% per year, it will double in 17-18 years. At 13% it will be just six years. Growth at that rate, if allied to a reasonable distribution of wealth, can rapidly persuade the majority of a population to support the *de facto* government.

Much rubbish has been written about the duration of insurgencies and COIN campaigns. It results in sayings such as 'fast in war, slow in COIN'. It tends to confuse correlation with mechanism. It may be entirely possible to change the military situation quite quickly (but see below). At best, that creates the conditions for political, hence social and economic, development. Those developments will take longer. But the protracted nature of many COIN campaigns resulted largely from a failure to make the necessary political changes in any timely fashion. Consensus may be hard to reach. Politicians may prevaricate or not agree to change. Mrs Thatcher made no political initiatives in Northern Ireland in almost 12 years. When such things happen it becomes hard to sustain a military campaign which is largely limited to containing violence.

Doctrine written for regular warfare will need to be applied wisely, if at all. For example, 'concentration of force' is generally considered to be a principle of war. It may apply in COIN. If it does, it applies in limited circumstances. That is, when the enemy can be clearly and unambiguously identified; and struck without harming innocent civilians, causing unnecessary damage to their property, or being perceived as unjust. That may be quite rare. Hence the notion that the principles of war need to be interpreted in an almost metaphysical sense in COIN. It would probably be better to say that the principles of war need better definition. Alternatively, paradigms of regular and irregular warfare need revision.

Many armies have COIN doctrines. They have been applied with varying degrees of success. What may have been more important was the writing of theatre directives to unify activities across all relevant lines of operations for a given campaign. Where such directives or plans have been well-considered, simple and clear they have generally contributed to overall success. That extends into the early 21st Century. The American Generals David Petraeus and James Mattis oversaw the writing of a new COIN Manual, the Army's FM 3-24 (the USMC's MCWP 3-33.5) for operations in Afghanistan and Iraq. It may have more important that Petraeus wrote, and oversaw the execution of, campaign directives for both theatres.

Regular forces have often been required to operate in 'non-traditional' roles. Sappers and gunners acting as infantry is one example. Another example is sappers building schools. Those kind of tasks frequently occur because the circumstances are dangerous, there is nobody else, or both. But there is a limit. Sappers can build schools, but cannot staff them. In a sense using soldiers in 'non-traditional' roles is too easy. It can delay the real political, social and economic development needed to address the causes of the insurgency and prevent a recurrence of violence.

In the 1950s Britain deployed up to about 40,000 regular troops in Malaya, and 400,000 indigenous security forces. At independence, the population of Malaya was perhaps 13 million. It is now over 33 million. At the end of the Mau Mau uprising Kenya's population was about four million. It is now about 40 million. Irregular warfare has long required indigenous security forces in large numbers. That requirement has grown as populations have grown. It may not, if insurgencies can be contained within restricted sectors of the population.

Population growth has probably also contributed to a different phenomenon. As populations grew it became easier for terrorist groups to live and to operate hidden amongst the people.

Terrorist incidents are fleeting. The perpetrators may have left the scene before the violence occurs (for example, if they place time bombs). They generally exploit the advantage of surprise and do not stand and fight. They have typically planned their withdrawal in advance. Any forensic evidence created may be destroyed in the resulting explosion or fire. Terrorism (and to some extent insurgency) is fundamentally difficult to defeat.

Whoever controls the ground can control the narrative. Control of the air is irrelevant to that. Control of the air did not give decisive advantage to COIN forces. The evidence before 1939 is, at best, ambiguous. The evidence from after 1945, of more than 100 campaigns, is not. As in regular warfare, air support was very useful for reconnaissance and intelligence gathering. It was hugely useful for tactical air transport. The helicopter revolutionised COIN. But helicopters may have prompted a perception that COIN forces can come and go at will. Many airmobile operations in Vietnam only lasted a few hours. Coming, staying and defeating the insurgents might have been better.

Air attack has had a very mixed impact. It can be helpful in support of ground troops in contact. That may be counterproductive when its use becomes the default tactic. Air attack can be very popular with the domestic population of a non-indigenous COIN force. It looks dramatic on TV, the consequences are rarely visible, and it rarely has a cost in terms of lost aircrew. It can divide non-indigenous and host-nation authorities, because of collateral casualties and damage.

Air attack in COIN is only really effective where the insurgents can be made to stand and fight. That is rare. The damage may be transient. The resulting resentment is not. Air attack is typically an ineffective substitute to the real business of defeating insurgents and bringing about political, economic and social change. It tends to be largely unnecessary, only effective in limited circumstances, and costly. Air support has made very little difference to the outcome of COIN at the campaign level. We should, nonetheless, expect its supporters to continue to overstate its effects and underplay its failures. They have done so for decades.

Broadcast media developed slowly in the early 20th century. Development accelerated in the 1990s with the advent of digital and satellite technology. Real-time broadcast news was only common at the end of the century. Terrorists and insurgents generally exploited the media faster than governments and their agencies reacted. In the 1970s, for example, British government media and public influence activities in Northern Ireland were described as woeful and inadequate. The approach was naive: 'gentlemen don't do that'. It was frequently amateur by the standards of best practice in other sectors. Their opponents were less principled. Government failures and omissions handed cheap wins to the opposition. If the only message was the insurgents', that would be the only message to be heard.

The news media were complicit. Practically every terrorist or insurgent incident was unthinkingly translated into a 'spectacular'. The media learnt to rush to the scene like sheep. They competed to be the first with the news. Damage (and sometimes casualties) made good footage. Interviews with casualties, survivors or eyewitnesses added to the drama. Pious pronouncements that it is the journalist's duty to convey the truth were undermined by the theatrical techniques which they, and their production teams, use to dramatize the events. Some individual journalists have been very professional in the way they disguise their deeply-held partisan biases. That includes some working for highly respected international broadcasting organisations. It still happens.

The media has generally been quick to profess its independence (where that is the case). However, by the manner of its reporting, it has done much of the terrorist's or insurgent's job for him. After Pearl Harbor, Hollywood saw it as its patriotic duty to support the US war effort. That may be somewhat extreme in conflicts which are not wars of national survival. Changing the way in which terrorist or insurgent actions are reported by news media might be a more responsible and even-handed response.

There is little evidence that government media and influence activities have had much positive effect on the course and outcome of COIN campaigns. There have, of course, been excessive claims from proponents. Public information *can* reassure the uncommitted middle portion of the population. It can counter, and help to neutralise, the insurgent's messages. But government talk is not action. There is some evidence that government information operations can work well when they reinforce real pain or damage to insurgents, inflicted in other lines of operations. It is typically one of the few ways that government forces can exploit tactical success. It is another reason to ensure that all lines of operation are properly coordinated across a COIN campaign. The seemingly quaint system of District Action Committees and Sub-District Action Committees developed by the British in colonial COIN operations was, at the time, the method used to achieve that integration.

Insurgent tactics were described briefly above. They are typically the tactics of necessity and of the reality of being, at least initially, quite weak. Success can breed success as they capture more weapons, attract more recruits and develop new and better tactics. Terrorist and insurgent groups are probably quicker and more likely to adapt and evolve than regular security forces. They may have an existential reason to adapt: if they fail, they lose and perhaps die. They generally do not have cultural or professional baggage. Insurgent groups are also likely to deploy 'political' agents tasked to persuade, cajole, indoctrinate or coerce the population into supporting the insurgency.

Criminality can be a major feature of insurgencies. Insurgents have already crossed the line into unlawful action. A generalised breakdown of law and order can give rise to opportunism. Crime can be used to generate funding through bank robbery and extortion. It can be used to extend authority through racketeering and protection. That can lead to a degree of social control. Drug-dealing may be taken over, or suppressed. Suppressing drug dealers prevents social control by rival groups. It can also be presented as morally beneficial ('the police did nothing to stop drug dealing; we have'). Conversely governments can, and should, go to considerable lengths to identify and eliminate the funding of insurgent movements.

Searches, sweeps and raids have been typical COIN tactics. They can be gloriously unsuccessful unless accurately targeted. Insurgent groups rarely chose to stand and fight. Indications such as the sound of helicopters often suggested the need to melt away; any fighting became unintentional. It is difficult to fix insurgents in order to strike them. An approach based on a large number of foot patrols saturating an area presents insurgents with a considerable problem. They may be locally outnumbered. It will be difficult to track all the patrols, and therefore difficult to avoid them. Fighting any one patrol (by accident or design) will attract the others. Failing to fight surrenders both credibility and the initiative. It may therefore surrender control of territory and popular support. Switching patrols rapidly from area to area by helicopter or vehicle makes the insurgents' task far more difficult.

This is a deliberate tactic designed to engage the insurgent. It may result in him being found and fixed in unpredictable and serendipitous ways. He is fixed in a different sense, because he needs to engage the security forces. An insurgent group which does not fight is not an insurgent group. When the insurgents do so, they can be struck. Naturally they will counter such tactics by, for example, denying freedom of movement. Clearing mines and booby traps gives the insurgent further opportunities to engage the security forces. That then gives the security forces further opportunities to engage the insurgents. That should be seen as success.

What emerges is a framework of operations which should reassure and protect the population. In doing so it should force the insurgents to either come out and engage the security forces (attracting defeat), or desist. The framework will consist of static observation posts (for both security and intelligence gathering) and mobile patrols. Just as in regular warfare, reserves should be held at every level, to engage insurgents when they show themselves. The balance has often been wrong. Too many troops were tied up in static security and too few were available to patrol. Reserves were committed to clear up after incidents, rather than to fix and strike the insurgents when they exposed themselves.

Armies do not just fight. They manipulate the use, and the threat of the use, of force. Manipulating the threat of the use of force is the arena of information operations. All military operations in irregular warfare are underpinned by the ability to employ force if necessary. Many armed forces displayed a naïve approach to manipulating the threat of the use of force in irregular warfare. Probably none managed to integrate it into their core doctrine. It was generally a bolt-on or afterthought, if present at all.

The term 'minimum use of force' is a misnomer. It is more appropriate to say 'restraint and judgement in the use of force'. That is especially important in terms of the need to avoid collateral damage and civilian casualties. Many of the techniques of regular warfare can be used where doing so does not alienate the uncommitted middle.

Protecting the population is not an end in itself. COIN is a contest for the support of the population. To gain and retain their support, the security forces do need to protect them. But protecting them, like defeating the insurgents, is largely done in order to allow political, hence social and economic, development.

Military culture can get in the way. So-called 'Special Forces' can have a propensity for direct action. They can see targeted raids and 'decapitation operations' to kill or capture insurgent leaders as being their *raison d'etre*. That can be unhelpful. Targeted raids *can be* useful. But if the population's main experience of the security forces is of doors being kicked in at dead of night, they will consider the security forces to be worse than the Gestapo. 'Decapitation' rarely works at more than a local level. Leaders will be replaced; often by younger but brighter, more capable and more committed people. 'Decapitation' has worked very well where the operation targets the whole leadership of an insurgent group in a region simultaneously.

As a COIN campaign develops, more and more reliance will have to (and should) be placed on indigenous security forces. Just as within the general population, there will be a small proportion of the indigenous security forces who are unquestionably loyal to the government; a small proportion who are corrupt; and an uncommitted middle whose loyalty is critical to success. Indigenous security forces can often be infiltrated by one faction or another. The biggest risk may not be of infiltration by insurgents, but by pro-government militias. One of the earliest reform actions taken in Northern Ireland was to disband the (largely Loyalist) paramilitary police reserve, the 'B Specials'.

Distributing indigenous security forces in small detachments has at times made infiltration and corruption worse. It may be better to restrict the numbers of those local police forces. The bulk of the indigenous forces should then be formed into army or gendarmerie units which can be moved as required, and which are easier to oversee.

What does tactical success in COIN look like? Successes include the death, capture or imprisonment of insurgents; preventing recruitment; deterring and interdicting operations; and capturing or destroying arms and supplies. Higher-level military success is reflected by pacified areas where insurgents cannot operate. That means that they can no longer influence, coerce or intimidate the population. In those areas political, social and economic development can, and should, take place. The overall military mission should be to deny the insurgents the ability to operate; in order to permit political, social and economic development.

Training is critical. Soldiers trained for general war need to be trained in restraint in the use of force. They, and their units, need to be trained in theatre-specific tactics; the techniques of searching; of detecting and avoiding IEDs; and of how to interact with the civil population. In the 1980s British infantry battalions would cease training for general war and undergo about three month's bespoke training before deploying to Northern Ireland, despite typically having undertaken operational tours there only two to three years before.

Intelligence is critical to COIN. Insurgents are often not numerous, act covertly, and hide amongst the population. Finding out who they are, where they are, and what they are doing is critical to being able to act against them. Predicting what they are about to do is difficult. It can create rare opportunities to surprise and shock them. Intelligence gathering and intelligence staff work can be major activities. By the 1990s roughly one in every seven soldiers in Northern Ireland was directly involved in intelligence work. Sharing intelligence between security services, and between indigenous and non-indigenous forces, has sometimes been problematic but highly beneficial when done well. Building up a critical mass of such human intelligence (HUMINT) can take considerable time. That is one reason why military operations in irregular warfare are not likely to be as quick as in regular operations.

Much useful intelligence can be obtained by interrogation. Interrogation methods have inevitably tended to be close to the limits of what is lawful, in order to extract the maximum benefit. Methods must be kept secret, so that insurgents cannot develop counters them. The products must also be kept secret, not least so that the insurgents do not know what the security forces have learnt. There is also an issue of counterintelligence: the security forces may have learnt about the insurgent's intelligence and security operations, and wish to keep that secret. So there are several valid reasons why interrogation methods and products are kept secret.

Well-intentioned liberal academics may not understand that. Some commentators may chose to ignore it. Both groups may overlook the fact that those who have been interrogated are often unreliable witnesses (having a tendency to exaggerate); may have an interest in (or benefit from) lying; and may (quite understandably) have difficulty in being objective.

Soldiers are not lawyers. Some are highly disciplined. Where that discipline has been based on military law which is consistent with international humanitarian law (IHL), and the army prides itself on maintaining the rule of law, soldiers have worked within legal constraints very effectively. Indeed, that should be the goal. Most other circumstances make them less, rather than more, effective; at least in the long term. There may be short-term advantage to be gained by beating up or executing insurgent suspects. It will be no more than that.

In practice, despite (or perhaps because of) the possession of doctoral degrees in this or that subject, some academics seem to have understood the practical application of IHL less well than serving subalterns.

The human experience of COIN can be very much like that of war. 'Low-intensity operations' may have seemed highly intense to those participating, at certain times and in certain places. But there are differences. Regular war tends to result in more casualties overall, a greater proportion of the casualties being killed, and also a greater proportion as immediate psychological cases. Of the wounded, more are severely wounded. It has not been unusual, however, for battalions to return from a few months of COIN operations with one or two dozen dead and several dozen wounded. Front-line strengths were just as likely to be below establishment as in regular warfare. It is just as ridiculous, and just as avoidable.

Just as in regular warfare, COIN expertise could be built up over decades. British intelligence staff in the Balkans in the 1990s had generally all served in Northern Ireland. They served there under officers who had been trained by a generation who had served in Malaya, Kenya, Aden and Cyprus. That generation had served under officers who in turn had served in Ireland, Iraq and Palestine. They had learnt their intelligence skills in the Great War. The same was true in principle for operations staff and front-line units.

Military behaviour relating to the use of force was, obviously, a highly important issue. Excessive or unlawful force alienated the population like little else. Three incidents involving British troops stand out. On 13 April 1919 a British brigadier ordered Indian troops to open fire on a crowd at Amritsar in the Punjab, killing hundreds. The order was probably lawful. The use of force was clearly excessive by modern standards. On 21 November 1920 British police auxiliaries opened fire on a (Gaelic) football crowd at Croke Park in Dublin. 14 civilians were killed. Dozens were wounded. The shooting almost definitely resulted from a failure of fire discipline (ie, firing in the heat of the moment without lawful cause).

On 30 June 1972 British paratroopers shot and killed 13 civilians in Londonderry[2]. The circumstances strongly suggest another breakdown of fire discipline[3]. Those three incidents alienated large sections of the local population and are remembered to this day. The murders of 13 British soldiers and police in the morning before the Croke Park incident tends to be overlooked. Looking elsewhere, the My Lai massacre in Vietnam on 16 March 1968 resulted in the murder of over 300, and perhaps 500, civilians. The circumstances were not well known at the time, but the incident is no less notorious.

Overall, however, the most important insight relating to tactics in COIN relates to adaptation and evolution. Insurgent groups adapt and evolve. The tactics used by the security forces will not be a perfect fit at first. They will become irrelevant, unless the security forces also adapt and evolve. Probably the most important single factor in success over the long term is managing that process. It requires an open mind, an awareness of the need to adapt, and scientific and technical support. On one occasion a British EW operator in Northern Ireland predicted that PIRA would soon change the frequencies it was using for radio-controlled IEDs. He then predicted exactly which frequency would be adopted. That prediction both saved lives and gave technical intelligence staff a critical advantage.

2   Another civilian later died of wounds. 12 other people were injured.
3   The battalion involved had shot another 11 civilians over three successive days the previous August.

Discussion of COIN campaigns and tactics tends to conceal a simple, but critical, anomaly. It is that some irregular forces have persisted, and continued to operate for many years, despite the actions of seemingly more powerful security forces. Indeed, some have eventually won.

In March 1982 all 300 or so PIRA Volunteers took on a British Army brigade in Northern Ireland in open battle. Within hours the whole of PIRA was dead or in captivity. Clearly that did not happen. Described that way, however, the anomaly is obvious (and in 1982 there was nearer a division than a brigade of the British Army in Northern Ireland). Many insurgent groups have existed in what can be described as an evolutionary niche. It is a niche in the sense that the security forces cannot, in practice, bring their strength to bear. It is evolutionary in that the insurgents adapt and evolve to exploit local conditions for their own protection.

Those conditions may in part be geographical. Columbia is a relatively large country with a large population. It has a dozen or so large cities. They, and most of the population, lie in (or west of) the Andes. More than half of the land area, but only six per cent of the population, lies east of the Andes. Much of that area is jungle. So Columbian insurgents could hide either in the cities, or the jungles, or both.

The niche conditions may in part be social. In many countries, ethnic or other social divisions dictate that (in practice) sections of the population will hide and protect insurgents from government and non-indigenous security forces. Such divisions may be indicated by religious affiliation.

Economic aspects may also be important. Some governments simply cannot afford protracted COIN operations (in which case the apparent anomaly is explained: government forces are actually not powerful enough to prevail). In some cases the insurgents have access to funding which allows them to continue long after they would otherwise have capitulated. Drug crops, or subsidies from other countries, may provide the funding.

There may be legal aspects to the niche. Tactically, many terrorist suspects in Northern Ireland remained at liberty because the security forces would not arrest them. Operationally or strategically, that was because legislation was not changed to allow their conviction.

In practice every evolutionary insurgent niche will be different. Political, legal, social and economic conditions in every country are unique. Each insurgent force will adapt and evolve differently, not least because it faces a unique array of security forces. Those security forces will adapt and evolve in a unique way, and so on. The precise conditions of an evolutionary niche will be a unique balance of geographical, political, social, legal and economic factors. Analysts and security forces should therefore be very cautious about applying templated solutions to insurgencies.

If a niche does not form, the security forces will be able to prevail; probably quite quickly (a matter of a few months). That begs the question as to how government forces should respond. A list of empirical 'do's and 'don't's is at Figure 12-1 above. Another approach, however, would be to investigate quite explicitly what prevents the security forces from prevailing. That is, how to close the niche.

The immediate answer might be, for example, a lack of HUMINT. But the underlying reason for that might be social (that the population won't betray the insurgents). The government and security forces might then address the reasons why that is the case. Alternatively, if geography is a major factor then better surveillance, improved mobility and better tactics may reduce or eliminate the niche.

If the answer is political (that the government cannot, or will not take, sufficient action) then analysis has reached the real core of the problem. Foreign intervention might affect the situation (for example, by invading or imposing a regime change). But without substantive political change, the situation will not be resolved definitively.

In Northern Ireland the problem was not a lack of intelligence. There was a lack of political will during the Thatcher government. But terrorist suspects could not be convicted without revealing evidence, or sources, which the government or security forces were not prepared to reveal; or for lack of witnesses willing to testify; or similar. Changes to the law might have overcome that. There was legal conservatism, a commendable reluctance to infringe human rights, a lack of understanding of the dynamics of the problem, and resistance from lawyers with Republican sympathies. But, more importantly, there does not seem to have been a recognition of the nature, scope and scale of the issue. Had there been, there might have been a reasoned debate as to how to resolve it. That could have addressed ethical, legislative, security and jurisprudential concerns. Tragically that debate never took place. Between 59 and 125 people died in the Troubles in each year that Mrs Thatcher was PM.

Irregular warfare in the 20th century was understudied; widespread; but generally less consequential globally than general war. Individual conflicts were often protracted and sometimes indecisive: a country might fall back into conflict a few years later. Irregular warfare was generally indecisive both tactically (few engagements achieved anything) and operationally (fighting did not settle the campaign). What the security forces could achieve by fighting was to do suppress the insurgency. That would allow political, hence also economic and social, development to take place.

Insurgencies, and COIN, are resolved through political developments. Where those developments do not take place, conflict *may* be interrupted by military action. It will probably break out again in a few years. That is because the underlying grievances, which caused a section of the population to resort to violence, were not addressed.

Insurgencies are not resolved by military means. The military mission is to defeat the insurgents in order to allow political, hence economic and social, development. Defeated insurgents cannot effectively influence the uncommitted bulk of the population. Insurgency and COIN are two sides of a single struggle for the support of the population.

We know what wins. We also know that military success may take a long time, because insurgent groups can occupy evolutionary niches where security forces cannot in practice bring collective armed force to bear. In each individual campaign the government and security forces should seek to identify what factors constitute that niche. Those factors will typically be a unique mixture of geography, law, sociology, economics and politics. Identifying the niche is the first step to forcing the insurgents out of it, or bringing it down around their heads. We should not expect it to work immediately. Insurgent groups adapt and evolve. Smart operational planning would ensure that the measures taken to eliminate the environmental niche are some of the same measures needed to address the underlying grievances: the grievances which caused a section of the population to resort to violence. That would be both effective and efficient. It would also save lives.

13

'It Is Clearly Illegal ...'

The 20th century was the first century of air warfare. Technological developments were impressive. By 1945 Lancaster bombers could carry up to 14,000lbs of bombs. They could fly up to 2,500 miles at up to 280mph. Just 20 years later a Phantom could carry up to 18,000lbs of bombs and fly at up to 1470mph. Unrefuelled range was not remarkable, but Phantoms could carry drop tanks or be refuelled in flight, extending range considerably. In the 1990s digital technology improved sensors, weapons, communications and the ability to control aircraft over wide areas dramatically. The next technological development (the widespread use of composite materials in air structures) was just around the corner.

In another sense, however, not much had changed. By 1915 aircraft could shoot down enemy aircraft or attack surface targets. By the end of the century the technology had developed enormously, but the basic proposition had not: aircraft attack, and then fly home. Aerial (that is, air) warfare is conducted as raids.

Air warfare is inherently a very technical discipline. That can lead to difficulties. There is a tendency to dwell on the technology and the techniques. That is to overlook the purposes to which they are employed, which are more important. A related issue is the tendency to report air warfare in terms of effort (such as sorties flown) or performance (bombs dropped) rather than effect (targets destroyed) or, most importantly, outcome achieved. The latter is difficult. For that and other reasons, it is often overlooked.

The RAF's central air warfare doctrine was encapsulated in AP 3000, 'British Airpower Doctrine'. Its Third Edition was published in 1999. It was the RAF's endorsed version of its central warfighting doctrine at the end of the century. In listing 16 factors that underpin the effective exploitation of airpower the first was 'aircraft carriers' (an interesting positional statement). Critical among them, however, was 'impermanence'. Air warfare is conducted as a series of raids. Air attack is transient. Its effect is episodic.

The tactic of raiding relies on the accumulation of many small combat or logistic successes. Thus with air warfare: sorties in which enemy aircraft are shot down; or sorties in which logistic stocks, surface forces, factories or transport infrastructure are damaged. Air raids benefit from the ubiquity of flight. Aircraft can attack any relevant target, whilst defenders might try (and generally fail) to defend them all. Individual raids have no tactical impact other than the immediate objective of the raid, possibly accompanied by some psychological effect (the defenders may become demoralised, or similar).

Bombing is raiding. Bombing offensives such as the Allied Combined Bomber Offensive (CBO) of the Second World War rely on an accumulation of logistic and infrastructure damage. That is the methodology reported by Bomber Command. However it typically overlooks repair, rebuilding, replenishment and reinforcement. Damage is generally transient, and largely tactical. Operationally Germany could, and did, rebuild its factories. Indeed bombing could be counterproductive. In the German case it not only encouraged, but to an extent forced, planners to re-prioritise and rationalise production. Industrial production grew, especially in critical areas such as tank production.

Raiding depends on both physical and psychological effects for operational success. Both are transient. It is extremely difficult to exploit such transient effects using aircraft. After a raid, they fly home. The main recourse is repeated attack. That becomes protracted and costly. There have been very few 'knockout blows'. They have largely resulted from either massive material superiority or operational surprise. When raiding becomes protracted and costly, the advantages of the approach are largely lost. That is broadly what happened to Bomber Command by 1943 or so. That is the point at which Britain failed to make the strategic decision to scale back its bomber offensive. It was no cheaper than land attack. It did not work by itself. It resulted in both wasted resources and wasted lives.

It is entirely possible to adopt persisting (rather than raiding) logistic approaches. That is, permanently denying the enemy the use of logistic resources. It is done by capturing them. By early 1944 iron ore from the Donbass and oil from Ploieşti were, literally, critical to the German war economy. Cutting off Romanian oil and overrunning the Donbass with T34s did more harm to German industrial production than any number of Lancasters over the Ruhr.

Raiding forces may be objectively weaker than the defenders. They can, however, persist and even prevail because they can choose the location and timing of their attacks. Air attackers might not, however, be weaker than the defenders. The destruction of the German day fighter force in 1944 allowed the USAAF to deploy superior force and then prevail. That, however, was very much an issue of sheer numerical superiority. If the Luftwaffe had been able to build, train and fuel more fighters than the USAAF the outcome would have been very different.

Raids rely heavily for surprise for their effectiveness. Where surprise is lost, their tactical and operational effectiveness is reduced sharply. After 1941 few long-range bombing raids achieved surprise on German cities. Air forces did, nonetheless, continue to achieve surprise in other campaigns and other wars. Operationally it generally wore off quite quickly (in the early 1970s, even North Vietnam could predict USAF air raids).

Raiding can be gratifyingly dramatic, but that often obscures the critical point. It did not really matter how many sorties the RAF flew against Rommel's fuel supply, nor how many bombs were dropped. Nor did it matter how many fuel trucks were destroyed. What mattered was whether Rommel was critically short of fuel. Naturally those air raids had some effect. But Rommel withdrew from Alamein when he was beaten on land, and successfully withdrew all the way to Tunisia. The only important question is therefore to what extent fuel (or other logistic) shortages contributed to his decision to withdraw. (He had been short of fuel before. The facts that 8th Army was about the break through, and that the Torch landings had taken place, were somewhat more pressing.)

There is no question that raiding can contribute to the success of fighting by other services. The contribution can be damage to surface forces, to logistics, or to infrastructure. There have been several excellent examples. What has generally made the approach operationally devastating in an air-land campaign is a combination of rapid ground movement with aerial attack. Ground and air forces act together to create the conditions for breakthrough and encirclement. In that phase the air contribution is principally to deny enemy observation, and therefore create or maintain surprise. The land force breakthrough is then heavily supported from the air, typically by preventing enemy reinforcement. Land force manoeuvre (typically envelopment or encirclement) prompts enemy ground forces to move, either to counterattack or to withdraw. They are then devastated by air attack. Enemy land forces begin to abandon equipment, lose their cohesion, surrender, or flee. Ground encirclement concentrates targets for more effective air attack. It is an operationally devastating approach. It is not new. Think of Megiddo in 1918, Falaise in 1944 or the Basra Highway in 1991. The key is synergy between ground and air forces.

Understanding air attack as raiding is not new, either. Dr Noble Frankland was one of the two authors of the British history of the 'strategic' air offensive of the Second World War. He had been awarded the DFC as an RAF navigator in the Second World War. He then returned to Oxford. In 1951 he was awarded a doctorate for research into Napoleonic *Guerre de Corse* (commerce raiding against British maritime trade). Frankland's view can be summarised as saying that the CBO did not work because raiding does not work; the evidence being *Guerre de Corse*. That has been criticised as claiming that that the CBO did not work simply because Frankland's DPhil said that *Guerre de Corse* did not work.

That is cheap and belittling.

A more comprehensive understanding of raiding was provided by the American Professor Archer Jones. Jones was visiting professor at the US Command and General Staff College in the 1970s. His seminal work encapsulates over 30 years of researching and teaching military history and over 2,500 years of warfare[1]. Raiding is just one of several themes that Jones discusses at considerable length. It is Jones' finding (for example) that without a mechanism of shock, warfare is often protracted and rarely decisive. It is, of course, quite possible to belittle, talk down or ignore such analysis.

---

1   Jones, Archer, *The Art of War in the Western World*, (London: Harrap Limited, 1988).

At the end of the 20th century air forces started to introduce long range, high-attitude, long-endurance and highly vulnerable reconnaissance drones. Air enthusiasts started to suggest that the impermanence of air effort was coming to an end. Many of the lessons about the use of airpower could now be set aside. That is to ignore one of the most fundamental of those lessons. Any surveillance aircraft (whether tethered balloon or long range, high-attitude, long-endurance drones) can only operate where the operator has air superiority. The dynamics of air warfare have not changed.

A comparison of the classic purposes of raiding and the specific case of the long-range bombing of industry and infrastructure in the Second World War is enlightening. See Figure 13-1:

Serial	Purpose of Raiding	Bombing
1.	To gain economically (typically by removing and making use of resources).	Not possible. At best, to inflict cost on the defender (but at considerable cost to the attacker).
2.	To extract political benefit.	No benefit extracted from Germany. Some benefit obtained by Britain in relation to the USA, and by the Western Allies in relation to the USSR.
3.	To deplete or destroy enemy supplies.	Limited success at an operational or strategic level. Only possible with continued re-attack.
4.	To live at the enemy's expense.	Not possible. Hugely expensive.
5.	To compel battle.	The USAAF succeeded in 1944. The RAF did not.
6.	To substitute for battle (for lack of alternative).	The RAF did so, successfully, from 1940 to about 1942.

Figure 13-1 Raiding.

No form of raiding (from Attila's Huns to Sherman's March to the Sea and beyond) has ever met the ideal. Long-range infrastructure bombing, however, falls short in many aspects. Less ambitious goals, and particularly air interdiction, can meet the fifth purpose (to compel battle) very well. Nonetheless, aircraft attack, and then fly home. Air warfare will inevitably remain a form of raiding. Its actions will remain episodic, its effects transient. That is not obvious when one reads standard texts on air warfare theory.

As early as February 1917 an officer in the German long-range bomber force predicted that his unit would only be able to operate in daylight (with a new generation of aircraft) for three months before the 'English' forced it to fly at night. He was not quite right. It took three months and nine days. Professionally-trained and perceptive officers were quite capable of understanding the dynamics of the new discipline.

More generally, however, the early years of air warfare were notable for a series of conceptual mistakes. There was a strong flavour of well-intentioned error resulting from the exploration of a novel phenomenon, linked to the deliberate but mistaken claims of enthusiasts.

In August 1917 the (second) Smuts Report advocated the creation of an independent air force. It consisted of just 11 paragraphs. The last paragraph contained advice to conceal the real reason for the change (a projected surplus of aircraft). Presentational issues therefore accompanied the very genesis of the world's first independent air force. The logic of the report is weak. It would not merit a pass mark if presented at a staff college today. Sir Maurice Dean, Principal Under Secretary to the Air Ministry from 1955 to 1963, wrote that the Report was based on several assumptions that turned out to be seriously wrong. The RAF was, actually, created for domestic political reasons. They included a wish by the government to be seen to be doing something about German air raids on London. Lloyd George's motivation seems to have been to undermine the positions of the existing armed forces. He was probably entirely indifferent as to any long-term or military consequences.

Trenchard considered the creation of the RAF 'the culmination of a German plot' and '... a more gigantic waste of manpower as has ever been', or words to that effect (he was not particularly articulate). Trenchard was appointed CAS (Designate). He resigned on 19 March 1918, 12 days before the creation of the RAF. Lord Rothermere (a newspaper owner appointed President of the Air Council, a ministerial post, by Lloyd George) had attempted to persuade Trenchard to help undermine Haig. Inter-service political backstabbing reared its ugly head even before the birth of the RAF. As a serving major general, Trenchard quite rightly objected. He later apparently had a somewhat Damascene conversion, to express belief in the power of long-range bombing. He served as CAS for 11 years. There is a strong suggestion that he was effectively a figurehead for the bright young officers he gathered around him. Several of the views on air warfare attributed to him can be seen to be flawed.

Early thinkers used the term 'strategical' (sic) to mean 'long range'. Practically anything appreciably beyond artillery range became 'strategic(al)'. The operational level wasn't really understood. So when early air warfare thinkers used the term 'strategic' it is not clear that they understood the term as it would be understood today. Some early air power thinkers do seem to have believed that long-range infrastructure or logistic bombing could achieve strategic goals directly. They were mistaken. Long-range bombing raids achieve tactical results, such as damage to roads, bridges and factories. Such raids may contribute, incrementally, to the goals of long-range bombing campaigns. They, in turn, may contribute to achieving to achieving strategic goals. Or they may not.

Adopting the term 'strategic' had significant but unfortunate results. One was an excessive claim to national resources in time of war. Another was to reinforce calls for independent air forces. Believing that long-range bombing could have strategic effect led to the development of heavy bombers (due to the technology of the day) and to the acceptance of low standards of accuracy and of dubious (and very limited) effectiveness. Air warfare in general, and long-range bombing in particular, has long existed in a tension between imagined possibilities and technical realities. That underlines the importance of aspiration to air warfare adherents. Over time it has led to a degree of self-delusion and even deception. The way to overcome that is through rigorous examination of empirical evidence.

There is perhaps a view that the progression to long-range infrastructure bombing was planned in advance and inevitable. It wasn't. There were rudimentary plans and there were aspirations. Britain didn't have a single four-engined bomber in service in May 1940. Other alternatives could have been developed. America had some four-engined bombers. Given its strategic geography (requiring the defence of Alaska, Hawaii and the Panama Canal) that is unsurprising.

War is adversarial and evolutionary. Air warfare is warfare. It is not an exception. Air warfare theory seems to be flawed in a number of areas. They merit examination.

War is adversarial. Surface-based air defences can be lethal. At the end of the 20th century, Coalition aircraft did not operate below 15,000 feet against Iraq initially, and Kosovo at all. That was against second-rate air defences. Commanders rightly measure risk against potential gain. In that instance they took a low-risk approach. Such considerations limit what air attack can actually achieve in the real world. In general it demonstrates the superior power of the tactical defence. Air warfare is not an exception. Archer Jones would characterise it as the general superiority of 'missile' (ground-based air defence) forces against 'raiding' (air) forces. Air attack *can* prevail; generally at the cost of very expensive technology; tactics which reduce the overall effectiveness of the air campaign (such as operating above 15,000 feet); or both.

The underlying failure is the failure to understand the nature of raiding. A few highly mobile raiders can cause disproportionate harm, and force the opposition to protect a wide array of targets at considerable cost. That is true of the early stages of an air offensive. But what happens where the defender can resist effectively? Figure 13-2 demonstrates the case of the German air offensive against Britain in 1940-41.

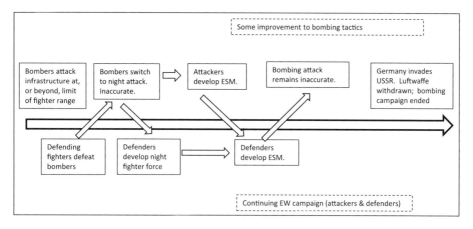

Figure 13-2 The German Air Offensive of 1940-41.

The long bold arrow represents time. The attacker's actions are above the line, the defender's below. Diagonal arrows indicate actions, or developments, which have an effect on the opposition. Figure 13-3 is the equivalent case for the early stages of Bomber Command's attack on Germany.

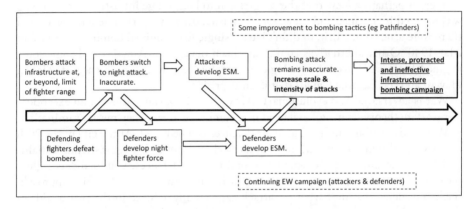

Figure 13-3 The Early Stages of Bomber Command's Attack on Germany.

Note that, in both cases, both sides had to respond to the other's actions: war is adversarial. Also note that, over time, the nature of the offensives changed: war is evolutionary. However, now consider the case of the first year or so of the USAAF's offensive, at Figure 13-4:

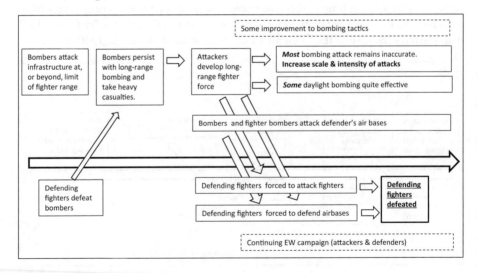

Figure 13-4 The Early Stages of the USAAF's Attack on Germany.

War and warfare is still adversarial and evolutionary, but the details are significantly different. Finally, consider the CBO in the last 18 months or so of the War, at Figure 13-5:

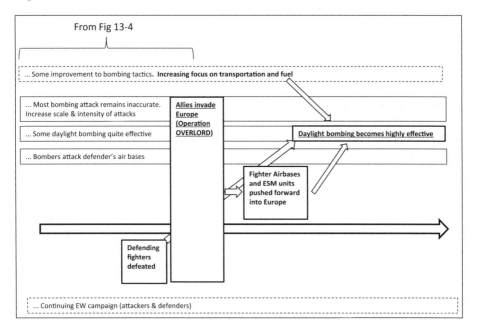

Figure 13-5 The Later Stages of the Combined Bomber Offensive.

Bombing did reduce German industrial production in the last months of the war (see Figure 7-1). But this does not point to strategic decision: air attack did not resolve nor settle the war. But the discussion helps us understand what happened. At this level of abstraction, air warfare is like land and naval warfare. Airmen are not exempt from behaving like other human beings in the way they respond to collective violence.

Failing to understand that warfare is adversarial and evolutionary has led airmen to overpromise. Responses and counters to air attack are inevitable. Achieved performance will be less than what was initially expected. Some over-promising results from an unspoken and perhaps unthinking assumption that the use of aircraft will be one-sided. It is shades of Hillaire Belloc's 'whatever happens we have got – the Maxim gun, and they have not'. It is naive. It is not the most general, nor the most demanding, case. Unfortunately, even when it has occurred (typically in COIN) the results have still been disappointing. Conceptual limitations to the effectiveness of raiding are not just due to air defences.

Air forces have great difficulty in fixing their peer opponents. How do you fix an air force? What stops it just flying away, to resist damage? The general method is to attack something you believe he is bound to protect: his airbases, his sovereign territory, or his surface forces. The nub of that problem, however, is 'belief'. Trenchard advised the conduct of 'Flying Circuses' over France in late 1940 and 1941. Up to 200 RAF fighters would escort perhaps half a dozen bombers attacking a Luftwaffe airbase. Many such operations were conducted. However, the Luftwaffe didn't believe they were obliged to defend the bases, except on their own terms. About 400 RAF fighter pilots (many of whom who had survived the Battle of Britain) were shot down for no real gain and the loss of just 103 German fighters. In 1990-91 the Iraqi air force did not feel obliged to stand and fight. That is why so many Iraqi aircraft survived, and why no-fly zones were needed for years afterwards

Air warfare theory seems to lack a defeat mechanism. On land, fixing and striking the enemy effectively will typically make him desist or face destruction. It is not at all clear what equates to that in air warfare, either in air-to-air combat or in the attack on ground forces. Perhaps there is no defeat mechanism.

Conveniently, there is typically no perceptible end to an air operation either, except perhaps a 'fly past'. That means that failure can be hidden. Air forces can simply stop bombing, fly home and say nothing. That's what they did, for example, in Vietnam.

Air forces misuse the term 'strategic'. Air forces have used the term 'strategic' to mean 'long range' too easily and for too long. It entered the lexicon unthinkingly. Its continued use is either sloppy or deliberate misdirection. The RAF had a 'strategic air transport' fleet for many years. How can passenger aircraft contribute directly to the conduct of wars? 'Strategic air attack' almost always means 'long range bombing of industry, infrastructure, and occasionally command and communication facilities'. If one replaces 'strategic' with 'long range' in most cases, the error is exposed.

Two other misuses of the term 'strategy' are insightful. One is in the context of 'airpower strategies'. It normally means no more than alternative tactical approaches. An alternative definition of 'strategy' is 'the art of the General' (or admiral, or air marshal). If that is so, strategy means 'what generals (etc) do'. Hence 'air warfare strategy' becomes just 'the operational or tactical use of aircraft'. However the ambiguity (between strategy as 'the art of the general' and as 'the use of collective armed violence, *at the national level*, for the purposes of the state') is useful to airmen. It is quite possibly deliberate. If it is not deliberate it reflects ignorance or lack of thought.

A further misuse of the term is a piece of masterful misdirection. Part One of the 1999 version of AP 3000 covers 'the strategic context'. It contains three chapters. The first covers the nature of war and armed conflict. The second is called 'Air Power'. That is: *air power forms part of the strategic context of RAF operations*. That is a wonderful piece of presentation. Air power *is* strategy. Wow! It begs the question of what air power actually is.

A more insidious piece of clever presentation appears in an interesting piece of analysis prepared for the USAF by RAND[2]. It suggests that the air component (ie,

---

2   Johnson, David E, *Learning Large Lessons. The Evolving Roles of Ground Power and Air Power in the Post-Cold War Era*, (Santa Monica, California: The RAND Corporation, 2007), p140.

the USAF) predominates at the operational level, whilst the land component (the Army, Marines, or both) predominates at the tactical level. How subtle! The fallacy is, once again, mistaking geography for taxonomy. In this case the report mistakes 'long range' for 'operational'. Long-range operations have, typically and understandably, been dominated by air forces. However, the report contradicts itself. It goes on to describe how, in Iraq in 2003, the operational level was dominated by the 600km advance of a single US Army division.

This discussion of 'strategic', 'operational' and 'long range' begs the question of 'how much is enough?' Since air forces have rarely if ever resolved wars directly, do nations need large air forces? There is an interesting analogy with armoured divisions in the Second World War. By about 1942 the tank strength of German panzer divisions had been halved. Soviet equivalents had more tanks. But, critically, German divisions had far more antitank guns. They both negated Russian tanks and freed up German tanks to undertake other, offensive tasks. The synthesis was far more effective. The analogy is that nations' armed forces might be far more effective if they had far fewer long-range aircraft and better air defences. A long-range air attack capability using manned aircraft can easily cost a third of a nation's defence procurement budget. If long range operations contribute little in strategic terms, nations' armed forces might be more effective if they invested elsewhere.

Euphemism can be a very powerful tool. During the Second World War the USAAF frequently used the term 'non-visual bombing'. It meant the inaccurate, radar-directed bombing of city-sized targets. The USAAF repeatedly attacked so-called 'rail marshalling yards' in western Europe. The term suggests that cities conveniently had all their 'railroad' infrastructure located outside or beyond the 'city limits', helpfully laid out to facilitate air attack. European cities aren't like that. Railway sidings and goods yards were built wherever convenient: close to factories (and, coincidentally, their worker's homes) where possible. That is, almost inevitably in and amongst existing built-up areas. In practice the USAAF's devotion to precision bombing was merely an ideal, which was sacrificed as and when required. Alternatively, its policies were interpreted so widely as to be meaningless.

Logical or conceptual flaws were greatly assisted by euphemism and obfuscation. Airmen have sometimes watered down the word 'decisive' by modifying it to 'partially decisive'. 'Decisive' is categoric. Something either settles or resolves an issue, or it does not. 'Partially decisive' means 'contributory'. If the writer had written 'contributory' instead of 'partially decisive' air operations, the conceit would have been exposed. Another interesting and revealing use of terminology refers to the 'auxiliary' roles of air forces. They include all the things that aircraft should be doing, rather than the things which air warfare exponents want them to be doing. They include, for example, anti-submarine warfare. Describing them as 'auxiliary' implicitly degrades them in the eyes of the reader.

Such lack of clarity, deliberate or otherwise, was one of the factors which led to moral hazard. That had tragic consequences. The primary RAF doctrine manuals of the 1920s discussed the question of targeting civilians at length. They concluded that it was ineffective and immoral. One document stated that it was clearly illegal to bombard a populated area in the hope of hitting a legitimate target. 'Illegal' and 'immoral' are not the same thing. The way to prohibit acts considered immoral is to make them illegal. Doing so provides the legal sanctions required to prevent, deter, or if necessary punish them.

Article 24(4) of the 1923 Hague Rules of Air Warfare states:

> In the immediate neighbourhood of the operations of land forces, the bombardment of cities, towns, villages, dwellings or buildings is legitimate provided that there exists a reasonable presumption that the military concentration is sufficiently important to justify such bombardment, having regard to the danger thus caused to the civilian population.[3]

That is reasonably clear, but does allow some room for interpretation. For example, what about targets distant from the operations of land forces? The Hague Rules were never ratified, but make an important statement about the desirability of avoiding civilian casualties.

In the Second World War bombing was described to the British population in terms of attacking targets of military or economic value. If German civilians got in the way, that was regrettable. The reality was somewhat different. The German population was the target, in the hope that that would lead to a collapse in German economy and morale. The St Valentine's Day directive of 13 February 1942 ordered the CinC of Bomber Command to concentrate all of his efforts on the morale of the enemy population. Harris didn't actually believe in that. He believed in destroying German factories, and hence war production. But the Directive effectively allowed him to do that.

The intention was hidden from the British public. The Government did not believe that the population would support it. Concealing the realities of warfare has long been a way of maintaining public morale and retaining the moral high ground. Deliberately concealing a morally questionable policy, however, is a different matter.

It was not a war crime. Harris was not a war criminal, in the sense that what he did was not against the wars of law in any categoric sense. He seems to have been a deeply unpleasant character and what he did seems deeply immoral. But not criminal.

The bombing can be seen as a sincere, albeit mistaken, attempt to defeat Germany. But it was also far more than that. Institutional aspirations on the part of the RAF and USAAF became institutional imperatives. Bombing became a mechanism for demanding, and acquiring, resources. It became a career path for Regular officers. It became a toxic combination of all of those things.

---

3   *The Hague Rules of Air Warfare.* Unpublished, but see for example Spaight, J M, *Air Power and War Rights*, third edition, (London: Longmans, Green & Co, 1947).

By 1944 or so bombing tactics deliberately targeted fire, rescue and medical personnel. It was deliberate. Given their remoteness from the highly centralised control of bombing, there was no crime and little, if any, immorality on the part of the bomber crews. The immorality, gross though it was, came from the commanders and their staff. They had followed their doctrine, and their organisational imperatives, into immorality. They had manipulated legal opinion into exploiting ambiguity and supporting their wishes.

One hears a strong cry that it is wrong to make moral judgements. 'You weren't there: you don't know what it was like'.

'Hogwash'; to put it politely.

One didn't have to feel the heat of the ovens at Auschwitz to know that that was wrong. One didn't have to watch the village church at Oradour sur Glane burning, and hear the screams of those inside, to know that that was morally wrong. (To repeat: reprisals were not illegal at the time). One could reasonably suggest that in some ways the aircrew of the Second World War were emotionally too close to the events. Hitler *had* bombed their chippy.

There is a quaint little town in the Black Forest called Neustadt. Today its population is less than 9,000. Much of it was built of wood. In early 1945 it was attacked by bombers with incendiaries. The memorial in the town square describes the effect as a '*Brandmeer*': a sea of flames. Neustadt lies on one of what were the few road and rail routes through the Forest. One can see why it was attacked. But why did it have to be turned into a sea of flames, a month or two before the end of the war?

Human beings are quite capable of making moral judgements. Before we do so, we should assemble and examine the facts. When we do that, it is difficult to escape the conclusion that the CBO was grossly immoral.

The senior diplomats, lawyers and politicians of the late 1970s were of the generation who fought the Second World War. Some would have worked in the Allied Control Commission, or similar. The Geneva Convention of 1949 was specifically 'relative to the Protection of Civilian Persons in Time of War'. It was not comprehensive, however, regarding indiscriminate bombing. Hence the Additional Protocols of 1977[4]. The 1998 International Criminal Court (ICC) Statute further outlaws death, injury or damage which is not proportionate to the military effect sought.[5] It would not have been possible to pass the 1949 Conventions, nor the 1977 Additional Protocols, nor the ICC statute, without the agreement of the USA and Britain. So the USA and Britain knowingly signed conventions which outlawed what they had done in the Second World War.

The 1923 Hague Rules, and RAF doctrine in the 1920s, clearly indicated that attacking civilians was considered immoral. The 1949 Fourth Convention and the

---

4   See Articles 51(5)(b) and 85(3)(b) of the 1977 Additional Protocol I of the Hague Conventions.
5   See Article 8(2)(b)(iv) of the 1998 ICC Statute.

1977 Additional Protocol criminalised attacks on civilians, and specifically area bombing. They were both clearly considered to be immoral. So, they were considered immoral both before and after the Second World War. Why should we think that attacks on civilians and area bombing were *not* immoral during the War?

Misunderstanding the dynamics of war; misuse of the term 'strategy' (and perhaps 'operational'); use of euphemism and obfuscation; being dragged into immorality. Does it all matter? It does. We are not about to un-invent aircraft. What is needed is a better understanding of how air attack works, and therefore how best to use military aircraft, free from institutional imperatives.

What is 'air power'? The term was scarcely used before the 1990s. Histories of air power are now quite common. People forget, or overlook, the history of the term itself. However, armed forces love to define things. The 1999 version of AP 3000 defined it as 'the ability to project military force in air or space from a platform or missile operating above the surface of the earth'. The projection of military force is warfare. Airpower is the ability to use aircraft or missiles for military purposes. So air power is the potential to conduct air warfare. Or is it?

No. Most human beings do not use narrow definitions of terms. So, what is the wider use of the term? The very existence and widespread use of the term is indicative. The equivalent term 'land power' is very rarely used. Why is the term 'air power' necessary, or useful? One quickly finds a number of elements. 'Air Power' is aspirational: a series of assumptions or desires as to what its adherents would want it to be. It is series of assertions: a series of sometimes explicit, sometimes implicit statements as to what air forces claim they can do. Lastly, air power proselytises: it attempts to teach what air forces can, or should, do. Why else would the RAF have a 'Centre for Air Power Studies' and publish an 'Air Power Review' three times a year? To that extent, air power is institutional propaganda.

A colleague once spoke at air warfare conference and suggested that 'airpower' is nothing more than the use of aircraft for military purposes. The apparent power of the term stems from the implications made or drawn around it. In his words, however, his remark went down like finding something deeply unpleasant in a punchbowl. Tellingly, *nobody disagreed* (it would have been difficult to do so). Nobody, however, wanted to agree.

'Air power theory' is largely 'air warfare theory'. It tends to be rich in assertion and light on evidence. 'The bomber will always get through' was an early example. Air warfare theorists do seem to believe what they are saying. They produce simplistic models which cannot hope to describe something as complex as warfare. Their theories are full of abstract nouns without concrete meaning. Their work has a strong degree of circularity: they refer frequently to other theorists. It is highly rationalistic. Thus the whole edifice will fall down when exposed to empirical reality. The work of the American theorist John Warden is a good example. His 'five rings' model falls apart the moment it is examined (see Figure 13-6):

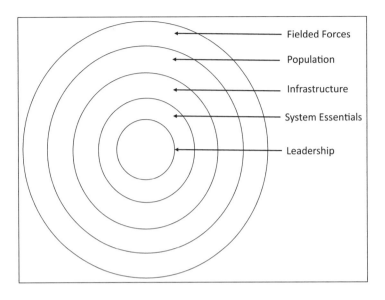

Figure 13-6 Warden's Five Rings Model.

Why are the target elements rings, and why are they concentric? Why, or how, does the population surround the infrastructure? Surely, in some figurative way, the infrastructure surrounds the population?

Warden wrote well after the 1977 Additional Protocol. The population is protected by international law. Warden assumed a ripple effect. According to his model, attacks on the infrastructure would affect the population. That might be the case, but would be illegal. It is not at all clear how (illegal) attacks on the population would affect the fielded forces. Warden's model also repeats a practical fallacy: it ignores the effects of the enemy. It ignores the superior power of the tactical defensive. It assumes massive material superiority, as does his advocacy of multiple, simultaneous attacks. Warden also explicitly proposed information operations against his own government and population.

The USAF and RAF are not unique. At an air warfare conference in 2015 an IAF speaker derided his predecessors of the 1960s and 1970s for being nothing more than 'bombing contractors for the army'. That overlooks the fact that they were extremely effective bombing contractors. The IAF had subsequently fallen for a very shallow appraisal of the events of 1991 (in Iraq) and 1999 (Kosovo), though the roots of the new thinking were in place before then. The subsequent failure of the early phases of the Second Lebanon War of 2006 was very largely driven by flawed IAF ideology. In short, the IAF fell victim to its own propaganda.

As previously mentioned, the Soviets and the the Germans looked at this subject in the 1920s and 30s, and were far more cautious in their findings. Some air warfare theorists have argued since before the Great War that their favoured military tools can deliver all the military effect needed for strategic and political decision in war. They have never been able to prove those claims. It is unlikely that they ever will.

Air control, the bombing of Germany and the creation of the V-Bomber force were all products of institutional dynamics: finding roles or missions that support the independence of the RAF. Similar considerations applied in other countries. The tendency is repeated and generational. It has become self-sustaining, due to the creation of air staffs, officer academies and staff colleges. Inflated and repeated claims of the effectiveness of air warfare occurred in the Second World War, then Korea, Vietnam, the Gulf War and Kosovo. It continues into the 21st century. It is not new. Trenchard has been described as the master of the unsubstantiated statistic. There is a strong suggestion he also that fed false data to the authors of the official history of the RAF in the Great War, and then quoted that data back to officials in the interwar period.

It was the Butt Report in 1941 which showed that less than 5% of Bomber Command's bombs were falling within five miles of the target. The RAF's response was defensive, organisational, and existential. The consequence of that response was a tragedy for both Bomber Command aircrew and for German civilians. During the Second World War the Air Ministry sought to avoid public discussion of 'strategic' bombing policy, whilst being quite happy to report tactical events such as the Dams raid. It was an understandable bureaucratic response to a subject known to be contentious. The USAAF's actions were similar in kind. In 1943 Arnold ordered Spaatz to do nothing for Overlord which would detract from the formation of an independent air force after the war.

Some other weaknesses are also institutional. After the Second World War one senior and very highly decorated RAF officer criticised post-war aircrew selection on the basis that it was preferring aircraft handling over leadership. He called the post-war generation of officers (with whom he served for another 25 years or so) 'a bunch of garage mechanics'. Such selection policies, if institutionalised and perpetuated, would ensure that eventually everyone became a garage mechanic.

A colleague, an RAF officer, commanded a flight at the RAF College, Cranwell in the 1980s. According to that officer, any student who had passed aircrew selection would pass the commissioning course, no matter how poorly they performed. (Since just after the Second World War, all pilots and navigators, and some other crew members, have been commissioned.) The problem is not just that some pilots and navigators are poor officers. It is that it inevitably drags standards down across the force.

The USAF is not blameless. The head of the USSBS was not impartial. He became a strong advocate of an independent air force. Mindful of that, the heads of the GWAPS were far more circumspect. They were reasonably effective in restraining the efforts of the staff of the Chief of Staff of the Air Force to modify GWAPS' findings. His staff clearly recognised that they weren't getting the report they wanted.

The USAF has been relentless in its efforts at self-advancement. After the Gulf War it attempted to get a 'halt phase' written into joint doctrine. That was an assertion that an initial enemy ground attack would be halted by the USAF, gaining time for the Army to deploy and counterattack. Something like that *had* happened in Korea and the Gulf War. It *might* happen again. By getting it written into doctrine, however, it would become something that *should* happen and therefore should be relied upon and resourced. Unsurprisingly, the US Army fought it off.

Another colleague was in the audience at the first-ever USAF aerospace symposium at Maxwell Air Force Base in 1998. The USAF speaker gave a brilliant pitch. He claimed that 'airpower' could ensure that ground forces would never have to do anything except mop up after 'airpower' had, essentially, solved the problem. He appealed to motherhood ('your sons won't have to fight a dug-in enemy; just the remnants of a beaten force'); infatuation with technology ('all airpower is based on technology and we, the USAF, have what it takes to ensure ground forces don't have to really fight any longer'); and cost effectiveness ('we – the Air Force – can do this if you'll only give us a fraction of the ground forces' budget; which they won't need now that we can solve their problems for them'). He spoke very convincingly and well.

However, General Paul Van Riper, USMC had opened the symposium with the keynote address. After a strong opening he proceeded to discuss every leading air warfare theorist and show that they were wrong in most of their promises. The USAF clearly hadn't received an advanced copy of his script.

Serving, or former serving, air force officers almost always defend their own service: the so-called 'blue suit' tendency. They tend to overstate on the one hand and play down on the other. Defending one's service is entirely understandable and, to an extent, reasonable. However, air warfare history has become a matter of defending the history of the RAF, or the USAF, or whatever. It tends to overstate the nobility of air warfare and understate its legacy, positive and negative. That does a disservice to the study of air warfare as a discipline. It has a marked influence on the way that the public views the subject and the services which conduct it. Put another way, it is reasonably effective propaganda.

'It will work next time', or 'maybe next time', is another institutional dynamic. Professor Richard Holmes once remarked that the history of air warfare is one of technological determinism that never quite delivers. But, 'maybe next time'. It is a useful device. In practice defence ministries will not remember that air forces have repeatedly made promises that they have not delivered, at various intervals, over decades. If to that one adds a habit of over-stating successes and airbrushing failure, then a repeatedly optimistic stance will repay the effort in terms of roles and resources gained.

The issue of organisational dynamics is structural. It is not auxiliary to, but central to, the way that the USAF and RAF do their business. It has been so as long as those services have existed. Unfortunately 'being a service' becomes more important (in practice) than the nature or quality of service they provide. Being an independent force has become more important than the best way to deliver force. If it is true of the RAF and the USAF, it is probably also true to some extent in all independent air forces.

Military historians and theorists tend to be fairly objective and honest people. Air warfare seems to provide the few exceptions. We could take some of what they say or write at face value if they were not misleading, disingenuous or simply lied. One air power historian said at a conference that the St Valentine's Day directive was not written for, or by, Harris. Harris only took over as CinC Bomber Command a week or so after the Directive was issued. That statement was, at the very least, disingenuous. The historian would have known that Portal had spoken to Harris about taking over Bomber Command the previous December. The Directive was clearly written with Harris in mind.

Listening and watching air historians over decades, one notices patterns. One tendency is to deploy considerable factual knowledge but split hairs in doing so. There is also a tendency to undermine perspectives negative to air forces, present no credible alternative, and leave a strong perception of 'not proven'. That probably means that the speaker rarely actually has to lie, and does not have to try to defend the indefensible.

Contributions to peer-reviewed journals that are critical of air forces can be rejected on spurious grounds. Responses to invitations to present papers at conferences can be rejected if it is suspected that the speaker will be critical. Ministerial correspondence can be full of the standard tropes of airpower theory, deployed in an obvious and easily-detected fashion. It is clearly drafted by bright, educated but seemingly unwise air force staff officers. One writer did not even bother to investigate the credentials of the correspondent.

Such correspondence can expose the most monumental arrogance. Apparently members of the RAF are able to think freely about how best to employ airpower, applying its range, flexibility and agility to achieve the right effects not only in the immediate battle but also for simultaneous strategic results. Seemingly this 'air-mindedness' cannot simply be bolted on to existing knowledge or organisations. How disgustingly patronising! It suggests that no-one else is capable of thinking freely about how best to conduct air warfare. That is undermined immediately by the fact that RAF initial officer training is only 24 weeks long. The Royal Navy's is 30 weeks. The Army's is 44 weeks. Since 'Air Power Studies' is only a part of the RAF curric-ulum, presumably the Royal Navy or Army could get those it needed to 'think freely' about air warfare to do so in six weeks or so. There is an even greater disparity in the length of initial command and staff courses.

In the 1960s it was alleged that the RAF had a briefing map re-drawn to show Australia much further west. The intention was to persuade ministers that all of the Indian Ocean was within range of land-based aircraft, thus the Royal Navy's proposed aircraft carriers were not needed (they were, in fact, cancelled). Since then there have been several similar tales. Such stories may, or may not, be true. The subjects are always the RAF; never the Army nor the Royal Navy. The underlying theme is always the same: the RAF, its theorists, its staff and historians are at times driven well beyond the limits of reasonable behaviour to protect, or enhance, the standing of the Service. Nor are such stories unique to Britain. Are they disingenuous, lying, or simply trying too hard? Many individuals are none of the above. A few seem to display all three tendencies. Some will be somewhere in between.

Objective analysis should attempt to see through and beyond such behaviour. Air forces have several strengths. They include:

- That they can make a major contribution to campaign success through reconnaissance and surveillance. By the end of the century that included long range, wide-area surveillance and airspace control. The latter allowed fighters engage enemy aircraft, safely, beyond visual range: a huge advantage.
- That they can make a major contribution to the attack on shipping and submarines. Long-range aircraft were a significant factor in the defeat of the U-boat. Torpedo bombers were very important in Japan's conquest of south east Asia in 1941; or in American anti-shipping campaigns in the Pacific; or similar British operations in the Mediterranean.
- That no land campaign should be undertaken without a major air contribution. All land campaigns should be joint air-land campaigns. Aircraft are peerless at pursuing a broken land force, largely due to their greatly superior mobility. Under those conditions, that more than offsets the general tactical superiority of the defence.
- Usefully, air effort can be scaled up (or especially down) quite easily, normally at little cost in terms of aircrew casualties. The *monetary* cost can become eye-watering.
- That air operations are extremely useful in allowing politicians to be seen to be doing something, without fixing the problem. That may be bad (the problem does not get fixed) or good (the politicians don't really want the problem to be fixed).
- Political signalling is more than just being seen to be doing something. Air operations can send important political signals. Unfortunately the effectiveness of political signalling may be undermined once recognised for what it is. To some extent it is bluff.

Air forces also have several weaknesses:

- They have not resolved or settled any substantive strategic issue calling for the application of collective armed violence. That is: they have not won wars.
- They repeatedly failed to have significant outcome in any of the hundred or so low-level COIN campaigns since 1945.
- They have a strong and repeated tendency to over-promise and under-deliver. That they continue to do so tells us that it is institutional.

This is not a criticism of the military use of the air. To the contrary: it should have been more effective than it was. That failure arises from two causes. The first is a failure to understand war, perhaps coupled with a perception that air warfare is different. It isn't. Air warfare is warfare. The fact that the platforms and some of the weapons are different are purely tactical issues. The apparent exceptionalism ('air warfare is different') is to some extent wilful. It derives from the second cause: continued and entrenched institutional imperatives. Such imperatives have got in the way, and continue to get in the way, of operational effectiveness. A superficial view that there is a requirement for 'environmental' forces (that is, different services for land, sea and air) prevents proper integration.

None of the foregoing comments is a criticism of the bravery or dedication of the people involved. Nobody suggests that they are not competent, well trained, dedicated and brave. That is not the point.

The point is that air raiding has almost never been decisive at the operational or strategic level. And air forces justify their existence on their ability to conduct air raiding.

When surveying air warfare across the whole of the 20th century single issues, such as predicting the failure of the German day bomber offensive of 1917, are of little consequence. It is more important to try to understand the overall dynamics of air warfare and the institutional dynamics of those who wage it.

If one analyses the *substance* of the RAF's concept of 'strategic effect' and overlooks 'air mindedness' as largely a construct of air power propaganda, one quickly identifies that air forces can conduct outstanding operational and tactical surveillance, reconnaissance, and raiding. It's what they are good at: they have no equal. To do that well they need to achieve air superiority early. Soldiers and sailors have understood that for a century.

The problem, however, is that independent air forces always have their own agenda. What they call 'strategy' invites them to do things to demonstrate their own independent capability. That is counterproductive. What is required is truly integrated air-surface campaigns. That doesn't happen when (say) the FSCL is not just a corps-level formation boundary but an inter-service boundary.

By the time of Operation Desert Storm, expeditionary forces had corps HQs, land component HQs, and air component HQs. The particular air-land integration issue described in chapter 10 seems to call for a 'deep (that is, long-range) operations command' responsible for all military activities beyond the FSCL. The command should have a commander and staff and be given all the assets required to conduct those operations. The orders given to that commander should be operational, not tactical. His forces might include long-range artillery, attack aviation and airmobile units or formations. They should be assigned and reassigned just as for any other formation. The FSCL, or whatever replaced it, would be an operational and a formation boundary. It would not be an inter-service boundary.

Unfortunately the agenda problem is institutionalised. It is a strategic problem. It impacts negatively on the way that nations apply force at the national level. It persists because airmen teach the next generation of airmen to think like they do. That needs to change. It won't change as long as the institutions persist.

The issue of independent air forces is one of politics: the politics of identity. 'Air mindedness' and 'air power debate' are not issues of military doctrine any more than so-called 'religious' politics are about theology. Just as the Troubles in Northern Ireland were not about the Miracle of the Transubstantiation, the existence of independent air forces is not about air warfare theory. It is an issue of identity. It is unhelpful.

The East German National People's Army was disbanded in 1990. Many units were amalgamated into the Bundeswehr. Officers of the rank of colonel and above were pensioned off. They were seen to be too thoroughly indoctrinated into communist ideology.

Smuts' second report was published on 17 August 1917. The RAF came into existence on April Fool's Day, just over six months later. That happened in the middle of the largest war Britain had ever fought (to date). It was a major strategic mistake. Today, the mistake would be to allow it to persist. It should be absorbed back into the Royal Navy and the Army.

That should be done within six months; Britain is not at war. Group captains (colonels) and above should be retired. Separate uniforms, ranks, colleges and schools should all go. Within months, bright young airmen would see that they have a career in air warfare *within* the other services; not alongside them. Appropriate, properly-integrated operational and tactical approaches would quickly evolve. The same should apply to the USAF, and elsewhere.

This is not a question of cost, or overheads. It is a question of effectiveness. The conceit of air power, and strategic effect, needs to be dismissed. Allowing it to persist would be a major strategic mistake.

14

Business in Great Waters

They that go down to the sea in ships, that do business in great waters; these see the works of the Lord, and his wonders in the deep.[1]

By 1900 the world was, in a very real sense, globalised. Much of its surface was covered by a network of shipping routes. Notwithstanding the advent of air transport, shipping volume and value continues to grow. In the 20 years from 1964 to 1984, for example, volume grew from 137 million tons to 419 million tons annually. The use of the sea was highly important. In 1914 Britain imported two thirds of its food. To Britain, retaining the use (and hence, when necessary, the control) of the sea was vitally important.

Several aspects of naval warfare were just as important in 1999 as they had been in 1900. Some are not obvious.

Firstly, hull life dominates long-term planning. Ships are typically built with an expectation of 20-30 years of useful life. They are expensive to build, so the cost dynamics strongly supports building for decades of use. It is not just a matter of hull life. The propulsive machinery is also large and expensive. Engines, electronics and armament can all be replaced. For warships that can be a virtue, as mid-life upgrades increasingly became a planned aspect of a ship's useful life.

The British *Queen Elizabeth* class battleships are a good example of service life. HMS *Queen Elizabeth* was probably the only British Dreadnought battleship in service to miss Jutland: she was undergoing maintenance. The other ships in the class, HMSs *Barham, Valiant, Warspite* and *Malaya*, did fight at Jutland. All five then fought in the Second World War. The USSs *Arkansas* and *Texas* served even longer. *Arkansas* was commissioned in 1912, *Texas* in 1914. Both fought at Normandy, Iwo Jima and Okinawa. They were decommissioned after the war. The issue is not just one of longevity. It takes years to design and build ships and then fleets. As soon as (or

---

1   The 107th Psalm, verses 23 and 24. The Authorised, or King James, version of the Bible.

even before) the first ships are built their refit, modernisation, disposal and replacement have to be considered.

Block obsolescence is a related problem. If a navy builds a group of ships in a short period they will all become obsolete at about the same time. That then creates either a capability gap or a (possibly unaffordable) spike in spending, as replacements are procured. Hull life dominates naval planning possibly even more than operations and tactics.

Dreadnoughts were expensive, but that should be put in perspective. The British naval estimates for 1912-3 were for about £44 million, including £15 million on new construction. What does that mean? The 28 British Dreadnought battleships at Jutland cost Britain about £4 billion in 2017 terms. The six Type 45 destroyers which Britain built from 2010 cost about £6 billion. Thus the battle line at Jutland cost about the same as four destroyers in 2010. However, GDP had grown about six-fold over the century. So £4 billion equates to about £24 billion of government spending as a part of GDP. But British defence spending in 2017 was about £47 billion. The Dreadnoughts at Jutland cost about half a year's defence spending in 2017 terms. They were expensive, and would have been hard to replace; but were actually cheap in terms of GDP. The cost of crewing and operating them was a different matter.

Cost dynamics had other implications. Given both their high capital cost and long lead times, admiralties tended to procure large warships, rather than smaller classes, in peacetime. One reason is the difficulty of getting naval budgets passed through parliaments. It is probably easier to gain funding for 'big ticket' items such as battleships or aircraft carriers rather than for a cash equivalent in small ships. Three battleships per year might succeed where, for example, a similarly-priced bid for several dozen destroyers might be cut down. Another reason is the lead time. Smaller ships could be, and were, produced quickly in response to changing circumstances. British destroyer building in the Great War, or corvette and frigate building for the Second World War, are good examples.

'Fleets in being', particularly of large warships, become major national assets. No one nation successfully challenged the British fleet of 1914 nor that of 1939 (admittedly, America did not try.) In the Second World War Japan raised a significant challenge, to the USN rather than the Royal Navy, but ultimately failed. Ironically its main legacy was the post-war USN. America was forced to expand its navy, and did so. That left it with a legacy on which it continued to build. 30 years later Reagan's 600-ship plan was never fully realised, but more than saw off the threat from the Soviet Navy. The USSR could not successfully challenge the American 'fleet in being'.

Seaworthiness and seamanship are also critical, and also often overlooked. Several navies have built seemingly more *impressive* ships than the Royal Navy, going right back to the Spanish Armada. It is hard, however, to point to consistently more *seaworthy* ships. In the action off the Lofoten Islands on 9 April 1940, HMS *Renown* had to cease firing her 'A' (forward) turret for 20 minutes of the three-hour battle due to heavy seas. Both *Scharnhorst* and *Gneisenau* lost the use of their 'A' turrets due to electrical failure: the power supply wasn't sufficiently waterproof. At the Battle of the

North Cape on 26 December 1943 *Scharnhorst* again lost the use of her 'A' turret for long periods due to bad weather. Her principal opponent, HMS *Duke of York*, kept her turrets in action throughout the 10½-hour battle. In both actions the weather was appalling (hence the quotation at the beginning of this chapter). The Royal Navy fought and won major engagements both further north (off the North Cape) and south (off the Falklands: *twice*) than any other navy. Good ship design helps. So does knowing how to operate those ships in big seas.

Even at the height of the Second World War, the German Navy managed to get no more than 64% of its U-boats at sea at any one time. In peacetime, ship schedules are typically announced as 'one in three' or 'one in four'. That means one ship (or boat) on station, one working up and deploying, and one returning then undergoing maintenance. The fourth (typically quoted for nuclear submarines) represents the proportion in deep overhaul or refit.

Such schedules are clearly only gross approximations, meant for public consumption. Naval staffs plan them in considerable detail before a class of ships is commissioned. They then work continuously to achieve (or if possible exceed) them. The schedules do, nonetheless, conceal an obvious fact. It is that there was considerable leeway in such a 'top line'. That gave navies the ability to surge in response to war or crises. A good example occurred in 1964. Assume that the USN had 100 nuclear attack submarines (SSNs). That would imply 25 on station, 25 in refit and 50 others working up, deploying or returning. In response to an exercise alert, the USN surged 44 boats to sea within 24 hours. Now, in practice the USN never quite had a fleet of 100 SSNs, which makes 44 surged to sea quite remarkable. Having double crews for some boats must help. For example: since the four British SSBNs had two crews each, and one boat (with one crew) was at sea at all times, it should have been reasonably easy to schedule crews to surge a second and third boat at short notice.

Occasional catastrophes conceal that fact that well-designed warships were astonishingly tough. Yes, a few blew up (notably British battlecruisers). However, many took enormous punishment before sinking. *Prince of Wales*, *Repulse*, *Bismarck* and *Scharnhorst* all took several hits from bombs, shells or torpedoes. The cruiser *Belgrano* sank with only two torpedo hits: that points towards poor seamanship and (particularly) poor damage control.

There were notable failures. For the British battlecruisers the story is a combination of design, tactical use (up against enemy battleships) and operation (dangerous ammunition handling practices, in order to increase rate of fire). American aircraft carriers in the Second World War provide a second example. Seven were lost to a combination of fuel and ammunition fires. Put simply and judgementally, they blew up. The USN lost 14 carriers in the war. The Royal Navy lost eight, but none of them blew up. The reasons for American losses are not simple, but do seem to include critical differences in design and operation.

Not all navies are equal. Britain started the Second world War with 38 submarines; the Soviet Union had 75 and Italy 115. The Soviet and Italian submarine fleets achieved very little. For example, the 83 Italian submarines which operated in the

Mediterranean sank just 34 ships in four years. That was in part because there were relatively few unescorted Allied merchant ships in the Mediterranean. Italian ships also operated briefly in the Atlantic, with relatively more success. Russian submarines were woefully poorly handled. That continued for decades. Between 1975 and 1985 the Soviet Union had over 200 accidents involving submarines, several of which sank. Western submarines had remarkably few peacetime accidents.

There was considerable continuity in operational role. Throughout the century navies carried out five main tasks: the strategic movement of troops; the acquisition of advanced bases; the landing of armies on hostile shores; blockade; and contesting the mastery of local seas. Navies did not always do all of those things successfully, and the strategic outcome was not guaranteed. The Royal Navy successfully projected an army ashore at Gallipoli, sustained it, and brought it off safely. It successfully contested the Sea of Marmora: Turkish forces had to be supplied by mule and donkey over 100km from their railheads, due to British submarine operations. That is not to say that Gallipoli was a strategic success. The Royal Navy also failed to force the Dardanelles for surface ships.

The list of roles is presentationally modest. Unlike airmen, sailors do not seem to claim that their forces can win wars. Fisher may have said that the Army was a bullet to be fired by the Navy. Fisher paid more attention than most to how to actually defeat Germany. He was broadly correct in identifying that the most effective thing the Royal Navy could do was to conduct a blockade. He could see that extending that into the Baltic would make it more effective. He does not seem to have said that that would defeat Germany by itself. Nor, however, could he see how the small British Army could make a major contribution to defeating Europe's preeminent land power.

In the 1990s the Royal Navy's primary doctrine was described in the British Maritime Doctrine, BR 1806. Like the third edition of the RAF's AP 3000, the second edition of BR 1806 was published in 1999. A direct like-with-like comparison can be made. Strikingly, BR 1806 considers the maritime environment to have five dimensions of military-strategic relevance: economic, political, legal, military and physical. The sophistication of that world view, in comparison with the assertion that air power *is* strategy, could not be more marked.

Some things did change. The 20th century was the first century of naval aviation. Page 32 of BR 1806 contained just one line of text: 'air supremacy is a necessary precondition of the command of the sea'. The naval use of aviation is not surprising. All things being equal, bombs which can be delivered accurately out to 200 miles are more effective than shells which can only be fired 20 miles. The naval use of aviation can be seen as a sensible extension of technology, like submarines or radar. It required adaptation, and then the introduction of new ships and new tactics. The ability to use naval aviation to support amphibious operations, and over land forces, has been allowed to blur issues of inter-service roles and responsibilities. What is needed is integrated maritime-air operations, not turf wars. As with air-land operations, the best course of action would be to absorb independent air forces back into their respective armies and navies.

Electronic warfare was a significant feature of naval operations throughout the 20th century. A tension developed between the use of ships for intelligence gathering and as warships. Navies don't need expensive warships in order to have good intelligence platforms. However, a good intelligence platform could easily be a poor warship. Regrettably navies often seem to require the same ships to be both.

Challenges to predominant fleets did not succeed. Kaiser Wilhelm the Second's surface fleet, between 1897 to 1918, was an expensive failure that was never likely to challenge the Royal Navy. A more sober strategic assessment would have concentrated on coastal defence in the North Sea and the need to keep Britain out of the Baltic. Given the geography, that should have been straightforward and much cheaper. U-boat operations in both World Wars were based on the premise of narrow technical threats which were conceptually (and in practice) susceptible to broad-based counters. In the Second World War, German surface forces constituted a well-considered threat to British naval operations. British tactics had, however, been adapted well in advance. *Bismarck* was not sunk by a Jutland-esque line of battle, but by a series of independent forces coordinated over a vast area (from the Greenland-Iceland Gap to Gibraltar). But, as in the Great War, German surface naval forces were never likely to seriously challenge British and American use of the Atlantic. They became, effectively, very proficient raiding forces; with the strengths and weaknesses which that implies.

The IJN was somewhat different. It formed a reasonably coherent contribution to the armed forces of a mid-sized, industrializing, island nation. Unfortunately, collective self-delusion led Japanese policy makers to believe that they could defeat the nation with the largest economy, and strongest industrial base, on earth. The IJN planned an executed a brilliant naval aviation strike on Pearl Harbor. It had major operational consequences. Strategically, it virtually guaranteed Japan's defeat. The USN and the shipbuilding capacity which supported it (on both coasts of the USA) were far too strong to be defeated at one stroke.

The Soviet Union believed that it could successfully challenge the USN at sea. It could not. The plan was an expensive failure which made a significant contribution to bankrupting the Soviet Union. In 1948 its plan called for 1,200 submarines within 20 years, as well as sizeable surface forces. The advent of nuclear propulsion caused a major revision. By 1967 the Soviet Union had about 300 diesel ('SSK') and 107 nuclear submarines in commission. In 1990 it had 271, divided almost equally between SSBNs, SSNs, cruise missile submarines and diesel boats. Technological progress had been made, and there was some cause for NATO to be concerned. However, virtually all of NATO's submarines were technically and tactically much better than the great majority of their Soviet counterparts. The USN had about 89 SSNs and 36 SSBNs. Britain had about 15 SSNs, 4 SSBNs and 13 SSKs. The French fleet had several SSBNs and SSNs. Other NATO navies had several dozen diesel submarines between them, many of them excellent German boats. It is not at all ironic that post-war West Germany was probably the world leader in building diesel-electric submarines.

The war on trade showed some interesting dynamics. It is clear that in the Second World War both Japan and Italy failed to protect their merchant shipping.

Allied convoying of merchants ships across the Atlantic and to Russia was broadly successful, once it was introduced. Malta presented a different picture. The main requirements were to sustain Malta as a base and to feed the population (of 277,000 people). 30,000 tons of supplies were needed each month, and the siege effectively lasted for 43 months. The task for the Royal Navy was to escort convoys of up to about a dozen merchant ships, on five- or six-day journeys, through fairly narrow waters covered by land-based aircraft, submarines, motor torpedo boats and the distant threat of Italian surface ships. The convoys were run from either Gibraltar or Alexandria. 35 convoys were run; slightly less than one per month on average. Up to 45 warships (including 32 destroyers) escorted each convoy. 31 merchant ships were lost out of 110 sailings, as were 27 warships (including one battleship and two aircraft carriers). Casualties included about 2,200 Royal Navy sailors and 200 merchant seamen. It was quite possible to fight convoys through 'enemy' waters, but the price was high.

There are a number of myths about naval warfare. Several concern submarines. In 1945 Germany was trying, but failed, to bring the new Type XXI design into service. The Type XXI would have represented a major step forward. It could remain submerged for much longer. It was much faster submerged, and very quiet. It formed the basis of several post-war designs.

However, it was not all of those things at the same time. It could make 16 knots submerged. Unfortunately, at that speed it was so noisy that surface ships didn't even need active sonar to detect it: it could be heard with passive hydrophones. And although German engineers worked incredibly hard to get Type XXIs into service, the design was not mature when the war ended.

There are a series of half-truths about the attack on Pearl Harbor. On 6 December 1941 the USN had 17 battleships in commission. Eight were in the Atlantic and nine in the Pacific. Of those nine, one (USS *Colorado*) was undergoing repair in Bremerton navy yard in Washington State. The remaining eight were in Pearl Harbor. One of those was in dry dock. The other seven were alongside. By the end of the attack not a single ship was fit for sea. None would be ready for four months (the first returned to duty on 19 April 1942; *Colorado* returned to sea at about the same time). It was not until August that four of those attacked (USSs *Maryland, Nevada, Tennessee* and *Pennsylvania*) were fit for sea. One (*Arizona*) was a total write-off (sunk in Pearl Harbor and not refloated). One (*Oklahoma*) was refloated and towed towards the American mainland. It foundered and was then lost at sea. The last two (*California* and *West Virginia*) re-joined the fleet later in the war.

That chronology can be interpreted many ways. One is as praise for amazing work by the dockyard crews. Another is to put the tally as two sunk and six seriously damaged (any ship out of action for more than four months is, presumably, 'seriously damaged').

No other US Dreadnought battleship was ever sunk by enemy action: major warships were incredibly tough. To claim that 'no US battleship was ever sunk at sea' is, narrowly, true. It is equally true that on 8 December 1941 more than half (nine out of 17) of all the US Navy's battleships were out of action.

The final tally for British and American battleships in the Second World War was: USN, two battleships sunk by air attack. Royal Navy: one battlecruiser sunk by gunfire; two battleships sunk by submarine; one battleship and one battlecruiser sunk by air attack. That is all. The four lost to air attack were lost in one attack at Pearl Harbor (American) and one attack off Malaya (British). That is, all four were lost in five days in December 1941 under what can be described as conditions of technical and operational surprise. That apart, Britain and America did not lose a single battleship to air attack.

Of the 248 British warships sunk by enemy action in the Second World War, almost exactly a quarter were sunk by enemy ships. Just less than a quarter each were lost to submarines and mines. Just over a quarter were sunk by enemy aircraft. That is, 55 destroyers and just 15 other warships. Destroyers were, clearly, vulnerable to air attack. Other classes of ships were not.

It therefore came as a bit of a surprise to be told, in an after-dinner talk by a retired general, that 'aircraft had made battleships redundant'. If that is true, then it is not obvious how. Britain lost one aircraft carrier to naval gunfire and six to submarines. America lost one carrier to gunfire, three to submarines and eight to aircraft attack. Wasn't it more likely, given the statistics, that aircraft would have made *aircraft carriers* redundant? Or destroyers? Or perhaps that *submarines* would have made aircraft carriers redundant?

What is demonstrably true is that most battleships were retired and then scrapped, fairly quickly, after 1945. Aircraft carriers were not. That merits explanation. Consider the situation in September 1945. America and Britain had, between them, over 30 battleships. Germany, Japan and (looking not very far ahead) the Soviet Union had none. Not a single one. Neither did anyone else who America and Britain were likely to fight. Battleships were incredibly tough. They were very good for fighting other battleships. They were useful for shore bombardment. They had large crews and were very expensive to run. By comparison, aircraft carriers were far more flexible. Their ships' companies were often even larger (perhaps 2,000 – 2,500 for a battleship; perhaps 2,900 for a large carrier), but they could project force over a much larger area.

The last battleships to be laid down had plenty of hull life and represented a major investment. HMS *Vanguard*, the last British battleship, cost more than £9 million and was completed in April 1946. But there was nothing for her to fight and she was expensive to man and run. She was scrapped in 1960.

Perhaps the most important naval myth is that of major fleet actions. There was a major battle in the Tsushima Strait in 1905. There were eight naval actions in the Great War, and 37 in the Second World War. Including naval actions in the Balkan Wars and elsewhere might bring the total up to 50 in the whole century. Yet:

- In the Great War the Royal Navy lost 101 surface warships and 54 submarines. Germany lost 109 and 178 respectively. Over 5,000 merchant ships were sunk. But even including Jutland, a total of just 35 ships (about one in six of all warship losses) were sunk in those eight fleet actions.

- In the Second World War 708 surface warships, 1,129 submarines and 8,035 merchant ships were sunk. Just 133 warships (roughly one in eight losses) were sunk in those 37 fleet actions. 49 were sunk in the Mediterranean and Atlantic, and 84 in the Pacific.

Tens of thousands of sailors died in each war. For example, the Royal Navy lost 50,758 men killed, 820 missing and 14,663 wounded in action in the Second World War.[2] Merchant seaman losses were also high. However, major battles were rare and few ships were lost in them. Some of the battles had major operational significance. Midway was exceptional; not because seven ships were lost there, but because five of them were aircraft carriers (one American and four Japanese). The loss of four fleet carriers in one action was unparalleled. It fatally weakened the Japanese carrier force. It severely limited the Japanese Navy's ability to oppose further American operations. Fleet actions were generally significant in the extent that they supported the success of other operations, such as amphibious landings or constructing forward air bases.

In the 20th century, war at sea was fought and won (where it was won) as integrated naval-air (and often amphibious) campaigns. Those campaigns were often significant in winning the wars of which they formed part. But not decisive. Wars are not won at sea.

2   The Women's Royal Naval Service lost 102 killed and 22 wounded.

15

The Hall of Mirrors

There are three great truisms about war. It is an act of policy; it is fundamentally a human phenomenon; and it is not determined. To that we can add that war in the twentieth century was strongly characterised by the use of machines, and by the use of the air. It was also a century of great advances in the mobilisation of all elements of the state for warlike use, when required.

History is our best guide to the future, but it is an imperfect mirror. The history of war is rarely viewed directly. At a distance of decades we are, at best, looking at what people wrote. Typically we are looking at what people wrote about what other people had written. Often we are looking at what other people had written about that; and so on. It is like looking down a hall of mirrors. What one actually sees is largely reflections in the reflections of reflections.

None of the mirrors are perfect. Imperfections are often repeated again and again by reflection. We may well not see what we thought we were looking at. In a fairground, the mirrors are designed to distort. Distortion is deliberate and part of the attraction. Written history is not the same: many, probably most, historians do not set out to distort. Some do. In practice all distort to some extent: due to preconceptions, biases, heuristics and other very human issues. Additionally, no two people looking into a hall of mirrors see the same thing, not least because they are the subjects of their own reflections.

Looking back, it is easy to see the Great War as a consequence of the proclamation of the German Empire in the Hall of Mirrors at Versailles in 1871. Another way of seeing the same events, however, stresses continuity. It would see an extended peace starting in 1815 interrupted occasionally, briefly and violently; principally by the Franco-Prussian War, the Great War and the Second World War.

In that sense, not much changed in the twentieth century. Eight of the ten nations with the largest GDP in 1900 were still in the top ten in 1999. Japan was a late starter, but was in the top ten by 1914 and remained there. Britain and India were individually both present in 1900, but that was hidden by the existence of the British Empire. Russia was a poor sixth in the late nineteenth century. It only kept its place in the top ten in 1999 by comparison of purchasing power parity. That reflects poorly on the overall state of its economy.

252

Divesting its empire was not the only reason that Britain lost its economic prominence. It was also a consequence of other countries (notably America, Germany and Japan) overtaking Britain's early industrial lead. In other words, Britain's position in 1900 was not sustainable. However, its GDP grew six times in real terms in the 20th century. Its GDP per head tripled after the Second World War, despite its population growing by a half. Although Britain fell a few places down the league table, it has prospered hugely in real terms. The wider observation is that for almost all nations the best way to prosperity and security is through long-term economic growth.

The total number of independent states around the world has tripled since the 1920s, largely due to decolonisation. The newer, and particularly the smaller, states have benefitted as well as the larger and longer-established. Their security and their economic growth have depended on the working of adequate international institutions. The post-Napoleonic system worked moderately well for Europe. It worked moderately well for the rest of the world, when Europe owned much of it as colonies. The League of Nations was a brave attempt which didn't work. The United Nations was built on the lessons of the League and has served quite well since then. It is not perfect.

From that perspective, war did not change the world very much. The century was, nonetheless, punctuated by the two most destructive wars in history. They were followed by a unprecedented 45-year strategic standoff. For the western liberal democracies, the results were good. They defeated fascism in 1945 and the threat of communism by 1990.

Regrettably barbarism has often been not far below the surface. The last decade of the twentieth century showed that the UN did not always prevent it breaking out, notably in the Balkans and in Africa. It remains to be seen whether it can do so in future.

War clearly did have a major impact on the 20th century. This chapter considers some of the broader issues which emerge when looking at war and warfare across the century as a whole. It does so under three general questions. Firstly, how should we consider war and warfare, in order understand them better? Secondly, since war is a fundamentally human phenomenon, how does human behaviour affect its course and conduct? Thirdly, how should we best study war and warfare?

So, firstly, how should we consider war and warfare?

The discussion in this book has explicitly differentiated between strategic, operational and tactical levels of war. Yet the wars of the 20th century were not generally fought like that. Are we looking at war and warfare in the right way?

The word 'strategy' is ambiguous. In this book it has been used to relate to the conduct of war at the national level. The alternate meaning is basically 'the craft of the General'. That is, 'what generals (or admirals, or air marshals) do'. Much of that concerns operational or tactical issues. So, firstly, there is unhelpful ambiguity. Secondly, it allows some writers to write whatever they like about military matters and gloss it up as 'strategy': thus seemingly important. Thirdly, the ambiguity can be exploited ('air power *is* strategy': yes, but almost exclusively if 'strategy' concerns operational or tactical matters).

The division into strategic, operational and tactical does seem to be a useful perspective. It tells us, for example, that Napoleon was a woeful strategist. He and his generals were generally good tacticians. He, personally, was a gifted operational commander. The planning and conduct of his campaigns were first-rate. However he achieved no lasting strategic result. Not a single one of his wonderfully-executed campaigns brought France an advantageous, lasting peace.

The direct outputs of military strategy are largely military. They result in armed forces being committed to operations. The professional responsibility for the outcome, and the moral responsibility for the lives of the servicemen involved, lie with the military commanders. Military strategic planning should not be outsourced to civilians. But the opposition also applies: Politicians should not outsource grand strategy to military men. War is the extension of policy using other means, and the policy should be formulated by politicians. The grey line narrows, however, when the politicians are military or ex-military men.

Military strategy will inevitably be formulated in a political environment. That can cause difficulties. Policy can change quickly. Military operations cannot always respond as fast. More problematically, politicians who wish to change policy almost on a whim may not be aware of, nor be particularly concerned about, the military consequences. Furthermore, it is in a politician's nature to avoid responsibility for any negative consequences of policy decisions. Hence, for example, Churchill largely avoided mentioned the bombing of Germany in his memoirs. Holding politicians responsible for the negative consequences of their decisions will be difficult. The crown of military success, conversely, will be borne far more willingly. Victory has a thousand fathers.

Strategy is conducted as campaigns in theatres of operations. The 20th century tells us that that is done best when there is one commander per theatre. Where that does not happen, there are in practice multiple, simultaneous, probably uncoordinated (and even competing) campaigns in a theatre. Was Schwarzkopf, for example, the sole operational commander in Kuwait and Iraq in 1991? The single commander and his staff should have responsibility for planning and conducting the campaign. To that extent there is inevitably an operational level of war. The resulting plans and directives should translate strategic goals into tactical missions and tasks. That is the job of the theatre HQ. It follows that in any but the smallest theatre, its job is not tactical: subordinates do that. The operational level is the interface between the strategic (above) and the tactical (below). Hierarchically it should lie uniquely at the theatre headquarters.

There should be considerable doubt, however, as to whether there should be such a thing as operational art. Issues of higher-level tactics, such as army group-level encirclements, should be excluded. In one sense the debate is metaphysical: operational art exists if it has been invented and used. More pragmatically, however, the evidence is weak. It should be conceptually simple to translate strategic directives into tactical orders. Resourcing them is also often fairly mechanical (albeit not without difficulty at some points). One can, of course, dress that up and mystify it. The main risk in doing that is that the resulting direction to subordinates will not be simple and clear. It will be difficult to execute and therefore likely to fail. Operational art would *of itself* then lead to operational failure.

Perhaps the most important aspect of military planning is the golden thread of purpose: the logical linkage between national strategic goals and the activities of individual servicemen. Where that is missing, operations will almost inevitably be pointless or futile. That infers a question: how much, or how little, work is required to conduct strategic and operational planning?

One should be sceptical of prescriptive methodologies for campaign planning. Every campaign will be different. Indeed much of the insight displayed in good campaign planning lies in identifying the unique character of a given theatre, and campaign, and then preparing directives to commit forces successfully. The evidence does not necessarily suggest that commanders and staffs can be trained to do that. They may well be *educated* to do that.

Operational planning may well be conceptually simple, particularly where the campaign will be short and the theatre is small. The existence of large coalitions may obscure that, as may the existence of very large headquarters. Indeed the existence of large coalitions and large headquarters in the decade of the Balkans may have created the perception that campaign planning needs be complex, extensive, protracted and detailed. Viewed across the whole of the century, that seems to be a recipe for failure.

This book has generally avoided consideration of 'winning' and 'losing'. Although commonplace, the terms ('to win' or 'to lose', or 'to beat' or 'to defeat') are poorly defined and hence problematic. 'Success' and 'failure' have been used almost exclusively in their place. That is more useful. It avoids several problems, not least presentational or propaganda issues.

In August or September 480 BC a force led by the Spartan king Leonidas held the pass of Thermopylae against a much larger Persian force. After seven days, including three of battle, the Greek rearguard of about 1400 men was overrun and killed. It was clearly a tactical failure: the pass was cleared and the Persian army continued its advance. However it was an operational success. The other Greek states were united politically by the event (a grand strategic outcome). That led to the Greek tactical and operational naval success at Salamis, which forced the Persians to withdraw from Greece.

On 30 March 1918 a weak squadron of the Canadian Lord Strathcona's Horse, led by Lieutenant Gordon Flowerdew, charged five companies of German infantry supported by machineguns. The charge was, essentially, shot flat with heavy casualties. Thus it appears that Flowerdew's charge was a tactical failure. However, it halted the advance of two German divisions through Moreuil Wood. Surely it was a tactical success?

Success and failure are only meaningful in terms of the goals sought. By chance, Flowerdew's brigade commander was Brigadier General 'Galloper Jack' Seely, the British MP who had resigned as War Minister in March 1914. Seely's tactical goal in March 1918 was to stop the German advance. Flowerdew achieved that. (He was subsequently awarded the Victoria Cross.)

What do we mean by winning? Does capturing a position, but subsequently being thrown off it, constitute winning? Does shooting down an aircraft, but being shot down oneself? Using the words 'success' and 'failure' in terms of the mission or goal assigned appears to be more useful. It is, unfortunately, problematic for historians. The goals sought may be difficult to identify, not least due to the requirement for secrecy. Accounts may be dishonest (particularly in cases of failure). Goals may change during operations. An action which might be deemed successful in terms of the goals initially sought may be futile or irrelevant later on. Success or failure should, nonetheless, be judged in terms of achieving the goals sought at the time.

The goals of a strategic defensive may be especially problematic. Initially they may be the retention or restoration of the *status quo ante*. However, when a nation becomes closely involved in a war its goals may become more expansive, perhaps to include a degree of retribution. Hence, in part, continuing discussion as to what extent Britain 'won', or did not 'win' the Great War. Its goals probably changed. From what, and to what, have never been entirely clear.

There is no guarantee of success in war, so failure to achieve a mission does not necessarily imply bad planning or bad judgment. Operation Market Garden was tactically a failure. It did not achieve the intended operational effect. It (or something like it) was, however, well worth attempting.

Success and failure are not the same as decision. Something is decisive if it resolves or settles an issue. A campaign that decides a war is strategically decisive. A battle that decides a campaign is operationally decisive. An action that decides a battle or engagement is tactically decisive. In 1944 Operation Diadem was intended to result in an advance on Rome from Cassino and Anzio. The capture of the town of Cassino would not have achieved that; nor would the capture of Cassino Abbey. The capture of the ridge behind would. It would have led to the abandonment of the town and the Abbey. More importantly, it would have enabled the attackers to overlook the Liri valley from the east. It would have been tactically decisive (see Figure 8-1). In practice, the actions of Juin's French corps was decisive because it captured the hills overlooking the valley from the west. Hence 'decisive' can have two connotations. The first is the action which the commander *intends* to settle or resolve his operation favourably. The second is the action which is *seen to have done so*, after the event. The first is foreseeable and indeed planned for. The second is not.

It follows that large-scale encirclements will often be decisive. Where they result in the elimination of a sizeable enemy force, the opponent's ability to resist subsequent operations is reduced. That highlights another generalization. The decisive act may well not be the last in an operation or war. It may well be the exploitation of that act which brings the war or the campaign to an end. In the case of the campaign in north west Europe in 1944-5, the defeat of the German Ardennes offensive can be considered operationally decisive because it effectively neutralised the German armoured reserves in the west. By that analysis, the crossing of the Rhine early in the Spring of 1945 and the subsequent advance were operational exploitation.

A decisive act is something which forces, persuades or encourages an enemy commander to accede. That is unlikely to result from air attack. The direct psychological results of air attack are transient. The physical results may make the opposing commander chose an alternative course of action, but such effects are largely the somewhat limited effects of raiding.

What does 'strategically decisive' imply? In terms of military strategy it is something which resolves or settles the military goals of the war. The issue is more complex when considering grand strategy. It is an open question as to whether a military act can resolve or settle the political goals of a war, in many cases.

'Decisive' can be problematic; 'critical' even more so. 'Critical' can be a euphemism or synonym for 'decisive'. It can also relate to 'moments of crisis', or the usage in the phrase 'the critical path'. Thus, at the very least, 'critical' is ambiguous. 'Moments of crisis' can be used to imply drama. Military operations are often dramatic, but that can distract from objective analysis. If war is not determined then the idea that there is, or was, a critical path in the conduct of a battle, a campaign or a war is illusory. The term 'critical' is probably best left to healthcare professionals.

Armed forces are complex entities. Interactions between them, especially if violent, will be unpredictable. Thus, firstly, war is not determined. Secondly, there will generally be second- and third-order consequences. They may be predictable in nature (for example, there may well be casualties) but not in detail (how many, where, and when). They may be unpredictable. They may be beneficial or adverse. Second- and third-order consequences are different in kind from the intended outcome, yet directly related. They may be separated by time and space.

By that analysis, casualties are second-order consequences. In most actions, there will be some. But battles and engagements are not normally fought to achieve, nor suffer, casualties. The relation between casualties (of personnel or equipment) and success is especially problematic. Consider a company which captured a hill from the enemy. The company commander achieved his mission (to capture the hill), so his action was successful. However, he took so many casualties in the process that he could not hold it. His company was then thrown off by a counterattack. Does that mean that his action was not successful? No: it was successful: he seized the hill. But it was not decisive: it did not force nor persuade the relevant enemy commander to desist. Such argumentation can quickly become convoluted. But it can be said that discussion of 'winning' and 'losing' is simplistic. It should be avoided. Discussion of success or failure can be more useful, if used in terms of the goals sought

There may be other second- or third-order consequences. They include changes to morale, gaining experience, lessons identified, and civilian (population or political) support gained or lost. If they are unpredictable, they cannot be relied upon. If advantageous, they should be exploited. If disadvantageous, mitigation should be put in place. If they are unpredictable, however, they are not particularly praiseworthy. They are serendipitous. Thus (for example) Slim's Fourteenth Army may have learnt a lot during the Burma campaign, and its morale may have risen; but neither of those things were campaign objectives. They should be discounted when considering whether the campaign succeeded or failed in its strategic goals.

Unintended consequences abound. When America expanded its operation in Vietnam it did not consider that boatloads of refugees, nor that inherited disorders in children would result.

'Decisive' and 'critical' are adjectives. 'Victory' is a noun. It is often over-used, nebulous and ambiguous. It means more than 'military success'. If one uses 'military success' carefully and narrowly, one is left with the sense that victory is a declaratory political artefact. It is declaratory, in that it only exists if it is declared. It is political, in that its main use is for political purposes. It is an artefact, in that it is man-made. A military success that is not declared, by people, is not a victory.

Victory is not *merely* a political artefact. Wars are fought for political purposes. Declaring victory signifies that military operations have had successful, and by assumption useful, political outcomes. The declaration itself has political effect. 'Victory' can relate to tactical, operational or strategic success. Declaring a stream of victories (no matter how small the operation or the success) can create a perception of success. That may be useful in itself. The declaration may be untrue. It may have pre-emptive value: the German declaration of victory at Jutland echoes down to today. Conversely the absence of a declared victory might hide failure. Did people notice the end of the Vietnam War any less because there was no parade?

On 14 June 1940 elements of the German Sixth Army marched down the Champs Elysées in Paris. The campaign was not over: France surrendered on the 22nd. Nevertheless the German units marched in parade formation. Did Parisians, and anyone else who watched the film footage, know that Paris had fallen to the German Army? Absolutely.

In some circumstances both sides might declare victory. Why would they not, if it suited their purposes and was broadly credible? It may not be necessary to declare victory: a dominant narrative may be as, or more, effective. However if successes are not heralded, that is to say that victories are not declared as such, the political value of the operation may be foregone. That may be convenient. The British government seems not to have wanted to take political advantage of sinking hundreds of Italian merchant ships in the Second World War.

Whenever a victory is declared, or a military success announced in some similar fashion, the first response should not be to explore the events of the operation. It should be to examine the declarer's motive in announcing it. Similarly, one might usefully review any book or article about war and warfare and replace the word 'victory' with 'tactical (or 'operational', or 'strategic') success'. Any apparent difference in meaning would be enlightening.

As with 'winning', 'losing' and 'defeat', the term 'victory' is ambiguous, nebulous, and using it may prompt a lack of thought. Its use should be reserved for describing declaratory political acts.

Some historians use military terms loosely. That may in part reflect their training. It can be considered bad literary style to repeat the same word within a few sentences. A synonym, euphemism or similar would be preferred. That runs counter to the military usage in which given words have specific meaning. A historian's literary style may run counter to the need for terminological precision.

Using 'success' and 'failure' (at the relevant level), rather than 'winning', 'losing' and 'defeat', is an issue of terminology. So is choosing to restrict 'victory' to being a declaratory political artefact. Better use of terminology may assist debate and analysis in future. So might a better understanding of theory.

Much of Fuller's, Liddell Hart's, Mitchell's and Douhet's writings (and what followed from them) was rationalistic assertion. It was extrapolation from the facts, but a long way from those facts. It was typically based on some evidence, but the evidence base was narrow and sometimes selective. It led to deductions which were unsafe. They were unsafe in that the tactical and operational practices which they suggested did not work, and in that they resulted in unnecessary casualties.

Their thinking was highly influential. The writers often deployed powerful and persuasive arguments. They were generally not right. Unfortunately a bad idea, repeated by people in authority, can seem great. It is not. A bad idea is a bad idea. Much the same applies when bad ideas, particularly rationalistic extrapolations, are seized on by groups for institutional reasons.

There is no harm in extrapolation. It is a useful way of extending human under-standing. But extrapolation about warfare should remain close to the evidence base. That requires checking the evidence, analysis, and testing the hypotheses (or asser-tions) that result. Armed forces should proceed in small steps, checking as they go. That is, essentially, what the Reichswehr did. It had an existing requirement for rapid, high-tempo operations. It recognised practical problems of mobility across, and between, battlefields. It applied the evidence of the Great War towards overcoming that. Importantly, its thinking wasn't just about tanks. It included consideration of motorisation, antitank weapons, and several other things besides. The synthesis that the German Army had created by the mid-1930s, and tested in the Spanish Civil War, was grounded in the evidence that it had examined. Much the same applied to the Germans' understanding of air warfare.

The Soviets had done something similar. Much of their deep-battle theory was based on evidence, much of it first-hand. What the Red Army generally lacked was the tactical, and sometimes operational, competence required to make its solutions work.

However, wartime evidence is often ambiguous, tenuous, and can be discredited by those with an agenda to do so. Such agendas typically arise out of institutional dynamics.

A related problem arises from the actual experience of learning lessons in war. Before people learn a lesson, they may not understand what they are seeing. The outcome might not be identical next time. The observers may also not recognise the *significance* of what they have seen. That can be interpreted as a failure to learn lessons. It isn't: it is a failure to identify that a lesson exists. Identifying what the lesson was, then putting improvements in place, and perfecting them, may take time. It may require some repetition. There may be repeated failures along the way: war is complex. Put that way, the pace of improvement demonstrated by the major armies on the Western Front in the Great War seems quite understandable.

Things that succeed, or help armed forces succeed, will tend to attract attention. But the future is uncertain. We can broadly expect that the future will be mostly like the past, but not exactly, and that some things will change. That suggests a 'cone of probability', illustrated in Figure 15-1:

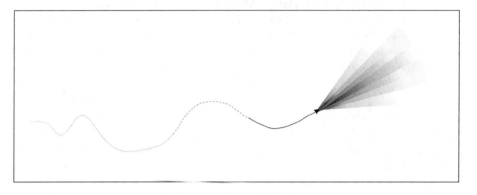

Figure 15-1 The Cone of Probability.

The snaking arrow represents the path of events. It is not straight: things do change, therefore so does the direction of the arrow. The future lies somewhere within the grey cones. Near to the present moment, the future will lie close to the direction of travel. Possibilities further off the present path are less likely, as are events further ahead in the future. Events further into the future are less likely to lie *directly* along the present direction of travel. Rationalistic extrapolations are possible futures which may be well off the present course, or well into the future, or both. Limited, empirical and pragmatic projections are nearer to the present course. Making such projections requires a well-developed understanding of what the present course is, and what recent history actually was.

War is an act of policy. Wars start when adversaries decide to start them. They finish when they decide to finish them. Those are political decisions. For much of the century that meant declarations of war and the signature of armistices or articles of surrender. So we know, for example, that the Great War started on 28 July 1914 (when Austria-Hungary declared war on Serbia) and finished on 11 November 1918 (with the armistice on the Western Front).

However, wars can have untidy beginnings and endings. Poland and the Baltic States were involved in fighting the Soviet Union long after the Armistice of November 1918. China had been fighting Japan for years before Japan entered the Second World War. Those actions were warlike. They were related to the events of the World Wars. But they were not part of those World Wars. They were a form of unfinished business.

Some writers question whether the Great War, for example, did start and finish as described above. Their argument is largely that the fighting either pre-dated, or continued after, those dates. Well, some fighting did. But such arguments overlook the dominance of politics, and hence major political acts, in war.

Wars may not resolve all issues of strategic relevance. The Great War did not put an end to Italian irredentism. It did not stop Japanese imperial expansionism. (If anything, it encouraged it). It assuaged Serbian irredentism for some time, only for it to re-emerge. The Paris peace conference imposed terms on Germany and the other Central Powers, but it did not leave a stable political situation in Germany. (Why would it?) The division of Vietnam after Dien Bien Phu did not create a lasting solution. 'Winning the peace' is an important aspect of diplomacy at the ends of wars. It is politically difficult, and armed forces may be of very little value in the process. The situations that they have created by the war's end may be enough to ensure success, and there may be some influence that they can continue to exert. However, negotiating a peace settlement is to a large extent diplomatic and, to that extent, political. There have been several examples of politicians being accused of throwing away the fruits of victory.

Other unfinished business continues in the background. For Britain, Irish independence was unfinished business before and after the Great War. So was Indian independence, before and after the Second World War. There will always be unfinished business in international affairs, and that is the stage on which wars are enacted. Change is the norm. Issues arise, achieve prominence, subside, and may re-emerge. Journalists and, increasingly, the visual news media will have been reporting throughout. Narratives will arise quickly: either at the time, or in the weeks and months after.

Given that war is a fundamentally human phenomenon, how does human behaviour affect its course and conduct?

Structuralist reasons tend to be used when considering the causes of the Great War. Issues of individual human agency tend to be used for the Second World War, particularly as they refer to Hitler. Neither are sufficient. A better-informed balance of the two is called for. Real people make decisions. Decisions have consequences which (not least) inform decisions made by other real people. People also create human institutions, which are run by people, who make decisions, and so on as above. However, human organisations develop emergent properties including their own dynamics or imperatives. The effects those institutions have can be, and often should be, greater than the sum of individuals' contributions. So, for example, when looking at Germany and the Great General Staff in 1914 we should also look at (for example) Moltke the Younger and the Kaiser. Similarly when looking at Hitler we should also look at the Nazi party and the German Foreign Ministry.

Governments have not necessarily been the most important strategic decision-making bodies. In the Great War Hindenburg and Ludendorff effectively sidelined the German government. The Japanese Army and Navy had been dictating strategy well before Pearl Harbor, not least because the prime minister was also a general. And in the early 20th century governments and parliaments were often not sovereign.

A single man can conceive of, plan, and order a war. In a modern state that is unlikely. Formulating, disseminating and executing plans calls for authority and consensus, in varying amounts. Neither authority nor consensus should necessarily be assumed, either at the time or in studying the events afterwards. Politics and war are complex and human. Unintended consequences abound in any large-scale human endeavour. Several factors are assumed to underpin the Law of Unintended Consequences (one version of which is 'let no good deed go unpunished'). One is complexity, leading to unpredictability. The others tend to result from human agency in some form.

Individuals and organisations can, and do, fail to apply so-called lessons of past conflicts. Reasons include: misapplying lessons that were identified; believing that they do not apply; failing to identify them; ignoring them; or dismissing them as speculation (for whatever reason. The reason may be political rather than pragmatic or logical). Sometimes organisations simply learn the wrong lessons.

One construct of strategy is that of a bridge: a link between the civilian government and senior military commanders. However, there may be no-one (or no-one competent) at the civilian end. The civilian end of the bridge may lead to a swamp. Strategy is difficult. Well-trained, experienced and well-advised senior officers can contribute to it very effectively. The civilian ministers at the other end may be more of a challenge. Robertson, CIGS during the Great War, described very succinctly how politicians overturn military advice. Rhetoric and rationalistic arguments are employed to win arguments presentationally, thus overcoming military advice based on years of accumulated experience. In the Cabinet discussion over the decision to undertake the Dardanelles campaign, military advice was overturned on the basis of evidence-free assertions. Claims were made about the development of aircraft and submarines which had supposedly taken place since the relevant studies (such as Callwell's) had been undertaken; based on no evidence whatever. Experienced politicians may quite possibly be better than senior officers at rhetoric and rationalistic argument. They may therefore be better at winning cabinet battles. The consequences may be severe.

Churchill did not lack self-confidence. As First Lord of the Admiralty he was 40 years old when the Dardanelles were discussed in cabinet. By 1940 he was 65 and had been a cabinet minister, on and off, for over 20 years. He used to employ his military experience, which was relatively limited, to overawe his civilian colleagues. He had little difficulty in outmanoeuvring many military officers. A few, including Alanbrooke, had the force of personality to stand up to him.

Churchill was an exceptional individual. Roosevelt had been Assistant Secretary of the (US) Navy in the Great War, Governor of New York for a term, and President for eight years by the time of Pearl Harbor. The west was extremely fortunate that two politicians of that standing were available. One would have to look hard to find similar people today.

Many commanders appointed in peacetime fail on the outbreak of war. In armed forces which expand rapidly (and in an unplanned way) there is often a rash of failures and sackings. That suggests that peacetime promotion processes are not sufficiently perceptive, and that that failing tends to persist on enlargement. It is not good enough to say that, for example, somebody would make a good wartime general but a poor peacetime general. Generals, admirals and air marshals earn their rank and their pay on operations. Furthermore, peacetime officers are not put aside on mobilisation. They are expected to perform. Competent people *are* generally available. Of those promoted rapidly, a proportion succeed spectacularly. Several of those who rose to prominence in the British Army in the Second World War came from unfashionable regiments.

The German Army was probably not typical, particularly in the Second World War. There were very few sackings for incompetence, and many commanders who rose rapidly. Friedrich von Mellenthin and Siegfried Westphal were both majors in 1940. Both served on Rommel's staff in North Africa. Von Mellenthin ended the war as a major general, Westphal as a general. Conversely several German officers who commanded divisions in 1940 were still commanding divisions in 1945. Appointment to corps command was clearly done on merit, not seniority.

Age and experience can be critical. Michael Carver was a 25 year old lieutenant when he first fought in the Western Desert in 1940. By June 1944 he was commanding an armoured brigade. In the interim he had been awarded the Military Cross, and the Distinguished Service Order twice. He was a man of undoubted competence: he went on to be CGS. If he had been ten years younger, he might have reached the same rank in due course. But he would not have been a 29-year-old brigadier.

'Leadership', like 'victory', is a much abused term. Its primary meaning denotes motivation and the inspiration of followers. But 'leadership' can also mean 'command'. The resulting ambiguity can be exploited. There is a particularly American habit of using 'leader' to mean 'commander'. Regrettably some commanders could not lead their way out of a paper bag. The important question is whether commanders are effective. It helps if they are liked. It helps if they are charismatic. It is more important that they are competent, and that they have authority. 'To respect' and 'to like' are not the same. Neither Patton nor Montgomery were particularly likeable people, but in very different ways. Both were highly competent. Both were respected by their subordinates. Both displayed authority: sometimes quite ruthlessly. Patton did not always control his temper; Montgomery generally seems to have done. Both were effective commanders. Good interpersonal skills can be useful. Both Eisenhower and Alexander had them in abundance. Alexander, however, could never have done Montgomery's job. Alanbrooke knew that.

The subject material for this book largely excludes detailed discussion of the processes of command, for several reasons. It should be said, however, that some armed forces have consistently produced more effective commanders than others, and that is very largely a result of the way that its officers are trained and educated.

People, and human institutions, forget. Collective memory lasts about 30 years for serving officers. I served with veterans of Aden and Malaya. I remember some administrative post holders who were retired veterans of Suez and Korea, and in one case a Second World War veteran. However, memory can play tricks. For a decade I used to recount an incident that had happened to me on active service. I now know that the details cannot physically be true. The incident cannot have happened to me. I believe that it did happen, but that I had (in good faith) put myself into the story. The incident reminds me forcibly of the fallibility of human memory.

Somewhat later, having retired from the Army, I was asked to discuss a subject with a general officer and his staff (all senior to the rank I had held.) I thought it sad that it fell to me to remind them that one of the functions of guard forces was to counter enemy reconnaissance. Armed forces slowly forget over time. The British Army gained a strong sense of the value and techniques of surprise in the Great War. The infantry training pamphlets for 1937, 1950 and 1960 all stress them strongly. So did the relevant formation tactics pamphlets. By the late 1970s that lesson tended to be overlooked. The value and use of barbed wire, identified in the Great War, was strongly stressed in the Second World War. By the 1980s that, together with outposts, reverse slope positions, the counterattack, all-round defence and night attacks were all being observed but not stressed strongly.

Doctrine is a spectrum from formal (expressed in training pamphlets) through informal (typically presented in lectures or written articles) to implicit (things that 'everybody just knows'). Unfortunately even if something is captured in formal doctrine it can be forgotten, or rather overlooked over time.

Handbooks and training pamphlets are explicit statements of doctrine. Armed forces also employ knowledge that is rarely written down. It covers issues that everybody in the organisation 'just knows'. In effect, it is belief. Some of it is unspoken. A good example comes from the Royal Navy. Its officers privately express respect for other navies which are considered thought to display standards of seamanship as good or better than it does; more than any other characteristic. Seamanship is held to be highly important by the Royal Navy. (The list of navies which they express respect for is not long. It excludes some obvious candidates.)

Doctrine is what is taught, but also an entirely human artefact. Doctrine can be well or poorly written. It can be prescriptive or descriptive. It can describe actual best practice, or it can be aspirational (it can describe practice which should be adopted). The quality of writing is probably best when done by one writer. A related question, however, is acceptance. Acceptance requires consensus. Having only one writer may fail to achieve consensus. Doctrine authorised by the highest military authority may be simply ignored if it has not been accepted both intellectually and emotionally across the service. Getting to that point requires it to be disseminated (not merely published), and adopted by senior commanders. That requires it to be organisationally acceptable, or at least not unacceptable. The description of some roles within air warfare as 'auxiliary' in Chapter 13 is probably a description which is organisationally acceptable to the RAF.

Formal doctrine is changed when there is a perception that it needs changing. The publishing history of a doctrine pamphlet can itself be informative. Of the 19 version of the US Army's Field Service Regulations, then FM 100-5 and FM-3 (covering high-level doctrine), the one which lasted longest was current from 1923 to 1939. Clearly there was little perception of any need for change.

The existence of corporate beliefs is an example of institutional behaviour. Institutions have dynamics and perhaps imperatives of their own. The dynamics include how an institution learns and forgets, and how it changes over time. Issues can include aspects of identity or self-image, the logic of position in relation to peer organisations, and competition for resources or prestige. All of those can result in strange consequences. They can affect the decisions which member of the institution make.

For air forces, motivating factors can include technological enthusiasm and the assumption of technological determinism. Independence resulted in competition for resources at the strategic level, and (in the case of the RAF and USAF at least) descent into moral hazard. As the 20th century closed new technology (such as drones and precision technologies) reawakened the spectre of technological determinism. Remember Belloc: '[w]hatever happens, we have got; the Maxim gun, and they have not.' That's fine until the adversaries get the Maxim gun. Moreover, even complete air superiority has not allowed air forces to dominate counterinsurgency campaigns.

Airborne forces provide another example. During the Second World War institutional imperatives were a significant driver for Operation Market Garden. Since then, airborne forces have repeatedly tried to justify their continued existence by proposing operations that will inevitably be risky and which could all be conducted by helicopter. One strange consequence of the continued existence of airborne forces was the development of the US M551 Sheridan light tank, designed to be air-dropped and probably the worst armoured vehicle ever fielded by the US Army.[1]

Over a million soldiers have been trained to parachute since 1945. Only few thousand have jumped in combat. Given developments in rotorcraft,[2] large-scale parachute operations are increasingly unlikely. Retaining airborne forces is an expensive luxury. Given their propensity for risky operations of questionable operational value, they should be seen as national liabilities rather than strategic assets. If airborne units were told that they could keep their insignia but lose their parachuting role, specialist training and competitive selection, one would quickly see whether they chose to survive or march into history with their dignity intact.

Institutional dynamics may have positive benefits. For air forces 'air mindedness' might be one. An emphasis on flying skills or aircraft engineering may be another. It is hard to know whether such characteristics simply reflect the role, national characteristics, or other factors. The British Army developed an emphasis on small arms shooting after the Boer War, but that seems to be shared with (for example) the Canadian, Australian and New Zealand armies, and the Royal Marines. There is good evidence that the soldiers of some other armies generally shoot better.

---

1   In the words of an officer who commanded a company of them.
2   Such as the MV-22 Osprey, which has characteristics similar to that of the Second World War Dakota (20-30 passengers and faster than 200 knots).

Regular, colonial or post-colonial armies display some characteristics that differ from conscript, metropolitan armies. They may include better levels of individual training and better unit cohesion, but reflect few opportunities to train at formation level. Coupled to tight budgets in peacetime (large exercises are particularly expensive), that can result in even seemingly professional armies being relatively small and poorly trained on the outbreak of war. Witness the British Army in 1939 and 1940, and the US Army in 1942.

Collective experience can be misleading. If personnel rotate between units every two years, there is no corporate memory within units after two years. If whole units rotate between stations, they may well remember incidents perhaps 20 years before. However they may have no memory of events in their current duty station even two months before. Ironically a British battalion serving in the Berlin garrison in 1988 had no memory of events there in 1987 (such as the death of Rudolf Hess and the consequent demolition of Spandau Jail); but some memory of President Kennedy's visit in 1963 (from a previous tour of duty).

Battles are won by fighting. Battles, and campaigns, are not won by moral forces. Institutions such as the Waffen SS show that it is perfectly possible to fight well without embracing western liberal ideals.

Strangely, armed forces are not in the first instance good at fighting (although they may be). They can, at best, be very good at *whatever it is that they have learnt to do*. That reflects the lessons which they have taught themselves. That reflects what fighting they have done; against who, where and when they fought, and so on. So a given armed force may seem to be highly proficient, but not as good at fighting as another force which had previously fought in the same war.

That is clearly not the whole story, not least because armed forces make choices as to how to fight. That affects what they learn. It introduces aspects such as cultural and social differences, and different conceptual approaches. A nation whose approach to thinking stresses the rationalistic over the empirical may have armed forces which stress the theoretical over the pragmatic or the experiential; unfortunately for them.

War is not determined by technology. The belief that it is persists in some quarters. Those who demonstrate such beliefs may be *technically* quite knowledgeable and even skilled; but *technologically* illiterate. Alternatively they wilfully ignore the evidence to suit their own purposes. Both may apply. There is no other reasonable explanation.

Better technology can, naturally, give armed forces considerable advantages. Technology, however, is essentially a human artefact. Any technological advantage can be countered, copied or neutralised. Countering, copying or neutralising are human activities. Some opponents cannot do any of those things, and may well lose. Defeating them that way is merely a sensible way of bringing strengths to bear.

Technology is not a 'given'. It is a product of many things, all of which are human. Culture is one. Technology is not just equipment in use. Its use depends on industrial and economic strength, supply and maintenance, training, and methods of employment (and hence integration into doctrine).

The early stages of the adoption of a technology reveals early adherents, proponents and enthusiasts. They will often be derided as nerds or cranks. Those early stages will also expose sceptics. Some may be Luddites. Others may be very well informed and may be right. Adoption will tend to be an adversarial and evolutionary process as soon as a potential enemy becomes aware that a technical advantage has been (or might be) gained. Development can increasingly be rapid; particularly where hardware becomes less important and software more so. However, the overall rate of progress may be quite slow outside major wars.

Being a generation behind has long been fatal: think pre-Dreadnoughts versus Dreadnoughts, biplanes versus monocoque fighters, or Centurions versus Panzer IVs (a feature of some fighting on the Syrian-Israeli border). As weapons systems become increasingly software-driven, a generation may be a very short time.

Getting intellectually or emotionally stuck in a technology may be equally dangerous. The RAF persisted with long-range, unescorted heavy bombers when long-range, fast medium bombers and long-range fighters were available. The Luftwaffe stalled its aircraft development in the middle years of the war and ended up with a generation of aircraft which were little better than those of 1939.

The best may be the enemy of the good. Cheap is not cheerful: good equipment costs money. However, at a certain point most of the major benefits have been paid for. A little extra money will buy small but significant improvements, perhaps in integration or ergonomics. Beyond that point, however, bigger changes have to be made. Costs increase dramatically. Over-specification may lead to very expensive equipment which is only marginally better, if at all, than something that is 'good enough'. It would be easy for a 'better' equipment to cost twice as much as an adequate one. In some areas, that may be critical. If so, a country should buy it if it can afford to. However, it would have to be a very good tank, say, to be so good that it is better than two similar but slightly less capable tanks. Such arguments may be valid, but hard to sustain in peace-time. That is one of many factors that leads to cost escalation in defence procurement, which is typically much higher than retail price inflation.

Enthusiasts ensure that advances in technology are typically overstated in the short term (but possibly understated in the long term). They tend to overstate the positives and understate the negatives. They also tend to disregard counters. Typically a technology will then not be as effective on the battlefield as on the drawing board. Technology can be copied by a competitor. But high-technology solutions cannot easily be copied by emerging nations. They can develop cheap counters; if the developer is stupid enough to design systems which are susceptible to simple technical counters.

How should we best study war and warfare?

Much of our understanding of warfare comes to us from the work of historians. Many people who write on historical matters have no academic qualification in history. Nevertheless it is useful to look at the academic discipline of history. One well-known British military historian remarked of his education at Cambridge University that it often appeared that *how* students wrote was more important than *what* they wrote.

Another history professor remarked whimsically that God is not so almighty that he can change history: therefore he created historians. Perhaps more tellingly:

> 'Humans are the most unobservant creatures in the universe. Oh, there are lots of anomalies ... but historians explain them away. They are so very useful in that respect.'
>
> 'Death', in *'A Thief in Time'*; Terry Pratchett.[3]

The pursuit of history (researching, analysing, writing and reading it) is human. We should not expect it to be perfect. All intellectual disciplines have blind spots, heuristics and biases. For example, a study of academic economists in America found that they were three times as likely to give politically left-leaning opinions, rather than right-leaning. Examples would include attitudes towards wealth distribution, as opposed to wealth creation. For anthropologists, the equivalent ratio was 30 to one. An informal survey of military historians suggested that (in Britain, at least) they tend to display:

1. a strong preference for written sources;
2. a tendency towards discourse about written sources;
3. preference for the results of the above over information gained elsewhere;
4. blind spots resulting from gaps or absences in the above;
5. a disinclination to study maps in depth;
6. a disinclination towards numerical analysis;
7. an ambivalence towards technology:
   a) a tendency of some to dwell, or even revel, in the small details of military hardware;
   b) a tendency of some to resort to technological determinism;
   c) an aversion towards technology by some others.

That may not be surprising. (1) and (2) can be seen as what historians do. (3) and (4) are natural consequences of that. (5) results from few of them being trained to do so (as most army officers, for example, are). (6) probably reflects the fact that very few academic historians have even A-level (high school) mathematics (a consequence of sixth form structures). (7)(a) and (b) result in part from the fact that exceptionally few are trained in military technology. (7)(c) is a reaction from mainstream historians, who feel that (7)(a) and (b) give military history a bad name.

A drunken man who has lost his keys in the dark will look under the nearest street light, because that is where he can best see. Unfortunately that can be a metaphor for military history. Blind spots result from a lack of written sources, or the lack of any reference to a particular issue in the sources. If the sources don't speak of it, the

---

3   Pratchett, Terry, *A Thief in Time'*, (London, Harper Collins, 2001), p66.

historian will not write of it. Similarly some historians do not see it as their responsibility to provide lessons or insight. That is not the purpose of history, as they see it. So for the purposes of studying war and warfare, military history alone is not sufficient.

Furthermore, 'Historie without Geographie like a dead Carkasse hath neither life nor motion at all'[4] (sic). The problem there is not just one of lifeless historical accounts. Military endeavour is directly related to location. Not studying maps leads to a poor understanding of warfare. It also leads to a poor understanding of what commanders and staffs actually did, because they *did* study maps (or nautical charts, etc).

There are (of course) lies, damned lies, and statistics. Numerical analysis has its own pitfalls, like any other discipline. But that can be an excuse for not looking at, or for, gross numerical trends. From them researchers can make simple but broad deductions, whilst being aware of the possible pitfalls in any insight they give.

The first 23 years' volumes of the journal 'War in History' provide a total of 911 articles and reviews relevant to the subject of this book. 24.8% relate to the Great War. 28.4% relate to the Second World War. 8.7% relate to general issues. The remaining 38.1% discuss the remaining 90 years of the 20th century. One can clearly see where the streetlights are.

It is perhaps reasonable for historians to only be prepared to go as far as the evidence takes them. Some branches of history (such as the cultural, or social, history of war) do not really look at warfare. Practitioners of those disciplines may, of course, do whatever their disciplines suggest to be appropriate; but that is of little use to the study of warfare. It would be nice to see more social, or cultural, analysis of warfare. The history of warfare would be a good place to look.

Some historians are, at least in part, aware of the shortcomings of their discipline. Historiography (the study of the writing of history and of written histories) is a part of what they do. Historians may be more aware that they have blind spots, heuristics and biases than members of some other disciplines. It would be nice to think that professors of military history are amongst the bright ones who carry torches, to see into the areas where the streetlights don't shine. They should train their students to look for, and into, the gaps. However it would also be naive to presume that academic military historians will change the way they practise their discipline, not least because of their interaction with other historians.

Historiography is important. We can now see somewhat more clearly how the post-war British public was influenced by Churchill's and Montgomery's versions of events. Historiography allows us to understand issues such as Haig's reputation, highly influenced by Lloyd George's memoirs. Regrettably that has not yet led to a really balanced understanding of Haig's strengths, to counter the prevailing exposure of his supposed weaknesses. The alleged negative consequences of Versailles take on a different perspective when one becomes aware of the actions of Maynard Keynes and

---

4   Peter Heylyn, 16th century English writer, in Blackbourn, David, *The Conquest of Nature. Water, Landscape and the Making of Modern Germany*, (London: Jonathan Cape, 2006), p15.

the German Foreign Office. Yet some issues remain unresolved. Professor Sir Henry Tizard, later the Chief Scientific Adviser to the Ministry of Defence, suggested in 1942 that the diversion of German resources to defend against Allied bombing could be achieved with a far smaller force of bombers. Yet the diversion of German resources is still cited as a key justification for the Combined Bomber Offensive, over 70 years later. Perhaps historians are not well qualified to judge such matters.

Historiography also tells us that, put simply, Russians lie. So often the Soviet official history of the Second World War concealed, overlooked or misled. It is ingrained. Much more recently a Russian military attaché became aware of the content of a British campaign narrative. He asked a British colleague, incredulously, "[i]n the British Army, you admit you made mistakes?" One wonders whether such behaviour is practiced by all Russian officials.

Some historical criticism is unjustified. The Channel Islands were occupied by the Wehrmacht in the Second World War. The Germans built a large number of bunkers and gun emplacements. One strident criticism has been that they were futile and pointless, because the British never attacked. Such criticisms are common, not least where they relate to permanent fortification; and not least because of the cost and effort they represent. However,

a. The defences might well have been a factor in deterring attack. A modern commentator cannot easily know whether they were, or not.
b. Building the defences was, surely, a reasonable precaution. Defending against an attack would be easier, and more likely to be successful, if they were in place.
c. The cost and effort may not have been a major factor, if the defenders had a large garrison (hence lots of labour available) and long periods of waiting[5].
d. It was, surely, the commanders' duty to protect their soldiers as best they could against likely threats.

Unreasonable criticism is a significant factor in military history. Another example is that of British yeomanry and light horse ('cavalry') regiments having to charge with nothing more than bayonets in the Middle East in the Great War. That has received severe criticism. However, those units had not been expected to charge, nor trained to do so. Therefore they were not equipped to do so, due to a sensible assessment of what training standards they could reach in peacetime. Their role was seen as being slightly more than that of mounted infantry. The issue actually reflects choices subsequently made by their unit and formation commanders. If, after mobilisation, they chose to employ their troopers in charges, they should have trained and equipped them to do so. Later in the war, they did. That particular criticism tells us that the writers were poorly informed.

---

5   A lot of directed labour, eg Russian POWs, was used in building the Channel Islands defences. From a German perspective, the effort may not have been a major factor.

Other criticism may reflect reasonable debate. Were the Allied landings in southern France in August 1944 necessary, or a major waste of effort? Seen from the perspective of northern France, where the Falaise pocket was about to close, it could be seen as unnecessary. That is hindsight. From the perspective of providing a mechanism to introduce the French Army into continental Europe; of opening another line of communication; of the situation pertaining when the operation was first planned (well before Overlord) or later (when it looked as if the Normandy campaign might become bogged down); of denying the use of French harbours to German naval forces; or as a mechanism to allow the transfer of forces from Italy (several divisions were, in fact, moved), the decision looks somewhat different.

Some myths spring up quickly and then persist. For decades it was common to assume that the plan for the Arnhem had been compromised, and the British 1st Airborne Division effectively betrayed, because of the speed of the German reaction. Now that German operations have been properly analysed, that myth has been exposed.

Such issues – unfair criticism, opinionated expression of reasonable debate, myths – are bound to occur. If history is no more than an interim report from the past, we can expect our view of the past to change, and hopefully to improve. We should not expect to ever have perfect knowledge. History does not seem to be like that.

Counterfactual history has been deployed in several places in this book. If the future is uncertain, we cannot know whether any alternative course of events would be more, or less, likely than whatever did in fact occur. No attempt has been made to say that any of the counterfactual versions of events could, or would, have happened. In each instance a few factors were altered to suggest a possible alternative outcome. All of those factors were technologically possible. The vignettes were only intended to explore the nature, and particularly the dynamics, of war and warfare in those circumstances.

Studying war and warfare can be interesting in itself. Its primary value, however, is to their practitioners. They appear to want a hybrid of what has happened in the past and what may happen in future. That should be shaped by their need to succeed: they need to know what wins. They do not get paid to come second. The future is unpredictable and history does not repeat itself; so they need to be able to *discover* how to win, in unfamiliar circumstances. Hence the emphasis on insight in this book.

Regrettably, most military history does not consider war*fare* directly. There does not seem to be an agreed, clear-cut discipline of war studies. What one observes is, primarily, a historical perspective together with a somewhat *ad hoc* admixture of other disciplines: perhaps security studies, intelligence, and environmental-specific studies (eg, maritime, air warfare or cyber). In some universities there is a preoccupation with policy and strategy. That may seem positive, but the vast majority of war studies practitioners will never be involved in grand strategy. Its value is questionable.

Over a century ago Professor G F R Henderson described the six benefits of the study of military history to be: to refine personal judgement; to understand the variety of potential (primarily tactical) methods; to anticipate future war; to develop a broad understanding of the component parts of the armed forces; to help educate subordinates; and to develop and understanding of the reality of war. Those six things all seem appropriate.

However, consider a debate between two military historians. What are they doing? Are they having an academic debate, with consequences of professional interest, papers published, esteem within the profession, and possibly departmental funding? Alternatively, are they having a historiological debate about the sources, the use of the sources, and how to interpret them? Or are they actually having a military debate about the tactical (and possibly operational) pros and cons of the various courses of action? The first two options are legitimate activities for academic historians. A problem arises, however, because very few academic historians are qualified to undertake the third option. Henderson was: he was a serving infantry officer, professor of military art and history at the Staff College, and served as director of intelligence to the commander in chief in the South African War. But are practitioners well served if academic historians undertake the third activity?

Problems also arise if practitioners discuss the events of the past. They may have no feeling for the conditions or dynamics of warfare in the past. They may not have the historical skills required to understand what probably did happen, as opposed to what historical accounts say. Thus any military history is necessarily an imperfect mirror.

Henderson's six benefits seem appropriate. However they do not all require military history as the subject matter. So an intellectual discipline of war studies *should* consider military history in depth and breadth; but not be limited to it. A strong focus on political science, politics or international relations is probably mistaken, except to provide context. The role of politics or international relations in other disciplines (such as security studies) is, of course, a different issue.

Some emphasis on military technology, and particularly the history of military technology in its human context, is also appropriate. Numerical analysis need not be particularly complex in order to be insightful. Many historical enquiries can be addressed with simple arithmetic. Advanced statistical analysis can be useful (hence the discussion of shock and surprise in Chapter 11, or counterinsurgency issues in Chapter 12). The most important single aspect, however, is the habit of looking at the numbers. Lots of numerical data is available for the 20th century, or can easily be assembled.

Subjects such as social history do little to inform the study of warfare. It might be helpful to discriminate between military sociology (the study of military institutions), conflict sociology (the study of human institutions in conflict) and war sociology (the study of human institutions which fight wars). Clearly there would be overlap between the three. See Figure 15-2.

Similarly for anthropology (culture) and psychology (human behaviour). The newly-identified sub-disciplines of war sociology, war anthropology and war psychology would be of direct value in the study of warfare. Very few sociologists, anthropologists or psychologists study their discipline as applied to warfare. The work of the few who do can be very insightful. It tends to be confined to defence research agencies, be

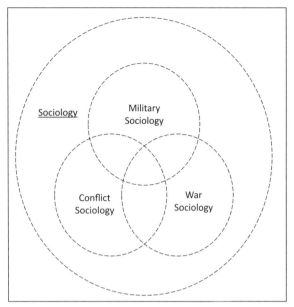

Figure 15-2 Military Sociology, Conflict Sociology and War Sociology.

classified, and rarely reaches a wide audience. The same applies to most government defence analysis.[6]

Whatever the balance of disciplines within war studies is or should be, it should have a broad span. The adherents of each discipline will have their own approaches. They will rarely agree over research methods. Heated argument can arise. That is a pity and sometimes a problem. Agreement to differ over methods, but to seek synergies and insights between and across disciplines, would be helpful. Pretentious twaddle, often wrapped up in obscurantist language, is already a feature of some war studies literature. The tendency to discuss the discourse is also common. Many writers do not seem to understand that they are doing it. They think they are using writers' names as an appeal to authority, if they think about it at all. In the study of warfare, the idea is generally more important than its provenance

It is also obvious that some writers do not really understand the practical workings of official secrets legislation They would, of course, proclaim that they do (especially if they are journalists). Governments, and their officials, are unlikely to correct them, so errors occasionally arise and persist. This does not seem to be a big problem, except where historians cannot or do not identify the reason for a gap in unclassified sources.

6   For a good example of war psychology see Murray, Leo, *Brains & Bullets. How Psychology Wins Wars* (London: Biteback Publishing, 2003).

Warfare is complex. Studying it is inevitably a human activity. That will be complex and will result in some error. Better-focussed military history, more examination of maps and human behaviour, some numerical enquiry, and a better understanding of military technology are all called for. Less study of politics and international relations would create syllabus space, and result in fewer armchair strategists. Much of the subject material currently found in masters' dissertations or doctoral theses does not help the practitioner understand the conduct of war in any conceivable way.

Controversy is inherent in war, but may be the best method we have for deepening our understanding of it. Make judgements, invite comment, and move the debate forward. Don't expect that to happen in any useful way in blogs.

To conclude, a broad trend has emerged. Nations generally improved their strategy between the Great War and the Second World War. The operational level of war was recognised with increasing clarity through the century. Tactics developed considerably. To that extent, it is reasonable to say that man's understanding of war and warfare improved. In some cases, nations and insurgent organisations got better at actually waging war. But that is a considerable generalisation.

Strategic success in two World Wars was not a given. Those wars *were* won, in the sense of strategic success. They were not won because the winners had right on their side. They were won by fighting. At the strategic level, that meant organising and deploying resources. That meant arranging alliances and coalitions as well as mobilising the home front. It meant well-considered military strategy: which campaigns, in which theatres, when, for which goals, and with which resources?

At the operational and tactical levels it meant fighting. Superior resources were useful, but were neither a guarantee nor essential. Tactical competence was not essential, but helped enormously: not least in keeping casualties down. However the golden thread of purpose is more important than numbers or competence. If tactical endeavour is not linked simply and clearly to strategic goals, war and warfare will be futile.

Wars are not won at sea, nor in the air. They are won on land, through well-integrated land-air campaigns. Access to the theatres where those campaigns are fought may require control of the sea. Control and exploitation of the air is essential, both over the land and over the sea.

Insurgencies, or counterinsurgency campaigns, are won by doing more of the right things and fewer of the wrong things. We know what those things are.[7]

War is basically an assault on the enemy as a collection of human institutions. It is an interaction between human organisations. War is adversarial, highly dynamic, complex and lethal. It is grounded in individual and collective human behaviour, and fought between human institutions that are themselves complex. The manner and extent to which technology is both deployed and employed is significant. War is not determined, hence uncertain, and evolutionary. Critically, and to an extent that we should never overlook, war is fundamentally a human activity.[8]

---

7   See Figure 12-1.
8   See Storr, Jim, *The Human Face of War*, (London: Continuum, 2009), p56.

Appendix I

Army Formations

It was remarked in Chapter Three that armies reduced the size of their divisions during the Great War, for a variety of reasons. That observation has been extended into a numerical and qualitative study of the formations fielded by armies in, and since, the Second World War. The unit of comparison was the division. Organisation charts for many different divisions are available, both real and proposed. For example, the US Army planned 12 reorganisations of its divisions between 1945 and 2000. Seven were implemented.

Details down to the level of individual men and vehicles can be found, or assembled. Those details can then be compared and contrasted. Such analysis can show whether a divisional structure is too big or to small. It can also, quite separately, show whether it is overmanned or undermanned. For example, comparing US and British armoured divisions in 1944, the Americans employed 46% more maintenance engineers per tank at battalion level, and 136% more across a division. The tanks were the same (M4 Shermans).

The fighting power of a division can be seen to be only loosely correlated with its size. It is more closely correlated with its mobility. Thus small size is an advantage, within reason. Large divisions put their reserves in the wrong place. They place a high proportion of the force in the places where they are doctrinally and historically unlikely to be needed.

The Second World War clearly showed that the optimal size for divisions was 20-25 'line' (combat; ie tank and infantry) companies in six to eight battalions. Many were larger than that. Some were smaller. The key problem for the Cold War, only obvious on reflection, was that governments or parliaments typically mandated the *number* of divisions. So, for example, there were to be 12 divisions in the Bundeswehr. Congress dictated the number of US Army divisions: typically between 10 and 16 in the Regular army. Army planners then made those divisions as big as possible, in order to make their armies as big as possible. It was an understandable error.

In 1946 the US Army identified that its armoured divisions were too small (18 line companies in 6 battalions). They were; but not by much. By the mid to late 1980s western divisions had 40 line companies (US); or 36-42 (Bundeswehr); or 30-36

(British). They were broadly twice as large as equivalent Second World War divisions. They might sensibly have been split in two. Detailed analysis suggests they should not be replaced 'two to one', but by about 1.7 to one. Thus the 12 Bundeswehr divisions could have formed about 20 smaller, more mobile divisions.

The general trend was for divisions to get larger over time. For example, a US armoured divisional was nominally 10,937 men strong in 1945, but about 19,000 by the end of the Cold War. The main difference was that the former had 18 line companies, the latter 40. There were other factors, some of them significant. However it is, broadly, that simple. The same was true in most other armies.

US late-war armoured divisions were too small, but also significantly overmanned. That is not obvious: their small size disguised the overmanning. US divisions have been overmanned ever since. They use an unnecessary number of people to man their units. Americans are by no means the only culprits. There has actually been a general but slight trend to reduce manning across western divisions over the decades. The divisions were, nonetheless, still too big.

Conversely, post-war Soviet divisions were too large (about 50 line companies in 15-17 battalions), but undermanned. They could not sustain or maintain themselves, nor even care for their wounded. That could work, but only if they were intended to be used once, burnt out and then rebuilt.

The French Army inherited divisional structures from the US Army, which equipped it in the Second World War. Interestingly, although there was some evolution, French armoured divisions did not grow much larger. By the 1980s they were typically 20-24 line companies in five or six battalions. The internal command structure was quite different from other western models. Smaller, wartime armoured divisions survived in the British Army until 1982. Some commentators derided them as being, in effect, large brigades. A more perceptive analysis might have remarked that they had evolved better than the archetypical NATO monstrosities with which they were compared.

In 1974 the Bundeswehr identified a tactical need for more, smaller battalions within brigades. Soon afterwards the British changed from four rifle companies to three in infantry battalions. That provided manpower for large numbers of specialist ATGW teams (20-28 per battalion). It was a very manpower-efficient solution. In professional, as opposed to conscript, armies manpower is often the most critical resource. Every single post on an establishment table has to be fought over at length. In conscript armies the rationale may be different. Large amounts of manpower might be available; the problem lies in trying to maximise the military potential. The two are subtly different.

Signal manpower grew markedly: in the US case, from 2% of a division to 3.5% of a larger division. That was a small problem by comparison with the growth of HQs. In the Yom Kippur war the forward HQ of the Israeli 252nd Armoured Division operated for 23 days, 60-100km forward of its logistic rear HQ. It consisted of six vehicles. By 1993 the equivalent HQ of the British 1st Armoured Division was 70 vehicles and 220 men. Which was the more effective?

There was some stupidity. In one case a medical battalion scaled to support a division of 13,000 men was the same size 50 years later, when it supported a division of 19,000 men.

German divisional reconnaissance battalions were reorganised from multipurpose units into specialised guard forces, appropriate for a defensive role on the Central Front. However, the right overall balance between small reconnaissance vehicles intended to gain information by stealth (and not equipped nor trained to fight), and tank-heavy guard forces, was probably not achieved by other NATO armies. The US Army had roughly twice as many 'reconnaissance' units as other armies. It was unnecessary.

In 1944, British tank battalions employed an average of 4.84 men per tank, over and above the tank crews. That is quite good; the Germans employed 7.53 men per tank during the war, but by the 1980s it was 5.07. However, the total number of such men employed in a British tank battalion scarcely changed (292, plus or minus 12) from 1945 to 1999; regardless of the number of tanks (between 67 and 43). Simple calculation suggests that when they got down to 43 tanks, each battalion might have employed perhaps a hundred fewer men. (A Bundeswehr battalion with two less tanks employed 184 fewer men.)

That concealed a different issue. At about the time that British tank crews were reduced from five men to four, the battalion maintenance platoon grew from about 40 to about 100. About 60 posts, roughly one per tank, were effectively moved from tank crews to the maintenance platoon. (The number of maintenance posts elsewhere in the division was broadly unchanged.) The fifth post in each tank had been the co-driver, who obviously had some role in tank maintenance. Effectively the Royal Armoured Corps sub-contracted parts of its tank maintenance to the Royal Electrical and Mechanical Engineers. The new tank, Chieftain, was notoriously unreliable. Or was it, in practice, just poorly maintained? It was scarcely more complex than Centurion. Its successor, Challenger (later 'Challenger 1'), was even less reliable. Yet when Challenger units were first employed on operations (for Operation Granby, that is Operation Desert Storm), availability shot up. Perhaps the culture of the famous regiments involved had got in the way of professionalism.

The cost of (say) 60 extra posts per battalion over 40 years equates to at least £1.344 billion across the Army. That was more than the entire cost of the Challenger 2 fleet.

To conclude, analysis strongly suggests that armies should have organised more, smaller divisions. That would allow a slight increase in the overall ratio of combat support (artillery and engineers) to line companies; and to match the provision of logistic support to demand. (Hence the figure of about 1.7 to one, above.) Analysis also suggests the organisation of more, smaller corps. That includes deleting corps-level armoured cavalry (brigade-sized) regiments from the US Army.

In practice, the organisation of divisions is not a question of objective, rational design. It is a matter of political social, and cultural issues. They can, and do, override empirical evidence.

Any debate over army size should not just look at the authorised number of divisions. That only prompts planners to make the divisions as large as possible. Discussion should centre on the design of small, powerful formations; and then procuring as many as can be afforded.

Appendix II

Post-War Tanks and Infantry Fighting Vehicles

After their rapid evolution in the Second World War, tank design showed surprisingly slow development. At first, armies had large inventories of wartime tanks. As the Cold War went on, they upgraded or replaced them. The process was fairly gradual when viewed from a distance. The exception was the US Army, which soon felt that it was outmatched by Soviet tanks, especially for Korea. Its large inventory of M4 Shermans, and a few M26s, were not considered to be a match for late-model T34s and T44s.

The M26 entered service in 1944. Design work for the M46 started in January 1948. The only real change over M26 was the Continental AV 1790 engine, initially petrol-fuelled (later models were diesel-fuelled, hence 'AVDS'[1]). The gun and hull were the same. The M46 was effectively a prototype. The M47 was ordered in September 1950. 8,736 M47s were built. It was replaced by the M48, which was ordered in December 1950. At most stages the production of the M48 was just eight or nine months behind that of the M47. The M47 had a slightly different hull and turret from the M46. M48 developed 16.6hp per ton on entry into service. The M48's hull was slightly different again. Both had the AV 1790 and a 90mm gun. The turret ring on the M48 was increased slightly. It was described as 'a radical technical departure' from the M47. How? M47 and M48 both had a 90mm gun, the 1790 engine, and looked practically the same. If the M47 was considered to be a stopgap, as has been claimed, why were almost 9,000 built and then discarded? By 1956 or so almost all M47s had been sold to other nations. Why? Was something wrong with it? If so, why was it sold to (for example) Germany and Turkey? Curiously, armour historians seem unaware of the issue.

The M60 entered service in 1959. It initially had the same turret as the M48, the 1790 engine, and a very similar hull with *less* armour. It had the British 105mm L7 gun: the first real improvement since 1948. The thinner upper hull armour was sloped slightly more than that of the M48 (ie, 65 versus 60 degrees), so had the same effective

---

1   Air cooled, Vee engine, Diesel, Supercharged, 1,790 cubic inch capacity

thickness. Overall, from M26 to M60 is a series of modest, incremental improvements. The M26 weighed 46 tons, the M60 50 tons.

Comparing the M60 with the Panther is interesting. Their weight and mobility were about the same. M60 had (effectively) about 220mm of frontal armour; Panther about 140mm. The M60's gun was 105mm versus the Panther's 75mm. In other words, M60 was a much better design for the same weight.

The M1 Abrams entered service in 1980. It was the first genuinely new post-war American design. It had a 1500hp gas turbine engine, modern 'Chobham' compound armour and soon had the German 120mm smoothbore gun. The turbine guzzled fuel. Tank units needed seven more fuel trucks per battalion. The turbine was badly unreliable. However, M1 achieved 27hp per ton. Its automotive performance was remarkable.

Soviet tanks also showed surprisingly slow and evolutionary development. By the end of the Second World War the T34 was being replaced by the broadly similar T44, and then the T54 in 1947. The T54 had a 100mm gun. By 1993 the T90 had succeeded the T80, the T72, T64, T62, T55 and T54 (although not necessarily in that order). They all looked fairly similar. T90's 125mm gun had entered service in 1968. At 46 tons T90 was only 14 tons heavier than T44. The engine, now highly uprated, had been in service for almost 60 years. On T90 it delivered 18hp per ton. T90 is the result of gradual, although occasionally punctuated, evolution over more than 50 years.

The British 105mm L7 gun could penetrate roughly twice as much armour as any similar gun when it entered service. Practically every Western army adopted it (including the Swiss and the Swedes).

The Chieftain represented a modest evolution from Centurion, which had been in service for 20 years. Centurion had been upgraded to mount the L7 gun in 1958. Chieftain entered service in 1967 with a 120mm rifled gun. Centurion was nominally a 50 ton tank; Chieftain weighed 55 tons. Chieftain had Centurion's main vice of being underpowered, at just 750hp; hence only 13.6hp per ton. It did, however, have the equivalent of 338mm of frontal armour.

If you take a Chieftain, give it a (Perkins CV12) 1200hp engine and Chobham armour, you get a Challenger: *literally*. Challenger 1 achieved a respectable 19.2hp per ton and had updated sights and fire control systems. It entered service in 1988. Challenger 2 is reputedly a completely rebuilt Challenger 1 with a modified 120mm gun.

If you take a Centurion, cut it down the middle (front to back) and widen it by 200mm, move the engine to the front and the turret to the back, you get a prototype Israeli Merkava. *Literally*. The prototype can be seen in the IDF Armoured Museum at Latrun. Israeli Centurions already had the 1790 engine and the L7 gun, so Merkava Mk 1 did as well. It was initially badly underpowered. Its weight was 60t due to improved protection, and that model of 1790 engine produced only 900hp. (Merkava now has the German 120mm smoothbore and the German MTU 1500hp engine).

The first German tank to be produced after the Second World War was the Leopard 1. It was two tons *lighter* than the Panther, had a 830hp engine (the Panther's had been an impressive 700hp), and the L7 gun against a 75mm. The Germans, given their Second World War experience, had deliberately produced a tank which had a much better gun, was much more mobile (at 20.7hp/t), but less well protected. Its hull front armour was only 22mm thick (equivalent to 70mm, due to its slope). The design requirement was only for protection against 20mm cannon.

Leopard 1 was replaced by Leopard 2 from 1979. It was a new tank. Its MTU engine developed 1500hp, and hence 27.3hp per ton. Its automotive performance was just as startling as that of the M1. Its new 120mm smoothbore gun slightly outperformed the British rifled gun. Its Chobham armour gave it roughly the same protection as M1 and Challenger.

Tanks are almost never re-engined in peacetime, nor are they up-gunned. The exceptions are interesting. Israel converted Centurions to the AVDS 1790. That appears to be partly to ensure access to an engine which they could guarantee to support, and partly to convert from petrol to diesel. The Leopard 2, M1 and Merkava all entered service with the L7 gun but were soon upgraded to the German 120mm smoothbore. That seems to be due to delays in producing the German gun.

Western tanks had become broadly similar the end of the century, but from different starting points. The biggest differences had been between British and German tanks. Chieftain had been very well protected, but slow. Challenger's CV12 engine overcame the mobility issue. Conversely, Leopard 1 had been highly mobile and had very good firepower, but only modest protection. Chobham armour allowed Leopard 2 to approach the same level of protection as Challenger. Its new engine allowed it to exceed the already impressive mobility of Leopard 1.

There is a consistent pattern. Officers are taught that tanks are a balance between firepower, protection and mobility. They are, but that is misleading. The first requirement is for a good enough gun (the German long 75mm; the 17pdr; the L7; the German 120mm smoothbore). Tanks then need a powerful and reliable engine that will deliver 20hp per ton or better to the intended tank. If the tank is to weigh 30t, it will need a 600hp engine. If it weighs 50t, it will need 1,000hp; and so on. The armour should then be designed to the weight limit.

That is, effectively, what Leopard 1 was; designed around a 40t tank. Germany's new 1500hp engine allowed Leopard 2 to do even better in a 50t tank. However:

- When Chieftain was designed at 55t, the CV12 (1200hp) was not available. It was fitted to export variants a few years later.
- When M1 was designed, the US did not have a workable high-power diesel, so chose a turbine. They could have had the British CV12, or the German 1500hp. The AVDS 1790 subsequently reached 1500hp.
- When Merkava was designed, Israel already had the 1790 (at 900hp). Israel preferred that to another foreign engine which it could not guarantee to support (although they did subsequently buy the MTU 1500hp). Israel's operational requirement for high road speed was probably less demanding that than of western armies.

- the Soviet Union has consistently accepted slightly under 20hp per ton, and done reasonably well with one reliable engine (although experimenting with others) and lighter tanks. T54/T55 was underpowered when that engine could only develop 500-600hp, but that was rectified when 840hp was achieved for T72 (and then T90).

The judgement of history? M1s and Challengers completely outperformed Russian tanks in the Gulf War. Israeli experience with Merkava is similar. Western tanks were, by 1999, typically slightly faster and had slightly better guns. But they also typically had 10 tons more protection. The tank is not the whole story: doctrine and training count for a lot. But the lesson is clear.

The development of armoured vehicles for the infantry tells a different story. The Wehrmacht had half-section and section half-track Armoured Personnel Carriers (APCs) in the Second World War. Tracked, enclosed APCs were among the first armoured vehicles the Bundeswehr procured. (Their first post-war armoured car had eight wheels, two drivers' stations, equal numbers of forward and reverse gears, a 20mm cannon and a four-man crew. So did their principal armoured car in the Second World War. Continuity in German armoured vehicle design is obvious, once identified.) The APCs had 20mm cannon instead of a machinegun. They weren't very good vehicles, and were replaced fairly quickly by the Marder. Marder could keep up with Leopard 1 and was well-armoured. It had a 20mm cannon and two machine-guns. Two in each platoon could mount their sections' Milan launchers.

At or about the same time, the Soviets designed a tracked, enclosed APC. They put a version of their recoilless antitank gun on it, and then a Sagger ATGW. That gave heavy antitank weapons to every dug-in infantry section in defence. It was a simplistic idea (not least, if the infantry platoon positions were neutralised by artillery fire, the antitank weapons would be neutralised as well). The resulting vehicle, the BMP, was poorly armoured (its armour could be penetrated by a 12.7mm heavy machinegun) but mobile and amphibious. When the Soviets identified NATO helicopters as a major threat, the gun was replaced by a cannon. A trend was emerging. Such vehicles became known as Infantry Fighting Vehicles (IFVs).

The US Army started development of an IFV the late 1960s. It was supposed to carry a nine-man section. It was decided that the new cavalry scout vehicle would be the same vehicle. It (Bradley) ended up with a 2-man turret, a cannon and TOW; but only seven dismounted soldiers. In order to carry three nine-man sections, they have to be distributed amongst the four vehicles in a platoon.

The British were the last to field an IFV: Warrior. It also needed a two-man turret for its powerful but old-fashioned Rarden 30mm cannon. Hence only seven soldiers can dismount.

There are two problems. The first is that no western army has developed an IFV that carries the number of dismounted soldiers it wanted. Isn't the primary purpose of an IFV to carry a section of infantry? IFVs, like all armoured vehicles, are a design compromise. They are clearly a bad compromise.

The second problem is more important. No army has ever successfully attacked with IFVs against a credible defence. When the Syrians tried, in 1973, they failed badly. The only other examples are from Iraq, in 1991 (and 2003), which is scarcely a rigorous test. Repeated analysis suggests that it simply won't work. In the attack IFVs will probably succeed in getting troops onto the objective; so long as that is all they do, and they don't try to use their weapons. In defence the vehicles will either suffer casualties from the attackers' tanks, leaving their dismounted infantry stranded; or they will remain concealed and not use their weapons. Those weapons are a bad idea. The one army with considerable relevant experience (the IDF) chose to procure the best-protected APC it could afford (eventually using Merkava hulls), typically mounting nothing more than a few machineguns. The IFV concept is a rationalistic experiment that has consumed considerable resources on the basis of poor thinking and no good historical precedent.

Bibliography

Section One: Books

Adan, Major General Avraham, *On the Banks of the Suez*, (London: Arms and Armour Press, 1980).

Alanbrooke, FM Lord; Danchev, Alex and Todman, Daniel eds, *War Diaries 1939-1945*, (London: Phoenix Press, 2002).

Ashworth, Tony, *Trench Warfare 1914-18. The Live and Let Live System*, (London: Pan Books, 1990).

Atteridge, A H, *Famous Modern Battles*, (London: Thomas Nelson, 1913).

Bailey, Maj Gen J B A, *Field Artillery and Firepower*, (Annapolis, Maryland: Naval Institute Press, 2004).

Badsey, Stephen, *Doctrine and Reform in the British Cavalry, 1880-1918*, (Aldershot: Ashgate Publishing Ltd, 2008).

Balck, Colonel; Kruger, Walter tr, *Tactics*, (Connecticut: Greenwood Press, 1977).

Banks, Arthur, *A Military Atlas of the First World War*, (London: Leo Cooper, 1989).

Bar-On, Colonel Mordechai ed, *The Israeli Defence Forces, The Six Day War*, (Slough: Foulsham and Co, 1968).

Barton, Peter; Doyle, Peter; and Vandewalle, Johan, *Beneath Flanders Fields. The Tunnelers' War 1914-18*, (Staplehurst: Spellmount Ltd, 2004).

Bauer, Cornelis, tr Welsh, D R, *The Battle of Arnhem. The Betrayal Myth Refuted*, (London: Hodder and Staughton, 1966).

Beca, Colonel; Custance, Captain A F tr, *A Study of the Development of Infantry Tactics*, (London: Swan Sonnenschein, 1911).

Beckett, Ian F W and Corvi, Stephen J eds, *Haig's Generals*, (Barnsley: Pen and Sword, 2006).

Beevor, Anthony, *Crete. The Battle and the Resistance*, (London: Penguin, 1992).

Beevor, Anthony, *Stalingrad*, (London: Penguin Books, 1998).

Beevor, Anthony, *Ardennes 1944. Hitler's Last Gamble.* (London: Viking 2015).

Behrendt, Hans-Otto, *Rommel's Intelligence in the Desert Campaign*, (London: William Kimber, 1985).

Bellamy, Christopher, *The Evolution of Modern Land Warfare. Theory and Practice*, (London: Routledge, 1999).

Bidwell, Shelford and Graham, Dominick, *Firepower: British Army Weapons and Theories of War 1904-45*, (London: Allen and Unwin, 1982).

Bijl, Nicholas van der, *Nine Battles to Stanley*, (Barnsley: Leo Cooper, 1999).

Billière, General Sir Peter de la, *Storm Command*, (London: Harper Collins, 1992).

Black, Jeremy, *War and the World. Military Power and the Fate of Continents, 1450-2000*, (New Haven: Yale University Press, 1998).

Black, Jeremy, *War. Past, Present & Future*, (Stroud: Sutton Publishing, 2000).

Black, Jeremy, *Introduction to Global Military History. 1775 to the Present Day*, (London: Routledge, 2005).

Black, Jeremy, *The Great War and the Making of the Modern World*, (London: Continuum, 2011).

Blumenson, Martin, *Patton – the Man Behind the Legend 1885-1945*, (New York: William Morrow, 1988).

Blumenson, Martin and Stokesbury, James L, *Masters of the Art of Command*, (New York: Da Capo Press, 1990).

Bond, Brian, *The Pursuit of Victory*, (Oxford: Oxford University Press, 1996).

Brown, Captain Eric 'Winkle' CBE DSC AFC RN, *Wings on my Sleeve*, (London: Weidenfeld and Nicolson 2006).

Brown, Captain Eric 'Winkle' CBE DSC AFC RN, *Wings of the Luftwaffe. Flying Captured German Aircraft of World War II*, (Manchester: Crécy Publishing, 2010).

Bryant, Arthur, *Triumph in the West*, (London: Collins, 1959).

Bungay, Stephen, *The Most Dangerous Enemy: A History of the Battle of Britain*, (London: Aurum 2001).

Bungay, Stephen, *Alamein*, (London: Aurum 2003).

Cameron, David W, *The Battle for Lone Pine. Four Days of Hell at the Heart of Gallipoli*, (Melbourne: Viking 2012).

Carell, Paul, tr Osers, E, *Invasion – They're Coming!*, (London: Transworld Publishers, 1963).

Carver, FM Lord, *Harding of Petherton, Field Marshal*, (London: Weidenfeld and Nicholson, 1978).

Carver, FM Lord, *The Apostles of Mobility*, (London: Weidenfeld and Nicholson, 1979).

Carver, FM Lord, *Britain's Army in the 20th Century*, (London: Pan Books, 1988).

Carver, FM Lord, *El Alamein*, (Ware: Wordsworth Editions Ltd, 2000).

Cattaruzza, Marina; Dyroff, Stefan; and Langewiesche, Dieter eds, *Territorial Revisionism and the Allies of Germany in the Second World War. Goals, Expectations, Practices*, (New York: Berghahn, 2013).

Cave, Nigel and Sheldon, Jack, *Ypres 1914: Messines*, (Barnsley: Pen and Sword Military, 2014).

Chamberlain, Peter and Doyle, Hilary, *Encyclopedia of German Tanks of World War Two. Revised Edition*, (London: Cassell & Co, 1999).

Chamberlain, Peter and Ellis, Chris, *British and American Tanks of World War Two. The Complete Illustrated Hiistory of British, American and Commonwealth Tanks 1933-1945*, (London: Cassell & Co, 2000).

Chaney Jr, Otto Preston, *Zhukov*. Norman, (Oklahoma: University of Oklahoma Press, 1971).

Chaseaud, Peter, *Mapping the First World War. The Great War Through Maps from 1914 to 1918*, (London: Harper Collins, 2013*)*.

Churchill, Winston S, *The Second World War. Abridged One-Volume Edition*, (London: Cassell, 1959).

Clark, Christopher, *The Sleepwalkers. How Europe Went to War in 1914*, (London: Allen Lane, 2012).

Clausewitz, Carl von; Rapoport, Anatol ed, *On War*, (London: Penguin Classics, 1982).

Clausewitz, Carl von; Howard, Michael and Paret, Peter trs and eds; *On War*, (New York: Alfred Knopf, 1993).

Clausewitz, Carl von; Howard, Michael and Paret, Peter trs and eds; Heuser, Beatrice ed, *On War*, (Oxford: Oxford University Press, 2007).

Clayton, Ann, *Chavasse Double VC*, (London: Leo Cooper, 1992).

Cohen, Susan, *Medical Services in the First World War*, (Oxford: Shire Publications, 2014).

Colville, J R, *Man of Valour: the Life of FM Lord Gort VC GCB DSO MVO MC*, (London: Collins, 1972).

Condell, Bruce and Zabecki, David T eds and trs, *On the German Art of War. Truppenführung*, (Boulder: Lynne Rienners Publishers, 2001).

Cordesman, Antony and Wagner, Abraham, *The Lessons of Modern War*, (London: Mansell Publishing, 1990).

Corum, James S, *The Roots of Bltizkrieg. Hans von Seeckt and German Military Reform*, (Lawrence: University Press of Kannsas, 1992).

Cox, Richard, *Sea Lion*, (London: Futura 1974).

Creveld, Martin van, *The Military Lessons of the Yom Kippur War*, (London: The Washington Papers, No 24, Saga Publications Ltd, 1975).

Creveld, Martin van, *Fighting Power. German and US Army Performance 1939-45*, (London: Arms and Armour Press, 1983).

Creveld, Martin van, *Command in War*, (London: Harvard University Press, 1985).

Creveld, Martin van, *The Transformation of War*, (New York: Macmillan, 1991).

Creveld, Martin van, *Supplying War. Logistics from Wallenstein to Patton*, (Cambridge: Cambridge University Press, 2004).

Crowley, Patrick, *Kut 1916. Courage and Failure in Iraq*, (Stroud: Spellmount, 2009).

Davies, David Twiston ed, *The Daily Telegraph Book of Military Obituaries*, (London: Grub Street, 2003).

Deacon, M G ed, *The Shiny Seventh. The 7th (Service) Battalion Bedfordshire Regiment at War, 1915-1918*, (Woodbridge: The Boydell Press, 2004).

Dean, Sir Maurice, *The Royal Air Force in Two World Wars*, (London: Cassell, 1979).

Delaforce, Patrick, *Churchill's Desert Rats. From Normandy to the Baltic with the 7th Armoured Division*, (Stroud: Alan Sutton, 1994).

Delaforce, Patrick, *Monty's Highlanders. 51st Highland Division in World War 2.* (Brighton: Tom Donovan Publishing, 1997).

Dennis, Peter and Grey, Jeffrey eds, *Raise, Train and Sustain: Delivering Land Combat Power. Chief of Army History Conference 2009,* (Australian Military History Publications, 2010).

Dennis, Peter and Grey, Jeffrey eds, *1911 Preliminary Moves. Chief of Army History Conference 2011,* (Big Sky Publishing, 2012).

Dennis, Peter ed, *Armies & Maritime Strategy. Chief of Army History Conference 2013,* (Big Sky Publishing, 2014).

Dixon, Norman F, *On The Psychology of Military Incompetence*, (London: Jonathan Cape, 1977).

Dixon, Norman F, *Our Own Worst Enemy*, (London: Jonathan Cape, 1987).

Doherty, Richard, *British Armoured Divisions and Their Commanders, 1939-1945*, (Barnsley: Pen and Sword, 2013).

Dupuy, Trevor N, USA (retd), *A Genius for War. The German Army and General Staff, 1807-1945*, (London: Macdonald and Janes, 1977).

Dupuy, Trevor N, *Elusive Victory. The Arab-Israeli Wars, 1947-74*, (London: Macdonald and Jane's, 1978).

Dupuy, Trevor N et al, *Hitler's Last Gamble. The Battle of the Bulge, December 1944-January 1945*, (Shrewsbury: Airlife Publishing, 1994).

Echevarria, Antulio J II, *Imagining Future War. The West's Technological Revolution and Visions of Wars to Come, 1880-1914*, (Westport: Praeger Security International, 2007).

Edgerton, David, *Britain's War Machine. Weapons, Resources and Experts in the Second World War,* (London: Penguin, 2012).

Ellis, John, *The Sharp End of War. The Fighting Man in World War II*, (Newton Abbot: David Charles, 1980).

Ellis, John, *The World War Two Databook*, (London: Aurum, 1993).

Ellis, John and Cox, Michael, *The World War One Databook*, (London: Aurum, 2001).

English, John A, *A Perspective on Infantry*, (New York: Praeger, 1981).

English, John A and Gudmundsson, Bruce I, *On Infantry*, (New York: Praeger, 1994).

Erickson, John, *The Road To Stalingrad* and *The Road to Berlin. Volumes One and Two* of *Stalin's War on Germany*, (London: Grafton, 1985).

Escott, Squadron Leader Beryl E, *The Heroines of SOE F Section. Britian's Secret Women in France,* (Stroud: The History Press, 2010).

D'Este, Carlo, *Fatal Decision. Anzio and the Battle for Rome*, (London: Fontana, 1992).

D'Este, Carlo, *Decision in Normandy*, (London: Robson Books, 2000).

Farrar-Hockley, Anthony, *The Somme*, (London: Pan Books, 1964).

Farrar-Hockley, Anthony, *Infantry Tactics*, (London: Almark, 1976).

Ferguson, Niall, *The War of the World. History's Age of Hatred*, (London: Allen Lane, 2006).

Foreman, D, *To Reason Why*, (London: Andre Deutsch, 1991).

Forty, George and Duncan, John, *The Fall of France. Disaster in the West 1939-40*, (Tunbridge Wells: The Nutshell Publishing Co, 1990).

Foss, Christopher F, *Jane's Tank Recognition Guide*, (Glasgow: Harper Collins, 1997).

Fleischer, Wolfgang, *Russian Tanks and Armored Vehicles. 1917-1945. An Illustrated Reference*, (Atglen: Schiffer Military History, 1999).

Fraser, David, *Knight's Cross. A Life of Field Marshal Erwin Rommel*, (London: Harper Collins, 1993).

Freedman, Lawrence ed, *War*, (London: Harper Collins, 1992).

Frieser, Karl-Heinz, *The Blitzkrieg Legend. The 1940 Campaign in the West*, (Annapolis: Naval Institute Press, 2005).

Fuller, Major General J F C, *Dragon's Teeth*, (London: Constable and Co, 1932).

Fuller, J F C,. *Armoured Warfare*, (London: Eyre and Spottiswood, 1943).

Fuller, Major General J F C; Terraine, John ed, *The Decisive Battles of the Western World and their Impact on History. Volume Two, 1792-1944*, (St Albans: Paladin, 1975).

Garbert, Dr Christopher R, *Seek, Strike and Destroy: US Army Tank Destroyer Doctrine in World War II*, Leavenworth Papers, Number 12, (Fort Leavenworth: Combat Studies Institute, US Army Command and General Staff College, 1985).

Gat, Azar, *A History of Military Thought. From the Enlightenment to the Cold War*, (Oxford: Oxford University Press, 2001).

Gelbart, Marsh, *Merkava. A History of Israel's Battle Tank*, (Erlangen: Tankograd 2005).

Geraghty, Tony, *The Irish War*, (London: Harper Collins, 1998).

Gerwarth, Robert ed, *Twisted Paths. Europe 1914-1945*, (Oxford: Oxford University Press, 2008).

Giblin, Hal, *Bravest of Hearts. Biography of a Battalion. The Liverpool Scottish in the Great War*, (Liverpool: Winordie Publications, 2000).

Gilbert, Martin, *The Routledge Atlas of the First World War. Second Edition*, (London: Routledge, 1994).

Glantz, David M, *Zhukov's Greatest Defeat. The Red Army's Epic Disaster in Operation Mars, 1942*. (Shepperton: Ian Allen, 2000).

Glantz, David M, and House, Jonathan M, *When Titans Clashed. How the Red Army Stopped Hitler*, (Lawrence: University Press of Kansas, 2015).

Gooch, J and Perlmutter, A eds, *Military Deception and Strategic Surprise*, (London: Frank Cass, 1984).

Gordon, Andrew, *The Rules of the Game. Jutland and British Naval Command*, (London: John Murray, 1996).

Graham, Dominick, *Against Odds. Reflections on the Experiences of the British Army, 1914-45*, (London: Macmillan, 1999).

Gray, Colin S, *Another Bloody Century. Future Warfare*, (London: Weidenfeld and Nicolson, 2005).

Gray, Colin S, *War, Peace and International Relations. An Introduction to Strategic History*. (London: Routledge. Second Edition, 2012).

Grehan, John and Mace, Martin eds, *The War at Sea in the Mediterranean 1940-44*, (Barnsley: Pen and Sword, 2016).

Griffith, Paddy. *Forward into Battle*, (Swindon: The Crowood Press, 1981).

Griffith, Paddy, *Battle Tactics of the Western Front – The British Army's Art of Attack 1916-8*, (London: York University Press, 1994).

Gross, Gerhard P, *The Myth and Reality of German Warfare. Operational Thinking from Moltke the Elder to Heusinger*, (Lexington, Kentucky: The University Press of Kentucky, 2016).

Grossman, Lt Col Dave, *On Killing. The Psychological Cost of Learning to Kill in War and Society*, (Boston: Little, Brown and Company, 1996).

Guderian, General Heinz; Fitzgibbon, Constantine tr, *Panzer Leader*, (London: Futura Publications Ltd, 1976).

Guderian, Major General Heinz; Duffy, C tr, *Achtung – Panzer!*, (London: Cassell, 1992).

Gudmundsson, Bruce I, *Stormtroop Tactics: Innovation in the German Army 1914-18*, (New York: Praeger, 1989).

Hackett, General Sir John, *The Profession of Arms*, (London: Sidgwick and Jackson, 1983).

Hamilton-Paterson, James, *Empire of the Clouds. When Britain's Aircraft Ruled the World*, (London: Faber and Faber, 2010).

Hamley, Sir Edward Bruce, *The Operations of War: Explained and Illustrated*, Facsimile reprint by Nabu Public Domain Reprints (undated).

Hanson, Neil, *First Blitz. The Secret German Plan to Raze London to the Ground in 1918*, (London: Corgi, 2009).

Harris, J P and Toase, F N eds, *Armoured Warfare*, (London: Batsford, 1991).

Harrison Place, Timothy, *Military Training in the British Army, 1940-44*, (London: Frank Cass, 2000).

Harvey, Trevor, *An Army of Brigadiers. British Brigade Commanders at the Battle of Arras 1917*, (Solihull: Helion and Company, 2017).

Hastings, Max, *Overlord. D-Day and the Battle for Normandy 1944*, (London: Michael Joseph, 1984).

Hastings, Max, *The Korean War*, (London: Michael Joseph, 1987).

Hastings, Max, *Bomber Command*, (London: Pan Books, 1999).

Hastings, Max, *Nemesis: The Battle for Japan, 1944-45*, (London: Harper Collins, 2007).

Hastings, Max, *Catastrophe. Europe Goes to War in 1914*, (London: William Collins, 2013).

Haythornthwaite, Philip J, *The World War One Source Book*, (London: Arms and Armour Press, 1992).

Herzog, Chaim, *The War of Atonement*, (London: Weidenfeld and Nicholson, 1975).

Heuser, Beatrice and Shamir, Eitan eds, *Insurgencies and Counterinsurgencies. National Styles and Strategic Cultures*, (Cambridge: Cambridge University Press, 2017).

Hogg, Ian V, *German Artillery of World War Two*, (London: Greenhill Books, 2002).

Holmes, Richard ed, *The Oxford Companion to Military History*, (Oxford: Oxford University Press, 2001).

Holmes, Richard, *Fatal Avenue. A Traveller's History of the Battlefields of Northern France and Flanders*, (London: Vintage Books, 2008).

Howard, Michael, *Clausewitz*, (Oxford: Oxford University Press, 1983).

Hutchinson DSO MC, Colonel G S, *Machine Guns: Their History and Tactical Employment. A History of the Machine Gun Corps, 1916-22*, (London: McMillan and Co, 1938).

Iliff, Jay ed, *The Daily Telegraph Airmen's Obituaries, Book Two*, (London: Grub Street, 2007).

Inauer, Josef ed, *The Swiss Army 2000*, (Frauenfeld: Huber, 2000).

Isby, David C, *Weapons and Tactics of the Soviet Army*, (London: Jane's, 1988).

Isby, David C, *Fighting In Normandy. The German Army from D-Day to Villers-Bocage*, (London: Greenhill Books, 2001).

Isby, David C, *The German Army at D-Day. Fighting the Invasion*, (London: Greenhill Books, 2004).

Jackson, Robert, *The Fall of France. May-June 1940*, (London: Weidenfeld & Nicolson, 1975).

Jacobsen, Hans-Adolf, *Documente der Westfeldzug*, (Berlin: Musterschmidt-Verlag, 1960).

James, Captain E A, *A Record of the Battles and Engagements of the British Armies in France and Flanders, 1914-1918*. (Aldershot: Gale and Polden, 1924). Reprinted Uckfield: Naval and Military Press.

Jary, Sidney, *18 Platoon*, (Bristol: Sidney Jary Limited, 1994).

Jeffery, Keith, *MI6. The History of the Secret Intelligence Service 1909-1949*, (London: Bloomsbury 2011).

Johnson, David E, *Fast Tanks and Heavy Bombers. Innovation in the US Army 1917-1945*, (New York: Cornell University Press, 1998).

Johnson, David E, *Learning Large Lessons. The Evolving Roles of Ground Power and Air Power in the Post-Cold War Era*, (Santa Monica, California: The Rand Corporation, 2007).

Jomini, Baron Antoine Henri de, *The Art of War*, (London: Greenhill Books, 1992).

Jones, Spencer ed, *Stemming the Tide. Officers and Leadership in the British Expeditionary Force 1914*, (Solihull: Helion and Company, 2013).

Jüngner, Ernst, *The Storm of Steel*, (London: Constable and Company, 1994).

Kahalani, Avigdor, *The Heights of Courage. A Tank Leader's War on the Golan*, (Westport: Praeger International, 1992).

Keegan, John, *The Face of Battle*, (London: Jonathan Cape Ltd, 1976).

Keegan, John, *Six Armies in Normandy. From D-Day to the Liberation of Paris, June 6th – August 25th, 1944*, (London: Book Club Associates, 1982).

Keegan, John, *A History of Warfare*, (London: Hutchinson, 1993).

Keegan, John, *The First World War*, (London: Hutchinson, 1998).

Keeley, Kevin, *The Longest War*, (Westport: Lawrence Hill, 1988).

Kennedy, Paul, *The Rise and Fall of the Great Powers. Economic Change and Military Conflict from 1500 to 2000*, (London: Fontana Press, 1989).

Kershaw, Robert, *It Never Snows in September. The German View of MARKET-GARDEN and the Battle of Arnhem, September 1944*, (London: Ian Allen, 2004).

Kitchen, Martin, *Europe Between the Wars. A Political History*, (London: Longman Group, 1988).

Kitchen, Martin, *The German Offensives of 1918*, (Stroud: Tempus Publishing Ltd, 2001).

Koch, Fred, *Russian Tanks and Armored Vehicles. 1946-to the Present[sic]. An Illustrated Reference*, (Atglen, Pennsylvania: Schiffer Military History, 1999).

Krause, Jonathan, *Early Trench Tactics in the French Army. The Second Battle of Artois, May-June 1915*, (Aldershot: Ashridge Publishing Ltd, 2013).

Jane's Fighting Ships of World War I, Foreword by Moore, Captain John, (London: Random House, 2001).

Jane's Fighting Ships of World War II, Foreword by Preston, Anthony, (London: Random House, 2001).

Larionov, V et al, William Biley tr, *World War II: Decisive Battles of the Soviet Army*, (Moscow: Progress Publishers, 1984).

Larson, Robert H, *The British Army and the Theory of Armored Warfare, 1918-40*, (London: Associated University Press, 1984).

Lavery, Brian, *The Royal Navy Officer's Pocket Book 1944*, (London: Conway, 2006).

Lewin, Ronald, *Man of Armour. A Study of Lieut-General Vyvyan Pope and the Development of Armoured Warfare*, (London: Leo Cooper, 1976).

Lewin, Ronald, *Slim the Standard Bearer. A Biography of Field Marshal the Viscount Slim KG GCB GCMG GCVO DSO MC*, (London: Leo Cooper, 1976).

Liddell Hart, Captain B H, *A Science of Infantry Tactics Simplified*, (London: William Clowes and Sons, 1923).

Liddell Hart, B H, *The German Generals Talk – [sic]*, (New York: Harper, 2002).

Lind, W S, *Manoeuvre Warfare Handbook*, (London: Westview Press, 1985).

Lindsay, Martin, *So Few Got Through. With the Gordon Highlanders from Normandy to the Baltic*, (Barnsley: Leo Cooper, 2000).

Lloyd, Nick, *Hundred Days. The End of the Great War*, (London: Viking, 2013).

LoCicero, Michael, *A Moonlight Massacre. The Night Operation on the Passchendaele Ridge, 2 December 1917. The Forgotten Last Act of the Third Battle of Ypres*, (Solihull, Helion and Company, 2014).

Lucke, Lt Fritz with Edwards, Robert and Olive, Michael, *Panzer Wedge. Volume One: The German 3rd Panzer Division and the Summer of Victory in the East* (Mechanicsburg: Stackpole Books, 2012)

Ludendorff, General [E], *My War Memories 1914-1918*, two volumes, (Uckfield: Naval and Military Press, 2005).

Luttwak, Edward and Horowitz, Dan, *The Israeli Army*, (London: Allen Lane, 1975).

Luttwak, Edward, *Strategy. The Logic of War and Peace*, (Cambridge: The Belknap Press, 1987).

Lyman, Robert, *Slim, Master of War. Burma and the Birth of Modern Warfare,* (London: Constable 2004).

Macintyre, Ben, *Operation Mincemeat. The True Spy Story that Changed the Course of World War II,* (London: Bloomsbury, 2010).

McMeekin, Sean, *The Berlin-Baghdad Express. The Ottoman Empire and Germany's Bid for World Power 1898-1918,* (London: Penguin, 2011).

McMeekin, Sean, *The Ottoman Endgame. War, Revolution and the Making of the Modern Middle East 1908-23,* (London: Allen Lane, 2015).

MacMillan, Margaret, *Peacemakers. The Paris Peace Conference of 1919 and its Attempt to End War,* (London: John Murray, 2001).

Magocsi, Paul Robert, *Historical Atlas of Central Europe,* (Seattle: University of Washington Press, 2002)

Manstein, Field Marshal Erich von, *Lost Victories,* (London: Methuen, 1994).

Manstein, Rudiger von and Fuchs, Theodor, *Soldat im 20. Jahrhundert,* (München, 1981).

Battles Hitler Lost. First-Hand Accounts of WW2 by Russian Generals on the Eastern Front. [Each battle described by a Marshal of the Soviet Union] (New York: Richardson and Steinman, 1986).

Marshall, S L A, *Armies on Wheels,* (London: Faber and Faber, 1942).

Mellenthin, Major General FW von; Betler, H tr, *Panzer Battles. A Study of the Employment of Armour in the Second World War,* (London: Futura Publications Ltd, 1979).

Melvin, Mungo, *Manstein. Hitler's Greatest General,* (London: Phoenix, 2010).

Merridale, Catherine, *Lenin on the Train,* (London: Penguin, 2017).

Messenger, Charles, *The D-Day Atlas. Anatomy of the Normandy Campaign.* (London: Thames and Hudson Ltd, 2014).

Middlebrook, Martin, *The Kaiser's Battle,* (London: Penguin, 1983).

Middledorf, Eike, *Handbuch der Taktik. Für Führer und Unterführer,* (Berlin: E S Mittler & Sohn, 1957).

Miller, Russell, *Uncle Bill. The Authorised Biography of Field Marsahl Viscount Slim,* (London: Phoenix, 2014).

Mileham, Patrick, *Difficulties be Damned. The King's Regiment 8th 63rd 96th,* (Knutsford: Fleur de Lys Publishing, 2000).

Montgomery of Alamein, Viscount Bernard Law, *The Memoirs of Field Marshal the Viscount Montgomery of Alamein KG.* (Cleveland: the World Publishing Company, 1958).

Montgomery of Alamein, FM the Viscount, *El Alamein to the Sangro. Normandy to the Baltic,* (London: Book Club Associates, 1973).

Moore, Captain JE and Compton Hall, Commander R, *Submarine Warfare. Today and Tomorrow,* (London: Michael Joseph, 1986).

Morgan, Hugh and Seibel, Jürgen, *Combat Kill,* (Cambridge: Patrick Stephens Ltd, 1997).

Mortimer, Gavin, *The SAS in World War II. An Illustrated History,* (Oxford: Osprey Publishing, 2011).

Moynahan, Brian, *The Claws of the Bear*, (London: Hutchinson 1989).

Murray, Leo, *Brains & Bullets. How Psychology Wins Wars*, (London: Biteback Publishing, 2013).

Murray, Williamson and Millett, Allan R eds, *Military Innovation in the Interwar Period*, (Cambridge: Cambridge University Press, 1998).

Murray, Williamson and Scales, Major General Robert H, Jr, *The Iraq War. A Military History*, (Cambridge: The Belknap Press, 2003).

Nafziger, George F, *The German Order of Battle. Panzers and Artillery in World War II*, (London: Greenhill Books, 1998).

Nafziger, George F, *The German Order of Battle. Infantry in World War II*, (London: Greenhill Books, 2000).

Nafziger, George F, *The German Order of Battle. Waffen SS and Other Units in World War II*, (London: Greenhill Books, 2001).

Neillands, Robin, *The Great War Generals on the Western Front 1914-18*, (London: Robinson, 1999).

Neillands, Robin, *The Bomber War. Arthur Harris and the Allied Bomber Offensive 1939-1945*, (London: John Murray, 2001).

Nordeen, Lon, *Fighters over Israel. The Story of the Israeli Air Force from the War of Independence to the Bekaa Valley*, (London: Guild Publishing, 1990).

North, John, *Northwest Europe 1944-5. The Achievement of 21st Army Group*, (London: HMSO, 1953).

O'Ballance, Edgar, *No Victor, No Vanquished. The Yom Kippur War*, (Novato: Presidio Press, 1978).

O'Gorkiewicz, R M, *The Technology of Tanks*, (Coulsdon: Jane's, 1991).

O'Gorciewicz, Richard, *Tanks. 100 Years of Evolution*, (Oxford: Osprey 2015).

Overy, Richard, *Why the Allies Won*, (London: Pimlico, 2006).

Overy, Richard, *The Bombing War. Europe 1939-1945*, (London: Allen Lane, 2013).

The Concise Oxford Dictionary, Sixth Edition, (Oxford: Oxford University Press, 1976).

Paice, Edward, *Tip & Run. The Untold Tragedy of the Great War in Africa*, (London: Weidenfeld and Nicholson, 2007).

Palmer, Michael A, *The German Wars. A Concise History 1859-1945*, (Minneapolis: Zenith Press, 2010).

Paret, P ed, *Makers of Modern Strategy*, (Oxford: Oxford University Press, 1986).

Passingham, Ian, *All the Kaiser's Men. The Life and Death of the German Army on the Western Front, 1914-1918*, (Stroud: Sutton Publishing, 2003).

Patton Jr, George S, *War as I Knew it*, (Cambridge: Houghton Mifflin Co, 1947).

Paul, Christopher; Clarke, Colin; and Grill, Beth, *Victory has a Thousand Fathers*, (Santa Monica: The Rand Corporation, 2010)

Perret, Bryan, *A History of Blitzkrieg*, (New York: Stein and Day, 1983).

Piekalkiewicz, Janus; Barker, H A and A J trs, *Arnhem 1944*, (London: Ian Allen, 1977).

Porter, David, *Soviet Tank Units 1939-45*, (London: Amber Books, 2009).

Prebble, Stuart, *Secrets of the Conqueror. The Untold Story of Britain's Most Famous Submarine*, (London: Faber and Faber, 2012).

Province, Charles M, *Patton's Third Army*, (New York: Hippocrene, 1992).

Rauss, Generaloberst Erhard and Natzmer, Generalleutnant Oldwig von; Tsouras, Peter G ed, *The Anvil of War. German Generalship in Defense on the Eastern Front*, (London: Greenhill, 1994).

Reynolds, Michael, *Steel Inferno. 1st SS Panzer Corps in Normandy*, (Staplehurst: Spellmount, 1997).

Roberts, Major General G P B, CB DSO MC, *From the Desert to the Baltic*, (London: William Kimber and Co Ltd, 1987).

Roberts, Geoffrey, *Stalin's General. The Life of Georgy Zhukov,* (London: Icon Books, 2013).

Roebling, Karl, *Great Myths of WW2*, (New York: Paragon Press, 1985).

Rogan, Eugene, *The Fall of the Ottomans. The Great War in the Middle East, 1914-1920*, (London: Penguin, 2016).

Rohwner, Jürgen, *Axis Submarine Successes 1939-45*, (Cambridge: Patrick Stephens Ltd, 1983).

Rolo, Charles J, *Wingates's Raiders. An Account of the Incredible Adventure that Raised the Curtain for the Battle for Burma*, (London: George Harrap, 1944).

Rommel, Erwin, *Infantry Attacks*, (London: Greenhill Books, 1990).

Roscoe, Theodore, *US Submarine Operations in WW2*, (Annapolis: US Naval Institute, 1949).

Rosinski, Herbert, *The German Army*, (London: Pall Mall Press, 1966).

Rowland, David, *The Stress of Battle. Quantifying Human Performance in Combat*, (Norwich: The Stationary Office, 2006).

Ryan, Cornelius, *The Last Battle,* (London: NEL Books, 1980).

Samuels, Martin, *Doctrine and Dogma, German and British Infantry Tactics in the First World War,* (New York: Greenwood, 1992).

Seaton, Albert, *The German Army 1933-45*, (London: Weidenfeld and Nicholson, 1982).

Senich, Peter R, *The German Sniper 1939-45*, (London: Arms and Armour Press, 1982).

Shamir, Eitan, *Transforming Command. The Pursuit of Mission Command in the U.S., British, and Israeli Armies*, (Stamford: Stamford University Press, 2011).

Sheffield, Gary, *The Somme,* (London: Cassell, 2003).

Sheffield, Gary and Todman, Dan eds, *Command and Control on the Western Front. The British Army's Experience 1914-18*, (Staplehurst: Spellmount Ltd 2004).

Sheffield, Gary and Bourne, John eds, *Douglas Haig. War Diaries and Letters 1914-1918*, (London, Weidenfeld and Nicholson, 2005).

Sheldon, Jack, *The German Army at Cambrai*, (Barnsley: Pen and Sword Ltd, 2009).

Sheldon, Jack, *The German Army at Ypres 1914,* (Barnsley: Pen and Sword Ltd, 2010).

Sims, Edward H, *The Fighter Pilots*, (London: Corgi, 1970).

Slim, Field Marshal Viscount, *Defeat into Victory,* (London: Pan Books, 2009).

Smith, Anthony, *Machine Gun A Story of the Men and the Weapon that Changed the Face of War,* (London: Piatkus, 2002).

Smith, John P, *Airborne to Battle. A History of Airborne Warfare 1918-71*, (London: William Kimber and Co Ltd, 1971).

Smith, General Rupert, *The Utility of Force. The Art of War in the Modern World*, (London: Allen Lane, 2005).

Smithers, A J, *Rude Mechanicals. An Account of Tank Maturity During the Second World War*, (London: Leo Cooper, 1987).

Spick, Mike, *The Ace Factor: Air Combat and the Role of Situational Awareness*, (Shrewsbury: Air Life Publishing Ltd, 1988).

Spiller, Roger J ed, *Combined Arms in Action Since 1939*, (Fort Leavenworth: US Command and General Staff College Press, 1992).

Stanton, Shelby, *The Rise and Fall of an American Army. US Ground Forces in Vietnam*, (Novato: Presidio Press, 1985).

Steinhardt, Frederick P Dr ed and trs, *Panzer Lehr Division 1944-45*, (Solihull: Helion and Company, 2010).

Stone, David, *Fighting for the Fatherland. The Story of the German Soldier from 1648 to the Present Day*, (London: Conway, 2006).

Storr, Jim, *The Human Face of War*, (London: Continuum 2009).

Strachan, Hew, *European Armies and the Conduct of War*, (London: George Allan and Unwin, 1983).

Strauss, Franz Josef, *Geschichte der 2. (Wiener) Panzer Division*, (Friedberg: Podzun-Pallas Verlag, 1987).

Stumpf, Reinhard, *Die Wehrmacht-Elite. Rang- und Herkunftsstruktur der Deutschen Generale und Admirale, 1933-45*, (Boppard am Rhein: Harald Boldt Verlag, 1982).

Sulzbach, Herbert; Thonger, Richard tr, *With the German Guns. Four Years on the Western Front*, (Barnsley: Leo Cooper, 1998).

Swinson, Arthur, *The Raiders. Desert Strike Force*, (London: The Pan/Ballantine Illustrated History of World War II, 1968).

Tarrant, V E, *The U-Boat Offensive, 1914-45*, (London: Arms and Armour Press, 1989).

Taylor, Brian, *Barbarossa to Berlin. A Chronology of the Campaigns on the Eastern Front 1941 to 1945*, two volumes, (Staplehurst: Spellmount, 2003).

Terraine, John, *To Win a War. 1918, the Year of Victory*, (London: Sidgwick and Jackson, 1978).

Terraine, John, *The Smoke and the Fire. Myths and Anti-Myths of War 1861-1945*, (London: Book Club Associates, 1981).

Terraine, John, *The Right of the Line. The Royal Air Force in the European War, 1939-1945*, (London: Hodder and Stoughton, 1985).

Thornton, Rod, *Asymmetric Warfare*, (Cambridge: Polity Press, 2007).

Tooze, Adam, *The Wages of Destruction. The Making and Breaking of the Nazi War Economy*, (London: Allen Lane, 2006).

Townshend, Charles ed, *The Oxford Illustrated History of Modern War*, (Oxford: Oxford University Press, 1997).

Trythall, Anthony John, *'Boney' Fuller – The Intellectual General*, (London: Cassell, 1977).

Tsouras, Peter G, *Changing Orders. The Evolution of the World's Armies, 1945 to the Present*, (London: Arms and Armour Press, 1994).

Vallance, Andrew G B, *The Air Weapon. Doctrines of Air Power Strategy and Operational Art*, (London: Macmillan, 1996).

Vigor, P H, *Soviet Blitzkrieg Theory*, (London: Palgrave MacMillan, 1983).

Watson, Bruce W; George, Bruce MP; Tsouras, Peter; and Cyr, B L, *Military Lessons of the Gulf War*, (London: BCA, 1991).

Waldrop, M Mitchell, *Complexity. The Emerging Science at the Edge of Order and Chaos.* (London: Penguin, 1994).

Westphal, General Siegfried, *The German Army in the West*, (London: Cassell, 1951).

Whitaker, Brigadier-General Denis et al, *Victory at Falaise. The Soldier's Story*, (Toronto: Harper Collins, 2000).

Williams, John, *The Ides of May. The Defeat of France May-June 1940*, (London: Constable, 1986).

Williamson, Gordon, *Aces of the Reich*, (London: Arms and Armour Press, 1989).

Winton, Harold R, *To Change an Army. General Sir John Burnett-Stuart and British Armoured Doctrine 1927-38*, (Lawrence: University of Kansas Press, 1988).

Wintringham, Tom and Blashford-Snell, J N, *Weapons and Tactics*, (London: Penguin, 1973).

Wynne, Captain G C, *If Germany Attacks. The Battle in Depth in the West*, (reprinted Westport: Greenwood Press,1976)

Zetterling, Niklas and Frankson, Anders, *Kursk 1943, A Statistical Analysis*, (London: Frank Cass, 2000).

Section Two: British Military Publications

Items are shown broadly in date order.

Musketry Regulations, (The War Office, HMSO, 1905).

Training and Manoeuvre Regulations, (The War Office. HMSO, 1909).

Musketry Regulations, Part 1, (The War Office. HMSO, 1909, Reprint 1912).

Field Service Regulations, Part 1, Operations, (The War Office. HMSO, 1909, Reprint 1912).

Trench Orders. 4th Division. Undated.

Bayonet Training 1916. (Provisional). (Headquarters Gymnasium, Aldershot, 1916).

Trench Orders. 55th (West Lancashire) Division, Jan 1918.

Instructions for the Training of Divisions for Offensive Action, (The War Office, December 1916. Reprinted Memphis: General Books LLC, 2012).

Platoon Training 1918. T/1919 and 40/WO/7172.

The Division in the Attack – 1918. SS 135. T/1635 and 40/WO/7036, (Reprinted as the Strategic and Combat Studies Occasional Number 53, 2008).

Statistics of the Military Effort of the British Empire During the Great War 1914-1920, (The War Office, 1922. Reprinted by the Naval and Military Press, undated).

The Official History of the War. Military Operations in France and Belgium 1914-18. Volume IX, The German March Offensive and its Preliminaries, (London: Macmillan and Co, 1935).

Infantry Training. Volume 2, War, (HMSO, 1931).

Report of the Committee on the Lessons of the Great War (The Kirke Report), (The War Office, 1932. Published as British Army Review Special Edition, April 2001).

Field Service Regulations, Vol. II, Operations – General, (HMSO, 1935).

Infantry Training. Training and War, (HMSO, 1937).

Infantry Section Leading, (HMSO, 1938).

Military Training Pamphet No. 23, Operations. Part II.- Defence, (HMSO, 1939).

Military Training Pamphet No. 23, Operations. Part IX.- The Infantry Division in the Attack, (HMSO, 1941).

Military Training Pamphet No.23, Operations. Part I.- General Principles, Fighting Troops and their Characteristics, (HMSO, 1942).

The German Armoured Division: Tactcial Handling. G.H.Q. M.E.F., 4 Feb 42. (Reprinted, Nottingham: Partizan Press, undated).

The Instructor's Handbook on Fieldcraft and Battle Drill (Provisional), Army Code 60314, Issued under the direction of CinC Home Forces, apparently dated October 1942.

Military Training Pamphet No. 3, The Defence, (HMSO, 1943).

The Regimental Officer's Handbook of the German Army, 1943, (The War Office, August 1943).

Infantry Training. Part VIII. – Fieldcraft, Battle Drill, Section and Platoon Tactics, (The War Office, 1944).

Some Notes on the Conduct of War and the Infantry Division in Battle, (Belgium, HQ 21st Army Group, November 1944). Reprinted under *Notes on War*, B L Montgomery, Nottingham: Partizan Press, undated.

Some Notes on the Use of Air Power in Support of Land Operations, (Holland, HQ 21st Army Group, December 1944). Reprinted as above.

The Armoured Division in Battle, (Holland, HQ 21st Army Group, December 1944). Reprinted as above.

79th Armoured Division Final Report 1945, (Germany, July 1945). Reprinted Nottingham: Partizan Press, undated.

The Story of 79th Armoured Division No author, no date, no publishing information; apparently written 1945.

Army Training Memorandum. War. January 1940 to May, 1945. Parts 28 to 52, (Uckfield: Naval and Military Press, undated).

Royal Armoured Corps Training. Volume I – Training Pamphlet No. 1 – The Armoured Regiment, (The War Office, 1948).

Royal Armoured Corps Training. Volume I – Training Pamphlet No. 2 – The Armoured Car Regiment, (The War Office, 1948).

Staff Duties in the Field, 1949, WO Code 8457, (The War Office, 15 December 1949).

Infantry Training. Volume I. Infantry Platoon Weapons. Pamphlet No. 6, The Light Machine Gun (All Arms) 1948. Reprinted with Amendments 1 to 3, (The War Office, 1953).

Infantry Training. Volume IV. Tactics. Infantry Section Leading and Platoon Tactics, (The War Office, 1950).

The Second World War 1939-45. Ordnance Services, (The War Office, 1950).

The History of The Second World War. Army Medical Services – Administration. Volume One, (HMSO, 1953).

The Second World War 1939-45. Army Signal Communications, (The War Office, 1954).

The Second World War 1939-45. Army Supply and Transport. (The War Office, 1954).

Order of Battle. The Second World War 1939-45, (HMSO, 1960).

Infantry Training. Volume IV. Tactics. The Infantry Platoon in Battle (Provisional) 1960, (The War Office, 1960).

Infantry Training. Pamphlet No. 1. General Introduction (All Arms) 1961, (The War Office, 1961).

Infantry Training. Volume IX. Infantry Tactics. Pamphlet 44 Part 1. The Infantry Battalion (General) 1975, Army Code 70740.

Infantry Training. Volume IX. Infantry Tactics. Pamphlet 44 Part 2. The Infantry Battalion (Basic Tactics) 1975, Army Code 70740.

Infantry Training. Volume IX. Infantry Tactics. Pamphlet 44 Part 3. The Infantry Battalion (Tactical Variations) 1975, Army Code 70740.

Command of Armour in World War II. Part 1: *North Africa* Part 2: *North West Europe*, (Films: British Defence Film Library C1404, C1405, 1979).

Design for Military Operations. The British Military Doctrine, Army Code 71451, 1989.

Army Doctrine Publication (ADP) Volume 1 Operations, Army Code 71565, 1994.

ADP Volume 2 Command, Army Code 71564, 1995.

Army Field Manual (AFM) Volume 1 Part 1, Formation Tactics, Army Code 71587, 1996.

Design for Military Operations. The British Military Doctrine, (Second Edition) Army Code 71451, 1996.

Bailey, Jonathan, *The First World War and the Birth pf the Modern Style of Warfare*, Strategic and Combat Studies Occasional Number 22, 1996.

AFM No 1 The Fundamentals, Army Code 71622, 1998.

AFM Volume IV Pt 5, Operations in Built-Up Areas. Army Code 71657, 1998.

Peach, Stuart ed, *Perspectives on Air Power. Air Power in its Wider Context*, (London, the Stationery Office, 1998).

British Air Power Doctrine. AP 3000 Third Edition, (London, the Stationery Office, 1999).

UK Doctrine for Joint and Multinational Operations, Joint Warfare Publication 0-10, Edition One, September 1999.

Gray, Peter W ed, *Air Power 21. Challenges for the New Century*, (London: the Stationery Office, 2000).

Staff Officer's Handbook, Army Code 71038, July 2001.

Gray, Peter W and Cox, Sebastian ed, *Air Power Leadership. Theory and Practice*, (London: the Stationery Office, 2002).

AP 3003. A Brief History of the Royal Air Force, (HMSO, 2004).

The First World War Battlefield Guide: The Western Front, Edition 1, August 2014, (UK MOD, 2014).

Section Three: US Army Publications

(With the exception of the official history *The United States Army in World War II*, items are shown in date order.)

Instructions for the Training of Platoons for Offensive Action. Washington: Government Printing Office, 1917.

Sixth [US] Armored Division 1944-5. Combat Record of the Sixth Armored Division in the European Theatre of Operations, 18 July 1944 – 8 May 1945. Compiled under the Direction of Major Clyde J Burke, Asst G3. (Aschaffenburg: Steinbeck-Druck, undated). [Foreword dated 30 July 1945].

US Army Order of Battle WW2. European Theatre, Divisions, (Paris: Office of the Theatre Historian, 15 December 1945).

The United States Army in World War II:

   Greenfield, Kent Roberts; Palmer, Robert R; and Wiley, Bell I, *The Army Ground Forces. The Organisation of Ground Combat Troops*. (Washington: Office of the Chief of Military History, United States Army, Department of the Army, DC, 1947).

   Palmer, Robert R; Wiley, Bell I; and Keast, William R, *The Army Ground Forces. The Procurement and Training of Ground Combat Troops*. (Washington: Office of the Chief of Military History, United States Army, Department of the Army, DC, 1948).

   Harrison, Gordon A, *European Theater of Operations. Cross Channel Attack*, (Washington: Office of the Chief of Military History, United States Army, Department of the Army, DC, 1951).

   Cole, Hugh M, *European Theater of Operations. The Ardennes: Battle of the Bulge*, (Washington: Center of Military History, United States Army, Department of the Army, 1965).

   Garland, Albert N and Smyth, Howard McGaw, *Mediterranean Theater of Operations. Sicily and the Surrender of Italy*, (Washington: Center of Military History, United States Army, Department of the Army, Washington DC, 1965).

   Fisher, Ernest F Jr, *Mediterranean Theater of Operations. Cassino to the Alps*, (Washington: Center of Military History, United States Army, Department of the Army, 1977).

Vigneras, Marcel, *Special Studies. Rearming the French*, (Washington: Center of Military History, United States Army, Department of the Army, 1989).

Miller, John Jr, *The War in the Pacific. Cartwheel: The Reduction of Rabaul*, (Washington: Center of Military History, United States Army, Department of the Army, 1990).

Clarke, Jeffrey J and Smith, Robert Ross, *European Theater of Operations. Riviera to the Rhine*, (Washington: Center of Military History, United States Army, Department of the Army, 1993).

Blumenson, Martin, *European Theater of Operations. Breakout and Pursuit*, (Washington: Center of Military History, United States Army, Department of the Army, 1993).

Blumenson, Martin, *Mediterranean Theater of Operations. Salerno to Cassino*, (Washington: Center of Military History, United States Army, Department of the Army, 1993).

Clarke, Jeffrey J and Smith, Robert Ross, *European Theater of Operations. Riviera to the Rhine*, (Washington: Center of Military History, United States Army, Department of the Army, 1993).

Cole, Hugh M, *European Theater of Operations. The Lorraine Campaign*, (Washington: Center of Military History, United States Army, Department of the Army, 1993).

Macdonald, Charles B, *European Theater of Operations. The Siegfried Line Campaign*, (Washington: Center of Military History, United States Army, Department of the Army, 1993).

Night Combat, Pamphlet 20-236, (Department of the Army, June 1953).

The German General Staff Corps, (Washington Military Intelligence Division, War Department, April 1946).

The Principles of Employment of Armor. Special Text No 48, The Armor School, 1948, in *Armor*, May-June 1998.

Combat in Russian Forests and Swamps. Pamphlet 20-231, (Department of the Army, July 1951).

Kearney, Thomas A and Cohen, Eliot A, *Gulf War Airpower Survey: Summary Report*, (Washington: US Government Printing Office, 1993).

Field Manual (FM) 100-5, Fighting Future Wars. Department of the Army, (McLean: Brassey's, 1994).

FM 101-5, Staff Organizations and Operations, (Washington: HQ, Department of the Army, June 1999).

FM 3-24 and Fleet Marine Force Manual 3-24, Counterinsurgency. (Washington: HQ, Department of the Army, December 2006).

Section Four: Theses, Papers and Presentations

164 conferences, seminars or lectures are not listed here. See 'Note on Sources'. Items are shown in date order.

Slim, FM Sir William, Higher Command in War. Address to US Army Command and General Staff Course, 8 April 1952. *Military Review*, Volume LXX No 5, May 1990.

Manstein, FM Erich von, Grundsätzliche Gedanken an der Organisationsplan Heer, November 1955. *Soldat im 20. Jahrhundert*, Rudiger von Manstein and Theodor Fuchs, (München, 1981). Ghislaine Fluck DERA CDA tr, with assistance from this author.

Lt Gen Paul van Riper, Commanding General of the US Marine Corps Combat Development Centre, prepared testimony to the House of Representatives National Security Committee, March 1997.

Jaya-Ratnam, Dr D D J J, Close Combat Suppression: Need, Assessment and Use. *Proceedings of the 34th Annual Gun and Ammunition Symposium*, 26-29 April 1999, Monterey, California.

Kiszely, Major General John, presentation at the RUSI (Battle Management Systems Symposium), 18-19 November 1999. *Journal of the Royal United Services Institute for Defence Studies (JRUSI)*, 144:4, December 1999.

In Praise of Attrition. Inaugural Lecture by Christopher Bellamy as Professor of Military Sciences and Doctrine, Cranfield University, 14 June 2001.

Section Five: Articles and Letters

911 articles, reviews and review articles from *War in History* are not listed here. See Note on Sources. Items are shown in date order.

Lindsay, Lieutenant Colonel (retd) Sir Martin of Dowhill Bt CBE DSO, Thoughts on Command in Battle, *British Army Review (BAR)* 69, December 1981.

Taylor CBE DSO, Brig (retd) George, Further Thoughts on Command in Battle, *BAR* 71, August 1982.

Lynam, Maj J M, Exercise King's Ride V: Initial Impressions. *Army Training News*, April 1986.

Kiszely, Major General John, The Meaning of Manoeuvre, *JRUSI* 143:6, December 1998.

Carver, Field Marshal Lord, The Boer War, *JRUSI* 144:6, December 1999.

Nicol, Captain J D, The Morale of the Australian Infantry in South Vietnam, 1965-72. *BAR* 127, Summer 2001.

Section Six: Reports

Items are shown in date order.

Effect of Artillery Fire in Attacks in Mountainous Country, (British) No. 1 Operational
Research Section report 1/24/A, 1945.

*The Contribution of Manned Armoured Reconnaissance to the Information Gathering Assets
of 1 (BR) Corps – Exercise White Ermine,* Final Report, DOAE Study 426, MOD
Defence Operational Analysis Establishment Memorandum R9003 dated June
1991.

The Effects of Shock and Surprise on the Land Battle, MOD Defence Operational Analysis
Establishment Memorandum R9301.

Rowland, D, et al. *Breakthrough and Manoeuvre Operations – Historical Analysis of
the Conditions for Success,* MOD Defence Operational Analysis Centre Report
R9412, October 1994.

Index